ESCAPING SHADOWS

Escaping Shadows

Jennifer E Roby

JRoby

1

Dedication

Escaping Shadows: Surviving a Sociopath and Stalker

By: Jennifer E. Roby, LPC, NCC, BC-TMH, C-DBT, CMHC, CCTP, CCBT, CBGT, C-PD, CEAP

To all the survivors who have endured the pain and fear of living with a sociopath or being stalked—your courage and resilience inspire hope for healing and freedom. You are not alone, and your story matters. To myself—for finding my strength in the face of unimaginable challenges, for surviving the darkness brought by a sociopath and a stalker, and for reclaiming my life. I AM JROBY. I am unbroken, unstoppable, and free.

This book is dedicated to every survivor of sociopathic abuse. Your strength, resilience, and courage in the face of unimaginable cruelty inspire me deeply. This work is a testament to your inherent worth and the power you possess to heal, to thrive, and to build a life free from the shadows of manipulation and control. It is a tribute to your unwavering spirit, your capacity for forgiveness, and your journey towards a future filled with peace, joy, and self-love. May these pages offer solace, validation, and a path towards the brighter future you

deserve. You are not alone. Your story matters. Your healing is possible.

Preface

As a survivor of sociopathic abuse, and a therapist specializing in trauma and abuse recovery, I understand firsthand the insidious nature of this form of manipulation. The experiences detailed within these pages are not fiction; they are born from lived reality, meticulously researched, and woven together with clinical expertise. The manipulation, gaslighting, and systematic erosion of self-worth are not easily recognized. They are subtle, complex, and often leave victims feeling isolated, confused, and questioning their own sanity. My aim in writing Escaping Shadows is to provide a lifeline, a roadmap to freedom for those caught in the web of sociopathic control, and a resource for those who seek to understand this often-misunderstood form of abuse.

This book combines personal narrative with clinically- sound advice and practical tools. It is designed to empower you, the reader, to recognize the signs, create a safety plan, escape the abuse, and ultimately, rebuild your life. This is not a journey for the faint of heart, but remember, you are stronger than you think. Your recovery is possible, and your future is waiting.

Introduction

Sociopathic abuse is a uniquely insidious form of trauma. Unlike physical abuse, its wounds are often invisible, leaving victims grappling with self-doubt and a pervasive sense of confusion. The abuser, often charming and charismatic, expertly manipulates their partner, eroding their sense of self and control. This book is not merely a theoretical exploration of sociopathic behavior; it's a practical guide designed to help you navigate the complexities of escaping such a relationship and beginning the long process of healing. Within these pages, you will find a detailed exploration of the tactics used by sociopaths, from gaslighting and financial control to technological stalking.

We will delve into the devastating psychological impact of this abuse and provide evidence-based strategies for recognizing the red flags early on. More importantly, *Escaping Shadows* offers a concrete action plan for creating a safety net, securing resources, and legally protecting yourself. The journey to recovery is long and challenging, but know that you are not alone. This book offers validation, hope, and a detailed roadmap to navigate this difficult path. Take your time, work through each chapter, and remember that reclaiming your life is not only possible, it is your right. This is your journey to healing and empowerment. Begin here.

Defining Sociopathy and its Traits

Sociopathy, also known as antisocial personality disorder (ASPD), is a complex personality disorder characterized by a pervasive pattern of disregard for and violation of the rights of others. It's crucial to understand that sociopathy isn't simply a matter of being "bad" or "selfish." It represents a deeply ingrained personality structure that significantly impairs an individual's ability to form genuine emotional connections, experience empathy, and conform to societal norms. This isn't to excuse the actions of a sociopath, but rather to contextualize the nature of the abuse they inflict.

Understanding the disorder helps survivors recognize the patterns of behavior and understand that the abuse they suffered wasn't their fault.

One of the most defining characteristics of sociopathy is the profound lack of empathy. Sociopaths struggle, often fail entirely, to understand or share the feelings of others. They don't experience the emotional pain or distress of their victims, making manipulation and abuse easier. This lack of empathy isn't simply a lack of compassion; it's a fundamental inability to comprehend the emotional experiences of other people. They may mimic empathy, expressing remorse or concern when it suits them, but this is usually a calculated performance, a tool for further manipulation rather than a genuine expression of feeling.

Closely linked to the lack of empathy is a profound ability to manipulate and deceive. Sociopaths are often masters of manipulation, using charm, charisma, and flattery to gain trust and control over their victims. They are adept at exploiting vulnerabilities and using emotional manipulation to achieve their self-serving ends. This manipulation can be

subtle and insidious, making it difficult for victims to recognize the abuse until considerable damage has been done. For instance, a sociopathic partner might consistently criticize a victim's appearance or accomplishments, gradually eroding their self-esteem until they become entirely dependent on the abuser for validation. This slow, methodical degradation of self-worth is a hallmark of sociopathic abuse.

Another key trait is a disregard for rules and consequences. Sociopaths often exhibit a pattern of impulsive and reckless behavior, disregarding the rights and well-being of others without remorse. They may lie, cheat, steal, or engage in other criminal activities without feeling any guilt or shame. This lack of moral compass is often paired with a sense of entitlement, believing they are above the law or societal expectations. Their actions are driven by a desire for immediate gratification, without considering the long-term consequences for themselves or others. For example, a sociopathic individual might repeatedly break promises, abandon responsibilities, or violate legal agreements without hesitation.

While charm is often associated with sociopaths, it's important to understand it is a manipulative tool, not a genuine reflection of personality. They can appear incredibly charming and likeable, making it difficult for victims to see the darkness beneath the surface. This façade of charm can mask their manipulative and exploitative behaviors, often lulling victims into a false sense of security. They may use charm to gain the trust of friends, family, and coworkers, reinforcing their image as a respectable and trustworthy individual, furthering their ability to conceal their abusive behavior. This charm is a carefully constructed persona, designed to serve their needs, and is easily discarded once their goals are achieved.

The diagnosis of sociopathy requires a specific pattern of behavior, not just a single instance of impulsive or unethical behavior. Professionals use established diagnostic criteria, typically from the Diagnostic and Statistical Manual of Mental Disorders (DSM-5) or the International Classification of Diseases (ICD-11), to assess for ASPD. Meeting the diagnostic criteria usually requires a history of exhibiting several key behaviors since the age of 15. These behaviors often include a pattern of deceitfulness, impulsivity, irritability, recklessness, consistent irresponsibility, and a lack of remorse. It's important to note that these diagnostic tools are just one piece of the puzzle in understanding sociopathic behavior and should be considered alongside an individual's entire history and context.

Differentiating sociopathy from other personality disorders is crucial. Narcissistic personality disorder, for instance, is characterized by an inflated sense of self-importance and a need for admiration, while sociopathy focuses on a pervasive pattern of disregard for the rights of others. While some overlap may exist, the core motivations and behaviors differ significantly. Similarly, borderline personality disorder involves intense fear of abandonment and unstable relationships, contrasting with the manipulative and exploitative nature of sociopathic interactions. A qualified mental health professional can make the necessary distinctions based on a comprehensive evaluation of the individual's history, behaviors, and interpersonal relationships.

Understanding the differences between these disorders isn't just an academic exercise; it's essential for victims of abuse to grasp the nature of the manipulation they've experienced. Recognizing the specific patterns of sociopathic behavior

allows survivors to validate their experiences, understand why they were targeted, and begin the crucial process of healing. The self-awareness gained from understanding sociopathy empowers survivors to establish healthier boundaries and build stronger defenses against future abuse.

It is crucial to remember that while the characteristics described provide a framework for understanding sociopathic behavior, it is not possible to definitively diagnose someone as a sociopath without a thorough professional evaluation. This chapter aims to provide information to help readers recognize potential red flags and seek appropriate support, not to label individuals.

The impact of sociopathic abuse extends far beyond the immediate physical or emotional harm. The subtle yet persistent manipulation can profoundly damage a victim's sense of self, leading to feelings of isolation, confusion, and self-doubt. Gaslighting, a tactic frequently used by sociopaths, systematically erodes a victim's trust in their own perception of reality. Victims may begin to question their sanity and memory, believing the abuser's version of events even when it contradicts their own experiences. This constant undermining of their self-perception can lead to significant psychological distress, including anxiety, depression, and post-traumatic stress disorder (PTSD). The isolating tactics employed by sociopaths further intensify this feeling of disconnect, leaving victims feeling alone and increasingly dependent on their abuser.

Furthermore, the financial control exerted by many sociopathic abusers can leave victims financially vulnerable and dependent, making it extremely difficult to escape the abusive relationship. This financial dependence is often coupled with threats and intimidation, further trapping victims in a cycle of abuse. The erosion of independence extends beyond finances; it often includes control over social contacts, limiting the victim's ability to seek support or build alternative relationships. The pervasive nature of this control creates a suffocating environment that prevents victims from accessing the resources and support necessary to break free.

The long-term effects of sociopathic abuse can be devastating. Many survivors grapple with lasting psychological trauma, impacting their self-esteem, relationships, and overall well-being. They may struggle with trust issues, difficulty forming healthy relationships, and a persistent fear of future abuse. The process of healing is complex and often requires professional intervention, such as therapy or counseling specializing in trauma and abuse recovery. The crucial first step, however, is recognizing the abuse for what it is—not the victim's fault but a result of the abuser's actions and disordered personality. Understanding the nature of sociopathic abuse empowers survivors to begin their journey towards healing and reclaiming their lives. The path to recovery is challenging but achievable, and help is always available.

Tactics of Manipulation and Control

The insidious nature of sociopathic abuse lies not just in its overt acts of cruelty, but in the subtle, pervasive tactics of manipulation and control employed to systematically dismantle the victim's sense of self. These tactics are rarely singular events; they are woven together into a complex web designed to isolate, confuse, and ultimately subdue the victim. Gaslighting, a cornerstone of this manipulative strategy, involves twisting reality to make the victim doubt their own perceptions and sanity. It's a slow, insidious poison, chipping away at the victim's confidence until they question their own memories and experiences, accepting the abuser's distorted version of events as truth. For example, a sociopathic partner might deny making a cruel remark or promise, insisting the victim is imagining things, creating a constant state of cognitive dissonance and confusion. The victim, overwhelmed by this constant undermining, begins to question their own sanity and relies increasingly on the abuser for validation.

Beyond gaslighting, emotional abuse is a core element of the sociopath's arsenal. This involves a range of tactics, from constant criticism and belittling to subtle put-downs designed to erode the victim's self-esteem. These comments aren't random outbursts; they're carefully calibrated to target the victim's vulnerabilities, chipping away at their confidence until they become entirely dependent on the abuser for validation. A sociopathic partner might consistently criticize a victim's appearance, intelligence, or accomplishments, making them feel inadequate and unworthy. This subtle, persistent negativity slowly breaks down the victim's self-worth, leaving them vulnerable and susceptible to further manipulation.

Isolation is another powerful tool used by sociopaths to exert control. This isn't simply about physical separation; it's about gradually severing the victim's ties to their support network. Sociopaths often work to alienate the victim from friends and family, convincing them that these relationships are negative influences or sources of conflict. They might spread lies or create false narratives to damage the victim's reputation amongst their loved ones, creating further isolation and dependency on the abuser. They might control access to communication, monitoring calls and texts, or even forbidding contact with certain individuals. The victim, left increasingly alone and isolated, becomes more dependent on the abuser for companionship and emotional support, making it more difficult to escape the abusive relationship.

Financial control is a common and devastating tactic. Sociopaths often exert control over the victim's finances, restricting their access to money, forcing them to seek the abuser's permission for even small purchases. They might conceal joint accounts, open secret credit cards, or manipulate the victim's income to maintain financial dependence. This financial control is not just about economic dominance;

it's about power and control over the victim's life. The financial dependence leaves the victim trapped, unable to leave the relationship without facing severe financial hardship. This dependence is often accompanied by subtle threats or intimidations, which further entrenches the victim's fear and prevents them from seeking help. The loss of financial independence is a significant barrier to escaping the abuse, leaving victims feeling powerless and trapped.

Control over communication is another tactic that reinforces the victim's isolation. This extends beyond monitoring calls and messages; it encompasses the manipulation of

information. The sociopath might control what the victim is allowed to read, watch, or listen to, limiting their access to information that could challenge the abuser's narrative or expose their manipulative behavior. They might filter information selectively, presenting only what suits their agenda and obscuring anything that could threaten their control. The victim's access to outside perspectives is curtailed, reinforcing their dependence on the abuser for information and interpretation of the world.

The impact of these tactics is cumulative and devastating. Each act of gaslighting, each instance of emotional abuse, each step towards isolation, each act of financial control further erodes the victim's sense of self and independence. The victim's reality is distorted, their confidence shattered, their support network dismantled, and their financial freedom curtailed. This systematic dismantling leaves the victim feeling helpless, confused, and deeply dependent on the abuser, making it extremely difficult to recognize the abuse, let alone escape it.

Consider the case of Sarah, a successful professional who fell prey to a charismatic sociopathic partner. Initially, he charmed her with his wit and apparent generosity. However, over time, he began subtly criticizing her work, her appearance, and her friendships. He manipulated her into isolating herself from her friends and family, convincing her they were jealous of their relationship. He exerted control over their finances, handling all the household bills and limiting her access to money. He would subtly gaslight her when she questioned his actions, implying she was too emotional or misunderstanding his intentions. Sarah found herself increasingly isolated, confused, and dependent on her partner, her sense of self completely eroded. She gradually lost confidence in her own judgment and accepted her

partner's distorted reality as truth, making it extremely difficult for her to recognize the abuse or seek help.

Another example is Mark, who experienced a different but equally insidious form of manipulation. His partner controlled the household narrative, consistently telling Mark he was ungrateful, lazy, or incompetent. This constant negativity, devoid of specific examples, was designed to break down Mark's self-esteem. His partner gradually isolated him from his friends by spreading malicious gossip and then took over managing his finances. This resulted in Mark becoming entirely financially dependent. He began to doubt his own perceptions, wondering if he was truly as flawed as his partner portrayed him to be. Mark's case illustrates how the insidious nature of sociopathic manipulation can manifest differently, subtly eroding a person's confidence and self-worth.

These examples underscore the subtle and insidious nature of sociopathic manipulation. The tactics are rarely blatant acts of aggression; instead, they're a series of carefully planned maneuvers designed to gain control and maintain dominance. The victim is gradually conditioned to accept the abuser's reality, making it difficult to recognize the abuse and escape its grip. The effects of this manipulative behavior are profound and long-lasting, impacting every aspect of the victim's life. Recognizing these tactics is the first critical step towards recovery and reclaiming one's life. Understanding the mechanisms of manipulation empowers survivors to break free from the cycle of abuse and begin the journey towards healing. The path to recovery is long and challenging, but with support and understanding, it is entirely possible. The knowledge gained from understanding these tactics is invaluable, providing the tools necessary to break the cycle and build a healthier, safer future.

The Impact of Sociopathic Abuse on Victims

The insidious nature of sociopathic abuse leaves a deep and lasting scar on the victim's psyche, extending far beyond the immediate physical and emotional trauma. The psychological and emotional consequences are profound and multifaceted, often manifesting as a complex array of symptoms that can significantly impair daily life. It's crucial to understand that these symptoms are not a sign of weakness or fault on the victim's part; they are entirely predictable and understandable responses to the systematic dismantling of one's sense of self, security, and reality. The experience is the result of the abuser's actions, not the victim's inherent flaws.

One of the most common consequences of sociopathic abuse is the development of Post-Traumatic Stress Disorder (PTSD). PTSD, traditionally associated with war or natural disasters, can also be triggered by the prolonged trauma of living with a sociopath. The constant fear, unpredictability, and emotional manipulation create a state of hypervigilance, leaving the victim constantly on edge, anticipating the next outburst or manipulation. Symptoms can include flashbacks, nightmares, intrusive thoughts related to the abusive relationship, and emotional numbness. Even seemingly mundane events or situations can trigger overwhelming feelings of anxiety or panic, transporting the victim back to the trauma. The inability to escape the emotional and mental grip of the abuser contributes significantly to the development of PTSD.

Anxiety disorders are another prevalent outcome. The constant uncertainty and fear created by the abuser's unpredictable behavior create a state of chronic anxiety.

Victims may experience generalized anxiety, characterized by persistent worry and nervousness, or panic attacks, characterized by intense fear and physical symptoms such as rapid heartbeat, shortness of breath, and trembling. The inability to trust one's own perceptions or judgment, a common consequence of gaslighting, further exacerbates anxiety, as the victim constantly questions their own reality and experiences. The resulting hyper-awareness of potential threats, even in safe environments, contributes to the persistent and debilitating effects of anxiety.

Depression is a common comorbid condition among survivors of sociopathic abuse. The systematic erosion of self-worth, the constant criticism and belittling, and the isolation imposed by the abuser contribute to feelings of hopelessness, worthlessness, and despair. Victims may experience persistent sadness, loss of interest in activities they once enjoyed, changes in appetite and sleep patterns, fatigue, and difficulty concentrating. The feeling of being trapped and powerless, coupled with the pervasive sense of shame and guilt often instilled by the abuser, deepens the depression, creating a vicious cycle of negativity and despair. The isolation often orchestrated by the abuser further prevents access to vital support networks, compounding the victim's distress.

Low self-esteem is a hallmark of the aftermath of sociopathic abuse. The abuser's constant criticism, subtle put-downs, and manipulation systematically erode the victim's confidence, making them question their judgment, abilities, and worth. The victim internalizes the abuser's negative messages, believing themselves to be flawed, inadequate, and unworthy of love and respect. This pervasive self-doubt extends to all aspects of their life, impacting their relationships, career, and overall well-being. The victim may struggle to make decisions, fearing they are

incapable of making the right choices. The erosion of self- esteem is one of the most enduring and devastating legacies of sociopathic abuse.

Beyond these specific diagnoses, sociopathic abuse leaves a broader impact on the victim's sense of self and their ability to navigate the world. Trust issues are widespread. The consistent betrayal and manipulation experienced in the abusive relationship make it difficult for the victim to trust others, even those who genuinely care about them. This distrust can extend to close friends, family members, and even professionals, creating barriers to seeking help and support. The constant deception and manipulation make establishing genuine connections difficult, resulting in feelings of isolation and loneliness, even within supportive environments.

Difficulties with intimacy and forming healthy relationships are also common. The victim may struggle to form close attachments, fearing the repetition of the abusive dynamics. They may subconsciously seek out partners with similar traits to the abuser, recreating the familiar, albeit toxic, pattern. Alternatively, they may become overly cautious and avoid intimacy altogether, fearing vulnerability and betrayal. The experience of abuse distorts the perception of healthy relationships, making it challenging to differentiate between healthy boundaries and abusive behavior.

Cognitive impairment, often subtle and overlooked, can also result from chronic stress and emotional manipulation. The victim may struggle with concentration, memory, and decision-making due to the persistent cognitive dissonance created by gaslighting. The constant questioning of one's perceptions and reality can impair cognitive function, making it challenging to process information and make sound judgments. This mental fatigue can contribute to feelings of overwhelm and further impede recovery.

Somatic symptoms, physical manifestations of psychological distress, are frequently reported by survivors. These symptoms can include chronic pain, gastrointestinal issues, sleep disturbances, headaches, and fatigue. The prolonged stress and anxiety associated with the abuse manifest physically, taking a toll on the victim's overall health. The body's inability to effectively manage the constant state of stress can lead to a range of physical ailments.

The recovery process from sociopathic abuse is a journey, not a destination. It requires patience, self-compassion, and access to appropriate support systems. Therapy plays a crucial role, offering a safe space to process the trauma, rebuild self-esteem, and develop healthy coping mechanisms. It is essential to validate the victim's experience, acknowledging the reality of the abuse and helping them understand that the symptoms they are experiencing are not their fault. Therapy provides the necessary tools to challenge the internalized negative messages and reclaim their sense of self.

Support groups offer invaluable peer support, creating a community where survivors can share their experiences, find validation, and learn from others who understand the intricacies of recovering from sociopathic abuse. Connecting with others who have lived through similar experiences can significantly reduce feelings of isolation and provide a sense of hope and resilience.

Rebuilding a sense of self requires active engagement in self-care. This includes prioritizing physical health through exercise, healthy eating, and sufficient sleep; engaging in activities that bring joy and foster a sense of

accomplishment; setting healthy boundaries and learning to say no to demands that compromise personal well-being. It involves cultivating self-compassion and recognizing one's own strength and resilience. The path to recovery involves challenging the ingrained beliefs and behaviors shaped by the abuse and creating a new narrative centered on self- worth, safety, and agency. The process is challenging, but with perseverance and the right support, a fulfilling and healthy life free from the shadow of abuse is entirely possible. The journey of healing is unique to each individual, but recognizing the common impact of sociopathic abuse is the crucial first step. Understanding that these experiences are not a reflection of personal weakness, but rather the direct consequence of abuse, is fundamental in embarking on the path towards recovery and reclaiming a life free from fear and manipulation.

Recognizing the Red Flags and Warning Signs

Recognizing the insidious nature of sociopathic abuse often proves challenging due to the abuser's mastery of manipulation and deception. They rarely reveal their true selves outright; instead, they employ a complex web of tactics designed to slowly erode the victim's sense of self and control their behavior. Identifying these red flags requires careful observation and a willingness to question seemingly innocuous behaviors. It's crucial to remember that not all of these signs will be present in every abusive relationship, and the presence of one or two doesn't automatically mean you're in an abusive relationship. However, the consistent presence of multiple red flags should serve as a serious cause for concern.

One of the most prominent red flags is a pervasive pattern of **gaslighting** . This involves systematically manipulating the victim's perception of reality, making them question their own sanity and memory. The abuser might deny events that happened, twist their words, or subtly alter the narrative to suit their agenda. For example, an abuser might deny making a specific promise, claim the victim is misremembering a conversation, or insist the victim is overly sensitive or imagining things. The cumulative effect of these manipulations can leave the victim feeling confused, disoriented, and increasingly dependent on the abuser for validation. The gaslighting isn't a single incident; it's a repeated pattern of undermining the victim's sense of self and truth.

Closely related to gaslighting is the abuser's tendency to **control and manipulate** the victim's life. This control can manifest in numerous ways: restricting access to friends and

family, monitoring phone calls and emails, controlling finances, dictating clothing choices, or limiting access to transportation or personal possessions. This control is often subtle at first, presented as concern or protectiveness.

However, over time, it becomes increasingly restrictive, isolating the victim and diminishing their independence. For instance, an abuser might initially claim to be concerned about the victim's safety when limiting their contact with family or friends. Later, this could escalate into preventing them from seeing loved ones altogether, under the guise of 'protecting them'. Financial control is another common form of abuse, where the abuser might withhold money, control all joint accounts, or prevent the victim from working.

The **lack of empathy and remorse** is a defining characteristic of sociopathic abusers. They rarely show genuine concern for the victim's feelings or well-being. They might dismiss the victim's emotions as irrational, overblown, or manipulative, further eroding the victim's sense of self- worth. Even when directly confronted with their hurtful actions, they may show little to no remorse, offering superficial apologies or blaming the victim for their own behavior. For example, an abuser might react to a victim expressing hurt feelings with a dismissive comment like, "You're too sensitive," or "You're making a big deal out of nothing." They lack the ability to genuinely understand and share the victim's emotional experience.

Another significant red flag is the abuser's **charming and charismatic** facade. They often present themselves as charming, intelligent, and successful, masking their manipulative and abusive tendencies. This initial charm helps to draw victims into the relationship and make it more difficult to recognize the abuse. The abuser may be exceptionally skilled at making a good first impression, leaving others unaware of their true nature. This duality

makes it difficult for victims and those around them to identify the abuser's abusive patterns.

Isolation is a tactic frequently employed by sociopathic abusers to increase their control and prevent the victim from seeking help or support. They might subtly undermine the victim's relationships with friends and family, creating distance and making them more reliant on the abuser. This isolation can be gradual, starting with criticisms of the victim's friends or family, leading to outright prohibitions on contact. The abuser might also make it difficult for the victim to leave the house, attend social events, or maintain their own independent social circle.

Pathological lying is a key component of the manipulative tactics used by sociopaths. They frequently lie, often without any apparent motive beyond the manipulation itself. These lies can be about big or small things, further eroding the victim's trust and confidence in their perception of reality.

The victim may find themselves constantly questioning the abuser's words and actions, further contributing to the confusion and disorientation caused by the abuse. Over time, this consistent deceit damages the victim's sense of security and self-trust.

Paranoia and projection are common mechanisms employed by sociopathic abusers. They often accuse the victim of behaviors that they themselves are guilty of, a tactic known as projection. This deflection shifts blame and distracts from their own actions. Similarly, they may display intense paranoia, distrusting the victim's intentions or accusing them of plotting against them. These behaviors are designed to confuse the victim and maintain control. For example, an abuser might accuse their partner of cheating when they are the one engaging in infidelity.

Threats, intimidation, and coercion can take many forms. These range from subtle threats to overt acts of violence or intimidation. The abuser might threaten to harm the victim, their family, or their pets; threaten to reveal embarrassing information; or use financial control to coerce compliance. These tactics are designed to create fear and maintain control over the victim. The constant fear generated through such threats impacts every aspect of the victim's daily life.

Controlling behavior extends beyond restricting social contacts and finances; it encompasses controlling every facet of the victim's life. This can include dictating what the victim wears, how they spend their time, who they can speak to, and even controlling their diet or sleep patterns. The abuser seeks to strip the victim of their autonomy, making them completely dependent.

Emotional volatility is another common red flag. The abuser's emotions can shift dramatically and unpredictably. They might switch from being overly charming and affectionate to angry and abusive within minutes or even seconds. This unpredictable behavior keeps the victim on edge, constantly anticipating the next outburst. This emotional rollercoaster creates a high level of stress and anxiety for the victim.

Lack of accountability and a refusal to take responsibility for their actions are crucial indicators. They will deflect blame, minimize the impact of their behavior, or rationalize their actions, shifting responsibility onto the victim or external factors. This prevents the relationship from ever being truly resolved and allows the abuse to continue.

Exploitation is a common element in sociopathic abuse. The abuser may exploit the victim financially, emotionally, or sexually. They might manipulate the victim into providing

money, favors, or emotional support without reciprocity. This exploitation is often intricately woven into the overall pattern of manipulation and control.

Love bombing , a period of intense affection and attention at the beginning of the relationship, is used to reel the victim in and create a false sense of security. This intense period of romantic gestures and compliments is then followed by periods of coldness, criticism, or abuse. This cyclical pattern of idealization and devaluation is a classic characteristic of sociopathic relationships.

Triangulation involves involving a third party in the relationship to create conflict and undermine the victim's sense of security. The abuser might talk to other people about the victim, pitting them against each other. They could also involve another person romantically to create jealousy or insecurity. This serves to weaken the relationship and increase the abuser's power.

Recognizing these red flags is a critical step towards escaping the cycle of abuse. While the presence of some of these warning signs doesn't automatically indicate sociopathic abuse, a consistent pattern of multiple red flags should be taken seriously. It's important to trust your instincts and seek help if you feel unsafe or manipulated.

Remember, escaping this kind of abuse is possible. The first step is identifying the problem and seeking professional support. The path to recovery is long and challenging, but it is a path worth pursuing. You deserve a life free from fear and manipulation.

Breaking the Cycle of Abuse The First Step

Breaking the cycle of abuse is a monumental task, often fraught with fear, uncertainty, and self-doubt. The insidious nature of sociopathic abuse leaves victims feeling trapped, their sense of self eroded, and their ability to make rational decisions compromised. However, understanding that you are not alone and that the abuse is not your fault is the crucial first step towards reclaiming your life. The manipulative tactics employed by sociopaths are designed to isolate and control, making it feel impossible to escape. But escape *is* possible. The path to freedom begins with recognizing the reality of your situation and accepting that you deserve better.

This isn't about blame; it's about empowerment. For years, I, like many others, struggled with the crippling guilt and self- reproach that accompany abuse. I replayed every conversation, every interaction, searching for my own flaws, the things I "could have done differently" to prevent the abuse. This is a classic manipulation tactic. Sociopaths expertly deflect blame, making you question your own sanity and perceptions. They'll paint you as the problem, the instigator, the emotionally unstable one, while they remain the seemingly rational, unaffected party. Let me assure you: this is a lie. The responsibility for the abuse rests entirely on the abuser's shoulders. Their actions are a reflection of their pathology, not a consequence of your shortcomings.

The decision to leave is rarely simple. It's often a process, a gradual awakening to the reality of the abuse and the recognition of its devastating impact. Fear is a powerful tool used by abusers, and it's understandable to feel terrified of the unknown. What will happen if you leave? Will you be

safe? Will you be able to support yourself? These are legitimate concerns, and addressing them is crucial to making a safe and successful exit.

Often, the first step isn't a dramatic escape but a series of small, incremental changes that gradually shift the balance of power. These subtle shifts can create space for self- reflection, allowing you to reassess the situation more clearly and begin to formulate a plan. Perhaps it's creating a secret email address, a discreet way to communicate with a trusted friend or family member outside the abuser's knowledge.

Maybe it's opening a separate bank account, securing a small amount of money to use for an eventual escape. Or it might be subtly researching local shelters or support organizations, learning about the resources available to you without alarming the abuser. These seemingly insignificant actions are actually steps towards reclaiming your agency, building a foundation for your escape.

Remember, creating a safety plan is paramount. This plan needs to be as detailed as possible, considering every aspect of your life. Where will you go? Who will you contact? Do you have access to transportation? What about your belongings? How will you secure your finances? Do you need to involve law enforcement? Creating a comprehensive safety plan minimizes risks and maximizes your chances of a successful escape. Don't underestimate the importance of having a detailed plan; it's the roadmap to your freedom.

It's imperative to start building a support network. Reach out to trusted friends, family members, or colleagues. Confiding in someone you trust, even if it's just one person, can make a world of difference. Sharing your experiences can provide validation, emotional support, and practical assistance. They might offer a safe place to stay, help with logistics, or simply provide a listening ear. This support network is crucial for

navigating the emotional and logistical challenges of leaving an abusive relationship. Don't be afraid to reach out; people who care about you want to help.

Connecting with support organizations specifically designed to help victims of domestic violence and abuse is also critical. These organizations offer a range of services, from emergency shelter and legal assistance to counseling and support groups. They provide a safe space to share your experiences without judgment and offer expert guidance on navigating the legal and emotional complexities of your situation. They can connect you with resources that you might not be aware of and help you develop strategies for moving forward. There is no shame in seeking help; it's a sign of strength and resilience.

Remember, the feeling of shame and guilt is a deliberate tactic used by abusers to keep you trapped. They want you to believe that you are somehow responsible for their behavior. You are not. The actions of the abuser are a reflection of their own character and personality disorders; your worth is not diminished by their actions. You deserve a life free from fear and manipulation. You deserve respect, kindness, and love.

The process of leaving an abusive relationship and rebuilding your life is a journey, not a destination. There will be setbacks, moments of doubt, and emotional challenges.

Healing takes time, patience, and self-compassion. Allow yourself to grieve the loss of the relationship you imagined, to feel the anger, the sadness, the confusion. These feelings are valid, and it's crucial to process them healthily, with the support of therapists or support groups.

Professional help is invaluable during this process. A therapist specializing in trauma and abuse recovery can

provide the necessary tools and techniques to cope with the emotional fallout of the abuse, to understand the impact on your mental and emotional well-being, and to develop healthy coping mechanisms. Therapy can help you unravel the complexities of the manipulation and rebuild your sense of self-worth. It offers a safe space to process your experiences without judgment and provides guidance on regaining your emotional equilibrium.

The path to recovery is paved with small victories, moments of self-discovery, and increasing self-confidence. It's about reclaiming your autonomy, your voice, your life. It's about redefining what a healthy relationship looks and feels like and setting boundaries to ensure you never fall prey to such manipulation again. It's about remembering your strength, your resilience, your inherent worth. This is your story, and you are writing the next chapter, a chapter filled with hope, healing, and a future free from the shadows of abuse.

Leaving an abusive relationship is never easy, but it is always possible. You are not alone. There are people who care, resources that can help, and a future waiting for you, a future where you can thrive and flourish. The first step, the most critical step, is recognizing the abuse, understanding that it's not your fault, and choosing to break free. That choice is the beginning of your journey to healing and recovery, a journey that is worth taking, a journey that leads to a life filled with love, respect, and peace. Remember your worth, believe in yourself, and know that you deserve a life free from the shadows.

Assessing Your Current Situation and Risks

Before embarking on the actual escape, a crucial step involves a thorough assessment of your present circumstances and the potential risks inherent in leaving. This isn't about dwelling on fear, but about strategically mitigating it. Understanding the potential dangers allows you to proactively build a safety plan that significantly increases your chances of a successful and safe transition.

Begin by honestly evaluating your living situation. Does your abuser have access to firearms or other weapons? Is there a history of violence or threats of violence? This information is critical for determining the level of immediate risk you face. If weapons are present, consider whether they are easily accessible, stored securely, or even hidden in places you wouldn't immediately suspect. The presence of weapons dramatically alters the safety equation, necessitating a more cautious and potentially more immediate escape strategy.

Next, analyze the level of control your abuser exerts over your daily life. This encompasses various aspects, from financial control to social isolation. Does your abuser control your finances, limiting your access to funds or preventing you from having a separate bank account? This financial dependence creates a significant barrier to escape, as it can leave you feeling trapped and unable to afford independent living. If this is the case, meticulously document any financial transactions, and begin subtly accumulating even small amounts of money. Consider creating a secret savings account, perhaps using a different financial institution, or utilizing prepaid cards.

Assess the extent of your social isolation. Have you been systematically cut off from friends and family? Does your abuser monitor your communications, restrict your access to technology, or control your movement? This isolation is a deliberate tactic to minimize your support network and increase your dependence on the abuser. If you're isolated, prioritize rebuilding contact with trusted individuals, even if it's initially through discreet methods, such as secret email addresses or coded messages. Re-establishing these connections is essential for providing emotional support and practical assistance during your escape.

Consider your abuser's personality and behavior patterns. Are they impulsive and prone to fits of rage? Do they exhibit a pattern of escalating aggression or violence?

Understanding these patterns allows you to anticipate potential reactions to your departure and factor those reactions into your safety plan. If they have a history of unpredictable behavior, you may need to take additional precautions, such as arranging for a temporary stay in a safe house or shelter, rather than going straight to a friend or family member's home.

Technological surveillance is a prevalent tool used by abusers. Assess your abuser's access to your digital devices, email accounts, and social media. Do they monitor your online activity? Do they have access to your passwords or location data through tracking apps? If so, take immediate steps to secure your digital privacy, changing all your passwords, deleting tracking apps, and limiting the personal information you share online. Consider using secure messaging apps that offer end-to-end encryption and using a different device if possible. It might be useful to research different applications and operating systems to better protect your privacy.

Your physical safety is paramount. Assess your home environment for potential escape routes and safe spaces. Identify potential escape routes from your home, noting the quickest ways to exit your apartment, house, or building safely. If you're staying in a shared residence, plan alternative routes. If you are being stalked, identify places where you are most vulnerable, and make plans to minimize your exposure to your stalker. Identify safe spaces within your home that offer a degree of privacy or refuge in case of an altercation. These safe spaces could be a locked room, a well-lit area, or a place where you can easily call for help.

Once you've conducted this self-assessment, it's crucial to identify specific risks associated with leaving. These risks can range from direct threats of violence to the more subtle forms of intimidation and harassment. It's imperative to recognize and address these risks systematically, incorporating preventive measures into your safety plan. The most crucial aspect of mitigating risk is careful planning and meticulous execution of that plan.

Consider the following potential risks and ways to mitigate them:

Physical violence: This is the most serious risk. If your abuser has a history of violence, leaving must be planned with utmost caution. Consider seeking assistance from law enforcement or a domestic violence shelter to ensure your safety during the escape.

Stalking and harassment: Your abuser may attempt to track your movements or harass you after you leave. Develop a plan to minimize your exposure and maintain your anonymity. This might involve changing your phone number, using a different email address, or temporarily relocating to a new address known only to a trusted few. Consider seeking a

restraining order to legally protect yourself from further harassment.

Financial hardship: If your abuser controls your finances, you'll need to secure your own financial resources before leaving. This might involve secretly opening a bank account, accumulating savings, or seeking assistance from family, friends, or social services.

Loss of housing and support systems: You may need to find a new place to live and rebuild your support network. Begin researching local shelters, affordable housing options, or the possibility of staying with friends or family.

Legal repercussions: If you're concerned about legal repercussions, consult with a lawyer specializing in domestic violence cases to understand your rights and options.

Emotional and psychological trauma: Leaving an abusive relationship is emotionally challenging. Begin building a support network of trusted friends, family, therapists, or support groups to provide emotional support and guidance throughout this process.

Your safety plan should be a detailed, personalized document addressing all these potential risks. It's not a single action but a multifaceted strategy covering every conceivable scenario. The more comprehensively you plan, the greater your chances of a successful and safe escape.

Begin creating your safety plan by listing all potential escape routes from your home, including alternative paths if your primary escape route is blocked. Consider the times of day when you are least likely to be observed or confronted and plan accordingly. If possible, consider having a backup plan in case your first attempt is unsuccessful. Don't

underestimate the importance of having a pre-determined location for your escape, whether it's a friend's house, a family member's home, or a domestic violence shelter.

This safety plan isn't static; it's a living document, subject to modification as circumstances evolve. Regularly review and update your plan based on any new information or changes in your situation. Remember, a dynamic, adaptable plan significantly improves your chances of a successful escape.

Remember that you are not alone in this, and seeking professional help is a sign of strength, not weakness. Therapists specializing in trauma and abuse recovery can provide invaluable support and guidance in developing a comprehensive safety plan and navigating the complexities of leaving an abusive relationship. They offer a safe space to process your fears, discuss your options, and develop coping strategies for the emotional challenges ahead.

The creation of a safety plan is a vital, life-affirming step toward reclaiming your life and breaking free from the abusive situation. It's a roadmap to your freedom, meticulously laid out to help you reach your destination safe and secure. Your journey towards freedom begins with one solid step: making a comprehensive safety plan.

Gathering Essential Resources and Support

Gathering the necessary resources and support is as crucial as crafting the safety plan itself. Your escape isn't just about leaving the abusive environment; it's about building a secure foundation for your future. This involves securing safe housing, assembling a dependable support network, and obtaining the legal and financial guidance you need to navigate this complex transition. Failing to adequately address these aspects can severely jeopardize your safety and well-being.

Let's begin with housing. Leaving an abusive situation often necessitates a change of address, even temporarily. The immediate priority is to find a safe place where your abuser cannot locate you. Domestic violence shelters offer a lifeline in these situations. These shelters provide temporary accommodation, meals, and often access to counseling and legal services. They are designed to offer a safe haven from immediate danger, giving you the space to assess your options and formulate a long-term plan. Finding a shelter requires research; many local organizations and hotlines can provide listings and referrals based on your geographical location and specific circumstances. Don't hesitate to utilize these resources; they are specifically designed to assist individuals in situations like yours. Remember, seeking help is a courageous act, not a sign of weakness.

If a shelter isn't immediately feasible, explore alternative temporary housing options. This could involve staying with trusted family or friends. Before approaching anyone, be sure you feel fully comfortable confiding in them. It's crucial to choose people who will prioritize your safety and offer unconditional support. Explain your situation honestly,

emphasizing the level of risk involved. This ensures they understand the gravity of the situation and can take appropriate precautions. It's vital to prepare your support network for potential contact attempts from your abuser. Provide them with strategies for deflecting any communication or visit attempts. If you have reason to believe your abuser may become violent or intrusive, your support network will need to be prepared to manage this possibility. A clear plan for handling any attempts from your abuser to contact them and you is crucial.

Finding long-term housing requires careful planning and consideration of your financial capabilities. Affordable housing options can be difficult to secure, especially if you lack financial independence. Explore housing assistance programs offered by your local government or non-profit organizations. These programs often provide subsidized housing or rental assistance to individuals in need. Research thoroughly and make sure you fully understand the eligibility criteria and application process. Be prepared to provide the necessary documentation, which might include proof of income, residency, and evidence of domestic violence.

Beyond housing, building a strong support network is vital. This network provides emotional and practical assistance during this difficult transition. Start by identifying trusted individuals who can offer unwavering support. This may include family members, close friends, colleagues, or members of your faith community. These individuals will offer a listening ear, practical help, and emotional strength during periods of vulnerability.

Reaching out to friends and family may feel daunting after a period of isolation imposed by your abuser. Remember, the isolation was a deliberate tactic designed to control you; it

does not reflect your true relationships. Your friends and family likely want to be helpful. Take the initiative to re- establish those connections. Start with short updates gradually explaining your situation. Don't feel pressured to reveal everything at once; take your time and share what you are ready to share. Prioritize those who you believe can be consistently supportive and understanding.

Consider joining a support group for survivors of domestic abuse. These groups offer a unique opportunity to connect with others who understand your experience. Sharing experiences and receiving empathetic support from others who've lived through similar situations can be incredibly powerful. Support groups provide a sense of community and validation. They can also offer practical advice and suggestions based on the lived experiences of others.

Finding professional support is essential. A therapist specializing in trauma and abuse recovery can offer invaluable guidance. Therapy provides a safe space to process the emotional trauma you've endured. A therapist can help you develop coping mechanisms to navigate the challenges of rebuilding your life. They can offer support and validation during this transition. Many therapists offer sliding-scale fees or pro bono services, ensuring access regardless of financial constraints.

Seeking legal counsel is also essential. A lawyer specializing in family law or domestic violence can advise you on your legal rights and options, particularly regarding restraining orders, child custody, and other relevant legal matters.

Having legal counsel can make a profound difference in securing your safety and protecting your rights during the separation and beyond. They can help you navigate the legal processes involved in severing ties with your abuser. A

lawyer can advise you on any potential legal repercussions related to the separation.

Financial independence is crucial for long-term safety and stability. If your abuser controlled your finances, you will need to begin rebuilding your financial security. Start by identifying your assets, including bank accounts, investments, and property. Secure these assets and take steps to prevent your abuser from gaining access to them.

Consider opening a new bank account and applying for credit cards in your name only. Explore financial assistance programs that offer grants or loans for survivors of domestic violence. These programs can assist in securing stable housing, paying off debts, or starting new careers.

Remember that rebuilding your life after escaping abuse is a marathon, not a sprint. Be patient with yourself and celebrate your progress along the way. It's important to acknowledge and validate the tremendous effort involved in creating a safe and stable future. Focus on taking small, manageable steps, one day at a time.

The process of gathering resources and support is integral to your safety and well-being. It's not a single step but a multifaceted strategy requiring ongoing effort. However, remember that each step you take is a demonstration of your resilience and strength. You are taking back control of your life, creating a foundation for your future free from fear and manipulation. This is a journey towards healing and empowerment, and you have the strength to succeed. Your commitment to rebuilding your life is a testament to your inner resilience and your determination to create a future free from abuse. Reach out to those who can support you, and remember that you are not alone.

Developing a Communication Strategy

Developing a communication strategy during the separation process from a sociopathic abuser requires careful planning and a deep understanding of their manipulative tactics. The goal is not to engage in protracted arguments or attempts at reconciliation, but rather to minimize contact while ensuring your safety and well-being. This means establishing clear boundaries and choosing communication channels strategically to protect yourself from further abuse or retaliation.

The first step involves recognizing that any communication with your abuser is inherently risky. Sociopaths are masters of manipulation, and even seemingly innocuous conversations can be used to exert control, gather information, or escalate conflict. Therefore, the ideal scenario is to eliminate direct contact entirely. This may involve utilizing a third party, such as a lawyer or a trusted friend, to handle all necessary communication. This approach removes the direct interaction that allows the abuser to exert their influence and minimizes the risk of emotional or psychological manipulation.

If direct communication is unavoidable—for example, regarding child custody arrangements or financial matters— it's crucial to maintain strict control over the interaction.

Choose a method that provides a written record, such as email or text messaging. Avoid phone calls, as they offer less control over the conversation and are more easily manipulated. Keep all communication concise, factual, and professional. Avoid emotional language or personal details that could be used against you. Respond only to essential

queries and refrain from engaging in lengthy discussions or arguments.

Before engaging in any form of communication, anticipate potential manipulative tactics. Sociopaths often employ gaslighting, blaming, and deflection to control the narrative and maintain their power. Prepare for these tactics by rehearsing your responses and having clear boundaries in mind. If the conversation veers into manipulation, immediately disengage. Politely but firmly state that you are not willing to engage in unproductive discussions and end the communication. Do not feel obligated to justify your actions or engage in debate.

Consider creating a template for your responses to frequently asked questions or common points of contention. This pre- prepared template ensures that your communications remain concise and avoids emotional responses. This is particularly helpful if you're dealing with multiple exchanges, ensuring consistency and preventing emotional outbursts that could fuel the abuser's manipulative behaviors. For instance, if the abuser repeatedly demands money, a prepared response outlining financial support arrangements and legal proceedings is more effective than a reactive, emotional response. Similarly, if questions arise about children, a consistent template that prioritizes the child's well-being and clearly outlines visitation plans minimizes the potential for manipulation.

Document every communication, including emails, texts, and any written notes. This record is crucial in case of future legal proceedings or if the abuser attempts to discredit your account of the abuse. It serves as irrefutable evidence of your interactions and demonstrates the pattern of their behavior.

Keep a detailed log of dates, times, the content of the communication, and any notable observations about the abuser's tone or demeanor. This comprehensive documentation not only protects you legally but also reinforces your awareness of the dynamics at play.

If the communication involves a third party, ensure they fully understand the situation and the abuser's potential manipulative tactics. Provide them with background information to help them manage the interactions effectively. This includes details about the abuse, the abuser's manipulative tactics, and any specific concerns about their safety. This collaboration helps to protect you and provides additional layers of support during the separation process.

It's essential to maintain emotional distance during all communications. Avoid showing any vulnerability or emotional reactivity that the abuser can exploit. This means responding to their communication in a calm, detached, and businesslike manner. This emotional detachment limits their opportunity to exert their control and minimizes the risk of emotional escalation. Remember, your emotional state is your responsibility. Do not let their communications dictate your emotions.

Establish a clear communication protocol. Decide on the preferred method of communication, the frequency, and the topics to be discussed. This helps establish boundaries and prevents the abuser from dictating the terms of interaction. Stick to this protocol strictly and do not deviate from it, even if pressured to do so. This consistency reinforces your boundaries and protects you from unpredictable escalation.

For example, you might stipulate that communication only occurs through a designated attorney and is limited to twice a week to discuss specific legal matters.

Consider seeking guidance from a therapist or counselor specializing in trauma and abuse recovery. They can offer

support and strategies for managing communications with your abuser. They can help you identify potential triggers, develop coping mechanisms for dealing with the emotional fallout from the interaction, and provide valuable insights on recognizing and responding to manipulative behaviors. This professional support helps you maintain emotional equilibrium and prevents the abuser's manipulations from undermining your progress.

After any communication, allow yourself time to process the interaction. Engage in self-care activities that help you regain emotional balance and manage the stress. This could involve spending time in nature, practicing mindfulness, engaging in creative pursuits, or talking with a trusted friend or family member. This self-care routine helps regulate emotional responses, preventing the abuser from further controlling your emotional well-being.

Finally, remember that you have the right to protect your safety and well-being. Prioritize your emotional and physical health over the needs of the abuser. If the communication becomes emotionally or psychologically damaging, disengage immediately. Don't hesitate to seek support from legal counsel or law enforcement if necessary. Your safety and well-being are paramount, and your strength and resilience will guide you through this challenging process.

The process of disengaging from a sociopathic abuser requires patience, resilience, and a strong commitment to self-preservation. By implementing a well-defined communication strategy, you're taking control of the situation, protecting yourself from further harm, and paving the way for a healthier and safer future. Remember, you deserve to live a life free from fear and manipulation.

Protecting Yourself from Technological Stalking

Protecting yourself from technological stalking requires a proactive and multi-layered approach. Sociopaths and stalkers are adept at using technology to monitor and control their victims, often employing sophisticated methods that require careful attention to detail to counter. This isn't about paranoia; it's about safeguarding your privacy and well-being in the face of deliberate, malicious surveillance.

The first step involves a complete overhaul of your digital security practices.

Begin by changing all your passwords. This isn't just about changing them; it's about creating strong, unique passwords for every online account. Avoid easily guessable passwords like birthdays, pet names, or sequential numbers. Instead, opt for a combination of uppercase and lowercase letters, numbers, and symbols. Consider using a password manager to generate and securely store these complex passwords.

Password managers generate robust passwords and can auto- fill login credentials securely, making this crucial task much more manageable. Remember to enable two-factor authentication (2FA) wherever possible, adding an extra layer of security to your accounts. This authentication method typically requires a second verification code, sent to your phone or email, in addition to your password. This significantly reduces the likelihood of unauthorized access even if your password is compromised.

Next, review and adjust your privacy settings on all social media platforms, email accounts, and online services. Most platforms offer detailed control over who can see your posts, messages, and location data. Limit the visibility of your personal information to trusted contacts only. Be particularly

mindful of location services. While convenient, sharing your location in real-time makes you vulnerable to stalking.

Disable location sharing on apps and services unless absolutely necessary, and check the settings of any apps you've downloaded, as some will continue to share location data even when it's not explicitly enabled. Even seemingly innocuous apps might have these features, so thoroughly review their privacy policies.

Consider the apps on your phone and computer. Many apps have access to far more information than you might realize. Review your installed applications and remove any that you no longer use or that you suspect might be used for tracking or monitoring your activity.

Pay close attention to apps with broad permissions, including access to your contacts, location, microphone, or camera. If you're unsure about an app's function, research it thoroughly online before continuing to use it. Uninstall any apps you deem suspicious and ensure that you are aware of every app installed on your devices.

Beyond reviewing your current apps, be vigilant about downloading new apps. Only download apps from reputable app stores, and carefully read reviews before installation.

Avoid apps from unknown or untrusted sources. Consider using a VPN (Virtual Private Network) to encrypt your internet traffic and mask your IP address. This makes it more difficult for someone to track your online activity and location. A VPN is a vital tool in preserving your digital anonymity and security, and it's a worthwhile investment.

Regularly scan your devices for malware and spyware. Use reputable antivirus and anti-malware software and keep it updated. These security programs can detect and remove harmful software that might be installed on your devices without your knowledge, potentially providing access to

your personal data and enabling surveillance. Ensure your operating systems are also updated regularly as these updates often include security patches to protect against known vulnerabilities.

Take extra precautions with your email. Be cautious about opening emails from unknown senders or clicking on links within emails, as these can lead to malware infections or phishing scams. Use strong and unique passwords for your email accounts and enable 2FA for added security. Consider setting up email filters to automatically move suspicious emails to your spam folder. Regularly review the "sent" folder and delete unwanted messages to prevent those messages from being easily accessible.

Be aware of smart home devices. Many modern homes are equipped with devices like smart speakers, security cameras, and smart televisions that can collect and transmit data about your activities. Be mindful of these devices and their privacy settings. Ensure you understand how they collect and use your data, and adjust their privacy settings to minimize the amount of data collected. In some cases, consider disabling these devices entirely if there is a significant risk of technological stalking. If you're unsure about the security implications of your smart home devices, consult a tech- savvy friend or professional.

Consider purchasing a new phone and/or computer. If you suspect your devices have been compromised by spyware or tracking software, it's wise to replace them. This is a significant step, but it's essential to ensure your complete digital security. While it requires an investment, the peace of mind gained by knowing you have devices that are truly yours and completely free of spyware is invaluable.

Finally, document everything. Keep a record of all suspicious activity, including emails, messages, and any unusual behavior of your devices. This documentation is crucial if you need to seek legal assistance or report the stalking to law enforcement. Note the dates, times, and details of any suspicious incidents. This detailed record will serve as crucial evidence of the abuser's actions and will greatly assist authorities in bringing them to justice.

This comprehensive approach to protecting yourself from technological stalking is crucial. It's a continuous process that demands vigilance and proactive measures. By adopting these strategies, you are significantly reducing your vulnerability and reclaiming control over your digital life and, by extension, your personal safety and well-being.

Remember, your safety is paramount. Don't hesitate to seek assistance from professionals – tech support, legal counsel, or a therapist specializing in trauma and abuse recovery – if you need help implementing these measures or feel overwhelmed. Your strength and resilience will guide you through this process. You deserve to live a life free from fear and manipulation.

Securing Legal Protection

Securing legal protection is a crucial step in escaping the clutches of a sociopathic abuser. It provides a tangible barrier against further harm and offers a pathway towards reclaiming your safety and autonomy. However, navigating the legal system can be daunting, especially when dealing with the manipulative tactics often employed by sociopaths. This section aims to equip you with the knowledge and strategies to effectively obtain legal protection and secure your future.

The first critical step involves understanding the types of legal protection available to you. In most jurisdictions, restraining orders and protective orders are the primary legal avenues for shielding yourself from abusive individuals.

While the specific terminology and requirements might vary slightly from state to state or country to country, the core purpose remains consistent: to prevent the abuser from contacting you, coming near your residence or workplace, and engaging in any other forms of harassment or intimidation.

Restraining orders, often referred to as temporary restraining orders or TROs, are typically granted quickly, often within a matter of days, following an initial court hearing. They provide immediate protection, but they are usually temporary in nature. A hearing is then scheduled to determine whether a permanent restraining order should be issued. To obtain a restraining order, you will need to demonstrate to the court that you are in immediate danger or have experienced credible threats of violence or harassment from the abuser. Detailed documentation of the abuse, including dates, times, specific incidents, and any

corroborating evidence (such as text messages, emails, photographs, witness statements, police reports, medical records), will be essential in supporting your application.

Protective orders, on the other hand, are often broader in scope and duration. They are frequently granted in cases involving domestic violence, stalking, or other forms of intimate partner abuse. They often include provisions beyond simple restrictions on contact, such as stipulations regarding child custody, visitation rights, firearm ownership, and access to shared property or finances. The application process for protective orders usually involves a more extensive investigation and hearing, but they offer stronger and more comprehensive protection.

Gathering evidence of abuse is paramount in your quest for legal protection. This evidence serves as the foundation upon which your case will be built. It is crucial to maintain detailed records of every interaction with your abuser, no matter how seemingly insignificant. This includes:

Detailed written accounts of every incident: Document the date, time, location, and a comprehensive description of what happened. Include specific details such as the abuser's words, actions, and any physical or emotional consequences you experienced. Be as specific as possible. Instead of saying "he yelled at me," write "on October 26th at 8:00 PM, in the kitchen, he yelled at me, calling me names including [specific names] and accusing me of [specific accusations]." **Copies of text messages, emails, and social media messages:** Save all communication, regardless of whether it's abusive or seemingly benign. These digital records often serve as irrefutable evidence of the abuser's behavior.

Screenshot everything. Don't delete anything; it can be used against you in court.

Photographs and videos: If you have any photographs or videos documenting injuries, property damage, or instances of harassment, these are powerful visual aids. If you take photos, ensure you take them immediately after the incident. **Medical records:** Document any injuries sustained due to the abuse. This includes physical injuries such as bruises, cuts, or broken bones, as well as psychological and emotional trauma. Make sure your doctor's records note the cause of your injuries.

Police reports: File a police report with every incident of violence or harassment. Keep a copy of the police report for your records. Even if the police don't make an arrest, the report serves as crucial documentation.

Witness statements: If anyone witnessed the abuse, obtain written or sworn statements from them. The testimony of independent witnesses can significantly strengthen your case.

Financial records: Document any financial control or manipulation by the abuser. This might include unauthorized withdrawals from joint accounts, control over finances, or preventing you from accessing money.

Organize all your documentation meticulously. Create a secure system for storing your evidence, and regularly back up your electronic files to the cloud. You might consider creating a dedicated file or folder, organized chronologically or by type of evidence. The goal is to have it readily available and easy to access when you're ready to approach the court system. Consider working with a therapist or advocate who can help you organize these materials into a cohesive and readily understandable file.

Beyond gathering evidence, seeking legal counsel is crucial. A lawyer specializing in domestic violence, stalking, or family law can provide expert advice, guide you through the legal process, represent you in court, and ensure that your

rights are protected. They can help you navigate the complexities of the legal system, explain your options, and help you develop a strategy for obtaining the most effective legal protection. Many legal aid organizations offer free or low-cost services to victims of domestic violence. Do not hesitate to seek professional legal assistance. This isn't a process to face alone.

It is imperative to understand your rights. You have the right to be safe, to be free from harassment and violence, and to seek legal recourse against those who abuse you. Familiarize yourself with your state's laws regarding restraining orders and protective orders. You are entitled to request an interpreter if you do not speak the language of the court and to be accompanied by a support person throughout the proceedings.

The process of obtaining legal protection might feel overwhelming and emotionally taxing. Remember that you are not alone, and seeking help is a sign of strength, not weakness. Lean on your support network—friends, family, therapists, support groups, or advocacy organizations—for emotional support and practical assistance. Take your time, focus on your well-being, and don't hesitate to seek help from professionals throughout this process. Securing legal protection is a crucial step in your journey towards safety and healing, and it's a testament to your resilience and your determination to build a life free from fear and control.

Remember that your safety and well-being are paramount. Never underestimate the power of seeking professional assistance; the support of qualified professionals can make all the difference in successfully navigating this challenging phase of your life.

The Escape Strategy A StepbyStep Guide

Leaving an abusive relationship with a sociopath is rarely a simple matter of packing a bag and walking out. It requires careful planning, meticulous execution, and a deep understanding of the potential risks involved. Your safety is paramount, and a well-defined escape strategy is crucial for minimizing danger and maximizing your chances of a successful and safe exit. This section will provide a detailed, step-by-step guide to help you navigate this challenging process.

First, understand that there's no one-size-fits-all approach. The best escape strategy will depend on your unique circumstances – the severity of the abuse, your abuser's personality and behavior patterns, your access to resources, and your personal support system. Some individuals might need to leave in a matter of hours, while others may require weeks or even months of careful planning. Don't feel pressured to follow a rigid timeline. Prioritize your safety and well-being above all else.

Assessing the Risks and Your Options:

Before you begin planning your escape, take some time to assess the level of risk you face. How unpredictable is your abuser? Are there instances of physical violence? Does your abuser have access to weapons? Have they threatened to harm you or others if you leave? Have they made threats via text or email? The answers to these questions will significantly influence your escape strategy. If you perceive an imminent threat of physical harm, prioritize contacting emergency services or a domestic violence hotline

immediately. They can provide immediate assistance and guidance on how to secure your safety.

Consider your available options for leaving. Do you have a safe place to go? This could be the home of a trusted friend or family member, a domestic violence shelter, or a safe house. If you don't have a pre-arranged safe haven, start identifying potential options now. Reach out to your support network and explain your situation. Don't be afraid to ask for help; it's a sign of strength, not weakness. Domestic violence shelters offer confidential accommodations and support services for victims of abuse. They can provide a safe space, counseling, and assistance with finding housing and other resources.

The Escape Plan: A Step-by-Step Guide:

1. **Gathering Essential Documents and Items:** Begin by compiling a list of essential documents and personal items you will need after you leave. This includes identification cards (driver's license, passport, social security card), birth certificates, bank information, medical records, legal documents (such as restraining orders or divorce papers), and any other crucial paperwork. Make copies of these documents and store them securely – ideally, outside your home and inaccessible to your abuser. Consider using a cloud storage service or a safety de-

posit box. Pack a small bag containing a few changes of clothing, toiletries, medication, and any other necessities. Leave this bag hidden, ready for a quick escape. Don't forget your phone and charger.

2. **Securing Financial Resources:** If your abuser controls your finances, discretely begin moving money to a separate account or securing access to emergency funds. This might involve opening a new bank account in your name only,

contacting your financial institution, or reaching out to trusted family or friends for financial assistance. This is crucial for your independence and safety post-escape. Keep records of all financial transactions, no matter how small. If your finances are intertwined and you require legal assistance to separate them, reach out to a lawyer immediately.

1. **Choosing the Right Time and Method of Escape:** The ideal time to leave will depend on your specific situation. If you live with your abuser, you might choose a time when they are not home, such as during their work hours or social engagements. If they are consistently home, leaving may require greater subtlety and more extensive planning. Leaving during the day might feel safer than leaving at night, depending on your specific circumstances. If you have children, carefully coordinate their safety and care in your escape plan. Consider involving a trusted friend, relative, or social service agency to assist with this.

Consider your transportation options. Do you have access to a vehicle? If not, arrange for alternative transportation, such as a taxi, rideshare service, public transportation, or a trusted friend or family member. Plan your route carefully, and avoid routes that your abuser might anticipate.

1. **Creating a Communication Plan:** Develop a secure communication plan with trusted individuals who can provide assistance and support. This might include friends, family, neighbors, your therapist, or a domestic violence advocate. Establish a code word or phrase that indicates you need immediate help. Keep your phone charged and readily accessible. If using your phone seems too risky, create alternate contact points, such as using a friend's phone to reach out to support.
2. **Seeking Support After Escape:** Once you're safe, reach out to your support network immediately. Let them know you've left, and seek the assistance you need. Consider connecting with a domestic violence shelter or support organization to access resources, such as housing assistance, counseling, and legal aid. Remember that recovery is a journey, and it's crucial to have a support system in place.
3. **Dealing with Potential Reactions from the Abuser:** Be prepared for potential reactions from your abuser after you leave. They may attempt to contact you, harass you, or even try to physically harm you. If you have a restraining order or protective order in place, make sure you understand its provisions, and report any violations to the authorities immediately. Maintain your safety plan and consistently follow its guidelines.
4. **Taking Care of Yourself:** The aftermath of escaping an abusive relationship is often overwhelming, both emotionally and physically. Prioritize self-care and seek professional help to process the trauma and rebuild your life. Trauma-informed therapy can provide you with the tools and support you need to heal and move forward. Don't underestimate the power of self-compassion; this is a monumental achievement and it's vital to celebrate that fact.

This step-by-step guide is intended to empower you, not overwhelm you. Remember that every situation is unique and there's no one-right answer. Adapt these steps to your specific circumstances. This escape plan is a testament to your strength and courage, and it's a critical step in reclaiming your life and your future. Don't hesitate to seek help from professionals, friends, and family—their support is invaluable. Your safety and well-being are your top priorities. Remember, you deserve to live a life free from fear and abuse.

Dealing with Immediate Threats and Emergencies

Dealing with immediate threats requires a different approach than the carefully planned escape outlined previously. While meticulous preparation is crucial for long-term safety, immediate danger necessitates swift action. Your priority in these situations is to get yourself and any dependents to safety. There is no room for hesitation; your well-being is paramount.

If you are facing an immediate threat of physical harm, your first course of action should always be to contact emergency services. This is not a time to hesitate. Dial 911 (or your country's equivalent) immediately. Clearly and concisely explain your situation, providing your location and describing the threat. Stay on the line with the dispatcher until help arrives. Even if you believe the situation might escalate if you call the police, prioritize your safety. Your life is far more important than potentially angering your abuser. The police can intervene and potentially provide immediate protection. If possible, safely leave the premises before the police arrive, but only do so if it is safe to do so.

If contacting emergency services feels impossible due to the immediate threat or your abuser's control, utilize any means available to get help. Texting a trusted contact with a pre- arranged code word ("Emergency - Code Red," for instance) can be effective, especially if you're unable to speak openly. This individual can then call emergency services on your behalf. Social media messaging, while potentially slower, can also work if your abuser doesn't monitor those accounts closely. However, be aware that evidence from social media messaging may not be admissible in court, but it can be helpful in building a history of abuse. Remember, even a

seemingly small action—a quick text, a silent alarm—can be a lifesaver.

The location you choose to flee to is vital in an immediate- threat situation. Your pre-planned safe house is your best bet; however, if that's not accessible, your options will depend on the specific circumstances. A neighbor's house, a nearby public space like a library or coffee shop, or even a crowded street can offer more immediate safety than staying in the current dangerous environment. Prioritize proximity and the visibility of other people.

Once you've reached safety, regardless of your location, inform the authorities and any relevant support networks. Detailed accounts of the incident are critical for legal action. If you have photographic or video evidence of abuse or threats—even if this information isn't currently accessible— note its existence and find a way to preserve it securely. This might involve uploading it to a cloud-based storage location accessed via a device other than your own, or confiding in a trusted individual to help you secure and preserve the evidence.

Creating a rapid response plan for urgent threats should be a crucial part of your overall safety strategy. This goes beyond the long-term escape plan discussed earlier. Think of it as your "Plan B" for when Plan A—a calm and meticulously executed exit—isn't feasible. This plan should include:

Pre-identified escape routes: Map out several different ways to leave your home or current location quickly and discreetly. Include alternative routes to avoid your abuser's anticipated path. This may involve exiting through different doors, windows, or even using back alleys if available.

Designated safe havens: Identify several locations besides your pre-planned safe house where you could go if an immediate escape is necessary. This could be a trusted friend's or family member's home, a public space with many people, or a 24-hour business that provides a safe environment.

Communication methods: Identify various communication strategies in case your primary method is compromised. This might include a pre-arranged signal with a neighbor, alternative phone numbers, or using public computers to contact support networks.

Emergency supplies kit: Keep a small bag containing essential items such as identification, medications, some money, and a phone charger in a readily accessible, hidden location. This kit is for quick grabs if you need to flee suddenly.

Pre-written emergency contact list: Keep a list of crucial contact numbers and information readily accessible, either physically or digitally. Include emergency services, domestic violence hotlines, trusted friends and family, and legal professionals.

Self-defense strategies: While not always ideal, learning some basic self-defense moves can provide a sense of empowerment and might give you a better chance to escape safely. There are many self-defense techniques available online or through community organizations that can provide this training. However, your primary goal is to escape, not engage in a physical confrontation.

Remember, your rapid response plan is a safeguard, a tool to help you get out of immediate danger, not a guaranteed solution. The plan should be flexible and adaptable to the

ever-changing circumstances of your situation. Regularly review and update it as your situation evolves.

Beyond these immediate actions, consider the long-term implications of the abuse. Seek professional help; a therapist specializing in trauma and abuse can help you process the experience, develop coping mechanisms, and create a more robust long-term safety plan. This help is not a sign of weakness but a testament to your strength and resilience.

The ability to acknowledge and address the damage done is essential to starting the long journey to healing and rebuilding your life.

The trauma you've experienced warrants significant support. Don't underestimate the depth of the impact. You may experience symptoms such as anxiety, panic attacks, depression, difficulty sleeping, flashbacks, and hypervigilance. These are all normal reactions to abnormal circumstances. It is imperative to seek professional help to navigate these challenges. A therapeutic alliance can offer a safe space to explore these feelings, unravel their root causes, and develop strategies to cope with them effectively.

Moreover, building a strong support network is crucial. Lean on your loved ones; let them be there for you. Explain to them what you've gone through in detail so they can understand the situation and provide the most appropriate level of support. They can become crucial allies in your recovery journey.

Healing from abuse by a sociopath is a marathon, not a sprint. There will be ups and downs, setbacks and progress. Be patient with yourself and celebrate your achievements along the way. Your ability to identify the abuse, to plan your escape, and to seek help are monumental steps toward reclaiming your life and your future. Remember, you deserve

to live a life free from fear and control, and the support is available to help you get there. It's a testament to your courage and strength that you've made it this far. Never forget that.

Managing the Aftermath of Escape

The adrenaline rush of escape often gives way to a profound sense of emptiness and disorientation. The immediate threat might be gone, but the emotional aftermath can be just as overwhelming, even more so. This isn't a time for self- criticism or second-guessing your decisions. You've survived. You've escaped. Now, it's about navigating the complex landscape of recovery. This phase involves a multitude of challenges, from dealing with the emotional trauma of the abuse to securing financial stability and rebuilding a life free from fear.

The first few weeks, even months, can feel like a blur. Sleep disturbances are common. You might find yourself constantly on edge, hyper-vigilant to any perceived threat, even in safe environments. Flashbacks – sudden, vivid memories of the abuse – can be terrifying and debilitating, pulling you back into the traumatic experiences you've worked so hard to leave behind. Anxiety and panic attacks may strike without warning, leaving you breathless and overwhelmed. These are not signs of weakness; they are normal responses to an abnormal situation. Your nervous system has been on high alert for a prolonged period, and it takes time for it to readjust.

It is crucial to understand that your emotional state is a direct consequence of the abuse you endured. Sociopathic abusers meticulously dismantle their victims' sense of self, creating a deep-seated feeling of inadequacy and self-blame.

Rebuilding self-esteem is a lengthy process, requiring patience, self-compassion, and professional support. Consider this phase as a marathon of healing, not a sprint. There will be moments of profound progress interspersed

with periods of regression. This is expected. The important thing is to keep moving forward.

One of the most immediate practical concerns is often financial instability. Sociopathic abusers frequently exert control over finances, leaving victims with little or no independent resources. This financial vulnerability can add another layer of anxiety and fear to an already precarious situation. Seek help immediately from local agencies dedicated to assisting victims of domestic violence. Many organizations provide emergency financial assistance, including temporary housing, food, and clothing. They can connect you with resources to help you open bank accounts, establish credit, and obtain essential necessities. Don't hesitate to reach out; these services are designed to help you regain your footing.

Finding secure housing is another critical step. If you left your home abruptly, you might find yourself without a place to live. Local shelters can provide temporary accommodation, offering a safe and supportive environment while you search for permanent housing. These shelters often offer additional services, such as counseling, legal assistance, and job training programs. Explore government assistance programs for subsidized housing; numerous options are often available depending on your location and circumstances. Reaching out to trusted friends or family members may also be a viable solution, but always prioritize your safety and comfort levels. Avoid situations that could put you at risk.

Navigating the legal system can seem daunting, but seeking legal assistance is vital to protecting yourself from future harassment and potential legal actions from your abuser.

Legal aid organizations offer pro bono or low-cost legal services, particularly in cases of domestic violence. These

services can help you obtain restraining orders, file for divorce (if applicable), and address any legal issues related to custody, child support, or property division. It is crucial to document every interaction with your abuser, keeping detailed records of any communication (emails, text messages, voicemails) and any instances of harassment or threats. This documentation will be essential in any legal proceedings.

Beyond the immediate practical issues, addressing the deeper emotional wounds left by the abuse is crucial for long-term healing. Therapy, preferably with a therapist specializing in trauma and abuse recovery, is paramount. This is not a sign of weakness; it's a testament to your strength and commitment to healing. A therapist can provide a safe and non-judgmental space to process the trauma, explore the impact on your self-esteem, and develop coping mechanisms to manage the emotional challenges you face.

They will help you understand the dynamics of the abuse and challenge the self-blame and negative self-talk that often accompany such experiences.

Cognitive Behavioral Therapy (CBT) is often highly effective in treating the psychological effects of trauma. CBT focuses on identifying and changing negative thought patterns and behaviors that contribute to anxiety, depression, and other symptoms related to trauma. Eye Movement Desensitization and Reprocessing (EMDR) is another effective therapy designed to treat trauma. EMDR uses bilateral stimulation (such as eye movements or tapping) to help process traumatic memories and reduce their emotional impact.

Building a support network is just as essential as professional therapy. Confiding in trusted friends, family members, or support groups can provide a sense of

community and belonging, helping to combat the isolation that often follows escaping an abusive relationship. Sharing your experiences with others who understand what you've been through can be incredibly validating and empowering. Support groups specifically for survivors of abuse can offer a safe space to connect with others who have had similar experiences and offer mutual support and encouragement.

Rebuilding your life after escaping abuse is a journey, not a destination. It requires courage, resilience, and a steadfast commitment to healing. There will be days when you feel overwhelmed and discouraged, but remember that you are not alone. Professional help, support networks, and self- compassion are your allies in this process. Celebrate your accomplishments, no matter how small they may seem. Each step you take toward healing is a victory. You have survived; now focus on thriving. Your strength and resilience are undeniable. Embrace your future, and know that a life free from fear and control is within reach.

Remember that reclaiming your life involves redefining your boundaries and establishing healthy relationships. This will require conscious effort and potentially professional guidance. Learning to recognize and assert healthy boundaries is vital in preventing future exploitation. The ability to say "no" without guilt or fear is a powerful tool in building a life free from manipulation. This may involve setting limits on contact with family members who enable or condone the behavior of your abuser. This will also involve creating a safe space for yourself physically and emotionally.

The process of rebuilding can involve many different aspects of your life. This might include returning to education, pursuing new career paths, or engaging in activities that bring you joy and fulfillment. Engage in activities that foster self-care and well-being. Exercise, meditation, yoga, and

spending time in nature can all contribute significantly to mental and emotional health. Make conscious choices that prioritize self-compassion and kindness. Treat yourself with the same empathy and understanding that you would offer a dear friend.

Finally, remember that your experience is not your fault. You did not deserve the abuse you endured. This understanding is fundamental to healing. The blame rests solely with your abuser. You are worthy of love, respect, and happiness.

Embrace this truth, and let it guide you as you navigate the path toward a brighter future. Your journey to recovery is a testament to your strength and resilience. Never underestimate the power of your inner strength and your capacity for healing. The life you are building is a life of freedom and self-determination. And you deserve that life.

Building a Support Network PostEscape

Building a support network is not merely beneficial after escaping abuse; it's essential for survival and healing. The isolation deliberately cultivated by sociopaths leaves victims feeling vulnerable and alone, even after the abusive relationship ends. Rebuilding your life requires actively creating a web of support that provides emotional sustenance, practical assistance, and a sense of belonging.

This support network acts as a crucial buffer against the lingering effects of manipulation and trauma.

The first step in building this network is often the most daunting: seeking professional help. Therapy, particularly with a therapist specializing in trauma and abuse recovery, provides a safe and confidential space to process your experiences. This isn't about weakness; it's a courageous act of self-care. A skilled therapist can help you understand the dynamics of the abuse, dismantle the self-blame that often accompanies such experiences, and develop coping mechanisms for managing the emotional fallout.

Finding the right therapist is vital. Don't hesitate to interview several therapists before making a decision. Look for someone who makes you feel comfortable, understood, and respected. A good therapist will validate your experience, offer non-judgmental support, and work collaboratively with you to develop a personalized treatment plan. Consider therapists with experience in treating complex post-traumatic stress disorder (C-PTSD), which is commonly associated with prolonged abuse by sociopaths. They will understand the intricacies of the manipulation and gaslighting you've endured.

Beyond individual therapy, consider the benefits of group therapy or support groups. Connecting with others who have experienced similar trauma offers immense validation.

Sharing your story in a safe and supportive environment can help you realize you're not alone in your struggles. Hearing other survivors' stories, their coping mechanisms, and their journeys to healing can be incredibly empowering and instill a sense of hope. These groups offer a unique opportunity to foster a sense of community and shared understanding, helping to combat the isolation and shame that are often lasting consequences of abuse.

Reaching out to trusted friends and family members can also be a vital part of building your support network. However, this step requires careful consideration. If your friends or family members were unaware of the abuse, or if they minimized or dismissed your concerns, their initial reactions might be unexpected or even unhelpful. It is important to prepare for this possibility and to prioritize your own emotional well-being. It might be necessary to communicate your boundaries clearly and directly.

Explain the impact of the abuse, the need for your privacy, and your need for their unconditional support. Choose individuals who demonstrate empathy, understanding, and a willingness to learn about the complexities of sociopathic abuse. They will need to appreciate the subtlety of manipulation and the effects of gaslighting without minimizing your experiences. If you find that certain relationships are not providing the support you need, it's okay to create some distance or temporarily limit contact until you're in a stronger position emotionally.

Rebuilding healthy relationships is a significant part of recovery. These relationships must be based on mutual respect, trust, and clear boundaries. You'll need to learn to

identify red flags and establish healthy patterns of communication. This may involve setting limits on contact with those who enabled or excused your abuser's behavior. It may involve saying "no" to requests that compromise your well-being or your boundaries. This process requires assertiveness, setting limitations, and maintaining a deep commitment to your own self-worth.

Rebuilding your life requires a proactive approach to self- care. Engage in activities that nourish your body and soul. Exercise regularly – it's a powerful antidote to stress and anxiety. Practice mindfulness techniques like meditation or yoga, which can help calm your nervous system and promote emotional regulation. Spend time in nature, engage in hobbies that bring you joy, and prioritize activities that restore your sense of peace and well-being. Self-compassion is crucial during this process; treat yourself with the same kindness and understanding that you would offer a cherished friend.

Consider seeking support from specialized organizations dedicated to assisting survivors of abuse. These organizations offer a wealth of resources, including hotlines, support groups, legal assistance, and financial aid. Many provide crisis intervention services, offering immediate support during moments of distress. They can also connect you with therapists, attorneys, and other professionals who specialize in working with survivors of abuse. These organizations often have extensive experience and understanding of the complexities of sociopathic abuse, offering a level of support tailored to your specific needs.

Remember, building a strong support network is an ongoing process. It will evolve and adapt as you heal and grow. There will be times when you need more support than others, and that is perfectly acceptable. Don't hesitate to reach out for

help when you need it. Embrace the strength that comes from connecting with others who understand and care. Your support network is an investment in your healing journey, and a testament to your resilience and your commitment to a future free from abuse.

Learning to recognize and establish healthy boundaries is a vital skill in rebuilding your life. Boundaries protect your physical, emotional, and mental well-being. They create a sense of safety and control in your life, which can be especially important after experiencing the manipulation and control characteristic of a sociopathic relationship.

Boundaries are not about being selfish; they are about self- respect.

These boundaries can extend to many aspects of your life. They might involve setting limits on how much time you spend with certain people, limiting communication with those who are toxic, or refusing requests that compromise your values or well-being. Boundaries might also involve protecting your personal space, possessions, and time.

Learning to say "no" assertively and respectfully is crucial. Practicing self-advocacy, stating your needs clearly and directly, is important for establishing and maintaining boundaries.

Rebuilding trust takes time, and it's a process that involves both the people in your support network and yourself. You might find yourself hesitant to trust others, and that's understandable given your experiences. Be patient with yourself and allow yourself to rebuild trust gradually. As you engage in therapy and connect with supportive individuals, you'll gain the confidence to discern healthy relationships from unhealthy ones. Look for individuals who respect your boundaries, listen without judgment, and are supportive of

your healing journey. Focus on nurturing these relationships, knowing that they are integral to your long-term well-being.

The journey of recovery from sociopathic abuse is not linear; it's a process marked by both progress and setbacks. There will be days when you feel strong and empowered, and days when you feel overwhelmed by memories or anxieties.

Acknowledge and validate these feelings; they are a part of the healing process. Remember that setbacks don't negate your progress. They are opportunities to learn, adapt, and grow stronger. Celebrate the small victories, and be compassionate towards yourself during moments of difficulty. You deserve kindness and understanding during this transformative journey. Your resilience is a testament to your strength, and a foundation for the bright future you deserve.

Finding Stability and Independence

Finding a safe and stable place to live is often the first and most crucial step towards independence after escaping an abusive relationship. The sense of security a stable home provides is paramount in the healing process. If you've been forced to leave your home abruptly, you might initially find yourself in a shelter or temporary housing situation. This is perfectly normal, and these resources are available to help you transition. Don't hesitate to utilize them; they are a vital part of your safety net.

Many shelters offer a range of services beyond just a place to stay. They often provide assistance with finding permanent housing, connecting you with support services, and helping you navigate the legal processes associated with escaping an abusive situation. It's important to remember that these are temporary solutions designed to give you the time and space you need to build a foundation for your independent life.

Once you've secured temporary housing, begin the process of finding more permanent accommodation. This might involve searching for apartments, houses, or shared living spaces. Consider factors such as safety, affordability, proximity to support systems, and your personal comfort level. If possible, visit potential housing options before signing any lease agreements. Trust your instincts; if something feels wrong or unsafe, look for another option.

Securing stable employment is another cornerstone of independent living. The income you generate will provide financial security and a sense of accomplishment. If you have job skills and experience relevant to your desired field, start your job search immediately. If you need to acquire new

skills or update your resume, consider taking advantage of resources available through local employment agencies, community colleges, or online training programs. Many organizations dedicated to assisting survivors of abuse offer job training and placement services.

During your job search, be prepared to address any employment gaps that may have occurred during your abusive relationship. Frame these gaps honestly but positively, focusing on the personal growth and resilience you gained during that challenging period. Highlight your transferable skills and your willingness to learn and contribute. Remember, your past experiences do not define your future potential. Employers often value resilience and adaptability, qualities you've undoubtedly developed.

Establishing financial stability goes hand-in-hand with secure employment. If you've experienced financial control during the abusive relationship, begin by creating a budget and tracking your income and expenses. This allows you to gain clarity about your financial situation and make informed decisions about your spending. Consider opening a separate bank account and obtaining credit cards in your own name, establishing your independent financial identity.

If you're struggling with debt or other financial difficulties, seek assistance from credit counseling agencies or non-profit organizations that provide financial literacy programs and guidance. These services offer a safe space to explore your financial challenges and develop a plan for long-term financial stability. They can often help you negotiate with creditors and explore options for debt management.

Remember, seeking help is a sign of strength, not weakness.

Beyond practical aspects like housing and employment, fostering your overall well-being is crucial for long-term

stability and independence. This is not merely about surviving; it's about thriving. Engage in activities that promote self-care and personal growth. Regular exercise is an excellent stress reliever and can contribute significantly to both physical and mental well-being. Even a short walk daily can make a difference.

Mindfulness practices, such as meditation or yoga, can help calm your nervous system and reduce feelings of anxiety or overwhelm. Numerous apps and online resources provide guided meditations suitable for all experience levels. Explore different techniques until you find what works best for you.

Remember, the goal is not to eliminate stress entirely, but to learn healthy ways to manage it.

Nutrition plays a pivotal role in your overall health. Focus on consuming a balanced diet rich in fruits, vegetables, and whole grains. Avoid excessive caffeine or alcohol, which can exacerbate stress and anxiety. Make time for regular meals, and try to cultivate mindful eating habits; pay attention to the flavors and textures of your food, savoring each bite.

Prioritize sleep. Adequate rest is essential for physical and mental restoration. Aim for 7-8 hours of quality sleep each night. Establish a regular sleep schedule, creating a relaxing bedtime routine to signal your body it's time to rest. A quiet, dark, and cool bedroom can also significantly contribute to better sleep.

Engage in activities you enjoy. Hobbies and leisure pursuits provide an outlet for stress, promote relaxation, and foster a sense of personal fulfillment. Whether it's reading, painting, gardening, or playing a musical instrument, make time for activities that bring you joy and replenish your energy. These activities are not luxuries; they are essential components of self-care and healing.

Consider reconnecting with old hobbies or exploring new ones. Learning a new skill can be a powerful source of self- esteem and accomplishment. This could involve taking a class, joining a club, or pursuing an online course. These pursuits provide structure, engagement, and a sense of purpose.

It is also essential to cultivate self-compassion during this process of rebuilding your life. Be patient and understanding with yourself. Recovery is a journey, not a race. There will be days when you feel overwhelmed or discouraged.

Acknowledge these feelings, and allow yourself to feel them without judgment. Remember, progress isn't always linear.

There will be setbacks and challenges along the way, but these are opportunities for growth and learning.

Celebrating your small victories along the way is incredibly important. Acknowledge and appreciate your progress, no matter how small it may seem. This could involve securing a job interview, paying a bill on time, or simply having a good night's sleep. These accomplishments contribute to your sense of self-efficacy and reinforce your belief in your ability to rebuild your life.

It's important to remember that you deserve a life free from fear and control. The journey towards independence and healing requires courage, resilience, and self-compassion. By focusing on your well-being, building a solid support system, and taking proactive steps to secure housing, employment, and financial stability, you can create a brighter future for yourself. Your strength and your journey are testaments to your resilience, and the life you create will be a testament to your remarkable capacity for healing and growth. This is not simply about escaping the past; it's about building a future that you deserve – a future defined by your

own strength, your own choices, and your own unshakeable self-worth.

Processing Trauma and Healing from Abuse

Processing trauma after escaping an abusive relationship with a sociopath is a deeply personal and multifaceted journey. There's no one-size-fits-all approach, and the healing process unfolds at its own pace. What's crucial is recognizing that healing is possible, and that you are not alone. Many resources and therapeutic approaches can support you in reclaiming your life and rebuilding your sense of self.

One of the most effective therapeutic approaches for trauma recovery is Cognitive Behavioral Therapy (CBT). CBT focuses on identifying and challenging negative thought patterns and behaviors that contribute to emotional distress. In the context of abuse, this often involves confronting the insidious lies and manipulations perpetuated by the abuser. CBT helps you reframe your understanding of the abuse, separating the abuser's distorted perceptions from your own reality. It equips you with coping mechanisms for managing triggers and flashbacks, allowing you to regain control over your thoughts and emotions. A skilled CBT therapist can help you understand how your responses to past trauma are impacting your present life, and guide you in developing healthier coping strategies. This may involve techniques like cognitive restructuring, where you actively challenge and replace negative thoughts with more balanced and realistic ones, and behavioral experiments, where you gradually confront feared situations in a safe and controlled manner.

Trauma-focused therapies, such as Eye Movement Desensitization and Reprocessing (EMDR) and somatic experiencing, are particularly effective in addressing the lingering effects of trauma on the body and mind. EMDR uses bilateral stimulation, such as eye movements or tapping, to help process traumatic memories and reduce their emotional intensity. This technique assists in breaking the cycle of re-experiencing traumatic events and helps you develop a healthier perspective on the past. Somatic experiencing focuses on addressing the physical sensations associated with trauma. It helps you safely release trapped emotions and bodily tension that can manifest as physical symptoms, such as chronic pain, digestive issues, or sleep disturbances. These therapies recognize the interconnectedness of mind and body and provide tools to regain a sense of bodily safety and regulation.

Beyond formal therapy, various self-help techniques can complement your healing journey. Mindfulness practices, such as meditation and deep breathing exercises, can be profoundly beneficial in managing PTSD symptoms like anxiety, hypervigilance, and intrusive thoughts. Mindfulness encourages you to focus on the present moment without judgment, helping you to ground yourself in the here and now and reducing the power of distressing memories. Even short periods of mindful meditation can significantly reduce feelings of anxiety and overwhelm. Many guided meditation apps are readily available to support you in practicing mindfulness.

Journaling can be a powerful tool for processing emotions and gaining self-awareness. Writing down your thoughts and feelings, without the need for judgment or editing, provides a safe and private space for emotional expression. It can help you identify patterns of thinking and behavior, track your progress, and gain a deeper understanding of yourself.

Journaling can be particularly helpful in documenting your healing journey, providing a tangible record of your progress and reminding you of your strength and resilience.

Physical activity plays a crucial role in both physical and mental health, particularly in the context of trauma recovery. Exercise releases endorphins, which have mood-boosting and stress-reducing effects. Regular exercise can help regulate sleep patterns, reduce anxiety and depression, and improve overall energy levels. Finding an activity you enjoy, whether it's walking, swimming, dancing, or yoga, can be a powerful form of self-care. Exercise provides a healthy outlet for emotions and promotes a sense of physical well- being, which can be particularly helpful after experiencing the emotional and physical toll of abuse.

Building a strong support system is paramount during this process. Connecting with trusted friends, family members, or support groups provides a sense of belonging and reduces feelings of isolation. Support groups specifically for survivors of abuse offer a safe space to share experiences, connect with others who understand, and learn from one another's journeys. These groups can provide validation, empathy, and practical advice, fostering a sense of community and shared resilience. Remember, seeking support isn't a sign of weakness; it's a testament to your strength and desire for healing.

Healthy boundaries are essential in protecting your well- being and preventing further harm. Learning to assertively communicate your needs and limits helps you safeguard your emotional and physical safety. This might involve setting limits on contact with the abuser, declining invitations that feel unsafe, or expressing your discomfort when others overstep your boundaries. Setting boundaries takes practice, and it's important to be patient with yourself as you learn to advocate for your needs.

It's vital to remember that healing is not a linear process; there will be setbacks and good days, and moments where

you feel strong and moments when you feel vulnerable. Allow yourself to feel the full spectrum of emotions without judgment. Acknowledge your progress, no matter how small, and celebrate your victories along the way. Be kind to yourself, and remember that self-compassion is a crucial component of the healing journey. Recovery from trauma is a marathon, not a sprint. Be patient with your progress and remember that you deserve a life free from fear and abuse.

The journey to healing is profoundly personal, and the timeline varies greatly for each individual. Some individuals may require intensive therapy to fully process their trauma, while others may find sufficient support through self-help techniques and support groups. The key is to find what works best for you and to be persistent in your commitment to healing.

Remember, you are not alone in this journey. Numerous resources are available to support you, including therapists specializing in trauma and abuse, support groups, hotlines, and online resources. Don't hesitate to seek professional help; it's a sign of strength, not weakness. With patience,

self-compassion, and the right support, you can heal from the trauma of abuse and build a fulfilling and joyful life.

The process of rebuilding your life after escaping abuse involves more than just securing housing and employment. It involves reclaiming your sense of self, rediscovering your passions, and redefining your future on your own terms. This process requires courage, resilience, and a steadfast belief in your capacity for healing and growth. You deserve to live a life filled with joy, peace, and empowerment. The journey may be challenging, but the reward—a life free from fear and control—is worth every step of the way. Remember to celebrate every milestone you achieve, no matter how small, and to honor your own remarkable strength and resilience.

Your future is yours to create, and it will be a future built on your terms, a testament to your enduring spirit.

Recovering Your SelfEsteem and Identity

Recovering your self-esteem after the insidious erosion caused by a sociopathic abuser is a monumental task, but it is absolutely achievable. The manipulation you endured wasn't your fault; it was a deliberate tactic used to control and dominate you. Understanding this crucial fact is the first step towards reclaiming your sense of self.

The process involves a multifaceted approach that incorporates self-compassion, positive self-talk, and a conscious effort towards self-discovery and personal growth. This isn't a quick fix; it's a journey of rebuilding, one brick at a time.

Self-compassion is paramount. You've endured unimaginable hardship, and it's vital to treat yourself with the kindness and understanding you would offer a close friend facing similar challenges. Forgive yourself for any perceived failures or weaknesses that the abuser exploited. Remember, you survived. Your survival is a testament to your resilience and strength, not a measure of your worth. Cultivate self- compassion by actively challenging negative self-talk, replacing it with affirmations of your inherent worth and capabilities.

Positive self-talk is a powerful tool for reshaping your internal narrative. The abuser likely bombarded you with negativity, criticism, and lies, designed to erode your confidence and self-worth. Counter this by consciously engaging in positive affirmations. Start small. Instead of dwelling on perceived inadequacies, focus on your strengths and accomplishments, no matter how insignificant they might seem. Did you manage to get out of bed today? That's a victory. Did you make a healthy meal? That's an

accomplishment. Celebrate these small victories, as they build momentum and reinforce your sense of agency.

Journaling can be a transformative tool in this process. Write down your thoughts and feelings without judgment. Explore the emotions that arise - the anger, the sadness, the fear - and allow yourself to feel them without trying to suppress them. Journaling allows you to process your experiences, identify patterns of negative self-talk, and track your progress as you begin to build a healthier self-image. Use your journal to chronicle your successes, no matter how small. Over time, you'll begin to see a pattern of resilience and growth. This tangible record will serve as a reminder of how far you've come.

Engage in activities that bring you joy and a sense of accomplishment. This might involve rediscovering old hobbies or exploring new interests. Anything that sparks your curiosity and allows you to express yourself creatively can be profoundly healing. Whether it's painting, playing music, writing, gardening, or hiking, prioritize activities that nurture your spirit and reconnect you with your passions.

Remember the things that brought you happiness before the abuse, and actively seek opportunities to engage with them again.

Self-discovery is an essential part of reclaiming your identity. The abuser worked to strip you of your individuality, making you dependent on them for validation and direction. Now is the time to rediscover who you are, independent of their influence. This process might involve exploring your values, beliefs, and aspirations. What truly matters to you? What are your goals and dreams? Consider seeking professional guidance through therapy or counseling, as a therapist can provide a safe and supportive

space to explore these questions and work through any lingering emotional wounds.

Personal growth is a continuous process, and this is an opportunity to focus on self-improvement in areas where you feel you might have been held back. This might involve developing new skills, pursuing educational opportunities, or setting personal goals for physical and mental health.

Consider taking a class, learning a new language, or volunteering your time to a cause you care about. These activities not only build confidence and skills but also contribute to a stronger sense of self and purpose.

Building healthy relationships is another crucial aspect of rebuilding your life. Focus on cultivating connections with individuals who support and uplift you. Surround yourself with people who treat you with respect, empathy, and genuine care. Set healthy boundaries in these relationships, protecting your emotional and physical well-being. Don't hesitate to distance yourself from relationships that feel draining or toxic. Building a supportive network of friends and family, or joining a support group for survivors of abuse, can provide the validation and encouragement you need as you navigate this journey.

Remember, physical health is intrinsically linked to mental well-being. Prioritize self-care through regular exercise, a healthy diet, and sufficient sleep. Physical activity releases endorphins, which have mood-boosting and stress-reducing effects. Engage in activities you enjoy, whether it's walking, swimming, yoga, or dancing. Focus on nourishing your body with healthy foods that fuel your energy levels. Aim for a regular sleep schedule, ensuring adequate rest for your mind and body. These seemingly small acts of self-care are crucial to your overall well-being and contribute significantly to your emotional recovery.

Consider professional help. Therapists specializing in trauma and abuse recovery can provide invaluable support and guidance. They can help you process the trauma, develop healthy coping mechanisms, and build resilience. Don't hesitate to reach out for professional support; it's a sign of strength, not weakness. A therapist can offer a safe and non- judgmental space to explore your experiences, address lingering emotional wounds, and develop strategies for building a healthier and happier future.

The journey of rebuilding your self-esteem and reclaiming your identity is a marathon, not a sprint. There will be setbacks and challenges along the way. Be patient with yourself, celebrate your progress, and remember that you are worthy of love, respect, and happiness. You are stronger than you think, and you deserve to live a life free from fear and control. Embrace this journey of self-discovery and growth with courage and self-compassion, knowing that you are not alone, and a brighter future awaits you. Your strength and resilience are remarkable; never underestimate your capacity to heal and thrive. Trust in your ability to rebuild your life, on your terms, and create a future that reflects your strength and worth. This journey is about reclaiming your narrative, rewriting your story, and celebrating the incredible person you are.

Setting Healthy Boundaries and Relationships

Building healthy relationships after escaping an abusive situation requires a fundamental shift in how you interact with others and how you perceive yourself within those interactions. The trauma you experienced likely distorted your sense of self-worth and your ability to recognize healthy dynamics. Rebuilding trust and establishing healthy boundaries are crucial steps in creating a safe and fulfilling future.

One of the first and most vital steps is learning to recognize red flags. These aren't always obvious acts of aggression; subtle behaviors can be equally dangerous. For instance, excessive jealousy or possessiveness, even in the early stages of a relationship, is a significant warning sign. A healthy partner celebrates your independence and supports your personal growth; they don't try to control your friendships, your work, or your personal choices. Similarly, belittling comments disguised as "jokes" or constant criticism, however seemingly minor, erode your self-esteem and create an environment of negativity. Pay attention to how the person makes you feel; if you constantly feel anxious, insecure, or even slightly uncomfortable, take note. Your gut feeling is a powerful indicator; don't dismiss it. Remember the patterns of manipulation you experienced previously— learn to recognize these tactics in others before they escalate into abuse.

Furthermore, look for controlling behaviors. Does the person attempt to isolate you from friends and family? Do they monitor your communications, demanding access to your phone or social media accounts? Do they constantly check your whereabouts or make unreasonable demands on your

time? These actions aren't about care; they are about control. A healthy relationship respects individual autonomy and privacy. Control is a hallmark of abusive relationships, no matter how subtly it is presented. Another subtle but crucial sign is the constant need for validation or excessive reassurance. Someone who continuously seeks validation may be insecure, but a deeper issue might be their need for control and manipulation. They might use your need for reassurance against you, subtly manipulating your emotions to gain power.

Learning to say "no" is a powerful tool in setting boundaries. Many survivors of abuse struggle with assertiveness due to the constant pressure to comply with the abuser's demands.

Practice saying "no" in small ways, even to insignificant requests, to build confidence and solidify your boundaries. It's okay to decline invitations you don't feel comfortable attending or to refuse requests that make you feel uncomfortable or pressured. Start with low-stakes situations and gradually increase your comfort level. If someone pressures you to do something you don't want to do, it's a red flag. Remember, you have the right to refuse any request that violates your personal comfort level or goes against your values.

Communication is key to establishing healthy relationships. Be clear and direct about your needs and boundaries. Don't shy away from voicing your discomfort or displeasure if something bothers you. If someone is repeatedly disregarding your boundaries, it might be time to reconsider the relationship. Healthy communication is not just about expressing your needs but also about actively listening to the other person's perspective. This doesn't mean you have to agree with everything they say, but actively listening is essential for understanding and building trust. However, remember that in unhealthy relationships, there's often an

imbalance of communication where one person dominates the conversation or shuts down important dialogues.

Consider assertiveness training. Many resources are available online, including workshops and support groups, which focus on developing assertive communication skills. These programs help you learn to express your needs and opinions in a calm and respectful way without being aggressive or passive. They teach techniques for dealing with difficult conversations and setting clear boundaries, empowering you to take control of your interactions. Role- playing exercises can help you practice these skills in a safe and supportive environment. This is essential as it helps you navigate challenging interpersonal dynamics confidently and effectively.

Beyond individual assertiveness, it's important to establish clear and consistent boundaries within the relationship.

These boundaries should cover various aspects, including physical touch, emotional intimacy, time commitment, financial decisions, and personal space. Clearly articulate your limits to the other person and enforce them consistently. For example, if you're uncomfortable with physical affection in public, say so. If you need personal space to recharge after work, let them know. Don't feel obligated to explain yourself extensively; a simple, clear statement of your needs is sufficient. If these boundaries are consistently crossed, it signals a disregard for your wellbeing and an unhealthy dynamic.

Building a strong support system is essential for navigating the complexities of new relationships. Reach out to trusted friends and family members who provide emotional support and a safe space for expressing your feelings. They can help you process experiences, offer perspectives, and hold you accountable for maintaining your boundaries. Sharing your

experiences with others who understand what you've been through can be incredibly validating and empowering.

Consider joining a support group for survivors of abuse. These groups provide a community of like-minded individuals who share similar experiences, offering a unique level of understanding and encouragement. In a safe group environment, you can share your anxieties, successes, and challenges without judgment, gaining strength and inspiration from others on similar paths.

Don't underestimate the power of professional support. A therapist specializing in trauma and abuse recovery can provide invaluable guidance in identifying red flags, developing healthy communication patterns, and setting boundaries. They can provide a safe space to work through the emotional baggage from previous experiences and develop coping mechanisms for navigating difficult situations. They can help you understand why you might be drawn to certain patterns in relationships and guide you toward healthier, more fulfilling connections. Therapy is an investment in your well-being and provides a non- judgmental space to process your experiences and develop strategies to avoid future harm.

Remember, rebuilding your life and establishing healthy relationships is a process, not a destination. There will be setbacks and challenges along the way. Be patient with yourself, celebrate your progress, and trust that you're moving in the right direction. Learning to recognize red flags, setting clear boundaries, and practicing assertive communication are essential skills for building a future free from fear and control. Your journey to healing and happiness is a testament to your resilience and strength; embrace it with courage, self-compassion, and the unwavering knowledge that you deserve a life filled with respect, love, and healthy relationships. Your ability to build healthy

connections is not just possible; it's your birthright. Embrace the process, learn from each step, and celebrate the remarkable person you are becoming. Your future is bright, and it's yours to create.

Forgiving Yourself and Moving Forward

The journey out of the shadows of abuse is rarely a straight line. It's a winding path, sometimes arduous, sometimes exhilarating, but always leading toward a brighter future.

While escaping the immediate danger is a monumental achievement, the internal work of healing is equally, if not more, important. A significant part of that healing involves forgiving yourself. This isn't about condoning the abuser's actions; it's about releasing the self-blame, the guilt, and the shame that often accompany surviving abuse.

Many survivors struggle with the pervasive feeling that they somehow deserved the abuse, or that they could have prevented it. This is a common and deeply ingrained consequence of manipulative tactics used by abusers. They systematically erode your self-worth, twisting your perception of reality until you believe you are at fault. The insidious nature of gaslighting and other forms of manipulation means that you internalize their lies, accepting their distorted version of events as your own truth. This self- blame can be incredibly debilitating, hindering your ability to move forward and build a healthy life.

Understanding this is the first crucial step. Recognize that the abuse was not your fault. No one deserves to be subjected to the cruelty and manipulation inflicted by a sociopath. Your abuser's actions were a reflection of their own pathologies, not a judgment of your worth. Repeating this affirmation to yourself, daily, is a powerful tool. Write it down, say it aloud, believe it in your heart. The repetition helps solidify this truth in your mind, slowly chipping away at the layers of self-blame that have accumulated over time. Consider writing a letter to your past self, acknowledging the

pain and reassuring that individual that they are worthy of love and respect. This act of self-compassion can be remarkably healing.

Seeking professional help is invaluable in this process. A therapist specializing in trauma and abuse recovery can provide a safe and non-judgmental space to explore these feelings of guilt and shame. Through therapy, you can begin to unravel the tangled web of lies that your abuser spun, replacing them with a more accurate and compassionate understanding of your experience. Techniques like cognitive behavioral therapy (CBT) can help reframe negative thoughts and beliefs, replacing self-criticism with self- acceptance. Eye Movement Desensitization and Reprocessing (EMDR) can be particularly effective in processing traumatic memories and reducing their emotional intensity. Remember that seeking help is a sign of strength, not weakness. It takes courage to confront the pain of the past and work towards a healthier future.

Forgiveness, however, is not solely an act of self- compassion; it also involves understanding the dynamics of the abusive relationship. This understanding does not require empathy for the abuser, but rather, a cognitive understanding of how manipulation works and how it affects its victims.

Learning about the psychological mechanisms employed by sociopaths helps neutralize the power of their tactics.

Understanding that they skillfully exploit vulnerabilities and emotional triggers allows you to see the situation more objectively, removing the personalized shame and replacing it with a clearer understanding of the power dynamics at play. This knowledge empowers you to recognize the situation was not a personal failure, but rather, a carefully orchestrated manipulation.

Beyond therapy, journaling can be a profoundly effective tool. Writing down your thoughts and feelings allows you to process them in a safe and private space. This can be particularly helpful in identifying recurring patterns of self- blame and challenging those thoughts. Try to describe your feelings in detail, without judgment. Allow yourself to feel the emotions without trying to suppress them. The act of writing itself can be therapeutic, allowing you to externalize the internal chaos and begin to make sense of it. Consider starting a gratitude journal as well. Focusing on the positive aspects of your life, however small they may seem, helps shift your focus away from the negativity of the past and fosters a sense of hope for the future.

Developing healthy coping mechanisms is crucial for moving forward. This might include engaging in activities you enjoy, spending time in nature, practicing mindfulness or meditation, engaging in creative pursuits, or connecting with supportive friends and family. Anything that brings you joy and peace is a valuable tool for healing. Remember that self-care is not selfish; it's essential for your recovery and well-being. Engage in activities that nurture your mind, body, and spirit. It's a powerful step to actively choose activities that replenish your energy and bring a sense of calm and peace to your life. This active commitment to self- care is a crucial act of self-love.

Moving forward doesn't erase the past; it acknowledges it, learns from it, and uses that knowledge to build a stronger, healthier future. Setting realistic goals is a key element.

Don't try to overhaul your entire life overnight. Start with small, achievable goals. This could involve setting a routine, creating a budget, pursuing an educational goal, or simply committing to a daily walk. Each small victory builds confidence and momentum, paving the way for bigger achievements. Celebrate these accomplishments, no matter

how small they may seem; acknowledge your resilience and strength.

Forgive yourself for the things you couldn't control, and learn from the things you could. This journey involves introspection, understanding your own vulnerabilities, and recognizing that you are not defined by the abuse you endured. Your worth is inherent; it cannot be diminished by the actions of another. Remember the strength you showed in escaping the abuse; that same strength will guide you in rebuilding your life.

Creating a vision for your future is a powerful way to foster hope. Imagine the life you want to create, the person you want to become. Visualize yourself living a life free from fear and control, filled with joy, love, and fulfilling relationships. This vision should be specific and personal, reflecting your dreams and aspirations. Write it down, create a vision board, or simply hold it in your mind. This act of envisioning a brighter future provides direction and motivation, fueling your journey toward healing.

Remember, you are not alone. There are many people who understand your experience and want to support you. Reach out to friends, family, or support groups. Connect with others who have survived similar situations; sharing your story can be incredibly cathartic and empowering. Knowing that others have walked a similar path and emerged stronger offers invaluable hope and inspiration.

Rebuilding your life after escaping abuse is a testament to your incredible resilience. The journey will have its ups and downs, but your strength and determination will carry you through. Embrace the process, celebrate your progress, and remember that you deserve a life free from fear and control. You are worthy of love, happiness, and a future filled with

possibilities. The journey is long, but you are on the right path, towards a future filled with the kind of happiness you deserve.

Creating a Future Free from Fear

Creating a life free from the pervasive fear instilled by your abuser requires a multifaceted approach. It's not merely about escaping a physical situation; it's about reclaiming your autonomy, rebuilding your sense of self, and cultivating a future defined by your choices, not your abuser's manipulations. This process demands patience, self-compassion, and a commitment to personal growth, but the rewards—a life filled with genuine peace, joy, and authentic connections—are immeasurable.

One of the most crucial aspects of this rebuilding process is prioritizing self-care. This isn't about indulging in frivolous luxuries; it's about actively engaging in practices that nourish your mind, body, and spirit. This might involve establishing a regular sleep schedule, ensuring you eat nutritious meals, and incorporating regular physical activity into your routine. Exercise, in particular, serves a dual purpose. It not only improves physical health but also releases endorphins, which have mood-boosting effects and can help alleviate symptoms of anxiety and depression— common consequences of prolonged abuse. Find an activity you genuinely enjoy, whether it's yoga, swimming, dancing, or a brisk walk in nature. The key is consistency, even if it's just for a short period each day.

Beyond physical self-care, nurturing your mental and emotional well-being is paramount. This could involve engaging in mindfulness practices, such as meditation or deep breathing exercises. These techniques help to center you in the present moment, reducing the power of intrusive thoughts and anxieties related to the past trauma. Consider journaling as a means of emotional processing. Writing

down your thoughts and feelings allows you to externalize them, making them less overwhelming and providing a safe space to explore your emotional landscape without judgment. Don't worry about grammar or eloquence; the act of writing itself is therapeutic.

Cultivating a strong support system is equally essential. Lean on trusted friends, family members, or support groups.

Sharing your experiences with others who understand can be incredibly validating and empowering. Find a therapist specializing in trauma and abuse recovery who can provide a safe and non-judgmental space for you to process your emotions and develop coping mechanisms. Therapy provides a structured framework for healing, offering tools and techniques to navigate the complexities of trauma recovery. Group therapy, in particular, can offer a sense of community and shared experience, helping you to feel less alone in your journey.

Remember that establishing healthy boundaries is a crucial aspect of creating a future free from fear. This means learning to say "no" to requests or demands that compromise your well-being. It means protecting your time and energy, prioritizing your needs, and setting limits on interactions with individuals who are toxic or draining. This process may feel uncomfortable at first, especially if you're accustomed to placating others or prioritizing their needs above your own.

However, establishing these boundaries is an act of self- respect and a vital component of creating a life free from manipulation and control.

Setting and achieving goals is a powerful way to build self- esteem and a sense of accomplishment. Begin with small, attainable goals, gradually working your way up to larger aspirations. This could involve anything from completing a small home improvement project to pursuing a new hobby or

enrolling in a course. Each accomplishment, no matter how small, reinforces your sense of agency and reinforces the belief in your ability to create positive change in your life. As you achieve these milestones, celebrate your progress and acknowledge your resilience. This positive reinforcement helps to build momentum and instills confidence in your ability to overcome challenges.

Consider pursuing personal growth opportunities that align with your interests and passions. This might involve taking a class, learning a new skill, volunteering for a cause you believe in, or engaging in creative pursuits. These activities not only provide a sense of fulfillment but also help you to rediscover your passions and connect with your authentic self. They can help to shift your focus away from the past and towards a brighter future, fostering a sense of hope and purpose. Investing time in your personal growth is an investment in your future happiness and well-being.

As you begin to rebuild your life, remember that forgiveness

—both of yourself and your abuser—is a crucial step in the healing process. Forgiving yourself is not about condoning the abuse; it's about releasing the self-blame, guilt, and shame that often accompany such experiences. It's about recognizing that you were a victim of manipulation and that your worth is not diminished by the actions of another.

Forgiving your abuser, on the other hand, is not about condoning their behavior; it's about releasing the anger, resentment, and negativity that they may still hold over you. This doesn't mean you need to reconcile or have contact with them; it simply means freeing yourself from the emotional weight of their actions. It's about choosing to move on and not letting their toxicity continue to impact your life.

Building financial independence is often a critical element in escaping and staying free from an abusive relationship. If you experienced financial control during the abuse, focus on regaining your financial autonomy. This might involve creating a budget, seeking financial counseling, or exploring educational opportunities to enhance your earning potential. Becoming financially independent empowers you to make your own choices, free from the manipulation and control of another. It is a powerful symbol of your newfound freedom and self-sufficiency.

It's essential to remember that the journey to rebuilding your life after escaping abuse is rarely linear. There will be setbacks, moments of doubt, and periods of intense emotion. Be patient and kind to yourself throughout this process.

Acknowledge your progress, celebrate your successes, and don't be afraid to seek support when you need it. The strength you demonstrated in escaping the abusive situation is a testament to your resilience, and that same strength will guide you as you navigate this next phase of your life.

Creating a future free from fear requires courage, determination, and self-compassion. It requires actively working to build a life that reflects your values, priorities, and dreams. It's a journey of self-discovery, healing, and personal growth. Remember that you are not defined by your past experiences; you are capable of creating a bright, fulfilling future filled with joy, peace, and genuine connection. Embrace the process, celebrate your progress, and know that you are worthy of a life free from fear and control. The path ahead may seem daunting, but with each step you take, you move closer to the life you deserve.

Remember, your strength is inherent; your value is undeniable; and your future is bright. The journey is long, but the destination—a life free from the shadows of abuse— is worth every step. You have survived the unimaginable; now, it's time to thrive.

Finding the Right Therapist or Counselor

Finding the right therapist is crucial in your journey to healing after escaping abuse. It's not a simple task; choosing a therapist is like choosing a partner—you need to feel comfortable, safe, and confident in their abilities. This section will guide you through the process, equipping you with the knowledge to make an informed decision. The wrong therapist can inadvertently retraumatize you; the right one can be your anchor in the storm. Remember, you deserve to be heard, understood, and supported by a professional who truly gets it.

The first step is researching therapists in your area who specialize in trauma and abuse recovery. Start by utilizing online directories such as Psychology Today, GoodTherapy, and the websites of professional organizations like the American Psychological Association (APA) or your country's equivalent. These platforms often allow you to filter your search by specialization, insurance acceptance, and even treatment modalities. You can refine your search by keywords such as "trauma-informed therapy," "complex PTSD," "sociopathic abuse," or "relationship abuse." Look for therapists with specific experience working with victims of the type of abuse you've endured.

Don't be afraid to cast a wide net initially. Look at several therapists' profiles, paying close attention to their bios. A good therapist's profile will clearly articulate their experience and approach. It should be more than just a list of credentials; it should offer insight into their philosophy and the types of clients they feel best equipped to serve. Look for statements reflecting an understanding of the nuances of

abuse dynamics, especially if you've experienced gaslighting, coercive control, or other manipulative tactics.

Once you've compiled a list of potential therapists, it's time to schedule initial consultations. Many therapists offer a free 15- to 30-minute introductory call or consultation. This initial contact is crucial; it's your opportunity to gauge the therapeutic rapport and determine if there's a good fit. Before the consultation, jot down questions that are important to you. These questions may include:

What is your experience working with survivors of sociopathic abuse or similar situations? Be specific about the type of abuse you experienced.

What therapeutic modalities do you utilize? (e.g., Cognitive Behavioral Therapy (CBT), Dialectical Behavior Therapy (DBT), Eye Movement Desensitization and Reprocessing (EMDR), Trauma-Focused Cognitive Behavioral Therapy (TF-CBT)). Different modalities cater to different needs and preferences. Research which modalities might be most helpful for your specific situation.

What is your approach to setting boundaries within the therapeutic relationship? This is crucial, especially if you've experienced difficulties setting boundaries in the past.

How do you handle emergencies or crises that might arise between sessions? What is your protocol for after-hours support?

What is your cancellation policy? This is a practical consideration, but also provides insight into the therapist's approach to their practice and client management.

What is your fee schedule, and what insurance plans do you accept?

Can you provide references? While unlikely to be explicitly offered, you can ask if you have significant concerns.

How long do you typically work with clients before considering termination of therapy? Understanding their

approach to the length of therapy helps in managing expectations.

What is your approach to working with trauma? How do you assess the impact of trauma on different facets of the client's life and personal relationships?

During the consultation, pay attention to your gut feeling. Do you feel safe and comfortable talking to this person? Do you feel judged or understood? A good therapist will create a safe and non-judgmental space for you to share your experiences, even if those experiences are extremely difficult to recount. They should listen attentively, validate your feelings, and avoid minimizing your trauma. They should not interrupt your narrative excessively, but respectfully guide the conversation. They should demonstrate empathy and a genuine interest in helping you heal.

It's vital to clarify their approach to confidentiality and mandated reporting. Understand the limits of confidentiality and under what circumstances they would be legally obligated to report information to authorities. This is essential for establishing trust and ensuring your safety.

If, during the consultation, you feel uncomfortable, uneasy, or that the therapist isn't a good fit, don't hesitate to end the session and seek out another professional. Finding the right therapist may take time and involve speaking to several practitioners before you find the right match. Don't lose heart; finding the right support is a critical part of healing. The time and effort spent searching for the correct professional is an investment in your long-term well-being.

It's also important to consider the therapist's cultural competency. If you identify with a specific cultural background or have unique cultural needs, ensure the therapist understands and respects your culture and beliefs.

Lack of cultural understanding can create barriers to effective treatment. If you feel unsure, directly inquire about their experience working with people from diverse backgrounds.

Beyond the initial consultation, consider researching the therapist's credentials. Verify their licenses and certifications with the relevant licensing board in your state or country.

Check online reviews, but remember that online reviews should be considered as one piece of information among many and not the sole determiner.

Once you find a therapist with whom you feel comfortable and confident, establish clear communication. Express your needs and expectations openly and honestly. Don't hesitate to provide feedback about your experience. A strong therapeutic relationship is built on mutual trust, respect, and open communication. Remember that the therapeutic relationship is a partnership, and both you and your therapist should be actively engaged in the healing process.

Finding a therapist is a journey in itself, a necessary step in your broader journey of healing. Be patient, persistent, and proactive in your search. Your mental and emotional well- being is worth the investment. The right therapist will provide a safe space to unpack the complexities of your trauma and equip you with the tools you need to navigate your recovery journey. Remember, healing is possible, and you deserve to experience a life free from the shadows of the past. You are strong, resilient, and deserving of a future filled with peace and happiness.

Types of Therapy for Abuse Survivors

Having found a therapist you trust, the next step is understanding the various therapeutic approaches available to help you process the trauma you've endured. There isn't a one-size-fits-all solution; the most effective therapy will depend on your individual needs, preferences, and the specific nature of your trauma. However, several therapeutic modalities have proven highly effective for survivors of abuse, particularly those perpetrated by sociopaths.

One widely used approach is **Cognitive Behavioral Therapy (CBT)** . CBT focuses on the interconnectedness of thoughts, feelings, and behaviors. In the context of abuse recovery, CBT helps you identify and challenge negative or distorted thought patterns that might be contributing to your emotional distress. For example, if you're struggling with feelings of self-blame or worthlessness – common after enduring abuse – CBT provides strategies to reframe these thoughts and replace them with more realistic and empowering ones. This might involve journaling, cognitive restructuring exercises, or behavioral experiments designed to test the validity of your negative beliefs. A CBT therapist will guide you in developing coping mechanisms to manage anxiety, depression, and other symptoms often associated with trauma. They might also help you establish healthy boundaries and develop assertive communication skills – skills often eroded during an abusive relationship. The strength of CBT lies in its practical, action-oriented approach, making it a highly effective tool for building resilience and self-efficacy.

Another highly effective modality is **Eye Movement Desensitization and Reprocessing (EMDR)** . EMDR is a

specialized therapy designed specifically to address trauma. It involves bilateral stimulation, often through eye movements, while you recall traumatic memories. The theory behind EMDR suggests that the bilateral stimulation helps your brain process the traumatic memories, reducing their emotional intensity. EMDR isn't just about remembering the traumatic event; it's about changing how your brain processes and stores that memory. While the exact mechanism isn't fully understood, research strongly supports EMDR's effectiveness in treating PTSD and other trauma-related conditions. It's particularly useful for processing specific traumatic events and reducing the intrusive thoughts, flashbacks, and nightmares often experienced by abuse survivors. Unlike some other therapies, EMDR often works relatively quickly, providing noticeable relief in a shorter timeframe. It's important to note that EMDR is usually not a standalone treatment and is often used in conjunction with other therapies such as CBT.

Trauma-Focused Cognitive Behavioral Therapy (TF- CBT) integrates elements of both CBT and EMDR, tailoring the approach to the specific needs of trauma survivors. It specifically addresses the cognitive, emotional, and behavioral consequences of trauma. This modality is especially effective in cases where trauma has significantly impacted a person's ability to function daily, affecting areas such as sleep, concentration, or relationships. TF-CBT uses a combination of techniques from CBT, including psychoeducation, relaxation techniques, and cognitive processing, to help survivors understand their trauma and develop healthy coping mechanisms. It incorporates aspects of EMDR to process traumatic memories directly, working to reduce the emotional impact of these experiences. The collaborative nature of TF-CBT—working closely with the therapist to establish goals and track progress—makes it a

powerful tool for regaining control and rebuilding one's life after abuse.

Dialectical Behavior Therapy (DBT) is another effective modality, particularly helpful for those struggling with intense emotions, self-harm, or suicidal ideation. DBT emphasizes mindfulness, emotional regulation, distress tolerance, and interpersonal effectiveness. These skills are crucial for managing the overwhelming emotions that often accompany trauma recovery. DBT helps you develop a broader range of emotional coping strategies, enabling you to manage intense feelings without resorting to self- destructive behaviors. The core principles of DBT involve acceptance of your current state alongside a commitment to making positive changes. This balanced approach is especially beneficial for individuals who might be struggling with feelings of shame or self-criticism, common after surviving abuse. It focuses on building a stronger sense of self, reducing reactivity, and improving relationships with others.

Somatic Experiencing (SE) is a body-oriented approach that focuses on the physical sensations associated with trauma. Unlike other therapies that primarily focus on cognitive or emotional processing, SE acknowledges that trauma is stored in the body. Through gentle movements and mindfulness techniques, SE helps you release the physical tension held within your body as a result of trauma. This can manifest as muscle tension, chronic pain, or other physical symptoms. SE helps you become more aware of your body's sensations and develop coping strategies for managing these physical manifestations of trauma. Because sociopathic abuse frequently involves physical and emotional control, SE can be particularly valuable in addressing the lingering physical effects of the abuse. It's a more gentle, non-invasive approach which can be particularly beneficial for individuals

who find traditional talk therapies triggering or overwhelming.

Beyond these core modalities, several other therapeutic techniques can be integrated into your treatment plan. These might include:

Narrative Therapy: This approach focuses on helping you reframe your story and create a more empowering narrative about your experiences. Instead of viewing yourself as a victim, narrative therapy helps you reclaim your agency and see yourself as a survivor who has overcome adversity.

Attachment-Based Therapy: This approach focuses on understanding how early childhood experiences and attachment patterns may have influenced your vulnerability to abuse and your responses to it. It helps to address underlying issues that might be perpetuating unhealthy relationship dynamics.

Group Therapy: Connecting with other survivors can be incredibly powerful. Group therapy provides a safe space to share your experiences, learn from others, and realize you're not alone in your journey.

The decision of which therapy, or combination of therapies, is best suited to your needs will be a collaborative process between you and your therapist. They will consider the nature of your trauma, your personal preferences, and your goals for therapy. It's crucial to be open and honest with your therapist about your experiences, your challenges, and what you hope to achieve through therapy. Don't hesitate to ask questions, voice concerns, and advocate for your needs. Your therapist is a partner in your healing journey, and the right therapeutic relationship is built on mutual trust, respect, and open communication. The path to healing is not always

linear; there may be setbacks and challenges along the way. Remember that progress is progress, and celebrate every step you take towards a healthier and more fulfilling life. Your resilience is a testament to your strength, and with the right support, you can reclaim your life and build a future free from the shadows of the past. You deserve to live a life filled with peace, happiness, and genuine connection. Don't underestimate the power of seeking help, and trust in your ability to heal and thrive. The journey is long, but the destination—a life free from the grip of abuse—is worth the effort. Remember, healing is a journey, not a destination, and it's okay to take your time, adapt your approach, and adjust your goals as you progress.

Support Groups and Peer Support

The therapeutic journey, as powerful as it is, doesn't exist in a vacuum. While individual therapy provides a deeply personal and focused space for healing, the added support of a community can be transformative. This is where support groups and peer support networks come in, offering a unique and invaluable dimension to your recovery. These groups provide a safe and understanding environment where you can connect with others who have lived through similar experiences. This shared understanding transcends the limitations of even the most empathetic therapist, offering a sense of validation, belonging, and hope that is incredibly powerful.

The value of connecting with fellow survivors cannot be overstated. It's a fundamental truth of trauma recovery that you are not alone. Feeling isolated and misunderstood is a common experience for survivors of sociopathic abuse, a consequence of the abuser's deliberate attempts to isolate their victims and erode their sense of self. Support groups actively counter this isolation, creating a space where sharing your story, hearing others' stories, and finding solidarity can be profoundly healing.

In a support group, you'll encounter others who understand the nuances of sociopathic manipulation, the insidious gaslighting, the pervasive control, and the lasting effects of the emotional and psychological damage. You'll hear stories that mirror your own, validating your experiences and helping you normalize your reactions. This shared validation can be incredibly powerful, dismantling the self-doubt and shame that often accompany abuse. You'll discover that your experiences are not unique, that your feelings are valid, and that your reactions are completely understandable given the circumstances. This simple realization can be a monumental step toward healing.

Beyond validation, support groups provide practical support and advice. Members often share coping strategies, resources, and information about legal and other assistance. This exchange of knowledge and experience can be a valuable lifeline, especially during the early stages of recovery when you're still navigating the complexities of leaving an abusive relationship and rebuilding your life. The collective wisdom within a support group can help you navigate practical hurdles, from finding safe housing and securing financial independence to dealing with legal issues and rebuilding your support network.

Furthermore, the peer-to-peer support offered in these groups is unique and invaluable. While your therapist provides professional guidance, your fellow survivors offer a different kind of support – a shared experience of understanding. This doesn't diminish the importance of therapy, but it complements it. The shared experiences and empathy within the group offer a sense of camaraderie and understanding that can be both comforting and empowering. You'll find yourself less alone in your journey, empowered by the collective strength and resilience of the group. This can build confidence and create a sense of hope that extends far beyond the confines of individual therapy sessions.

Many support groups are specifically designed for survivors of domestic violence and abuse. These groups often offer specialized support tailored to the unique challenges faced by those who have survived relationships with sociopaths or narcissists. They often delve into the intricacies of manipulative behaviors and offer strategies for recognizing and avoiding similar patterns in future relationships. This

specialized focus provides a level of understanding that is simply unavailable in more general support groups. Finding a group that caters to your specific experience is crucial in finding a supportive and understanding community.

However, finding the right support group is critical. It's essential to find a group that feels safe and comfortable for you. Look for groups that are facilitated by trained professionals who understand trauma and abuse. A well- facilitated group will provide a structured and supportive environment, ensuring that conversations are respectful and productive, and that boundaries are maintained. It's equally important that the group environment fosters a sense of trust and mutual respect. Some groups might adopt a strict confidentiality policy, ensuring that shared information remains within the group. Others might have more flexible guidelines. Understanding these nuances before joining is essential in ensuring a positive and beneficial experience.

Investigate any group thoroughly before participating.

Finding these groups may involve some research. A good starting point is to search online for "support groups for survivors of sociopathic abuse" or "support groups for domestic violence survivors" in your local area. Many organizations dedicated to domestic violence prevention and support offer online and in-person support groups. Your therapist can also provide valuable recommendations or referrals to local groups, leveraging their knowledge of your specific circumstances and needs. It's not uncommon for therapists to suggest or even refer patients to support groups as part of a holistic treatment plan. This collaborative approach significantly enhances the effectiveness of therapy and strengthens your overall recovery.

Moreover, online support groups and forums offer a broader reach, connecting you with individuals across geographical

boundaries. This is especially valuable if local resources are limited or if you prefer the anonymity and flexibility that online platforms can offer. Online communities can also provide ongoing support outside of scheduled group meetings, offering a sense of connection and community 24/7. However, it's crucial to approach online support groups with caution. Ensure the platform prioritizes safety and has measures in place to address potential harassment or inappropriate behavior. Some platforms provide moderation to ensure a safe and respectful environment. Always prioritize your safety and well-being when participating in online communities.

Remember that finding the right support group might take time. Don't be discouraged if the first group you try isn't a good fit. It's crucial to find a group where you feel comfortable, accepted, and understood. The feeling of acceptance and belonging is fundamental for healing. A supportive environment can help you to share your story, process your emotions, and connect with others on a meaningful level. This process might require trying out several groups before finding the one that resonates with you and feels like a true sanctuary.

The benefits of support groups extend far beyond the immediate feeling of connection and validation. The ongoing support you receive can empower you to navigate challenges more effectively, build resilience, and maintain momentum in your recovery. The lasting connections forged within these groups can provide a powerful source of strength and encouragement during difficult times. By creating a community around you that understands your experiences, you are creating a safe space where your healing can flourish and ultimately lead to a future free from the shadows of your past. The collective resilience found in such groups can be a

significant driving force in your continued healing and personal growth.

Beyond formal support groups, you can also find valuable support through informal networks. This might involve connecting with trusted friends, family members, or colleagues who understand your situation and offer consistent support. Even casual conversations with people who have shown empathy and understanding can be helpful. This approach is especially useful if formal groups aren't readily accessible, or if you find group settings overwhelming or triggering. Remember that any support is valuable, and building a supportive network, however informal, can substantially contribute to your healing journey.

Cultivating a personal support network is a cornerstone of successful recovery. It doesn't have to be a large group; rather, it's the quality of the relationships that matter most. These individuals, whether friends, family, or colleagues, provide a sense of normalcy and stability in your life, helping you feel connected and understood. The support you receive from your personal network can act as a buffer, mitigating the negative impacts of trauma and promoting your sense of self-worth. It's crucial to build a network of people who will listen without judgment and provide unwavering support during challenging times.

In summary, seeking support from both formal groups and informal networks is a critical element of healing from the trauma of sociopathic abuse. The validation, practical advice, and emotional support you gain from these groups can be instrumental in your recovery, and their contribution shouldn't be underestimated. By embracing these supportive communities, you're taking a proactive step toward reclaiming your life, strengthening your sense of self, and

building a future free from the grip of abuse. Remember, seeking help is a sign of strength, and you are not alone in this journey.

Working with Legal Professionals

Navigating the legal system after experiencing abuse from a sociopath can feel like entering a minefield. The complexities of the law, coupled with the emotional toll of the abuse, can be overwhelming. However, understanding your legal options and seeking skilled legal representation is crucial for protecting yourself and securing your future. This section will guide you through the process of working with legal professionals, empowering you to take control and safeguard your well-being.

The first crucial step is finding a lawyer specializing in domestic violence or abuse cases. These lawyers possess a deep understanding of the dynamics of abusive relationships and the specific legal challenges faced by survivors. They are equipped to handle the nuances of cases involving sociopathic abusers, who often employ sophisticated manipulation tactics to undermine their victims' credibility. Don't hesitate to interview several lawyers before making a decision. Ask about their experience with similar cases, their approach to working with trauma survivors, and their fee structure. A good lawyer will prioritize your safety and well- being, demonstrating empathy and understanding throughout the process.

One of the most effective legal tools available to survivors is a restraining order, also known as a protection order. A restraining order is a court order that legally restricts the abuser's contact with you. This can include prohibiting them from contacting you directly or indirectly, coming within a certain distance of your home or workplace, or even possessing a firearm. The specific terms of the order vary depending on your jurisdiction and the details of your case.

However, the primary goal is to create a physical and emotional barrier between you and your abuser, minimizing the risk of further harm.

Obtaining a restraining order requires providing evidence of abuse. This evidence can include photos, videos, medical records documenting injuries, police reports, emails, text messages, or even witness testimonies. Your lawyer will help you gather and organize this evidence, ensuring it is presented effectively in court. Be prepared to detail the instances of abuse, providing specific dates, times, and descriptions of the events. It is crucial to be accurate and consistent in your testimony, maintaining a calm and clear demeanor. Your lawyer will guide you through this process, offering support and reassurance along the way.

Remember that even if you've never reported the abuse to the police previously, you can still seek a restraining order. The court will consider all available evidence, even if it is solely based on your testimony and supporting documentation. Your lawyer can help you navigate the process of presenting your evidence effectively and persuasively. It's worth noting that obtaining a restraining order is not always a guarantee of complete safety, but it serves as a significant deterrent and provides a critical legal layer of protection.

Beyond restraining orders, legal professionals can play a vital role in securing your financial safety and independence. If you shared finances with your abuser, you might need assistance in disentangling your joint accounts, dividing assets, and obtaining financial support. This can involve seeking alimony, child support, or other forms of financial assistance. The process can be complex and legally demanding, requiring expert legal guidance. Your lawyer

will help you navigate the legal requirements, protecting your financial rights and ensuring a fair settlement.

Furthermore, if you experienced financial abuse – such as controlling access to funds, manipulating credit cards, or coercing you into financial decisions that benefited your abuser – your lawyer can help you address this specific aspect of your situation. This might involve seeking reimbursement for financial losses incurred during the abusive relationship, or addressing fraudulent activity. The legal process can help you reclaim financial control of your life, laying a secure foundation for your independent future.

In situations involving custody of children, legal representation is even more critical. Navigating child custody arrangements during and after a relationship with a sociopathic abuser can be incredibly challenging. Child custody cases are often highly emotional and contentious, requiring a strong legal team that understands the dynamics of abuse and can effectively advocate for your child's well- being. A lawyer specializing in family law can help you navigate the complexities of the legal process, ensuring the safety and best interests of your child are prioritized.

Your lawyer can help determine the most appropriate custody arrangement, considering the abuser's manipulative tendencies and any history of violence or abuse. They can assist in constructing a comprehensive parenting plan that safeguards your child's physical and emotional well-being, limiting the abuser's access if necessary. They can also advocate for your rights as a parent, ensuring that your voice is heard and that your concerns are addressed fairly and effectively.

Beyond individual legal action, your lawyer can also guide you through the potential benefits of seeking legal assistance

through domestic violence shelters or advocacy organizations. These organizations often provide pro bono or reduced-fee legal services to survivors, making legal representation more accessible. They can also offer comprehensive support services, including counseling, housing assistance, and financial assistance. Leveraging these resources can significantly enhance your ability to rebuild your life and secure your future.

Remember that the legal process can be long and emotionally draining. It's crucial to maintain open communication with your lawyer, keeping them informed of any new developments or concerns. Don't hesitate to ask questions or express your anxieties. Your lawyer's role extends beyond the courtroom; they are there to provide guidance, support, and a sense of stability during a challenging time. They are your advocate, helping you navigate a complex legal landscape while you focus on your healing and recovery.

Furthermore, consider the possibility of criminal charges against your abuser. If you have evidence of criminal activity, such as assault, stalking, or theft, you can report it to the police. Your lawyer can work with law enforcement to build a strong case, guiding you through the process of providing evidence and testimony. While it's not guaranteed that criminal charges will be filed, pursuing this avenue can provide a sense of justice and accountability, contributing to your healing process.

Finally, remember that seeking legal help is a sign of strength, not weakness. It's a proactive step toward protecting yourself and creating a safer future. Don't let fear or intimidation prevent you from accessing the legal support you deserve. With the help of a skilled and compassionate legal professional, you can navigate the complexities of the

legal system, securing your safety and laying the foundation for a life free from abuse. Your journey towards healing and empowerment begins with taking this critical step. The support you receive from your lawyer will prove invaluable as you continue to rebuild your life and reclaim your future. You deserve peace, safety, and a life free from the shadow of your past.

Accessing Community Resources and Services

The legal process, as crucial as it is, forms only one part of your journey to recovery. Equally vital is accessing the wealth of support available within your community. These resources, often overlooked in the immediate aftermath of abuse, can provide the lifeline you need to rebuild your life and reclaim your sense of self. Domestic violence shelters, hotlines, and advocacy groups offer a network of support, practical assistance, and a safe haven where you can begin to heal.

Domestic violence shelters provide temporary safe housing for survivors of abuse, offering a refuge from immediate danger. These shelters vary in size and the services they offer, but typically include a safe, secure environment, meals, clothing, and basic necessities. More importantly, they often provide access to crucial support services, including counseling, legal advocacy, and assistance with finding employment and housing. The shelter environment itself offers a powerful sense of community, allowing survivors to connect with others who have shared similar experiences. This shared experience can be incredibly validating and empowering, reminding survivors that they are not alone in their struggles and that healing is possible.

Finding a shelter can be as simple as a quick online search, but it's also vital to be mindful of safety and discretion. If you're concerned about your abuser's ability to track your location, utilize a trusted friend or family member's computer or phone for your search, or seek assistance from a trusted professional who can provide resources without compromising your safety. Many shelters maintain confidential databases of available beds and services,

ensuring that your location and contact information remain private. This privacy is paramount, understanding that maintaining confidentiality is crucial to your safety and well- being. Shelter staff are trained to understand and respond to the unique needs of survivors, maintaining a strict confidentiality protocol and ensuring that your privacy is safeguarded at all times.

Beyond physical shelter, many organizations offer crisis hotlines. These hotlines operate 24/7, providing immediate support and guidance to individuals experiencing abuse. A call to a hotline can offer immediate emotional support, helping you to feel less isolated and alone. Hotline counselors are trained to provide crisis intervention, helping you to develop a safety plan, access resources, and navigate immediate challenges. They can offer a calming voice amidst the storm, providing a safe space to vent your emotions and process your experiences without judgment.

They are invaluable resources, offering immediate assistance and helping to connect you to more sustained support.

Remember that reaching out is a sign of strength, not weakness, and that there are people who care and want to help.

Advocacy groups play a crucial role in supporting survivors of abuse. These groups work to raise awareness about domestic violence, advocate for policy changes, and provide direct support to survivors. They often offer a wide range of services, including counseling, legal advocacy, support groups, and educational workshops. Participating in a support group can be incredibly therapeutic, allowing you to share your experiences with others who understand, providing mutual support and validation. These groups offer a safe space to process emotions, build resilience, and foster a sense of community. The shared experience within the

group can be transformative, allowing you to move forward in healing with the support of your peers.

Many advocacy groups also provide legal advocacy services, working in conjunction with legal professionals to ensure survivors have access to justice and appropriate legal representation. They may provide assistance with obtaining restraining orders, navigating custody battles, or securing financial assistance. These groups can be a powerful ally, navigating the complexities of the legal system alongside you and providing unwavering support. They often have strong networks within the legal community, ensuring that survivors have access to the best legal professionals available and can assist in finding lawyers who specialize in domestic violence and abuse cases.

Accessing these services can sometimes feel overwhelming, especially in the midst of trauma. However, it's essential to remember that you are not alone. There are people who care about your well-being and want to help. Don't hesitate to reach out to multiple organizations, explore various resources, and find the support systems that best fit your individual needs. Your safety and recovery are paramount, and taking the step to seek assistance is an act of incredible strength and courage.

Beyond shelters, hotlines, and advocacy groups, many community organizations offer additional support services relevant to your situation. Food banks can address immediate food insecurity, while housing assistance programs can help you find safe and affordable housing. Job training and placement services can help you rebuild your financial independence, and mental health services can provide ongoing support for your emotional well-being. Reaching out to your local community center or social services agency can provide information on these and other vital resources.

It's important to acknowledge that the process of accessing and utilizing these services might feel overwhelming, particularly during the initial stages of your recovery. The emotional impact of abuse can make it difficult to navigate complex systems and make crucial decisions. Allow yourself time, be patient with yourself, and remember that every small step forward is a victory. Don't hesitate to reach out to a trusted friend, family member, or therapist for support and guidance in navigating these resources. Their assistance can be invaluable in helping you to organize your thoughts, prioritize your needs, and access the support that you deserve.

Remember, seeking help is not a sign of weakness, it's a sign of strength and resilience. Taking this step demonstrates your commitment to healing and rebuilding your life. The road to recovery is not always easy, but it is a journey filled with hope and the possibility of a brighter future. By accessing the resources available within your community, you are taking control of your life and empowering yourself to move forward with strength and confidence.

Furthermore, consider the potential benefits of online support groups. These online communities offer a sense of anonymity and accessibility that can be particularly beneficial for survivors who may feel hesitant to participate in in-person support groups. These online platforms can provide a sense of connection and shared experience, offering opportunities to build resilience and learn from others who have overcome similar challenges. These online resources can be a valuable supplement to other forms of support, providing readily accessible emotional support and practical advice.

It is crucial to remember that the healing process is personal and takes time. There is no prescribed timeline, and it's important to be patient and compassionate with yourself throughout this journey. Celebrate small victories, acknowledge your progress, and allow yourself to grieve the losses you've experienced. Embrace the support of the community and continue to seek out resources and services as needed, recognizing that your needs will likely evolve as you heal and move forward. The path toward healing is unique to each individual, and the journey itself will contribute to shaping your sense of self and building a stronger, more resilient future. Your resilience and strength are undeniable; embrace them and celebrate the progress you make each day. You are capable of healing, and you deserve a life filled with peace, safety, and joy. The resources mentioned are stepping stones on your path to reclaiming your life and building a stronger, healthier future for yourself. Remember to reach out for assistance – you don't have to walk this path alone.

Assessing Your Financial Situation

Rebuilding your life after escaping an abusive relationship requires a multifaceted approach, and financial independence is a cornerstone of that process. While the emotional and psychological wounds of abuse can take time to heal, regaining control of your finances can provide an immediate sense of empowerment and security. This section will guide you through a process of assessing your current financial situation, identifying your assets and liabilities, and exploring potential avenues for financial stability.

Remember, this is a process, and it's crucial to be patient and kind to yourself throughout. Each step you take, no matter how small, contributes to your journey toward financial independence.

The first step is to take a deep breath and gather your resources. Find a quiet, safe space where you can focus without distractions. It may be helpful to have a notebook and pen, or to use a computer spreadsheet program, to keep track of your information. Don't feel pressured to complete this process in one sitting. If you feel overwhelmed, break it down into smaller, manageable tasks, taking breaks as needed. Remember to prioritize self-care throughout this process. Engage in activities that help you relax and de- stress; this will help you to stay focused and avoid feeling discouraged.

Begin by creating a comprehensive inventory of your assets. This includes any bank accounts, savings accounts, retirement funds, investment accounts, and other financial holdings. List the account numbers, the current balances, and the institution where the account is held. Include any physical assets such as vehicles, property, jewelry, or other

valuable possessions. Estimate the value of these assets, taking into account depreciation where necessary. If you are unsure about the value of a particular asset, you can seek assistance from a financial advisor or a trusted professional. Detailed records will be helpful if you decide to seek legal advice or need to support financial claims later. Keeping this information organized will not only help you understand your current financial standing but also assist you in making informed decisions moving forward.

Next, create a list of your debts. This includes credit card debt, loans (personal, student, auto, mortgage), medical bills, and any other outstanding financial obligations. For each debt, record the creditor's name, the amount owed, the interest rate, and the minimum monthly payment. This clear picture of your outstanding debts will be essential in developing a strategy to manage and ultimately eliminate them. It's important to be thorough, even if some debts seem insignificant. A complete record will assist you in evaluating your overall financial situation effectively.

Once you have a comprehensive list of your assets and debts, you can calculate your net worth. This is simply the difference between your total assets and your total liabilities (debts). A positive net worth indicates that your assets exceed your debts, while a negative net worth indicates the opposite. Your net worth provides a snapshot of your current financial health and can be a useful tool for tracking your progress as you work towards financial independence. Don't be discouraged by a negative net worth; this is a starting point, and with a plan, you can gradually improve your financial situation.

Now, turn your attention to your income. Identify all sources of current income, whether it's employment, alimony, child support, social security, disability benefits, or any other

forms of financial support. Record the amount of income you receive from each source, as well as the frequency of payment (weekly, bi-weekly, monthly, etc.). This comprehensive income analysis will help you accurately assess your budget and plan for the future. It's also important to consider potential future income sources; do you have skills or qualifications that would enable you to find new employment opportunities? Exploring job training programs or enhancing your resume might open the doors to new income streams.

After compiling the information, it's time to create a budget. This should be a realistic budget reflecting your actual spending habits. You can use budgeting apps or spreadsheets to track your income and expenses. Categorize your expenses (housing, food, transportation, utilities, healthcare, debt payments, entertainment, etc.). It's important to be honest with yourself about your spending habits. Identify areas where you can cut expenses and adjust your budget accordingly. Remember, even small adjustments to your spending habits can make a significant difference in your overall financial picture. Creating a detailed budget not only provides financial clarity but also allows you to plan for the future and prioritize your needs effectively.

Consider exploring resources available to assist you during this financial assessment and budgeting process. Financial literacy programs and workshops can provide guidance on budgeting, debt management, and financial planning. Local community organizations and non-profit agencies often offer free or low-cost financial counseling services. These resources can be invaluable in navigating the complexities of personal finance, providing support and guidance as you work toward achieving financial independence. Utilize these resources to equip yourself with the knowledge and skills necessary to take control of your financial future.

If you are facing overwhelming debt, consider seeking professional help. Credit counseling agencies can help you develop a debt management plan, negotiate with creditors, and explore options such as debt consolidation or bankruptcy. These agencies can provide valuable guidance and support in navigating your debt and securing your financial stability. Seeking help doesn't signal failure, but rather displays your proactive approach towards gaining control over your financial situation. Remember, addressing debt head-on, with the appropriate professional assistance, will enable you to rebuild your financial health effectively.

Protecting your credit is also crucial during this period. Regularly review your credit report for errors or signs of fraudulent activity. If you discover any inaccuracies, take immediate action to correct them. Understanding your credit score and working toward improving it is essential for securing loans, securing housing and gaining access to financial services. Taking proactive steps to improve and maintain your credit score can contribute greatly to your financial stability.

This detailed assessment will empower you to navigate the financial aspects of your recovery. Remember, this process is a journey, and it's important to celebrate your achievements along the way. As you gain financial stability, you'll build confidence and resilience, contributing to your overall well- being and creating a future free from financial anxieties. The path to financial independence is attainable; with careful planning, persistence, and the utilization of available resources, you will achieve your financial goals. Your strength and perseverance in overcoming abuse extend to this new chapter of your life. Embrace this journey, acknowledge your progress, and celebrate the future you are

building for yourself, financially secure and independently empowered.

Creating a Budget and Managing Finances

Building a budget is more than just tracking income and expenses; it's about creating a roadmap for your financial future. This is particularly crucial after escaping an abusive relationship, where financial control may have been a significant tool of manipulation. Regaining control of your finances is a powerful step towards reclaiming your autonomy.

Start by meticulously documenting your income. This includes all sources—employment wages (including overtime and bonuses), alimony, child support, social security benefits, disability payments, rental income, any interest earned, and any other regular financial inflows. Note the frequency of each payment—weekly, bi-weekly, monthly, or annually. Be thorough; even small amounts add up. Consider setting up separate bank accounts for different purposes – one for necessities, another for savings, and perhaps a third for discretionary spending. This can improve your ability to track income and expenses. This segregation can also help you avoid overspending in one area while neglecting others.

Next, create a detailed list of your monthly expenses. Be brutally honest with yourself. Categorize your expenses to gain a clearer picture of your spending habits. Major categories often include:

Housing: Rent or mortgage payments, property taxes, homeowners insurance, renter's insurance, maintenance and repairs. If you're facing housing instability, explore options like subsidized housing, shelters, or transitional housing programs. Document all housing costs, even small ones, to

have a clear financial picture. If you shared housing with your abuser, you may have to reassess your housing needs and budget accordingly.

Food: Groceries, eating out, and any subscriptions to meal delivery services. Consider creating a meal plan to minimize food waste and reduce expenses. Look for budget-friendly recipes and explore options like bulk buying or utilizing food banks if your budget is particularly tight.

Transportation: Car payments, insurance, gas, public transportation fares, maintenance and repairs. If possible, consider carpooling, biking, or walking to reduce transportation costs. Explore public transportation options to cut down your costs.

Utilities: Electricity, gas, water, internet, phone, cable. Consider energy-efficient practices and negotiate with providers for better rates. Explore alternatives such as cheaper internet plans or switching to a more cost-effective phone provider.

Healthcare: Medical insurance premiums, co-pays, medications, dental care, vision care. If you're uninsured or underinsured, research available government programs like Medicaid or affordable care options in your area. Consider a health savings account (HSA) to plan for future medical expenses, a great tool for long-term savings.

Debt Payments: Minimum payments on credit cards, loans, and any other outstanding debts. List each debt separately, including the creditor, the balance, the interest rate, and the minimum monthly payment. This detailed information will assist you in formulating a comprehensive debt management strategy.

Childcare: If applicable, include daycare expenses, babysitting fees, or any other childcare-related costs. Research and find affordable childcare options such as subsidized programs or in-home care.

Personal Care: Toiletries, clothing, haircuts. Look for discounts and sales to minimize these expenses.

Entertainment: Movies, concerts, subscriptions, hobbies. This is often the first area to cut back on when budgeting is tight. Explore cost-effective alternatives like borrowing books from the library, enjoying free outdoor activities, or finding free or inexpensive community events.

Other Expenses: This category will encompass everything else, such as pet care, gifts, subscriptions, personal care products, and any miscellaneous expenses. A dedicated category for unforeseen expenses is wise.

Once you've compiled a complete list of your income and expenses, subtract your total expenses from your total income. A positive number indicates that you have a surplus, meaning you're earning more than you're spending. A negative number indicates a deficit, meaning you're spending more than you're earning. Don't panic if you have a deficit.

This is a common starting point and can be addressed through careful budgeting and financial planning.

If you have a deficit, you need to identify areas where you can reduce expenses. This may involve making difficult choices, but remember that this is a step towards financial independence and self-sufficiency. Examine each category closely, looking for areas where you can cut back without significantly impacting your quality of life. Consider reducing your entertainment budget, negotiating lower bills

with service providers, or switching to cheaper alternatives for everyday items.

Creating a realistic budget requires honesty and self- discipline. Don't set unrealistic expectations for yourself. Start small, track your expenses diligently for at least one month to get a clear picture of your spending patterns, and gradually work towards your financial goals. There are many budgeting apps and tools available to help you track your spending. Many offer insights into your spending habits and help you identify areas for improvement.

Consider building an emergency fund. Aim for 3-6 months' worth of living expenses. This fund will provide a safety net in case of unexpected job loss, medical emergencies, or other unforeseen circumstances. Start small and gradually build up your emergency fund over time. Even small regular contributions will make a difference in the long run.

Managing debt is another crucial aspect of financial independence. If you have high-interest debt, prioritize paying it down as quickly as possible. Consider strategies like the debt snowball or debt avalanche method. The debt snowball involves paying off your smallest debt first, regardless of interest rate, to build momentum and motivation. The debt avalanche method involves paying off your highest-interest debt first to save money on interest in the long run.

Seek professional guidance if needed. Financial advisors and credit counselors can offer personalized advice and support. Many non-profit organizations offer free or low-cost financial counseling services. Don't hesitate to seek help if you're struggling to manage your finances.

Remember, rebuilding your financial stability after escaping an abusive relationship is a marathon, not a sprint. Celebrate your progress, no matter how small. Each step you take toward financial independence is a victory in reclaiming your life and your future. The journey towards financial empowerment will build your confidence and resilience, further solidifying your independence and setting the stage for a more secure and fulfilling life. This financial independence is a tangible manifestation of your strength and capacity for recovery.

Seeking Financial Assistance and Resources

Rebuilding your financial life after escaping an abusive relationship requires more than just budgeting; it necessitates accessing available resources and support systems. Many organizations and government programs are specifically designed to help survivors navigate the complex financial challenges that often accompany such situations.

Understanding and accessing these resources is a crucial step towards achieving lasting financial independence.

One of the first places to explore is your local government's social services department. These departments often administer various programs, including emergency financial assistance, housing subsidies, and food stamps (SNAP).

Eligibility requirements vary depending on location and individual circumstances, such as income level and family size. It is crucial to gather all necessary documentation, such as proof of income, identification, and proof of residence to ensure a smoother application process. The application process itself can be daunting, filled with complex paperwork and potential delays. However, many social service departments offer assistance in navigating this process. Don't hesitate to ask for help; their staff are often trained to support individuals in need. Consider seeking assistance from a local advocate or volunteer organization to help you navigate the bureaucracy. They can act as an intermediary, providing support and reducing the emotional strain often associated with applying for benefits.

Beyond local government assistance, several federal programs offer financial support to abuse survivors. One of the most significant is the Temporary Assistance for Needy Families (TANF) program. TANF provides temporary

financial assistance for low-income families, including those escaping domestic violence. The program often includes job training and placement services to help recipients become self-sufficient. Eligibility requirements are similar to those of state-level programs, emphasizing income level and household size. Again, assembling all necessary documentation is vital for a successful application. It's highly recommended to familiarize yourself with the specific requirements of your state's TANF program before starting the application. Many states offer online applications and resources to guide you through the process.

Another crucial federal program is Medicaid, which provides healthcare coverage to low-income individuals and families. Healthcare costs can be substantial, and the lack of insurance can be a significant barrier to recovery. Medicaid helps alleviate this burden by covering essential medical, dental, and mental healthcare services. For those fleeing abusive situations, access to mental health services is particularly important, as trauma counseling is a vital part of the healing process. Navigating the Medicaid application process can be intricate, with varying eligibility requirements depending on your state. However, numerous resources are available online and through local health departments to assist in the application and understanding of the program.

In addition to government programs, many non-profit organizations across the country provide financial support specifically to victims of domestic violence. These organizations often offer a range of services, including emergency shelter, financial counseling, and assistance with job searching. Many of these organizations are locally based, offering a personalized approach to support. A simple online search for "domestic violence services [your city/state]" will likely yield a list of organizations in your area. These groups often have websites providing details about their services

and contact information. Don't hesitate to reach out to multiple organizations to explore the full range of support available. They often have a deep understanding of the unique financial challenges faced by survivors and can offer tailored solutions.

Some charitable organizations provide broader financial assistance, without necessarily focusing solely on domestic violence victims. Organizations like the Salvation Army and the United Way often offer emergency financial aid for various needs, including housing assistance and utility bill payments. Eligibility criteria vary, but these organizations often have flexible guidelines and prioritize assisting those facing immediate financial hardship. Their websites usually provide detailed information about their aid programs, including application processes and eligibility requirements. These broader charities may be particularly helpful if you are facing immediate financial emergencies while navigating the more specialized programs designed for domestic abuse survivors.

Beyond financial aid, many organizations provide crucial non-financial support. Legal aid societies often offer free or low-cost legal services to survivors, including assistance with obtaining protective orders or pursuing legal action against their abusers. Access to legal assistance is crucial for securing your safety and protecting your rights. Many legal aid societies offer services in various areas, such as housing law, family law, and employment law, areas often impacted by domestic abuse. Their services can alleviate the significant financial burden often associated with legal representation.

Job training programs are another invaluable resource for abuse survivors. Many organizations provide job skills training, resume building workshops, and job placement

assistance. These programs can help you gain the skills and confidence needed to secure stable employment, a crucial step towards financial independence. Many government agencies, such as the Workforce Development Boards, and non-profit organizations offer such programs, often with additional support such as childcare assistance and transportation assistance to help remove the barriers to obtaining employment. Check with your local workforce development board for available programs in your area.

They often offer a comprehensive list of services geared towards helping individuals achieve economic self- sufficiency.

Financial literacy workshops and counseling are also critical resources. Many organizations offer free or low-cost financial literacy workshops to help survivors learn about budgeting, debt management, and financial planning. These workshops can equip you with the tools you need to manage your finances effectively and build a secure financial future. These workshops are often offered through local community centers, libraries, and non-profit organizations. Look for workshops focusing on budgeting, saving, credit repair, and investing to build a solid financial foundation.

Remember, accessing these resources requires initiative and persistence. The application processes can be complex and time-consuming, and there may be initial rejections. Do not be discouraged. Seek help from advocates or caseworkers who can guide you through the process and provide emotional support. Their expertise in navigating these systems can significantly increase your chances of success. Consider keeping a detailed record of all your applications, communication, and deadlines. This will help you track your progress and ensure you don't miss any important steps. It is also helpful to keep a binder with all necessary

documentation to make the application process more efficient.

Finally, prioritize your mental and emotional well-being throughout this process. Rebuilding your life after escaping an abusive relationship is a marathon, not a sprint. Allow yourself time to grieve, heal, and adjust to your new reality. Support groups, therapy, and self-care practices can be invaluable tools during this challenging time. Remember that seeking financial assistance is not a sign of weakness but a sign of strength and resilience. You deserve to be safe, secure, and financially independent. Utilizing these resources is a testament to your commitment to building a brighter future for yourself and your family. The journey to financial freedom will be challenging, but with determination and access to the appropriate resources, it is entirely achievable.

Rebuilding Credit and Managing Debt

Rebuilding your credit after escaping an abusive relationship can feel like climbing a steep mountain, especially if your abuser controlled your finances. However, it is entirely possible, and vital for your long-term financial well-being.

The first step is obtaining a copy of your credit report from each of the three major credit bureaus: Equifax, Experian, and TransUnion. You can obtain these reports for free annually at AnnualCreditReport.com. This is crucial because it reveals the current state of your credit, identifying any negative marks left by your abuser or the financial challenges you faced during the relationship.

Examine your credit report meticulously. Look for accounts opened without your knowledge or consent, instances of fraudulent activity, late payments that might not reflect your own actions, and any inaccuracies. Dispute any entries you believe are incorrect. Each credit bureau provides a process for disputing information. You'll need to document your claims thoroughly with evidence, and be prepared for a potentially protracted process. While it may seem daunting, persistence is key. Remember, your abuser's manipulative behavior doesn't define your financial future.

Once you've cleaned up inaccuracies on your credit report, focus on rebuilding your credit score. This is a gradual process, but every positive step counts. Start by paying all your bills on time. This is the single most significant factor influencing your credit score. Set up automatic payments if necessary to avoid accidental late payments, a common pitfall during stressful periods of life. Consider using a budgeting app to track your spending and ensure you have

sufficient funds to meet your financial obligations each month.

Next, aim to keep your credit utilization ratio low. This ratio represents the percentage of your available credit that you're currently using. Ideally, you should aim to keep this ratio below 30%, and preferably even lower. For example, if you have a credit card with a $1,000 limit, try to keep your balance under $300. Paying down existing debt will significantly improve this ratio. Explore strategies for managing and paying down your existing debt. If you find yourself overwhelmed by the amount of debt, don't hesitate to seek professional guidance. Credit counseling agencies can provide personalized debt management plans, often offering debt consolidation or negotiation with creditors.

Debt consolidation can streamline your payments by combining multiple debts into a single loan with a potentially lower interest rate. This can simplify your finances and make it easier to stay on track with repayments. However, carefully evaluate the terms of any consolidation loan before agreeing to it. Some consolidation loans may carry significant fees or unfavorable interest rates, potentially making the situation worse in the long run.

Thoroughly compare offers from multiple lenders to ensure you're getting the best deal. Understand the implications before making any commitment. Do not rush into a deal simply because of the pressure to resolve debt quickly.

Negotiating with your creditors directly is another option, particularly if you're facing financial hardship. Many creditors are willing to work with individuals who demonstrate a sincere commitment to paying off their debt. You might be able to negotiate a lower monthly payment, a reduced interest rate, or even a settlement for a smaller amount than your total debt. Be prepared to provide

documentation of your financial situation and your willingness to stick to a repayment plan. Remember to keep a record of all communication with creditors.

Opening a secured credit card can be a helpful strategy for rebuilding credit. With a secured credit card, you make a security deposit, and your credit limit matches this deposit. This minimizes the risk to the lender, allowing individuals with poor credit history to build their credit gradually.

Consistent and responsible use of a secured credit card will gradually improve your credit score. However, remember to always pay your balance in full and on time to maximize the positive impact on your credit.

Building a positive credit history requires consistent effort and attention to detail. Set realistic goals, track your progress, and celebrate your successes along the way.

Remember, rebuilding your credit is a marathon, not a sprint. It will take time and patience, but the rewards of financial independence are well worth the effort. Financial independence is a powerful tool for protecting yourself from future abuse. It reduces your reliance on others, enabling you to make independent choices and maintain a sense of autonomy.

Beyond rebuilding your credit, it's crucial to develop strategies for protecting yourself from future financial exploitation. This involves understanding your financial rights and responsibilities, practicing responsible financial habits, and learning to identify and avoid potential financial scams or manipulative tactics. Develop a solid understanding of your personal finances. Keep accurate records of your income, expenses, and debts. Regularly check your bank accounts and credit reports for any unauthorized activity.

Educate yourself about common financial scams and manipulative techniques. Many predators target vulnerable individuals, using deception and coercion to exploit their finances. Learning to recognize these tactics can help protect you from falling victim to similar schemes in the future. This includes understanding how to identify and report identity theft, phishing scams, or other fraudulent activities.

Consider seeking professional financial advice. A qualified financial advisor can help you develop a personalized financial plan, providing guidance on budgeting, saving, investing, and debt management. Financial planning is essential for building a secure and independent future. They can provide insight and strategies for managing your finances efficiently and effectively. It also allows for a neutral evaluation of your financial situation, providing objective support and encouragement as you rebuild your financial life.

Finally, remember that your financial well-being is intrinsically linked to your overall mental and emotional health. The journey to financial recovery can be emotionally challenging, but it's important to prioritize self-care throughout this process. Don't hesitate to seek support from friends, family, or mental health professionals. Trauma therapy can be especially beneficial in addressing the emotional wounds that often accompany financial abuse.

Support systems can assist with dealing with the emotional stress involved in managing finances after experiencing abuse.

Financial independence is not merely about numbers on a balance sheet; it represents a fundamental aspect of personal freedom and safety. By actively rebuilding your credit, managing your debt effectively, and taking steps to protect yourself from future exploitation, you are reclaiming control

over your life and building a secure foundation for your future. This process might seem daunting initially, but remember that with resilience, resourcefulness, and the support available to you, you can achieve financial independence and live a life free from the shadow of financial control. Celebrate each small victory along the way, recognizing the strength and perseverance you are demonstrating in overcoming adversity. Your journey towards financial freedom is a testament to your strength and a powerful step towards lasting independence.

Gaining Financial Literacy and Independence

Gaining financial literacy isn't just about balancing a checkbook; it's about understanding the intricate web of financial systems and how they impact your life. After escaping an abusive relationship where financial control was a weapon, rebuilding your financial independence requires a deeper understanding than simply paying bills on time. It requires actively learning about budgeting, saving, investing, and debt management. Think of it as learning a new language – the language of money – to navigate a world that previously felt hostile and confusing.

The first step is acknowledging that you deserve this knowledge. Your abuser intentionally kept you in the dark about finances, fostering dependence and disempowerment. Reclaiming control starts with actively seeking out resources to understand how money works. This is not a sign of weakness, but an act of profound self-respect and empowerment.

There are numerous free and low-cost resources available to help you build this financial literacy. Many community colleges and universities offer free or discounted personal finance courses, often online. These courses often cover budgeting, debt management, investing, and retirement planning, providing a comprehensive foundation. Libraries also offer valuable resources, including books, workshops, and online databases with financial information. Don't underestimate the power of these readily available tools.

Online resources are another incredible source of financial knowledge. Websites like Investopedia offer clear explanations of complex financial concepts, while many

reputable financial institutions provide free guides and webinars on various financial topics. YouTube channels dedicated to personal finance offer engaging tutorials and advice from certified financial planners. While not all online information is trustworthy, research carefully, prioritizing information from established organizations and government agencies.

Budgeting is the cornerstone of financial literacy. It's about understanding where your money goes and making conscious decisions about how to allocate it. Many budgeting apps can simplify this process, automatically categorizing transactions and providing visual representations of your spending habits. These apps can highlight areas where you might be overspending, allowing you to make informed adjustments. A simple spreadsheet or notebook can also suffice if you prefer a more hands-on approach.

The 50/30/20 budgeting rule is a helpful guideline. It suggests allocating 50% of your after-tax income to needs (housing, food, transportation), 30% to wants (entertainment, dining out), and 20% to savings and debt repayment. This is just a guideline; adjust it based on your individual circumstances and financial goals. The key is to be mindful of your spending and to track your progress consistently.

Regularly reviewing your budget helps you stay on track and make necessary adjustments along the way.

Saving is crucial for building a financial safety net and achieving long-term financial goals. Even small, consistent savings can accumulate significantly over time, thanks to the power of compound interest. Automate your savings by setting up regular transfers from your checking account to a savings account. Treat these automated transfers as non- negotiable expenses, reinforcing the habit of saving.

Consider opening a high-yield savings account to maximize your returns.

Understanding debt is essential, particularly if you are carrying debt from your abusive relationship. Differentiate between good debt (like a low-interest student loan for a degree that enhances your earning potential) and bad debt (high-interest credit card debt). Prioritize paying down high- interest debt first to minimize the long-term cost. Explore different debt repayment strategies, such as the snowball method (paying off the smallest debt first for motivation) or the avalanche method (paying off the highest-interest debt first to save money). Explore options such as debt consolidation or negotiating with creditors, but always thoroughly research the implications before making any decisions.

Investing allows your money to grow over time, potentially outpacing inflation. Start by researching different investment options, such as stocks, bonds, mutual funds, and exchange- traded funds (ETFs). Understand the level of risk associated with each option and align your investments with your risk tolerance and financial goals. Consider starting with low- cost index funds or ETFs, which offer diversification and generally lower fees than actively managed funds. Avoid

get-rich-quick schemes, a common tactic used to exploit financially vulnerable individuals.

Protecting yourself from future financial exploitation is paramount. Monitor your credit reports regularly, checking for any unauthorized activity or errors. Regularly review your bank statements for suspicious transactions. Be wary of unsolicited financial advice or investment opportunities that sound too good to be true. Educate yourself about common scams, such as phishing emails or fraudulent websites, to avoid becoming a victim.

Building financial independence is a journey, not a destination. It requires patience, perseverance, and a commitment to continuous learning. Celebrate your small victories along the way, acknowledging the significant progress you've made. Remember that financial literacy empowers you to make informed decisions about your finances, ensuring a secure and independent future free from the manipulative control of others. It is a symbol of your resilience and your strength in overcoming adversity. Each step you take toward financial literacy is a powerful step toward building a life where you are in control of your destiny, financially and emotionally. You deserve financial freedom, and the path to achieving it begins with education and a commitment to your own empowerment. This is not just about numbers; it's about reclaiming your life.

Finding Safe and Affordable Housing

Finding safe and affordable housing after escaping an abusive situation can feel like navigating a minefield. The urgency to secure a safe space, coupled with the potential financial constraints and emotional distress, can be overwhelming. However, with careful planning and the utilization of available resources, finding a stable and secure home is achievable. This process requires patience, persistence, and a belief in your ability to rebuild your life. Don't be afraid to ask for help; there are people and organizations dedicated to supporting you.

One of the first steps is identifying your immediate needs. How much space do you need? Will you be alone, or will you be bringing children or pets? Do you require accessibility features? Knowing your requirements allows you to target your search effectively. This self-assessment is crucial to narrowing down the search and avoiding options that might not meet your specific needs. Start by making a list. Be realistic about your needs and priorities, recognizing that compromises might be necessary.

Shelters provide immediate safety and temporary refuge. Domestic violence shelters offer confidential, short-term accommodation, often including support services such as counseling, legal aid, and assistance with securing long-term housing. These shelters are specifically designed to protect survivors from further harm and provide a supportive environment to begin healing. Finding a shelter is often the first step in establishing a secure foundation. Their locations are usually kept confidential for the safety of residents, but local helplines or social services can provide referrals.

Remember, contacting a shelter is a brave step, and it

signifies your commitment to prioritizing your safety and well-being.

Transitional housing programs offer a bridge between emergency shelter and permanent housing. These programs typically provide longer-term accommodation, often with supportive services designed to help residents gain financial stability and develop life skills. They might offer assistance with job searching, budgeting, and life skills training, helping residents establish the foundations for long-term independence. These programs recognize that stable housing is only one piece of the puzzle. Access to resources and support is equally crucial for achieving long-term stability.

Research programs in your area to find one that best aligns with your individual needs and circumstances.

Affordable rental options are a crucial aspect of securing long-term housing. This requires researching different options, such as government-subsidized housing, Section 8 vouchers, and non-profit housing organizations.

Government-subsidized housing programs offer rent assistance to low-income families and individuals. Section 8 vouchers, administered by local housing authorities, provide rental subsidies that help pay a portion of the rent in privately owned housing. Non-profit organizations often offer affordable housing options, sometimes with additional support services. Thorough research is essential to understand the eligibility requirements and application processes for each program.

When searching for affordable rental options, it's essential to be cautious and thorough. Verify the legitimacy of any listing, confirming the landlord's identity and the property's availability. Avoid paying large deposits or fees upfront without proper verification. Inspect the property thoroughly before signing any lease agreement, ensuring it meets your

needs and is safe and habitable. Read the lease carefully before signing, understanding all terms and conditions to avoid unforeseen complications. Document everything, keeping copies of all contracts and correspondence. This proactive approach protects you from potential exploitation and ensures a smoother transition into your new home.

Beyond formal programs, networking can prove invaluable. Reach out to friends, family, and community organizations. Many individuals and groups are willing to offer assistance, providing information about available resources or even temporary accommodation. Don't underestimate the power of personal connections. People who have gone through similar situations can offer invaluable support and guidance, fostering a sense of community and shared experience.

Online resources and databases can aid your search. Websites such as Zillow, Trulia, and Apartments.com provide extensive listings of rental properties. Filter your search by price, location, and amenities to find properties that match your needs. However, always verify the legitimacy of any listing before contacting the landlord. Compare different options, and don't rush into a decision. Take your time to assess each option thoroughly before committing to a lease.

Safety is paramount. When viewing properties, bring a trusted friend or family member for support and an extra pair of eyes. Trust your instincts; if a property or landlord feels unsafe or makes you uncomfortable, don't hesitate to walk away. Prioritize locations that feel safe and secure, considering factors such as proximity to public transportation, well-lit streets, and a sense of community.

Remember, finding a safe home is essential for your well- being and recovery.

After securing housing, focus on establishing routines and creating a nurturing environment. Personalize your space to make it feel like home. This contributes significantly to your sense of security and stability. Declutter and organize your belongings to create a sense of calm and order. Incorporate elements that promote relaxation and well-being. Consider adding plants, soft lighting, calming colors, and personal items that bring you comfort and joy. This act of creating a haven for yourself is a powerful step in rebuilding your life.

Remember that this process takes time and patience. There will be challenges along the way, and setbacks are possible. However, focusing on your progress and celebrating small victories is essential. Each step you take toward finding safe and affordable housing is a significant step toward reclaiming your independence and building a life free from abuse. Don't hesitate to seek professional support. Therapists and counselors specializing in trauma can provide emotional support and guidance throughout this challenging process, helping you navigate the emotional complexities of rebuilding your life and creating a safe, stable future. You are not alone; there is support available to help you every step of the way. Believe in your strength and resilience; you deserve a safe and peaceful place to heal and thrive. The journey might be challenging, but the destination – a safe and stable home – is worth the effort. Keep moving forward, one step at a time. Your future is brighter than the shadows of the past.

Relocation Strategies and Safety Considerations

Relocation is often a crucial step in escaping an abusive situation, offering a chance to break free from the abuser's control and establish a safe haven. However, the planning and execution of a move require careful consideration, balancing the urgency of escape with the need for a well- thought-out strategy. The decision of where to relocate should not be taken lightly; it's a pivotal choice impacting your safety, well-being, and future. Several factors must be carefully weighed to ensure the relocation effectively protects you from further harm and provides a foundation for recovery.

First and foremost, the distance from your abuser is paramount. Consider the feasibility and necessity of moving far away. While escaping to a completely new state or even country may seem ideal, it also presents logistical challenges and may be financially impractical. The goal is to establish enough physical distance to deter the abuser while remaining within a manageable relocation budget and support network. Consider using online mapping tools to visualize the distance between your current location and potential new residences. Consult with law enforcement or victim advocacy groups to assess your risk level and determine the optimal distance to ensure your safety. They can offer valuable insights based on your specific circumstances and the abuser's behavior patterns. In some cases, even a move across town or to a different county might be sufficient to create the necessary buffer, especially if your abuser has limited resources or mobility.

Community safety is another critical factor. Research potential neighborhoods thoroughly before making a

decision. Look for areas with low crime rates, well-lit streets, and a strong sense of community. Online resources, local police departments, and neighborhood watch programs can provide valuable information about the safety of different areas. Consider factors such as the proximity of police stations, hospitals, and 24-hour businesses – all of which can offer added safety and peace of mind. If you have children, research school districts and the overall family- friendliness of the community. Remember, selecting a safe and secure environment is paramount for your healing and recovery.

Access to support services is crucial during and after a relocation. Identify the availability of resources such as domestic violence shelters, therapists, support groups, and legal aid services in potential relocation areas. These services offer crucial assistance during the transition and help you navigate the emotional and practical challenges of escaping an abusive relationship. Online directories, local social service agencies, and victim advocacy organizations can provide information on the availability of these vital resources. The proximity to these services directly influences your ability to rebuild your life and manage the aftermath of abuse. Don't underestimate the value of a strong support network; having access to help nearby is essential during times of stress or crisis.

Financial resources significantly impact relocation planning. Create a realistic budget that considers moving costs, security deposits, first month's rent, and ongoing living expenses. Explore available financial assistance programs, such as government subsidies, rental assistance, and charitable organizations that aid victims of domestic violence. These programs can significantly reduce the financial burden and make relocation more feasible. Develop a detailed financial plan, tracking your income and expenses

to ensure you can maintain stability. Don't be afraid to ask for financial assistance from friends, family, or community support networks. Many organizations specialize in helping victims of abuse secure safe housing and financial stability.

Legal considerations are essential for your long-term safety and well-being. If you have a restraining order or other legal protection in place, ensure your new address is compliant with these legal requirements. Consult with an attorney specializing in domestic violence cases to discuss your legal options and ensure your relocation doesn't compromise your safety. They can help you understand your rights and navigate any potential legal issues that might arise. Consider consulting with a lawyer about changing your phone number, email address, and social media accounts to prevent your abuser from contacting you. This is particularly crucial if technology was used for stalking or harassment.

Securing a new place to live involves more than simply finding a house; it's about creating a safe environment. Prioritize features that enhance your security, such as sturdy doors and locks, working smoke detectors and alarms, and a secure neighborhood. Inspect the property thoroughly before signing a lease agreement, ensuring it meets your safety needs. If possible, visit the property at different times of the day to assess the neighborhood's level of activity and safety. Don't hesitate to ask questions about building security, and request information about the management company's procedures for handling safety concerns.

Maintaining confidentiality is vital during and after your relocation. Avoid sharing your new address or contact information with anyone who might inadvertently reveal it to your abuser. Inform only trusted individuals about your new location and take measures to protect your privacy online.

Consider using a PO Box for mail instead of your residential

address. Update your address with essential institutions like your bank and employer only once you're fully settled and confident in your safety. A proactive approach to maintaining confidentiality safeguards your privacy and reduces the risk of being discovered by your abuser.

The process of relocation, while essential, can be emotionally challenging. Consider the emotional toll it takes on yourself and any children or dependents. Seek professional support from a therapist or counselor specializing in trauma and abuse recovery. They can help you navigate the emotional complexities of leaving an abusive situation and provide coping mechanisms to deal with the stress and anxiety involved in relocation. Support groups for survivors of domestic violence can offer a sense of community and shared experience, helping you feel less isolated during this challenging transition. Remember, this is a journey, and it's okay to seek help along the way.

Remember that rebuilding your life after escaping an abusive situation is a marathon, not a sprint. There will be setbacks and challenges. Be patient with yourself, celebrate small victories, and never hesitate to ask for help. Finding safe and affordable housing is a significant step towards reclaiming your independence and building a future free from fear. Your safety and well-being are the top priorities; prioritize them throughout this process, and trust your instincts. You are stronger than you think, and you deserve a safe and peaceful life. The path ahead may seem daunting, but with careful planning, support, and self-belief, you can create a future free from the shadows of the past. Your journey to safety and healing begins with the brave step you've already taken; continue moving forward, knowing that a brighter future awaits.

Navigating Housing Applications and Rental Processes

Navigating the housing application process after escaping an abusive situation can feel overwhelming. The emotional toll of leaving behind a controlling environment often adds layers of complexity to what would already be a stressful task. However, understanding the process and preparing thoroughly can significantly alleviate some of the pressure and increase your chances of securing safe and stable housing.

First, familiarize yourself with the various housing options available to you. These might include subsidized housing programs, domestic violence shelters, transitional housing, affordable apartments, or renting a room in a shared house. Each option comes with its own set of requirements and procedures. Researching your local resources and understanding your eligibility for specific programs is crucial. Online searches, local government websites, and social service agencies are invaluable sources of information. Don't hesitate to contact several organizations to inquire about available assistance and eligibility criteria. Some agencies may even offer support throughout the application process, guiding you through the paperwork and providing additional resources.

Begin by gathering all the necessary documents well in advance of starting your applications. This usually includes a valid photo ID, proof of income (pay stubs, bank statements, social security benefits), references (previous landlords or employers), and possibly a background check. If you're applying for subsidized housing or assistance programs, you'll likely need additional documentation proving your income, family size, and need for housing assistance. Keep all your documents organized in a secure place; consider creating a digital copy as a backup. This will streamline the application process and make it easier to respond to requests quickly. Missing even one document can delay the process significantly.

When completing applications, read each section carefully and provide accurate information. Any inaccuracies or omissions can lead to rejection, so take your time and double-check everything before submission. If you encounter any questions or sections you don't understand, don't hesitate to contact the housing provider or agency for clarification. They're often willing to assist in clarifying the application process and ensuring your application is complete and accurate. Remember, honesty is essential, and seeking clarification is perfectly acceptable.

Understanding rental agreements is critical to securing safe and stable housing. Before signing any lease, meticulously read every clause. Pay close attention to the terms regarding rent, security deposits, lease duration, responsibilities for repairs and maintenance, and eviction procedures. If anything is unclear or seems unfavorable, don't hesitate to negotiate or seek legal advice. Many tenant rights organizations can provide guidance and assistance in interpreting rental agreements and ensuring fair treatment.

You have the right to understand your lease fully before committing to it. Take your time, and don't feel pressured to sign anything before you're entirely comfortable.

When inspecting potential housing, safety should be your top priority. Assess the security features, such as door locks, window locks, security systems, and neighborhood lighting. Note the overall condition of the property – look for signs of disrepair that could pose safety risks. Is the property well-

maintained? Are there adequate smoke detectors and carbon monoxide detectors? If you have children, prioritize properties that offer a safe and child-friendly environment. Don't hesitate to ask questions about the building's safety record, security measures, and the management company's procedures for addressing safety concerns. A thorough inspection can help you avoid potential problems and enhance your safety and peace of mind.

Beyond the physical safety aspects, consider the neighborhood's overall safety and security. Research the crime rates, proximity to police stations and hospitals, and the general atmosphere of the area. This can influence your sense of security and safety. Online resources, local police departments, and neighborhood watch programs can be invaluable sources of information. Visiting the neighborhood at different times of day can give you a better sense of its activity and safety levels. If possible, talk to neighbors to gauge their experience living in the area. Trust your instincts; if a property or neighborhood doesn't feel safe, don't hesitate to look elsewhere.

Finding affordable housing can be a significant challenge. Explore various resources and financial assistance programs available to assist victims of domestic violence.

Government-subsidized housing, rental assistance programs, and charitable organizations dedicated to helping victims of abuse can offer invaluable support. Research local and national programs to find options that align with your situation and needs. Many organizations offer guidance and assistance in navigating the application process for these programs. Don't be afraid to ask for help. Many individuals and organizations are committed to providing assistance to those escaping abusive situations.

Throughout the process, prioritize maintaining your confidentiality. Avoid disclosing your new address or contact information to anyone who could unintentionally reveal it to your abuser. Consider using a PO Box for mail instead of your residential address, particularly in the initial stages of relocation. Update your address with essential institutions such as your bank and employer only after you're settled and feel secure in your new environment. Remember, safeguarding your privacy is critical to your safety and well- being.

The emotional toll of finding new housing after escaping abuse should not be underestimated. The process can be extremely stressful and triggering. Seek support from a therapist or counselor specializing in trauma and abuse recovery. They can help you process your emotions, develop coping mechanisms, and navigate the practical challenges involved in securing safe and stable housing. Joining a support group for survivors of domestic violence can offer a sense of community and shared experience, reminding you that you are not alone in your journey. Don't hesitate to seek professional support and lean on your support network throughout this challenging process. Remember, you deserve a safe and peaceful place to heal and rebuild your life.

Finally, remember that securing safe and affordable housing is a significant step towards reclaiming your independence and building a future free from fear. Celebrate the progress you've made, no matter how small. Each step you take towards safety and independence is a victory. Be patient with yourself and trust in your ability to create a better life for yourself and your loved ones. The journey to recovery is not easy, but with perseverance, support, and self-compassion, you can build a life free from the shadows of the past. Your strength and resilience are commendable; believe in your capacity to create the future you deserve. Remember, you are deserving of peace, safety, and a life free from abuse.

The complexities of navigating the housing application process can be daunting, even without the added burden of escaping an abusive situation. However, by taking a proactive, well-informed approach, and by accessing the abundant resources available to survivors, you can significantly increase your chances of securing a safe and stable living environment. Remember, your well-being is paramount, and seeking assistance is a sign of strength, not weakness. This is a journey, not a race, and taking each step with care and consideration is crucial to achieving long-term safety and stability. Your efforts and your bravery deserve to be celebrated; embrace your journey toward a brighter future. You are resilient, you are strong, and you deserve a safe haven.

Securing Housing Assistance Programs

Securing safe and stable housing is a fundamental step in escaping an abusive relationship, and thankfully, numerous resources exist to help survivors navigate this crucial process. This section will explore various government and community-based programs designed to provide housing assistance to those fleeing abusive situations. It's important to understand that eligibility criteria vary depending on your location and specific circumstances, so thorough research and direct contact with relevant agencies are essential.

One of the most commonly utilized programs is the **Housing Choice Voucher Program (Section 8)** , administered by the

U.S. Department of Housing and Urban Development (HUD). This program provides rental subsidies to low- income families, the elderly, and people with disabilities. While not exclusively for victims of domestic violence, it's a valuable resource for those who meet the income requirements and need financial assistance to secure affordable housing. The application process can be lengthy, often involving a waiting list. However, by submitting a complete and accurate application and maintaining regular contact with the housing authority, you can increase your chances of securing a voucher. Remember to clearly indicate your status as a survivor of domestic violence in your application, as this may expedite the process in some areas. Each local housing authority has its own specific procedures, so it's critical to contact your local office directly for detailed information.

Beyond Section 8, many communities offer **public housing** , which are government-owned and operated housing units for low-income individuals and families. These apartments often

have waiting lists, and eligibility is based on income and family size. Similar to Section 8, clearly indicating your status as a survivor of abuse can be beneficial in some locations. The application process will typically involve income verification, background checks, and an assessment of your housing needs. Contact your local public housing authority for specific information on eligibility and application procedures within your area.

Many states and municipalities also operate **state and local housing assistance programs** , which can offer various forms of support, including rental subsidies, down payment assistance, and mortgage assistance. These programs often target specific populations, such as families with children, seniors, or individuals with disabilities. However, many of these programs also consider victims of domestic violence for priority placement or expedited processing due to the urgent need for safe housing. To find these programs, search online using keywords like "[Your State/City] housing assistance," "[Your State/City] rental assistance," or "[Your State/City] domestic violence housing." The websites of your state's housing agency and your local government will be invaluable resources.

In addition to government-funded programs, several **non- profit organizations and charities** dedicate their resources to assisting survivors of domestic violence with housing.

These organizations often provide a range of services, including emergency shelter, transitional housing, and long- term housing support. They may offer assistance with finding affordable housing options, navigating the application process, and providing financial assistance with rent or security deposits. These organizations frequently work in collaboration with government agencies, offering a more comprehensive support system. Searching online for "domestic violence shelters [your city/state]" or "housing

assistance for domestic violence survivors [your city/state]" will help you locate these vital resources in your community.

Domestic violence shelters offer immediate refuge and support for survivors. They provide a safe, temporary place to stay while you develop a longer-term housing plan.

Shelters often provide a range of services beyond safe housing, including counseling, legal assistance, and help with securing employment. Finding a local shelter is often best done through a national domestic violence hotline or through local social services.

Transitional housing programs provide temporary housing for a specified period, usually six months to two years, helping survivors rebuild their lives and gain financial stability before transitioning to permanent housing. These programs often offer support services such as job training, life skills workshops, and counseling, aiding in long-term stability. Transitional housing programs are frequently connected with local non-profits or government agencies that work with victims of domestic violence.

For those who qualify, the **Veterans Affairs Supportive Housing (VASH) program** offers rental assistance and case management services to homeless veterans and their families. If you are a veteran, this program offers priority and may greatly reduce the housing-related stress associated with escaping abuse. Contact your local VA office to explore eligibility criteria.

It's crucial to be aware of potential **scams** related to housing assistance. Be cautious of any organization that requests payment upfront for housing assistance or asks for sensitive personal information before you have thoroughly vetted them. Always verify the legitimacy of any organization with

your local government agencies or trusted non-profit organizations.

Remember that the process of securing housing assistance can be complex and time-consuming. Be persistent, and don't hesitate to seek help from advocates and professionals specializing in domestic violence. These professionals can provide guidance, support, and assistance in navigating the bureaucratic processes and securing the resources you need to create a safe and stable future.

Furthermore, consider the emotional impact of this process. The stress of finding housing, dealing with applications, and managing the aftermath of an abusive relationship can be emotionally draining. It's essential to prioritize your emotional well-being throughout this time. Lean on your support system, seek professional counseling, and remember to practice self-care. Take breaks when needed, celebrate your small victories, and be patient with yourself.

Finally, remember that you are not alone. Many resources are available to help you navigate the complexities of securing housing and rebuilding your life after abuse. Reach out for help, and know that your strength and resilience will guide you toward a brighter future. Your safety and well- being are paramount, and seeking assistance is a sign of strength, not weakness. You deserve a safe and stable home, and with perseverance and the support available to you, you will find it.

Creating a Safe and Comfortable Home Environment

Creating a safe and comfortable home environment after escaping an abusive situation is crucial for healing and rebuilding your life. It's more than just finding a roof over your head; it's about establishing a sanctuary where you can feel safe, secure, and empowered. This process requires careful consideration of both physical and emotional aspects, creating a space that fosters self-care and promotes a sense of belonging.

One of the first steps is to declutter and purify your new space. The physical act of cleaning and organizing can be incredibly therapeutic. It allows you to remove any remnants of the past, symbolically and literally clearing away the negativity and manipulation you may have endured. Discard items that hold painful memories or represent the abuser's influence. Don't feel pressured to do this all at once; take it one step at a time, focusing on small, manageable tasks. The act of decluttering can itself be a powerful form of self-care, offering a sense of control and agency that may have been lacking during the abusive relationship. Consider inviting a trusted friend or family member to help; the support and shared experience can be profoundly beneficial.

Consider the scents in your environment. Strong, artificial air fresheners might mask unwanted smells but can also trigger headaches or allergies. Instead, opt for natural, calming scents such as lavender, chamomile, or sandalwood. These scents have been shown to have relaxing and therapeutic properties, creating a more peaceful atmosphere. Essential oil diffusers, candles (used safely), or simply a bowl of potpourri can effectively enhance the sensory

experience of your space. Creating a pleasant aroma can be incredibly soothing after experiencing the often overwhelming stress of escaping an abusive relationship.

Lighting plays a critical role in creating a safe and comfortable atmosphere. Harsh, fluorescent lighting can be jarring and unwelcoming, while soft, warm lighting can be profoundly calming and relaxing. Use a combination of ambient lighting, task lighting, and accent lighting to create a layered effect that suits your needs. Lamps with adjustable brightness settings allow you to customize the lighting to match your mood and activity. Consider investing in dimmer switches to control the intensity of your overhead lights.

Remember that feeling safe and comfortable is paramount; the right lighting can be a significant contributor to this feeling.

Security measures are essential to building a sense of safety. Depending on your situation and resources, this might involve installing a security system, reinforcing doors and windows, or adding extra locks. Even simple measures, such as a sturdy door chain, can offer a sense of increased security. Consider getting to know your neighbors and building a supportive network within your community. If you have concerns about your safety, don't hesitate to contact local law enforcement or a domestic violence shelter for advice and support. Creating a safe physical environment is a foundation for emotional healing.

Beyond the physical aspects, cultivating a sense of emotional safety is paramount. This involves creating a space where you feel comfortable expressing your feelings without fear of judgment or reprisal. This might involve setting boundaries with others, prioritizing self-care activities, and engaging in therapy or support groups. Surrounding yourself with positive affirmations and inspiring quotes can help shift

your mindset from one of fear and self-doubt to one of hope and resilience. Consider creating a vision board that represents your goals and aspirations; a visual reminder of your progress can be incredibly motivating during the healing process.

Self-care is not a luxury; it's a necessity during this period of rebuilding. Prioritize activities that bring you joy and relaxation, whether it's reading, taking a bath, listening to music, spending time in nature, or engaging in creative pursuits. Remember that healing is a journey, not a destination, and self-compassion is crucial throughout this process. Allow yourself time to grieve the loss of the relationship, process your emotions, and adjust to your new reality. Don't be afraid to seek professional help; a therapist specializing in trauma can provide guidance and support as you navigate this challenging transition.

Creating a comfortable and supportive social network is equally important. Spend time with loved ones who offer unconditional support and understanding. Join support groups for survivors of domestic abuse, where you can connect with others who have shared similar experiences. Remember that you are not alone in this journey; connecting with others who understand can provide validation, hope, and a sense of community. Sharing your experiences and hearing others' stories can be incredibly validating and empowering.

Personalize your space to reflect your personality and interests. Hang artwork that inspires you, display family photos, and surround yourself with objects that bring you joy and comfort. Creating a visually appealing and aesthetically pleasing environment can significantly impact your mood and sense of well-being. Don't be afraid to express your creativity and individuality; this is an opportunity to reclaim

your identity and create a space that truly reflects who you are.

Consider incorporating elements of nature into your home. Plants have been shown to reduce stress and improve air quality. Choose plants that are easy to care for and that complement your decor. If you have a balcony or patio, consider creating a small outdoor garden. The act of nurturing plants can be incredibly therapeutic and a wonderful form of self-care. The presence of nature in your home can provide a sense of calm and connection to something larger than yourself.

As you create your new home, remember that this is a process of rebuilding, both physically and emotionally. There will be setbacks and challenges, but with perseverance and self-compassion, you can create a safe, comfortable, and nurturing environment where you can heal, grow, and thrive. Celebrate your progress, and remember that you deserve a space that reflects your strength, resilience, and potential.

Your home should be a haven, a place where you can feel secure, empowered, and free to live the life you deserve. This is your sanctuary, a testament to your journey of healing and your commitment to a brighter future. Never underestimate the power of creating a space that nourishes your mind, body, and soul. This space is your foundation for the next chapter of your life.

Identifying Career Goals and Skills

Rebuilding your life after escaping an abusive relationship involves many facets, and securing financial independence through meaningful employment is a crucial step. This process isn't merely about finding a job; it's about reclaiming your agency and building a future free from the control and manipulation you've endured. The journey starts with self- assessment – understanding your skills, interests, and aspirations. This self-discovery is empowering, as it allows you to define your future on your own terms, rather than based on the expectations or limitations imposed upon you by the abuser.

Begin by reflecting on your past experiences, not just the negative aspects, but also the positive contributions you've made. What were you good at in previous roles? What aspects did you enjoy? What tasks or responsibilities brought you a sense of accomplishment? Consider keeping a journal to help you track your thoughts and feelings. Write down specific instances where you excelled or felt fulfilled. This isn't about glorifying the past but about identifying your strengths and talents that can be leveraged in your future career. For instance, if you managed household finances effectively even amidst the chaos of an abusive relationship, that demonstrates strong organizational and budgeting skills – highly valuable assets in many job roles. Perhaps you excelled at multitasking, juggling household responsibilities with concealed attempts to plan your escape. These skills, honed under duress, are transferable and significant.

Don't underestimate the value of seemingly minor skills. Proficiency in specific software, strong communication abilities, or even meticulous attention to detail – all these attributes can make you a strong candidate for various jobs. Remember, your abuser likely tried to diminish your abilities and self-worth. Now is the time to actively counter that narrative and recognize your capabilities. Create a comprehensive list of your skills, both hard skills (technical or quantifiable abilities) and soft skills (interpersonal or character-related traits). Be specific. Instead of writing "good communication skills," note "effectively communicated complex information to diverse audiences, both verbally and in writing." This level of detail makes your skills more impactful when presenting them to potential employers.

Next, consider your interests. What genuinely excites you? What activities make you feel engaged and motivated? Don't limit yourself to what you've done before; explore new avenues. The abusive relationship may have stifled your passions and personal growth; this is your chance to rediscover them. If you've always dreamed of pursuing creative writing, now is the time to explore that potential. If you find peace in helping others, consider roles in social work or community services. If you're fascinated by technology, research career paths in software development or data analysis. Exploring online resources like career aptitude tests can offer additional insight and direction. These tests aren't definitive, but they can help you identify career areas that align with your interests and abilities.

Once you have a clear understanding of your skills and interests, begin brainstorming potential career paths.

Research different occupations that utilize your strengths and align with your passions. Explore job descriptions and requirements to understand the specific skills and qualifications needed for each role. Consider using online job search engines to browse available positions and gain further insight into the job market. Don't be afraid to explore fields that seem outside your comfort zone. The process of

rebuilding empowers you to take calculated risks and explore paths you may have previously deemed unattainable.

Setting realistic employment goals is crucial for success. Avoid setting overly ambitious targets that can lead to disappointment. Instead, focus on smaller, achievable milestones. For example, your initial goal might be to secure part-time employment to gain experience and build confidence. This can then transition to a full-time position or a career advancement once you feel more established. Your goals should be specific, measurable, achievable, relevant, and time-bound (SMART goals). For instance, instead of saying "get a better job," set a goal like, "Secure a full-time position as a marketing assistant within the next six months, earning at least $X per year."

Consider your financial needs and circumstances when setting your employment goals. Will you need to secure immediate income to cover basic expenses, or do you have a safety net that provides some financial flexibility? This will influence the urgency and type of work you seek. Remember that starting small is perfectly acceptable. Many survivors find part-time or freelance work helpful in regaining a sense of independence and financial security before transitioning to full-time employment.

Networking is incredibly valuable during this process. Reach out to friends, family members, former colleagues, and mentors for support and guidance. Let your network know about your job search and the types of roles you're targeting. They may be able to offer leads or provide valuable insights into various industries. Attend industry events, workshops, or conferences to connect with potential employers and learn more about available opportunities. Remember, building connections is about fostering mutual support and collaboration.

Don't hesitate to seek professional guidance from career counselors or employment agencies. These services can provide personalized support and assistance throughout your job search. They can help you refine your resume and cover letter, practice interview techniques, and navigate the complexities of the job market. Many organizations offer free or low-cost career services specifically designed to support survivors of domestic abuse. Research your local resources and take advantage of these invaluable supports.

As you navigate your job search, remember that setbacks are inevitable. There will be days when you feel discouraged or overwhelmed. Don't let these moments define your journey. Focus on your strengths, celebrate your successes, and learn from any challenges you face. Maintaining self-compassion and believing in your ability to overcome obstacles is crucial during this transition. Remember that you are resilient, capable, and worthy of a fulfilling career. This is not just about finding a job; it's about reclaiming your life and building a future where you are in control, financially independent, and thriving. Your past experiences have shaped you, but they do not define your future. You have the power to create a new narrative, a future filled with purpose, accomplishment, and lasting happiness. Believe in yourself, and embrace this opportunity to build a career that reflects your strengths, passions, and unwavering spirit. This is your chance to rewrite your story and build a future free from the shadows of the past.

Job Searching Strategies and Techniques

Now that we've explored self-assessment and goal setting, let's delve into the practical strategies for your job search. Finding employment after escaping abuse is a significant undertaking, but with a structured approach, you can significantly increase your chances of success. This isn't just about securing a paycheck; it's about regaining your autonomy and building a foundation for a secure and fulfilling future.

First, let's focus on your resume and cover letter. These are your first impressions on potential employers, so crafting them effectively is crucial. Your resume should be concise, highlighting your most relevant skills and experiences.

Avoid lengthy paragraphs; use bullet points to showcase your achievements in a clear and impactful manner. Quantify your accomplishments whenever possible. Instead of saying "Improved customer service," say "Increased customer satisfaction ratings by 15% through implementation of a new training program." Such quantifiable results demonstrate your abilities more effectively.

Tailor your resume to each job application. Don't send a generic resume; adapt it to match the specific requirements and keywords mentioned in the job description. Use Applicant Tracking Systems (ATS) keywords strategically – these systems scan resumes for specific words and phrases, so including them increases your chances of getting past the initial screening. Spend time researching the company and the role to understand their values and priorities, and reflect this understanding in your resume and cover letter.

Your cover letter is your opportunity to tell your story. It shouldn't simply reiterate your resume; rather, it should provide context and demonstrate your enthusiasm for the specific position and company. Explain how your skills and experience align with their needs, and showcase your personality and passion. However, remember to keep it professional and concise, focusing on the most relevant aspects of your background. Avoid dwelling on the negative aspects of your past; instead, highlight your resilience and adaptability in overcoming challenges. Think of your cover letter as a narrative demonstrating how your past experiences have prepared you for this opportunity.

Next, let's address interview skills. The interview is a crucial stage, where you can showcase your personality and demonstrate your capabilities. Prepare thoroughly by researching the company and the interviewers. Practice answering common interview questions, focusing on your strengths and accomplishments. Prepare examples from your past work experience or volunteer activities to illustrate your skills and problem-solving abilities. Remember to frame your answers positively, highlighting your resilience and resourcefulness even when discussing challenging experiences. Never disclose details of your abuse unless you feel safe and comfortable doing so and it is directly relevant to the role.

Practice your responses out loud. This helps build confidence and fluency. Consider practicing with a friend or family member to get feedback. During the interview, maintain eye contact, speak clearly and concisely, and listen attentively to the interviewer's questions. Don't be afraid to ask clarifying questions if you're unsure about something. It demonstrates your engagement and interest. Remember to dress professionally and arrive on time, or even slightly early. Punctuality demonstrates respect for the interviewer's

time and professionalism. After the interview, send a thank- you note reiterating your interest and highlighting your key qualifications.

Networking is often overlooked, but it's a powerful tool. Leverage your existing network – friends, family, former colleagues, mentors – and inform them of your job search. They might have valuable contacts or insights into different industries. Attend industry events, workshops, or conferences to connect with professionals. Online platforms like LinkedIn offer excellent networking opportunities.

Remember, building connections is about fostering mutual support and collaboration. Be genuine and authentic in your interactions; don't be afraid to share your story if you feel comfortable, but always prioritize your safety and well- being.

Consider utilizing professional career services. Many organizations offer free or low-cost career counseling and job placement assistance, particularly for survivors of abuse. These services can provide personalized support, resume and cover letter review, interview preparation, and guidance on navigating the job market. Don't hesitate to seek this assistance; it's a valuable resource that can significantly enhance your job search efforts.

Remember to celebrate your successes along the way. Acknowledge every milestone, no matter how small. Finding a job after experiencing abuse is a significant achievement.

Be kind to yourself; the process takes time and effort. If you face setbacks, don't be discouraged. Learn from the experience, adapt your strategy, and keep moving forward. Maintaining a positive mindset and self-compassion is crucial for overcoming challenges. Remember your strength and resilience; you've already overcome immense obstacles.

Throughout your job search, prioritize your safety and well- being. If you feel uncomfortable or unsafe during an interview or networking event, remove yourself from the situation. Trust your intuition; your safety is paramount.

Remember, you deserve a job that values and respects you.

Beyond traditional job searches, consider alternative avenues. Freelancing or contract work might be excellent starting points, providing flexibility and allowing you to build your portfolio and gain experience. Volunteer work can also be beneficial, providing valuable skills and networking opportunities while contributing to your community. Starting your own small business, if feasible, allows you to be your own boss and build something according to your own terms and timelines. Explore all available options that suit your skills, interests, and overall well-being.

Remember, your journey toward financial independence and career success is a marathon, not a sprint. Be patient with yourself, and celebrate every small victory along the way.

Each step forward is a testament to your strength and resilience. You deserve a fulfilling career, a career that reflects your abilities and aspirations. This is your opportunity to rebuild your life on your terms, to create a future where you are empowered, independent, and thriving. Believe in yourself, your abilities, and your potential. Your future is yours to create, and you have the strength to build it. The shadows of the past may linger, but they do not define your future. You are capable, resilient, and deserving of a life filled with purpose and joy. This is your new beginning.

Embrace it with courage and confidence.

Accessing Job Training and Education Programs

Building a new career often requires acquiring new skills or enhancing existing ones. The trauma of abuse can leave individuals feeling depleted and unsure of their capabilities, making the prospect of returning to education or training seem daunting. However, many resources exist specifically designed to support survivors in acquiring the skills and qualifications they need for fulfilling employment. These programs understand the unique challenges faced by individuals escaping abusive situations and offer tailored support to help them navigate the process.

One vital resource is vocational training programs. These programs offer practical, hands-on training in a variety of skilled trades, from carpentry and plumbing to healthcare and technology. Many vocational schools offer flexible scheduling options, recognizing that survivors may have other commitments or need to adapt their learning around therapy appointments or other support services. Furthermore, these programs often provide supportive learning environments, fostering a sense of community and encouraging peer support among students. The focus on practical skills and immediate applicability makes vocational training an especially effective route for those seeking quick entry into the job market, offering a sense of accomplishment and tangible progress that can be incredibly empowering after experiencing the disempowerment of abuse.

Consider researching local community colleges and vocational schools. They often have dedicated counselors or advisors who can help assess your skills and interests and guide you toward suitable programs. Many offer financial

aid and scholarships, recognizing that financial constraints can be a major barrier for survivors. Don't hesitate to inquire about these options; they can make the difference between achieving your career goals and falling short. Don't be afraid to express your concerns about adjusting to a learning environment; many vocational schools are experienced in supporting learners with various backgrounds and challenges.

Adult education courses offer another avenue for skill development and career advancement. These courses cover a wide range of subjects, from basic literacy and numeracy to advanced computer skills and professional development training. The flexibility of many adult education programs allows for personalized learning plans, accommodating the varying schedules and learning styles of students. This flexibility is crucial for survivors who may be juggling multiple responsibilities or dealing with the lingering effects of trauma. Some programs specifically cater to adult learners, creating a supportive and understanding environment that encourages participation and success.

Many adult education programs offer free or low-cost courses, making them accessible to individuals with limited financial resources. These programs often partner with local organizations and businesses to provide job placement assistance and networking opportunities. Exploring your local community center or library is an excellent starting point for identifying available courses. Online learning platforms offer additional options, providing flexibility and accessibility for those who may not have access to in-person classes. Remember that many online courses provide certificates of completion, which can be valuable additions to your resume and demonstrate your commitment to professional development.

Beyond formal educational programs, consider the value of informal learning opportunities. Workshops, seminars, and online tutorials can provide valuable skills training in specific areas. These often focus on practical skills needed in today's job market, such as digital marketing, social media management, or graphic design. Many such workshops are offered at low cost or even for free, and they can provide a less intimidating entry point into learning new skills.

Government agencies often play a significant role in supporting job training and education for survivors of abuse. Agencies like your state's department of labor or workforce development often offer job training programs, financial assistance, and job placement services. These resources are specifically designed to help individuals re-enter the workforce after experiencing challenging life circumstances. Contacting these agencies can help you understand the specific benefits and services available in your area. They may offer financial assistance for tuition, childcare, transportation, or other expenses that could otherwise prevent you from accessing training or education opportunities.

Non-profit organizations dedicated to supporting survivors of abuse often offer job training and education programs tailored to their specific needs. These organizations frequently provide a holistic approach, addressing not only the skill development but also the emotional and psychological support necessary for successful reintegration into the workforce. They often offer individualized career counseling, resume building workshops, and interview preparation sessions. The supportive environment these organizations provide can be invaluable in building confidence and self-esteem, which are crucial for success in the job market after experiencing trauma.

When searching for appropriate programs, it's essential to consider your own individual needs and circumstances.

Assess your strengths, interests, and career goals. Identify the skills you already possess and the areas where you need additional training. The right program will align with your unique aspirations and provide the support you need to succeed.

Networking with other survivors can also be invaluable. Support groups and online communities provide platforms to share experiences and learn from others who have successfully navigated the process of job training and career development. Hearing success stories and receiving advice from those who understand your unique challenges can be incredibly motivating and empowering.

Remember, seeking help is a sign of strength, not weakness. Don't hesitate to reach out to the many resources available. Your journey toward career success is a testament to your resilience and determination. Believe in your capabilities, and know that with support and perseverance, you can achieve your goals. The path may be challenging at times, but the rewards of building a fulfilling and independent future are well worth the effort. Every step you take is a step toward reclaiming your life and building a future free from the shadows of the past. Your strength, resilience, and courage are undeniable; embrace them, and build the future you deserve. You are capable, you are resilient, and you deserve a life filled with purpose, joy, and professional fulfillment. This is your opportunity to write your own success story – embrace it.

Overcoming Barriers to Employment

Overcoming the barriers to employment after surviving abuse by a sociopath presents unique challenges. The trauma itself can manifest in various ways that directly impact job seeking and performance. Understanding these barriers is the first step towards overcoming them. Many survivors grapple with debilitating anxiety, panic attacks, and PTSD, making the structured environment of a workplace feel overwhelming and triggering. Simple tasks, such as answering the phone or interacting with colleagues, can become insurmountable obstacles. The constant fear of judgment or re-traumatization adds another layer of complexity. The intense manipulation and control exerted by a sociopath often leaves survivors with deeply ingrained

self-doubt and a diminished sense of self-worth. This can lead to imposter syndrome, where they undervalue their skills and abilities, making it difficult to present themselves confidently during job interviews or in the workplace.

Moreover, the abuse often involves financial control, leaving survivors with limited resources and a lack of professional experience, which makes it incredibly hard to break free and rebuild their lives.

The insidious nature of sociopathic abuse often leaves its victims with a damaged credit history, limiting their access to housing, transportation, and other essential resources necessary for securing employment. The abuser might have intentionally sabotaged the survivor's career, damaging their professional reputation or preventing them from gaining experience. The lack of stable housing can also pose a significant barrier, making it difficult to attend interviews or maintain a regular work schedule. This instability creates a vicious cycle of hardship, hindering the survivor's ability to

find and keep a job. It's vital to remember that these difficulties are not a reflection of personal shortcomings; they are direct consequences of the abuse suffered.

Addressing these multifaceted challenges requires a multi-pronged approach. Therapy plays a crucial role in helping survivors process the trauma, develop coping mechanisms, and regain their self-esteem. Cognitive Behavioral Therapy (CBT) and trauma-focused therapies like Eye Movement Desensitization and Reprocessing (EMDR) have proven particularly effective in addressing the psychological impact of abuse. These therapies can help survivors identify and challenge negative thought patterns, manage anxiety and panic attacks, and develop healthier coping strategies for dealing with stress. A supportive therapist can provide a safe space to unpack the emotions and experiences, fostering healing and strengthening self-belief, paving the way for greater self-confidence in navigating the job market.

Beyond therapy, practical support is essential. Financial assistance programs can help address immediate needs such as housing, transportation, and childcare. Many government agencies and non-profit organizations offer these services specifically tailored to assist survivors of domestic abuse.

These services often include emergency housing, food assistance, and job search support. Survivors should explore local and national resources available within their community, often publicized online or through advocacy groups focusing on victims' rights and support.

Building a strong support network is also critical. Connecting with other survivors, whether through support groups, online communities, or individual mentorships, provides a sense of belonging and validation. Sharing experiences and learning from others who have successfully navigated similar challenges can be incredibly empowering

and reassuring. This network can offer emotional support, practical advice, and encouragement during the job search process. The sense of community fostered in these groups can also help combat the isolation that often accompanies abuse.

Developing effective job search strategies is crucial, and this often begins with honestly assessing one's skills and qualifications. It's essential to focus on accomplishments and transferable skills gained from previous experiences. Even if those experiences were disrupted by the abuse, focusing on skills like problem-solving, adaptability, and communication can highlight valuable strengths. Resume and cover letter writing workshops offered by community organizations or career services can greatly aid in crafting compelling applications that highlight these transferable skills.

Interview skills are equally crucial. Practicing answering common interview questions with a trusted friend or therapist can help build confidence and prepare for the experience. Focusing on demonstrating resilience and adaptability, qualities often strengthened by overcoming past adversity, can be powerful selling points to potential employers. Many organizations that support survivors offer mock interviews to provide practice and feedback in a safe and supportive environment.

In some cases, survivors may find it beneficial to seek career counseling. A career counselor can help identify suitable career paths aligned with individual skills and interests, considering limitations and potential triggers related to the trauma. They can provide guidance on job searching, resume building, and interview preparation, offering tailored support for specific circumstances. The counselor's unbiased perspective can also help survivors identify and challenge negative self-beliefs hindering their job search.

Creating a safe and supportive work environment is crucial for survivors once they've secured a position. Open communication with employers about any specific needs or accommodations, such as flexible work arrangements or quiet spaces for breaks, can significantly improve the work experience. The Americans with Disabilities Act (ADA) protects employees with disabilities, including those with mental health conditions related to trauma. Under the ADA, employers are often legally obligated to provide reasonable accommodations to enable survivors to perform their jobs effectively. Knowing and understanding these rights is vital in creating a workplace where healing and professional growth can thrive.

Returning to the workforce after escaping a sociopathic relationship represents a significant accomplishment. It signifies the survivor's strength, resilience, and determination to rebuild their lives. Recognizing the profound impact of abuse and implementing the strategies outlined above – therapeutic support, financial assistance, building a support network, developing effective job search skills, and fostering a supportive work environment – empowers survivors to reclaim their lives and achieve professional fulfillment. The path might be challenging, but the ultimate reward – a life of independence and purpose – is well worth the effort. The journey to healing is a testament to personal strength and a vital step towards reclaiming a future free from the shadows of the past. Believe in your ability to succeed; you are stronger than you think.

Building a Successful and Fulfilling Career

Building a successful and fulfilling career after surviving the trauma of a sociopathic relationship requires a shift in perspective.

It's not just about securing a job; it's about aligning your work with your values, passions, and newly discovered sense of self. The process of rebuilding your life after escaping abuse is a testament to your resilience, and your career should reflect this strength and newfound self- awareness.

One of the first steps is to engage in honest self-reflection. The manipulation and control experienced in an abusive relationship can distort your sense of self-worth and your understanding of your capabilities. Take time to rediscover your passions and talents. What did you enjoy doing before the abuse? What skills do you possess that you might not have fully appreciated? Consider creating a list of your strengths, both personal and professional, focusing on accomplishments rather than dwelling on perceived failures. Remember, your abuser likely actively minimized or sabotaged your aspirations, intentionally aiming to undermine your confidence and independence. Overcoming this sabotage is a huge victory.

Explore career paths that align with your values. After surviving such trauma, it's essential to build a career that resonates with your newfound sense of purpose and empowers you. This might mean choosing a career that aligns with your desire for autonomy, creativity, or social impact. Perhaps you've always wanted to work in a helping profession, inspired by your journey through therapy and recovery. Or maybe the experience has ignited a passion for advocating for victims of abuse. The possibilities are vast,

and choosing a path that aligns with your values will contribute to a far more satisfying career journey.

Consider the work environment. The aftermath of abuse often leaves survivors with heightened sensitivity to certain work dynamics. It's crucial to assess your tolerance for different work environments and prioritize your mental and emotional wellbeing. A supportive and understanding workplace culture is paramount. Research potential employers, seeking out organizations that prioritize employee well-being and have policies supporting mental health.

Look for companies with strong anti-harassment policies and a culture of respect. Consider the physical work environment as well; is it calm and organized or chaotic and overwhelming? Will the work involve close contact with others that might make you feel anxious? These are important questions to consider during your job search.

Networking can be a powerful tool in your job search, but it requires a nuanced approach. Don't feel pressured to engage with people who make you uncomfortable. Build your network slowly and strategically, focusing on connections with people who are supportive and understanding. Online networking platforms can provide a safer space to connect with individuals in your field than in-person networking events. Remember, you're not obligated to disclose your past trauma if you're not comfortable, but connecting with others who have faced similar challenges can provide invaluable support and encouragement.

Develop strategies for managing stress and anxiety in the workplace. This might involve setting boundaries, prioritizing self-care, and seeking support from supervisors or colleagues when needed. Be open about your need for accommodations if necessary, but also remember that you are not defined by your trauma. Focusing on your strengths

and your value as an employee is key to building confidence and maintaining a healthy work-life balance.

Continuously develop your skills and knowledge. The workplace is constantly evolving, and it's important to stay current in your field. Consider pursuing further education, attending workshops or conferences, or seeking out mentorship opportunities. This not only enhances your career prospects but also contributes to personal growth and self-esteem. It's a demonstration of your continued investment in yourself and your future, a powerful message of self-respect and resilience.

Celebrate your accomplishments, both big and small. Acknowledge the significant strides you've made in rebuilding your life and career. Every step forward, no matter how small, represents a triumph over adversity. Keep a journal to document your progress and celebrate your achievements. Acknowledge how far you've come, and remember that your strength and resilience are what got you here.

Seek mentorship and support. Connecting with a mentor or career counselor can provide invaluable guidance and support during this transition. They can offer personalized advice and resources to help you navigate the challenges of building a fulfilling career. Their perspective can be incredibly helpful in identifying potential career paths and developing the skills needed for success.

Remember that building a fulfilling career is a journey, not a destination. There will be setbacks and challenges along the way, but the goal is to create a career that is not only financially rewarding but also personally enriching and meaningful. Your resilience and strength will serve as your

guiding principles in creating a path that empowers you and honors your incredible journey of healing and self-discovery.

Don't underestimate the power of self-compassion. The process of rebuilding your life after abuse takes time and effort. Be patient with yourself and celebrate your progress. It's important to acknowledge that you may experience moments of self-doubt or anxiety along the way, and that's perfectly okay. Self-compassion allows you to acknowledge these feelings without judgment, allowing you to move forward with grace and understanding.

Consider volunteering or taking on freelance projects. This can provide valuable experience, build your confidence, and expand your network. Freelance opportunities offer flexibility and control, which can be particularly beneficial for survivors who may need to manage their time and energy levels effectively. Volunteering in a field you're passionate about allows you to make a difference while gaining experience and potentially discovering new career interests. Both avenues are great ways to test the waters and assess your suitability for different work environments.

Remember, your career is a reflection of your journey and a testament to your resilience. Your experiences have shaped you, and your path forward should celebrate your strength and empower you to build a life of purpose and fulfillment. It's a chance to reclaim your narrative, defining your future on your terms. The path may not always be easy, but the destination – a career that brings you both financial security and emotional satisfaction – is worth the journey. The freedom and independence you gain will be a powerful affirmation of your strength and a testament to your incredible journey of healing and recovery. Embrace this new chapter with courage and self-belief, knowing that you possess the inherent strength and resilience to achieve your

goals. The future is yours to shape, and you have the power to create a life that reflects your dreams and values.

Understanding Healthy Relationship Dynamics

Understanding healthy relationship dynamics is crucial for anyone emerging from the manipulative and controlling environment of a sociopathic relationship. The insidious nature of this abuse often distorts one's perception of what constitutes a healthy connection, leaving survivors vulnerable to repeating unhealthy patterns. Rebuilding trust and establishing healthy boundaries requires conscious effort and a deep understanding of what constitutes a truly supportive and equitable partnership.

First and foremost, mutual respect is the bedrock of any healthy relationship. This means valuing each other's opinions, feelings, and needs, even when they differ from your own. In a healthy relationship, partners actively listen to each other, seeking to understand rather than simply to respond. There's an absence of belittling, criticism, or attempts to control the other person's thoughts, actions, or choices. Respect extends to respecting each other's time, space, and personal boundaries. It acknowledges the individual autonomy of each partner and avoids the power imbalances inherent in abusive relationships. This respect manifests in everyday interactions: Considerate behavior, thoughtful gestures, and a willingness to compromise are all signs of a respectful partnership. It's about creating a safe space where both individuals feel valued and heard, free from the fear of judgment or intimidation. The absence of such respect—the consistent undermining of one's self- worth, the constant criticism and control—is a hallmark of the abusive relationship you've left behind. Learning to identify and actively cultivate this aspect is paramount to your healing journey.

Trust is another cornerstone of a healthy relationship. It involves a belief in the other person's integrity, honesty, and reliability. This is built over time through consistent actions that demonstrate dependability and trustworthiness. It's not simply about believing what someone says; it's about observing their behavior and witnessing their actions align with their words. In an abusive relationship, trust is systematically eroded, leading to a deep sense of insecurity and anxiety. Rebuilding trust requires patience and consistent effort. It's about choosing to believe in the potential for genuine connection, while also recognizing the importance of establishing clear boundaries to protect yourself. Start small. Trust can be built gradually, but it requires consistent reinforcement. This involves being truthful and transparent in your own actions, and carefully assessing the behavior of anyone you choose to be close to. If you've been betrayed consistently, building trust can feel nearly impossible, but it's not. Small acts of kindness, consistent reliability, and open communication will gradually rebuild it.

Open and honest communication is paramount in any healthy relationship. This goes far beyond simply talking; it's about actively listening, expressing your feelings honestly and respectfully, and working collaboratively to resolve conflicts. It means being able to share both positive and negative emotions without fear of judgment or retaliation. In abusive relationships, open communication is often stifled.

Manipulative tactics—gaslighting, silent treatment, or deflection—are employed to prevent honest dialogue. In a healthy relationship, you'll find a collaborative approach to resolving conflicts. Disagreements are addressed constructively, focusing on finding solutions rather than assigning blame. This process necessitates active listening, empathy, and a mutual commitment to understanding each other's perspective. It involves respectfully expressing your

own needs and feelings while being receptive to those of your partner. This involves learning to express your emotions clearly, calmly, and directly, while also developing skills in active listening and empathy.

Establishing and maintaining healthy boundaries is essential for protecting your emotional and psychological well-being. This means setting limits on what you are and are not willing to tolerate in a relationship. Boundaries should be clear, consistent, and communicated effectively. This might involve setting limits on time spent together, defining acceptable communication styles, or determining how disagreements will be handled. In abusive relationships, boundaries are frequently violated, leading to a sense of powerlessness and depletion. Rebuilding your capacity to set and maintain boundaries is a vital step in recovering from trauma. Start by identifying your needs and preferences, and then clearly communicate these limits to others. This might feel challenging initially, especially if you have a history of being compliant or people-pleasing. You need to learn to prioritize your well-being and refuse requests or behaviors that undermine your limits. Don't be afraid to say "no" if you feel uncomfortable or pressured. Practice setting smaller boundaries and gradually work your way up to larger ones.

Another crucial element of healthy relationships is emotional intimacy. This involves sharing your thoughts, feelings, and vulnerabilities with your partner in a safe and supportive environment. It's about feeling comfortable being your authentic self, without fear of judgment or rejection. This capacity for emotional intimacy is often damaged in abusive relationships, where emotional vulnerability is exploited and used against the victim. In the recovery process, it's essential to rebuild this capacity. Start by practicing self-compassion and self-acceptance. This foundation allows you to approach intimate connections with greater security. Then, start with

small steps, sharing with a trusted friend or therapist before engaging in emotional intimacy with a romantic partner.

Shared values and goals are also important for a healthy relationship. While differences can add richness to a partnership, having some shared values and aspirations can strengthen the bond. This doesn't mean you need to have identical life goals, but having some common ground creates a stronger foundation. For example, shared values regarding family, career aspirations, or ethical considerations can greatly enhance a relationship's resilience. However, the emphasis here is on *shared* , not forced conformity. You shouldn't feel compelled to compromise your core values to maintain a relationship.

Equitable distribution of power and responsibility is another critical aspect of a healthy relationship. In an abusive relationship, power is heavily skewed towards the abuser. In a healthy partnership, decisions are made collaboratively, with both partners having equal input and influence.

Responsibilities are shared fairly, and neither partner feels burdened disproportionately. This includes not just household chores or financial contributions, but also decision-making regarding important life choices. A fair and equitable distribution of responsibilities helps build a sense of partnership and mutual respect.

Finally, a healthy relationship allows for personal growth and independence. While intimacy and shared experiences are important, a supportive relationship also allows both partners to pursue their individual goals and interests. This means respecting each other's need for personal time, hobbies, and friendships. It allows space for individual self- discovery and growth without pressure to constantly be together or sacrifice personal aspirations. The ability to

maintain a healthy sense of self while nurturing a loving connection is a hallmark of a supportive relationship.

Recognizing these hallmarks of healthy relationships is the first step to creating them for yourself. Understanding the subtle differences between a healthy dynamic and a manipulative one will empower you to make informed choices about your future relationships, avoiding the pitfalls of the past. Remember, building healthy relationships takes time, effort, and self-reflection. Be patient with yourself and celebrate your progress along the way. The journey towards healthy connections is a testament to your resilience and a vital part of your recovery.

Identifying and Avoiding Toxic Relationships

Identifying and avoiding toxic relationships is paramount to your healing journey after escaping the clutches of a sociopathic partner. The insidious nature of abuse often leaves survivors with a distorted sense of normalcy in relationships, making them susceptible to falling into similar patterns. Recognizing the subtle—and not-so-subtle—red flags is a critical skill to develop, one that requires both self-awareness and a willingness to trust your instincts.

One of the earliest warning signs is a relentless pressure to isolate you from your support system. This can manifest in several ways. Your partner might subtly criticize your friends and family, sowing seeds of doubt about their loyalty or intentions. They might actively try to prevent you from spending time with them, creating obstacles or making you feel guilty for prioritizing your relationships. This isolation isn't accidental; it's a deliberate strategy to control you and make you more dependent on them. It's a way to sever your connection to people who might offer a different perspective or provide support if you ever choose to leave. Remember the feeling of being trapped? The sociopath created that by systematically eliminating your support structure. Do not repeat this mistake. If someone actively tries to distance you from your loved ones, take that as a colossal red flag.

Another crucial aspect to observe is the nature of the communication. In healthy relationships, communication is open, honest, and respectful. Disagreements are handled constructively, with both partners striving to understand each other's perspectives. In contrast, toxic relationships are often characterized by manipulative communication tactics.

Gaslighting—making you question your own sanity and

memory—is a classic example. Your partner might deny saying or doing something they clearly did, leaving you feeling confused and doubting yourself. Other manipulative tactics include silent treatment, constant criticism, blame- shifting, and deflection. These are not accidental communication errors; they are intentional tools used to control and undermine you. If you constantly feel like you're walking on eggshells, unsure of how to respond without provoking a negative reaction, that's a clear indication of a toxic dynamic.

Pay close attention to how your partner treats you emotionally. Do you feel consistently undermined, belittled, or criticized? Are your accomplishments dismissed or your feelings invalidated? Do you constantly feel the need to defend yourself or apologize for things that aren't your fault? Do you find yourself shrinking in your interactions with them to not trigger their displeasure? These are all signs of emotional abuse. A healthy relationship is built on mutual respect and support. If you feel consistently devalued and disrespected, it's a critical sign that the relationship is toxic.

The constant erosion of self-worth that you experienced during the abuse can be mimicked in other relationships, so paying attention to your emotional well-being in new contexts is critical.

Financial control is another common tactic in toxic relationships. Your partner might try to control your finances, limiting your access to money or making you feel guilty for spending on yourself. This financial control can take many forms, from preventing you from having a separate bank account to constantly criticizing your spending habits. This is not about shared finances; this is about control. In abusive relationships, this control can also extend to dictating your work choices, schooling, or volunteer work. It's not just about money; it's about the overall control they

exert over your independence and autonomy. This form of control is one of the most damaging aspects of the abuse, because it isolates you and ties your independence to their approval. Learn to be financially independent and safeguard your own financial security.

The ways in which your partner attempts to control your time is another significant indicator. Are you constantly being told what to do, how to spend your free time, or who to socialize with? Does this partner monopolize your free time, leaving you feeling suffocated and with no personal space? This constant intrusion on your time—along with attempts to dictate how you dress, what you eat, where you go—can be seen as control over your very life. This level of control is not about a "caring" relationship; it's about stifling your independence and reinforcing their dominance. This behavior is a stark departure from a healthy relationship where independence and personal space are respected and nurtured.

Consider the level of jealousy and possessiveness your partner displays. In healthy relationships, partners trust and support each other's autonomy. In contrast, toxic relationships are often characterized by excessive jealousy, possessiveness, and controlling behavior. Your partner might constantly check up on you, monitor your whereabouts, or interrogate you about your interactions with other people.

They might become irrationally angry if you spend time with friends or family or express any interest in activities that don't include them. This isn't a reflection of their love; it's a reflection of their desire to control and possess you. A healthy relationship respects personal boundaries and supports personal growth, not control and possessiveness.

Observe the patterns of behavior. Do you notice recurring cycles of abuse and remorse? Does your partner apologize

profusely after abusive incidents only to repeat the same behavior again and again? This pattern of abuse followed by a period of remorse is known as the cycle of violence. The apology is not genuine remorse; it's part of their manipulation tactic to retain control. It's essential to recognize this pattern and understand that it's unlikely to change unless the abuser seeks significant professional help. This is not your fault. Their actions are a reflection of their character, not a sign that you could have somehow avoided the abuse.

Stalking and monitoring are insidious forms of control and abuse that extend beyond the relationship itself. This can involve constantly checking your phone, social media accounts, or tracking your location. It can also involve showing up unexpectedly or contacting you incessantly. This behavior is a clear violation of your privacy and personal space, and it's a crucial red flag. If a partner exhibits any of this kind of intrusive behavior, removing yourself from the situation is crucial to your safety. Remember, even after escaping an abusive relationship, stalking can continue.

Understand and implement the digital safety measures described previously in the book.

Beyond these individual behaviors, pay close attention to the overall dynamic of the relationship. Does it feel balanced and equitable, or is it characterized by an imbalance of power? In a healthy relationship, both partners feel respected, valued, and heard. In a toxic relationship, one partner often holds disproportionate power, leading to a constant feeling of being controlled and manipulated. This power imbalance isn't always overt; it can be subtle and insidious. Recognize the patterns of control—the constant manipulation, the disregard for your feelings, and the pervasive sense of unease. This power imbalance isn't something that you "created"; it's a direct result of their abusive behavior.

Remember, you are not responsible for the abusive behavior of others. It's crucial to understand that you did not cause the abuse, and you cannot cure it. Toxic relationships are not your fault, and leaving them is a sign of strength, not weakness. Taking the time to carefully assess your relationships and learn to identify the red flags, can protect you from future trauma and allow you to build healthier, more fulfilling relationships. If you encounter any of these warning signs, do not hesitate to seek professional help and support from trusted friends and family. Your safety and well-being are paramount. The journey to rebuilding your life after escaping abuse is challenging, but it's a journey worth undertaking. Remember that healing is possible, and a future filled with healthy, respectful relationships is within your reach. Trust your instincts. You deserve safety and happiness.

Building Healthy Communication Skills

Building healthy communication skills is not just about learning new techniques; it's about unlearning the patterns of manipulative communication you likely experienced in your abusive relationship. The sociopath likely distorted communication to control and manipulate you—gaslighting, silent treatment, constant criticism, blame-shifting—were all tools used to undermine your sense of self and maintain their power. Rebuilding your ability to communicate effectively, authentically, and assertively requires conscious effort, patience, and self-compassion. It's a process of reclaiming your voice and learning to express yourself in a way that honors your needs and boundaries.

The first step is to become a more attentive listener. Active listening involves paying attention not only to the words being spoken but also to the nonverbal cues—body language, tone of voice, facial expressions. When you were in the abusive relationship, it's likely your attention was completely focused on attempting to preempt the next attack, rather than listening to what was being said. This often involves anticipating the sociopath's reaction to whatever you said and self-editing to avoid triggering negative responses. Now, you need to learn to receive information without the filter of fear.

In active listening, you reflect back what you hear to ensure you understand correctly. For example, if someone says, "I'm feeling overwhelmed by work," you might respond with, "So, it sounds like you're feeling stressed and burdened by your workload." This shows you are actively listening and validates the other person's feelings. This kind of validation was likely absent in your previous relationship. The

sociopath likely dismissed or invalidated your feelings consistently. Learning to actively listen, to truly hear someone, and to respond with empathy is a fundamental step toward building healthy communication.

Active listening isn't just about repeating words; it's about understanding the underlying emotions and needs.

Sometimes, what someone says is different from what they actually mean. It's crucial to listen for the underlying message. For instance, if someone says, "I'm fine," but their tone is flat and their body language is tense, they might not actually be fine. Paying attention to these incongruencies, which may have been normalized in the past, is crucial to understanding the true message. This requires you to become aware of your own emotional response to the communication as well. If you feel defensive or anxious listening to someone, consider this as a clue about what needs more attention.

Once you become comfortable with active listening, the next step is learning how to express your own needs effectively.

This is particularly important after experiencing abuse, where expressing your needs may have been met with criticism, punishment, or disregard. Assertiveness, the ability to express your needs and opinions respectfully and confidently, is a key communication skill. It's not about being aggressive or passive; it's about finding a healthy balance. Start with small steps. For instance, if you're in a restaurant and you don't like your meal, learn to politely and directly tell the waiter, instead of suffering in silence as you may have done in the past.

When expressing your needs, use "I" statements. Instead of saying, "You always make me feel bad," which is accusatory and likely to provoke a defensive response, try saying, "I feel hurt and misunderstood when..." This focuses on your own feelings and experiences without blaming the other person. This technique helps create a more constructive conversation. Remember that your feelings are valid, and you deserve to have them acknowledged. This concept can be radically different from your experience with a sociopath, where your feelings were consistently invalidated or used against you.

Learning to resolve conflicts constructively is another essential communication skill. Disagreements are inevitable in any relationship, but how you handle them determines the health of the relationship. In your past relationship, conflicts were likely characterized by manipulation, aggression, or avoidance. Now, you must learn to approach disagreements with a focus on understanding, empathy, and collaboration. Avoid personal attacks; instead, focus on the issue at hand.

Negotiation is a crucial element of constructive conflict resolution. It involves finding solutions that meet the needs of both parties. Compromise and collaboration should replace the manipulative power dynamics from your previous relationship. It requires a willingness to listen to the other person's perspective, even if you disagree with it. This can be incredibly difficult after experiencing manipulation and control. You may have learned to anticipate and predict reactions, making open, honest dialogue a frightening prospect. Therapy can provide a safe and supportive environment to explore these anxieties.

Setting and maintaining boundaries is crucial for healthy communication. Boundaries are the limits you set to protect your emotional, physical, and mental well-being. This might involve saying "no" to requests that make you uncomfortable, limiting contact with people who are draining, or setting clear expectations for how you want to be treated. After surviving abuse, it is likely your boundaries

were constantly violated and ignored. Re-establishing healthy boundaries requires courage, self-awareness and consistency. Enforcing your boundaries will feel empowering and validating. It's an important part of self- care and healing.

Learning to communicate your boundaries effectively involves being direct, clear, and firm. Don't apologize for setting boundaries; you have the right to protect yourself. For example, if someone is constantly calling you late at night and you need sleep, tell them, "I appreciate you reaching out, but I need to set a boundary around my sleep schedule. Please call me before 9 p.m. if you need to talk." This is direct, clear, and expresses your needs without being accusatory. Reinforce your boundaries consistently. If someone crosses a boundary, calmly but firmly remind them of your limits.

Nonverbal communication is as important as verbal communication. Your body language, tone of voice, and facial expressions all communicate messages, often more powerfully than words. In your abusive relationship, you may have developed coping mechanisms—becoming withdrawn, subdued, or over-accommodating—that now need to be addressed. Focus on developing a confident and congruent posture, maintain eye contact, and use a calm and steady tone of voice. This will not only assist in communication, but also reflect your inner sense of strength and self-worth.

Another crucial aspect of healthy communication is learning to recognize and manage your emotions. Emotional regulation involves identifying your feelings, understanding their triggers, and responding to them in healthy ways. This may have been intentionally disrupted during your abusive relationship, creating chaos and confusion. Learning to

manage your emotional responses, recognizing the origins of this reactivity, and employing healthy strategies to cope with difficult emotions is essential. This might involve deep breathing exercises, meditation, or journaling. Remember, emotional intelligence is an important element of self-care.

Healthy communication is a skill that takes time and practice to develop. It's a journey of self-discovery and personal growth, and it's crucial for building healthy relationships.

Remember to be patient and compassionate with yourself. There will be setbacks, but each time you practice these skills, you are reinforcing your ability to communicate effectively and build stronger, more fulfilling relationships. The process of rebuilding healthy communication after abuse is vital, not just for future relationships but for your overall well-being. This is an essential step toward reclaiming your life and achieving a sense of peace and security. You deserve healthy relationships and communication—and you are capable of achieving them.

Setting and Maintaining Healthy Boundaries

Setting boundaries is not merely about saying "no"; it's about actively protecting your physical, emotional, and mental well-being. After enduring the insidious manipulation of a sociopath, where your boundaries were consistently violated and disregarded, reclaiming this sense of self-protection is paramount. It's about recognizing your inherent worth and establishing limits to prevent further harm. This process is often challenging, requiring courage, self-awareness, and unwavering consistency. It's a conscious act of self-care, a declaration that you will no longer tolerate mistreatment.

The first step in setting healthy boundaries is self-reflection. Consider your past experiences. Where were your boundaries violated?

What situations, people, or behaviors consistently caused you pain or distress? Identifying these patterns is crucial because they provide valuable insights into your vulnerabilities. You need to recognize the red flags, the subtle manipulations that might have slipped by unnoticed in the past. These aren't isolated incidents; they are symptomatic of a larger pattern of abuse.

Journaling can be an invaluable tool in this process. Write down instances where you felt your boundaries were crossed. Detail the circumstances, your emotional responses, and the consequences. This process of externalizing your experience can illuminate the recurring themes and help you recognize your own vulnerabilities. This is not about dwelling on the past; it's about understanding it to move forward with a clear understanding of your needs.

Once you have identified your vulnerabilities, you need to start setting new boundaries. This doesn't happen overnight;

it requires a gradual process of re-education and reinforcement. Begin with small, manageable steps. For example, if you have a tendency to overcommit yourself, learn to say "no" to extra responsibilities. If someone consistently demands your time and attention, limit your availability. These small acts of self-preservation will reinforce your newfound strength and increase your confidence.

Communicating your boundaries effectively is equally important. This requires clarity, directness, and firmness. Avoid ambiguity or apologies. You are not obligated to justify your decisions. For instance, if someone is constantly texting or calling you late at night and disrupting your sleep, clearly communicate your need for rest. You might say, "I appreciate you reaching out, but I need to establish a boundary around my sleep. Please only contact me before 10

p.m. unless it's an emergency." This approach is assertive, respectful, and unambiguous.

It's crucial to anticipate potential pushback. Sociopaths and manipulative individuals thrive on bending and breaking boundaries. They may test your limits, attempt to guilt-trip you, or downplay the importance of your needs. In these situations, reaffirm your boundaries calmly but firmly.

Repeat your limits as needed. Don't engage in arguments or justifications; simply reiterate your position. Consistency is key. The more consistently you enforce your boundaries, the more likely it is that others will respect them.

Maintaining healthy boundaries is an ongoing process, not a one-time event. It requires vigilance and self-awareness. You might find yourself occasionally wavering or compromising your limits. This is perfectly normal; it's part of the healing journey. When this happens, don't beat yourself up; simply acknowledge the lapse and re-establish your boundaries. The

important thing is to recognize the deviation and recommit to protecting yourself.

Setting boundaries extends beyond interpersonal relationships. It also encompasses your personal time, space, and emotions. Learn to prioritize your own needs and well- being. This might involve saying "no" to activities that drain your energy, creating personal space for reflection and relaxation, or simply taking breaks when you feel overwhelmed. These practices are not selfish; they are essential for your self-care and recovery. They demonstrate self-respect and demonstrate the value you place upon your own well-being.

Protecting your emotional space is crucial after experiencing abuse. This means setting limits on emotional burden. You are not responsible for the feelings or actions of others. If someone tries to offload their negativity onto you, set a boundary. You might say, "I understand you're feeling [emotion], but I can't carry that burden right now. I'm here to listen, but I need to focus on my own well-being." This response is both empathetic and assertive, acknowledging the other person's feelings while safeguarding your own emotional health.

Learning to say "no" can be incredibly liberating, particularly after a period of abuse where your needs were consistently ignored or disregarded. It is a powerful act of self-assertion, a reclaiming of your autonomy. It's also an opportunity to practice self-compassion; remember, saying "no" doesn't make you selfish; it makes you self-aware. You are learning to prioritize your well-being, to respect your limits, and to understand that it's perfectly acceptable to put your own needs first.

It's important to remember that setting boundaries doesn't mean isolating yourself from others. In fact, the opposite is true. Healthy boundaries allow for the development of authentic and supportive relationships. When you set boundaries, you communicate your needs and expectations, creating a space for healthy interaction. This is also a form of self-respect; it creates space for genuine connections based on mutual respect.

Establishing boundaries also extends to digital communication. This could mean limiting your interactions with certain individuals online, avoiding social media platforms that trigger negative emotions, or carefully curating your online presence to protect your privacy and personal information. In the digital age, boundary setting should be a priority, as we're often more vulnerable online than we realize.

Remember that setting boundaries is a journey, not a destination. There will be setbacks and challenges. There may be times when you feel uncomfortable or uncertain about your limits. In these moments, it's important to be patient and compassionate with yourself. Seek support from trusted friends, family members, or a therapist. They can provide encouragement, guidance, and accountability.

The process of rebuilding healthy relationships after abuse is complex and multifaceted. Setting and maintaining boundaries is a cornerstone of this process. It's about reclaiming your power, protecting your well-being, and creating a future free from manipulation and control. It's about valuing yourself, respecting your limits, and creating a life where your needs are honored and respected. This journey takes time and effort, but the rewards—a life lived on your terms—are well worth it. The freedom you will experience by setting and maintaining healthy boundaries is

truly liberating. Embrace this power and begin to build a life free from the shadows of the past.

Fostering Healthy Relationships with Family and Friends

Rebuilding trust and connection after escaping an abusive relationship is a crucial step in your healing journey. The damage inflicted by a sociopath extends far beyond the immediate relationship; it often fractures bonds with family and friends. They may have been alienated, manipulated, or even subtly pressured to doubt your account of the abuse.

Reconnecting with these individuals requires patience, understanding, and a carefully considered approach. It's not about forcing reconciliation; it's about rebuilding bridges based on honesty, transparency, and mutual respect.

The first step is self-assessment. Before reaching out, take time to reflect on your relationships before the abuse. Which connections were truly supportive, and which were more superficial or even subtly enabling of the abusive dynamic? Identifying those who consistently stood by you, offering unwavering support and understanding, is key. These are the relationships worth prioritizing as you begin to rebuild.

It's important to recognize that your friends and family might have been manipulated or misled. The sociopath likely engaged in a campaign of disinformation, portraying you in a negative light to undermine your credibility and sow seeds of doubt. They may have used charm, gaslighting, or even outright lies to influence their perception of you. This is not a reflection on your worth; it's a testament to the manipulative tactics employed by the abuser.

When you reconnect, be prepared for potential misunderstandings. Your loved ones may have questions or concerns that stem from the misinformation they've received.

Approach these conversations with empathy and patience. Explain your experience in a calm, clear, and concise manner, avoiding overly emotional outbursts or accusations. Remember that they may need time to process the information, to reconcile their previous understanding with your current account.

Providing evidence might be helpful, but don't force it. If you have documented instances of abuse, such as emails, texts, or photos, carefully consider whether sharing them would be beneficial. However, remember that your experience is valid even without concrete evidence. The focus should be on your emotional state and the impact of the abuse, rather than solely on proving the abuser's wrongdoing.

Don't expect immediate forgiveness or understanding. Some family members or friends may struggle to accept what you've been through, particularly if they've been close to the abuser. This is a reflection of their own biases and limited understanding, not a judgment on your character. Give them the space and time they need to process their feelings, without pressing them for immediate acceptance.

Consider approaching the reconciliation gradually. A short phone call, a brief email, or even a simple text message can be a good starting point. Gauge their response before committing to a face-to-face meeting. This approach allows you to assess their willingness to listen and understand without overwhelming yourself or them.

If you feel comfortable, consider seeking support from a therapist or counselor during this process. They can provide guidance on navigating these complex interactions, helping you communicate your needs effectively and develop healthy coping mechanisms for potential emotional setbacks.

They can also help you process any residual feelings of guilt, shame, or self-blame that may arise during these interactions.

Rebuilding relationships is not about blame; it's about healing. Forgiving those who didn't fully support you during the abuse may not be possible immediately, or ever.

However, focusing on your own healing and well-being is paramount. Acceptance of their limitations and your own emotional state is a sign of your strength.

The process of repairing family relationships might require a different approach than rebuilding friendships. Family dynamics are often more complex and emotionally charged. You might need to set stricter boundaries with certain family members, especially if they have historically enabled or minimized the abusive behavior. It's okay to distance yourself from individuals who continue to undermine your well-being or refuse to acknowledge the reality of your experiences.

Consider involving a neutral third party, such as a family therapist, to facilitate difficult conversations. This can create a safe space for open communication and help mediate disagreements. A therapist can offer tools for healthy communication and conflict resolution, fostering a more constructive environment for reconciliation.

Remember that rebuilding these relationships is a marathon, not a sprint. There will be setbacks, moments of frustration, and times when you feel like giving up. Be patient with yourself and allow yourself to grieve the loss of what you thought these relationships were. Celebrate small victories and acknowledge your strength in facing these challenges head-on.

It's essential to establish clear boundaries in your rekindled relationships. Communicate your needs clearly and directly, avoiding ambiguity or allowing yourself to be manipulated. This is not about controlling others; it's about protecting your emotional and mental health. It is your right to establish healthy boundaries, and these boundaries should be respected.

Avoid falling back into old patterns of behavior where you put others' needs before your own. The process of recovery requires prioritizing your own well-being. This is not selfishness; it is self-preservation. Healthy relationships are built on mutual respect and understanding, where each individual's needs are valued and honored.

If a relationship proves consistently damaging or unsupportive, despite your best efforts, accept that it may be necessary to sever ties, or at least significantly limit contact. This is not a sign of failure; it's a sign of self-respect and a commitment to your own well-being. You are prioritizing your healing journey, and that is a courageous and necessary step.

Throughout this process, remember that you are not alone. Seek support from a therapist, support groups, or trusted friends who understand the impact of sociopathic abuse.

These individuals can offer invaluable encouragement, validation, and practical strategies for navigating the challenges of rebuilding healthy relationships. Their support can be crucial in helping you maintain perspective and remain focused on your journey towards healing and wholeness.

The goal of rebuilding relationships is not to erase the past but to create a healthier future. By setting boundaries, communicating openly, and prioritizing your well-being, you

can foster supportive and fulfilling connections with those who truly care about you. This process takes time, patience, and courage, but the reward—genuine connection and supportive relationships—is invaluable in your healing journey. Remember your strength, your resilience, and your unwavering determination to build a life free from the manipulation and control that defined your past. This new chapter of your life is a testament to your courage and commitment to a healthier, happier future.

Prioritizing SelfCare Practices

Prioritizing self-care after escaping a relationship with a sociopath is not a luxury; it's a necessity. The insidious nature of this abuse often leaves victims feeling depleted, emotionally exhausted, and struggling with a range of mental health challenges, including anxiety, depression, and PTSD. Rebuilding your life requires prioritizing your well-being, nurturing your physical and mental health, and establishing routines that support your recovery. This isn't about achieving perfection; it's about making small, consistent changes that accumulate over time, leading to significant improvements in your overall health and emotional stability.

One of the most powerful self-care tools is physical activity. Exercise isn't just about burning calories; it's a potent stress reliever, mood booster, and sleep regulator. Even moderate exercise, such as a brisk walk for 30 minutes most days of the week, can make a dramatic difference in your overall well-being. The endorphins released during physical activity have a natural mood-boosting effect, helping combat the feelings of anxiety and depression that often accompany trauma recovery. Finding an activity you enjoy is crucial.

Whether it's yoga, swimming, dancing, hiking, or simply walking in nature, the key is to find something that motivates you to move your body and engage in some form of physical exertion. Joining a fitness class can provide added social support and accountability, counteracting the isolation often imposed by an abusive partner.

Incorporating mindful movement practices, such as yoga or Tai Chi, can be particularly beneficial. These practices combine physical activity with mindfulness, encouraging you to focus on the present moment and release physical

tension. The deep breathing techniques often integrated into these practices can help calm your nervous system and reduce feelings of anxiety. It's not just about the physical postures; it's about the mental and emotional release they offer, helping to ground you in the present moment and interrupt cycles of negative thought patterns. Many free online resources and apps offer guided yoga and mindfulness meditations, making these practices accessible even if you have limited time or financial resources.

Alongside physical activity, nourishing your body with healthy food is crucial for recovery. The stress of escaping an abusive relationship can often lead to unhealthy eating habits. You might find yourself overeating, undereating, or relying on comfort foods high in sugar and processed ingredients. However, nourishing your body with nutrient- rich foods is essential for providing your body and mind with the energy and resources they need to heal. This doesn't mean strict dieting or deprivation; it's about making conscious choices to include more fruits, vegetables, whole grains, and lean protein in your diet. Prepare meals at home more often, reducing reliance on processed foods and takeout, which are often high in unhealthy fats, sugar, and sodium. Focus on whole, unprocessed foods and make gradual shifts towards a healthier eating pattern.

Consider keeping a food diary to track your eating habits and identify any patterns that might be contributing to emotional distress. This self-awareness can be a powerful tool for making healthier choices. If you struggle with disordered eating or have difficulty making healthy food choices, seek professional support from a registered dietitian or therapist specializing in eating disorders. They can provide guidance and support in developing healthy eating patterns tailored to your individual needs and circumstances. Remember that

nutritional support is a vital part of your overall healing process.

Sleep is often disrupted after experiencing trauma. The constant state of hypervigilance and anxiety associated with abuse can make it challenging to fall asleep and stay asleep. Prioritizing good sleep hygiene is essential for promoting physical and mental recovery. This involves creating a relaxing bedtime routine, avoiding screen time before bed, ensuring your bedroom is dark, quiet, and cool, and maintaining a consistent sleep schedule, even on weekends. If you continue to struggle with sleep difficulties, consider consulting a healthcare professional to rule out any underlying medical conditions and explore potential treatments such as cognitive behavioral therapy for insomnia (CBT-I).

Mindfulness and meditation practices are powerful tools for managing stress, anxiety, and trauma. These techniques involve focusing on the present moment without judgment, allowing you to observe your thoughts and feelings without getting carried away by them. Regular meditation practice can help reduce rumination, improve emotional regulation, and increase self-awareness. There are many guided meditation apps and online resources available, catering to different experience levels and preferences. Start with short sessions (even five minutes) and gradually increase the duration as you become more comfortable with the practice.

Journaling can serve as a valuable tool for processing emotions and gaining insights into your experiences. Writing about your feelings can help you articulate what you're going through, identify patterns in your thoughts and behaviors, and gain a sense of perspective. It doesn't need to be a perfect or eloquent piece of writing; it's a private space for you to explore your emotions without judgment.

Engaging in creative activities can be a powerful way to express yourself and process your emotions. This could include anything from painting and drawing to playing music, writing poetry, or knitting. Creativity provides an outlet for expressing emotions that might be difficult to articulate verbally. It allows for self-expression, distraction from negative thoughts, and a sense of accomplishment.

Connecting with others is essential for healing. Social isolation often exacerbates feelings of loneliness and anxiety. Reach out to trusted friends, family members, or support groups. Sharing your experiences with others who understand can provide comfort, validation, and a sense of community. Joining a support group specifically for survivors of sociopathic abuse can be particularly beneficial, providing a safe space to share experiences and learn from others who have gone through similar challenges.

Setting boundaries is crucial for protecting your well-being. This involves identifying your limits and communicating them clearly to others. It's about protecting yourself from further harm and ensuring your needs are respected. This might involve limiting contact with certain individuals or saying no to requests that drain your energy or compromise your well-being. Setting boundaries is an act of self-respect and self-preservation. It is not selfish; it is necessary.

Learning to say no is a vital component of self-care. It's often difficult after years of being manipulated to assert your needs. However, protecting your energy and well-being requires learning to politely but firmly decline requests that do not serve you. Practice saying no in low-stakes situations initially, building your confidence and ability to protect your time and emotional resources.

Remember that self-care is not a one-size-fits-all approach. Experiment with different activities and practices to find what works best for you. Be patient with yourself; healing is a process, not a destination. There will be good days and bad days. Celebrate your progress and be kind to yourself during setbacks. Remember that you deserve to prioritize your well- being and create a life free from fear and control. Your journey to recovery is a testament to your strength and resilience, and these self-care practices are essential tools to help you navigate this journey with grace, strength, and a renewed sense of self-worth. Seek professional support when needed; a therapist specializing in trauma can provide invaluable guidance and support during this process. Your healing journey is unique to you, and there is no one right way to heal. Embrace the process, celebrate your successes, and be compassionate with yourself as you rebuild your life.

Developing Healthy Coping Mechanisms

Developing healthy coping mechanisms is paramount in the aftermath of abuse by a sociopath. The manipulation and control experienced often leave survivors with a complex array of emotional challenges, making it crucial to develop strategies for managing difficult emotions and stressful situations. This isn't about suppressing feelings; rather, it's about learning healthy ways to process and navigate them, preventing them from overwhelming you.

One highly effective coping mechanism is journaling. The act of writing down your thoughts and feelings can be incredibly cathartic. It provides a safe space to explore your experiences without judgment, allowing you to untangle the complexities of your emotions. Don't worry about grammar or style; the goal is simply to express yourself honestly. You might find patterns emerging as you write, gaining valuable insights into your emotional responses and triggers. Consider dating your entries to track changes in your mood and emotional state over time. This can be a powerful tool for monitoring your progress and identifying areas needing further attention.

Journaling can also help to process traumatic memories in a safe and controlled environment. The act of writing can be a form of emotional release, allowing you to externalize painful memories and experiences. It's crucial to approach this gently, avoiding triggering memories that are too overwhelming. If you find yourself becoming excessively distressed while journaling, take a break and engage in a relaxing activity before returning to it later. Remember, the process is about self-discovery and healing, not causing further distress.

Beyond journaling, mindfulness and meditation offer invaluable tools for managing intense emotions. These practices encourage focusing on the present moment, gently redirecting your attention from distressing thoughts and feelings. Even a few minutes of daily meditation can help to calm your nervous system and reduce feelings of anxiety and overwhelm. Numerous guided meditations are readily available online or through apps, catering to all experience levels. Explore different styles to find one that resonates with you. The focus isn't about emptying your mind; it's about acknowledging thoughts and feelings without judgment, observing them as they arise and pass.

Mindfulness extends beyond formal meditation practices. You can incorporate mindful moments throughout your day, such as paying attention to your breath during stressful situations, noticing the sensations of your feet on the floor, or savoring the taste of your food. These small acts of mindful awareness can help you to ground yourself in the present moment and interrupt cycles of negative thinking.

They offer a subtle yet powerful antidote to the overwhelming rumination that can often accompany trauma recovery.

Creative expression is another powerful coping mechanism, providing an alternative outlet for processing intense emotions. This could involve any creative activity that you find engaging, whether it's painting, drawing, sculpting, playing a musical instrument, singing, writing poetry, photography, or knitting. The act of creation offers a form of emotional release and self-expression, allowing you to communicate emotions that might be difficult to articulate verbally. The process itself can be therapeutic, providing a sense of accomplishment and fostering self-esteem. It can be helpful to keep your creative work in a safe place, revisiting

it later to notice how your perspectives may change over time.

Engaging in creative activities can also be a way to reclaim your sense of self, reconnecting with aspects of yourself that may have been suppressed or neglected during the abusive relationship. The process of creation can be a deeply personal and empowering one, helping you to reconnect with your inner strength and resilience. Don't worry about producing a masterpiece; the focus should be on the process of creating and self-expression.

Physical activity remains a cornerstone of healthy coping. The endorphins released during exercise have a natural mood-boosting effect, helping to combat feelings of depression and anxiety. Regular physical activity can also improve sleep quality, further enhancing your overall well- being. Find an activity that you genuinely enjoy, whether it's dancing, swimming, hiking, cycling, or simply taking a brisk walk. The key is consistency rather than intensity. Even short bursts of activity throughout the day can accumulate to have a positive impact.

Consider joining a fitness class or group activity to foster a sense of community and social support. This can help counter the isolation often imposed by an abusive partner, providing a valuable opportunity to connect with others and build new, healthy relationships. The social interaction can be as beneficial as the physical activity itself.

Social connection is crucial for recovery. Isolation can exacerbate feelings of loneliness and vulnerability. Actively cultivate supportive relationships with trusted friends, family members, or support groups. Sharing your experiences with others who understand can provide validation, comfort, and a sense of community. Joining a support group specifically

for survivors of sociopathic abuse can be particularly beneficial, offering a safe and supportive environment where you can connect with others who have had similar experiences. The shared understanding and mutual support can be incredibly empowering.

Remember, recovery is not a linear process. There will be days when you feel stronger and more resilient, and other days when you experience setbacks. Be patient and kind to yourself throughout this journey. Celebrate your progress, no matter how small, and acknowledge that setbacks are a normal part of the healing process.

Learning to assert boundaries is essential for protecting your well-being. This involves identifying your limits and communicating them clearly and assertively to others. It is not selfish to prioritize your own needs and well-being. This may involve setting limits on contact with certain individuals or saying no to requests that drain your energy or compromise your well-being. This is an act of self-respect and self-preservation. Practice saying no in low-stakes situations first, building your confidence and ability to protect your time and emotional resources. Remember, healthy boundaries are a vital component of self-care.

Developing healthy coping mechanisms requires experimentation and self-discovery. Not every strategy will work for everyone, so it's essential to find what resonates with you and incorporates it into your daily routine. Be flexible, adapting your approach as your needs and circumstances change. The process of healing is a deeply personal one, and there is no one-size-fits-all approach. Seek professional support from a therapist specializing in trauma or abuse recovery if needed. Their guidance and expertise can provide invaluable support as you navigate your healing journey.

Remember, healing takes time. Be patient with yourself, celebrate your progress, and prioritize your well-being. Your resilience and strength are testaments to your ability to overcome this challenging experience, and you deserve to create a life free from fear and control. The tools and techniques discussed here are designed to empower you on your path to recovery, providing strategies for navigating difficult emotions, building resilience, and reclaiming your life. This is not just about surviving; it's about thriving.

Maintaining Physical and Mental Health

Maintaining physical and mental health is not a luxury after escaping an abusive relationship; it's a necessity. The trauma inflicted by a sociopath often leaves deep wounds, both visible and invisible. Neglecting your well-being, in either aspect, will only hinder your recovery and allow the insidious effects of the abuse to linger. Prioritizing self-care in this context isn't selfish; it's an act of radical self- preservation. It's about rebuilding your life, brick by painstaking brick, and ensuring you have a strong foundation to support your future.

This begins with regular medical check-ups. The stress and emotional turmoil of escaping a sociopath can manifest physically in various ways – from digestive issues and chronic headaches to sleep disturbances and weakened immunity. Regular visits to your primary care physician allow for early detection of potential health problems, enabling prompt intervention before they escalate. Don't dismiss any physical symptoms; even seemingly minor ailments can be indicators of underlying stress or trauma.

Your doctor can perform necessary tests, offer advice on managing stress, and provide referrals to specialists if needed. Open and honest communication with your doctor is crucial; they can provide valuable support and guidance during this challenging time. Don't hesitate to explain the context of your life, the trauma you've endured, and how it's affecting your physical health. This information is vital in helping them provide the most effective care.

Beyond regular check-ups, be proactive in seeking medical attention when needed. Don't delay seeking help if you experience any significant physical or psychological

symptoms. This is especially important if you've experienced physical abuse. Delayed treatment can lead to more severe complications, both physically and emotionally. This proactive approach demonstrates self-respect and highlights the importance you place on your well-being. Remember, your health is your responsibility, and seeking medical assistance is a sign of strength, not weakness. Finding a doctor you trust and feel comfortable with is also crucial.

Choose a medical professional who is empathetic, understanding, and willing to listen to your concerns without judgment. A supportive doctor can become a valuable ally in your recovery journey.

Beyond physical health, mental well-being is equally, if not more, critical. The psychological impact of sociopathic abuse is profound and long-lasting. The manipulation, gaslighting, and emotional manipulation can leave deep scars, affecting your self-esteem, sense of self, and trust in others. Engaging in regular therapy is crucial for processing these traumatic experiences and developing coping mechanisms. Seek a therapist specializing in trauma and abuse recovery. This is not just about talking; a skilled therapist can provide you with specific techniques and strategies for managing trauma responses, such as flashbacks, nightmares, and intrusive thoughts.

Cognitive Behavioral Therapy (CBT) is frequently recommended for trauma recovery. CBT helps you identify and challenge negative thought patterns and develop healthier coping strategies. Eye Movement Desensitization and Reprocessing (EMDR) is another effective therapy for processing traumatic memories and reducing their emotional impact. Both of these therapies can help to reframe negative thoughts, reduce anxiety, and build resilience. A therapist can guide you through these techniques and help you adapt them to your specific needs and experiences. Remember,

finding the right therapist is paramount. It may take some time and effort to find a therapist with whom you feel comfortable and connected. Don't hesitate to try different therapists until you find one who meets your needs.

In addition to professional therapy, fostering self-compassion is essential. The self-doubt and low self-esteem that often result from abuse require deliberate counteraction. Practice self-affirmations, speaking kindly to yourself, and focusing on your strengths and accomplishments. Remind yourself that you are not to blame for the abuse you experienced, and that your worth is not determined by the actions of your abuser. This isn't a quick fix; it's a gradual process that requires consistent effort and patience. But over time, practicing self-compassion will significantly improve your self-esteem and empower you to move forward.

Building a strong support network is also vital for maintaining mental well-being. Isolation is a common tactic used by sociopaths to control and manipulate their victims. After escaping the abuse, actively cultivate relationships with trusted friends, family members, and support groups.

Sharing your experiences with others who understand can provide validation, comfort, and a sense of community.

Joining a support group for survivors of sociopathic abuse can be particularly beneficial. The shared understanding and mutual support within these groups can be incredibly powerful and healing. The opportunity to connect with others who have had similar experiences provides a sense of belonging and shared resilience.

Remember, there is no shame in seeking help. In fact, it demonstrates courage and strength. Reaching out for support shows your commitment to healing and well-being. This support network can provide crucial emotional support, practical assistance, and guidance during challenging times.

It's crucial to surround yourself with people who understand, support, and encourage your healing journey.

Prioritizing sleep is often overlooked but is fundamental to both physical and mental health. Trauma can significantly disrupt sleep patterns, leading to insomnia, nightmares, and fatigue. Establish a regular sleep schedule, creating a calming bedtime routine to promote relaxation and restful sleep. Avoiding caffeine and alcohol before bed, creating a quiet and dark sleep environment, and practicing relaxation techniques such as deep breathing or meditation can significantly improve sleep quality. If sleep problems persist, consult your doctor or therapist to explore potential underlying issues or consider seeking professional guidance on sleep hygiene. Sufficient sleep is essential for your body and mind to repair and rejuvenate, which is crucial for recovery.

Nutrition plays a vital role in overall well-being. A healthy diet provides the essential nutrients your body needs to heal and function optimally. Focus on consuming a balanced diet rich in fruits, vegetables, whole grains, and lean protein.

Limit processed foods, sugary drinks, and excessive caffeine, which can exacerbate anxiety and other symptoms. Regular hydration is also critical for both physical and mental health. Adequate water intake supports bodily functions and helps regulate mood. A well-balanced diet contributes to better physical and mental stamina, energy levels, and overall health, essential for navigating the challenges of recovery.

Finally, incorporating regular physical activity is another crucial element of self-care. Exercise releases endorphins, which have mood-boosting effects, helping combat feelings of depression, anxiety, and fatigue. Regular physical activity can also improve sleep quality, reduce stress, and boost overall energy levels. Find an activity you enjoy, whether it's

yoga, swimming, dancing, walking, or something else entirely. The key is consistency rather than intensity; even short bursts of activity throughout the day can accumulate to have a positive impact on your physical and mental health.

Remember, prioritizing your physical and mental well-being is an act of self-love and self-respect, critical for a full and meaningful recovery. This is not just about surviving; it is about thriving, building a life that is strong, healthy, and free from the shadow of abuse.

Practicing SelfCompassion and Forgiveness

Practicing self-compassion after escaping the clutches of a sociopath is not merely an act of self-care; it's a revolutionary act of self-preservation. The insidious nature of the abuse often leaves victims feeling profoundly flawed, responsible for the abuse they endured, and unworthy of happiness. This deeply ingrained sense of self-blame must be actively challenged and dismantled. Forgiveness, both of yourself and your abuser, plays a crucial, albeit complex, role in this process.

Self-compassion begins with acknowledging the profound impact of the abuse. It's about understanding that the manipulation, gaslighting, and control weren't your fault. The sociopath's actions were a reflection of their pathology, not a judgment of your worth. This understanding is the cornerstone of healing. It's a process of gently untangling the web of lies and distortions woven by your abuser, replacing them with the truth: you are worthy of love, respect, and a life free from fear.

One powerful tool for cultivating self-compassion is self- affirmations. These aren't superficial pronouncements; they're intentional statements designed to counter the negative self-talk instilled by the abuser. Start by identifying the most pervasive negative thoughts and beliefs about yourself—the ones that whisper doubts and insecurities.

Then, craft affirmations that directly challenge these thoughts. For instance, if you constantly berate yourself for not seeing the red flags sooner, an affirmation might be: "I am not responsible for my abuser's actions; I am learning and growing from this experience." Or, if you struggle with

feelings of inadequacy, an affirmation could be: "I am strong, resilient, and capable of overcoming this challenge."

Repeat these affirmations regularly—in the morning, before bed, or even throughout the day as needed. Write them down, say them aloud, or even record yourself saying them and listen back. The key is consistency. The more you repeat these positive statements, the more likely they are to replace the negative self-talk that has become deeply ingrained. It's like retraining your brain to recognize and value your inherent worth.

Beyond affirmations, practicing mindfulness can be profoundly beneficial. Mindfulness encourages you to focus on the present moment, without judgment. This can help to interrupt the cycle of negative thinking and self-criticism.

Simple mindfulness exercises, such as focusing on your breath or noticing the sensations in your body, can help ground you in the present and reduce feelings of anxiety and overwhelm. Numerous guided meditation apps are available to help you learn and practice mindfulness techniques. Even five minutes a day can make a significant difference.

Another vital aspect of self-compassion is self-soothing. This involves engaging in activities that bring you comfort and a sense of calm. These activities will differ from person to person, but they might include taking a warm bath, listening to soothing music, spending time in nature, reading a favorite book, engaging in a hobby, or connecting with a supportive friend or family member. Identify your personal self-soothing activities and make time for them regularly.

This is not a luxury; it's a necessity for healing and building emotional resilience.

Journaling can also be a powerful tool for cultivating self- compassion. Writing down your thoughts and feelings can

help you process your emotions, identify negative patterns, and challenge self-critical thoughts. It can provide a safe space to express your pain, anger, and grief without judgment. You don't need to write beautifully or eloquently; the act of writing itself is therapeutic. Simply let your thoughts and feelings flow onto the page. Over time, you might notice shifts in your self-perception and a growing sense of self-acceptance.

Forgiveness, both of yourself and your abuser, is another critical aspect of the healing process. Forgiving yourself doesn't mean condoning what happened or minimizing the trauma you endured. It means releasing the self-blame and self-hatred that can consume you. It's about recognizing that you were a victim of a manipulative and abusive person, and that you did the best you could given the circumstances. This is a process, not a destination. It might involve acknowledging your past mistakes, learning from them, and practicing self-compassion.

Forgiving your abuser is even more challenging, and it's not something you need to rush. It doesn't mean you condone their behavior or reconcile with them. It means releasing the anger, resentment, and bitterness that consume you and hinder your healing. Holding onto these negative emotions keeps you tethered to the past and prevents you from moving forward. Forgiveness doesn't erase the abuse; it simply frees you from its grip. You might find it helpful to visualize letting go of these negative emotions, perhaps by writing a letter to your abuser expressing your feelings without sending it, or through guided meditation or visualization exercises.

Remember that healing is a journey, not a destination. There will be setbacks, moments of doubt, and relapses. Be kind to yourself during these times. Don't judge yourself harshly for

feeling sad, angry, or scared. Allow yourself to experience these emotions without judgment and know that they are a natural part of the healing process. Recognize progress, no matter how small, and celebrate your victories along the way.

Self-compassion and forgiveness are not acts of weakness; they are acts of immense strength. They are essential steps in breaking free from the lingering effects of sociopathic abuse and building a life filled with self-love, self-respect, and well-being. This process requires consistent effort, patience, and self-awareness, but the rewards are immeasurable: a life free from the shadows of the past, filled with hope, happiness, and a renewed sense of self.

Consider seeking professional guidance in practicing self- compassion and forgiveness. A therapist specializing in trauma recovery can provide tailored strategies and support to help you navigate these complex emotional challenges. They can help you identify and challenge negative thought patterns, develop healthy coping mechanisms, and process the trauma you have experienced. Remember, you are not alone, and seeking professional help is a sign of strength, not weakness.

In addition to professional support, explore various self-help resources, such as books, workshops, or online support groups. These resources can offer valuable tools and strategies for fostering self-compassion and forgiveness.

Connect with other survivors of abuse; their shared experiences and support can be incredibly powerful and healing. The shared understanding and mutual support within these communities can offer a sense of belonging and shared resilience, reminding you that you are not alone in your journey.

It's crucial to remember that healing takes time. There is no set timeline for recovery, and your journey will be unique to your experiences. Be patient with yourself, celebrate your progress, and remember that you are worthy of a happy, healthy, and fulfilling life, free from the constraints of the past. The path to recovery is paved with self-compassion and forgiveness, leading to a future where you can finally escape the shadows and embrace the light.

Building Resilience and Strength

Building resilience after surviving abuse by a sociopath is not a passive process; it's an active, ongoing commitment to strengthening your inner self. It's about cultivating a deep- seated belief in your ability to overcome adversity, to learn from setbacks, and to emerge stronger on the other side. This involves more than just coping mechanisms; it's about fundamentally altering your relationship with yourself and the world. It's about recognizing your inherent strength, even in the face of overwhelming challenges.

One of the first steps in building resilience is to acknowledge and validate the trauma you've experienced. Minimizing or dismissing the abuse only serves to prolong the healing process. Allow yourself to feel the full spectrum of emotions - the anger, the sadness, the fear, the confusion. Don't try to suppress these feelings; instead, allow them to flow through you, acknowledging their presence without judgment. This acceptance is the bedrock upon which resilience is built. It's a recognition that you are not broken, but that you have been profoundly wounded and are actively working towards healing.

This acknowledgment often leads to a deeper understanding of your own strength and resourcefulness. Think back to moments during the abuse when you found inner strength, even if it was seemingly small acts of defiance or moments of quiet resistance. These moments are invaluable; they are proof that you possess an inner wellspring of fortitude that can be tapped into again and again. Recall specific instances: perhaps you subtly resisted a controlling demand, or you found a small way to maintain a connection with the outside world, or you silently planned your escape. These are crucial

victories that should be celebrated, no matter how seemingly insignificant they may appear in retrospect.

Learning to identify and challenge negative thought patterns is another crucial aspect of building resilience. Sociopaths are masters of manipulation, and their abuse often leaves victims with distorted perceptions of themselves and the world. These distortions often manifest as negative self-talk, self-doubt, and a pervasive sense of worthlessness. Actively challenge these thoughts. Ask yourself: are these thoughts based on facts or on the manipulations of your abuser? Are these thoughts serving me, or are they holding me back? By questioning the validity of these thoughts, you begin to reclaim your own narrative and create a more balanced perspective. Cognitive Behavioral Therapy (CBT) techniques are incredibly helpful in this process, teaching you to identify and reframe negative thoughts into more realistic and positive ones.

Developing healthy coping mechanisms is also essential for building resilience. This involves finding healthy and constructive ways to manage stress, anxiety, and other difficult emotions. This might involve physical activity, meditation, spending time in nature, engaging in creative pursuits, or connecting with supportive friends and family. It's crucial to find activities that truly resonate with you and that bring you a sense of peace and calm. Experiment with various approaches; what works for one person might not work for another. The key is to find strategies that help you regulate your emotions and feel empowered to navigate challenging situations.

Building a strong support network is paramount. Isolation is a common tactic used by sociopaths, leaving victims feeling alone and vulnerable. Actively seek out connections with supportive individuals who can offer understanding, compassion, and a safe space for you to express your feelings. This might involve connecting with friends, family members, support groups, or therapists. Remember that you do not have to go through this alone. The empathy and shared understanding offered by others who have experienced similar trauma can be incredibly powerful.

Shared experiences often foster a deeper level of mutual support and understanding. Support groups offer a sense of community and belonging, reminding you that you are not alone in your journey of healing and recovery.

Setting boundaries is another critical step in building resilience. This involves learning to say no to requests or demands that compromise your well-being or safety. It's about prioritizing your own needs and establishing clear limits in your relationships. This may seem challenging initially, especially if you're accustomed to prioritizing the needs of others above your own. However, setting healthy boundaries is essential for protecting your emotional and mental health and creating a safe and empowering space for yourself. It requires both internal and external actions; internal strength to know what your boundaries are and the courage to communicate them clearly.

Forgiveness, while not a requirement for healing, can be an incredibly powerful tool in the process of building resilience. Forgiving your abuser doesn't mean condoning their behavior or forgetting what happened; it means releasing the anger, resentment, and bitterness that are holding you back from moving forward. It allows you to break free from the past and focus on building a brighter future. This is often a gradual process, and you don't have to forgive all at once.

Some may find that they never forgive their abuser and that's entirely acceptable. The key is to prioritize your own healing and well-being.

Self-care, often neglected during periods of abuse, is now paramount. Prioritizing your physical, emotional, and mental health is not a luxury; it's an essential component of your recovery. This encompasses all aspects of your well-being, including adequate sleep, healthy eating, regular exercise, engaging in activities you enjoy, and nurturing your spiritual side. It's about creating a life that is nourishing and supportive, replenishing your energy and vitality.

Finally, remember that building resilience is a process, not a destination. There will be setbacks, moments of doubt, and times when you feel overwhelmed. Be patient with yourself; celebrate your small victories and acknowledge the progress you've made. Don't be discouraged by setbacks; instead, use them as opportunities to learn and grow. Building resilience is a testament to your strength and determination. It's a testament to your ability to overcome adversity and create a life filled with hope, happiness, and a sense of self-worth.

You have survived, and you are capable of thriving.

Learning to recognize your strengths and acknowledging the progress you've made, no matter how small, builds confidence. Keep a journal, documenting not only the challenges but also your victories. Look back at past entries and see how far you've come. This self-reflection helps reinforce your progress and builds a sense of accomplishment. Remember, there's no competition in healing; it's a personal journey, and the pace is yours to set.

Embrace opportunities for self-discovery and personal growth. The trauma you've experienced has inevitably shaped your perception of yourself and your relationships. This is an opportunity to examine these perceptions with honesty and kindness. You might consider seeking additional therapy to address remaining issues, explore creative expression as a means of processing your experiences, or

delve into personal development resources. The focus is on creating a stronger, healthier, more authentic you.

Consider seeking professional help for Post-Traumatic Stress Disorder (PTSD) or other trauma-related conditions. A therapist can provide valuable support, equip you with coping strategies, and guide you through processing your trauma. Professional support can significantly enhance your journey toward resilience. Many different therapeutic approaches can assist in building resilience, including EMDR

(Eye Movement Desensitization and Reprocessing), somatic experiencing, and trauma-focused Cognitive Behavioral Therapy.

Actively cultivate positive relationships with individuals who value and respect you. These relationships provide a sense of belonging, support, and understanding. Nurture these bonds, and choose to surround yourself with supportive and uplifting people who acknowledge and validate your experience. Remember that healthy relationships are reciprocal, providing mutual support and understanding.

Remember that you are not alone on this journey. There are many others who have survived similar experiences and can provide support and understanding. Seek out support groups or online communities where you can connect with others who have been through similar challenges. Shared experiences offer a powerful source of strength and healing.

Building resilience is not about forgetting the past; it's about integrating it into your life narrative in a way that empowers you, rather than defining you. It's about learning from your experiences, accepting your vulnerability, and celebrating your strength. It's about creating a future that is shaped by your resilience, not your trauma. You are a survivor, and you

are capable of building a life that is meaningful, fulfilling, and free from the shadows of the past.

Protecting Children from Abuse

Protecting children is paramount when escaping an abusive situation involving a sociopath. The safety and well-being of children must be the absolute priority throughout the escape process and in the aftermath. Their innocence and vulnerability demand a meticulous and proactive approach, one that goes beyond simply leaving the abusive environment. The manipulative tactics of sociopaths often extend to controlling and isolating children, making their escape particularly complex and demanding.

The first step involves meticulous planning. This isn't a spontaneous decision; it requires careful consideration and strategy. Begin by creating a detailed safety plan, a document that outlines every step of the escape, including the timing, transportation, and destination. Identify safe houses or shelters specifically equipped to handle children's needs. These shelters provide a secure environment, often with trained personnel who understand the complexities of child trauma. Familiarize yourself with the resources available in your area, including child protective services and domestic violence shelters. Research these options well in advance to ensure a smooth and secure transition. Timing is crucial. Consider the sociopath's routine, their vulnerabilities, and any predictable patterns in their behavior to choose the most opportune moment for the escape. Ensure the children are well-prepared, with a change of clothes and any necessary medications or comfort items packed discreetly.

Financial security is another vital aspect. Sociopaths often control the family finances, leaving the victim with limited resources. Secretly secure funds, even small amounts, can be

a lifeline. Open a separate bank account, if possible, and deposit any money that can be moved without detection. Reach out to family or friends for financial assistance; let them know your situation in confidence and request their support in getting the children to safety. If immediate financial assistance is inaccessible, look into local charities and organizations that provide emergency financial aid to victims of domestic violence. Explore all avenues for support; even small contributions can make a significant difference.

Transportation plays a critical role in a successful escape. If you have access to a vehicle, ensure it's reliable and has enough fuel. Plan the escape route carefully, avoiding locations where the abuser might intercept you. If you don't have a car, arrange transportation in advance – a trusted friend, a taxi, or public transport. Ensure the children are aware of the escape plan, but only to the extent they can handle without undue anxiety. Keep the details simple, emphasizing their safety and the new, safe place they're going.

Upon reaching safety, immediate actions are necessary to safeguard the children's well-being. Report the abuse to the appropriate authorities. This involves contacting child protective services and law enforcement to file a formal report. Provide them with all the necessary details, including the abuser's identity, history of abuse, and evidence of the abuse. Cooperate fully with the investigation and follow their instructions diligently. Seeking legal counsel is also important. A lawyer can help secure a restraining order to prevent further contact with the abuser and assist with custody arrangements. Remember, the legal system is there to protect you and your children; use its resources to ensure their continued safety.

The emotional impact on children must not be underestimated. They have likely witnessed and experienced the abuse firsthand, suffering from trauma that requires specialized care. Seek professional help immediately from therapists experienced in treating child trauma. These therapists employ techniques designed to help children process their experiences in a safe and supportive environment, utilizing age-appropriate approaches. Child- centered therapy helps the children articulate their feelings, understand their experiences, and develop coping mechanisms. Providing a consistent routine, maintaining stability, and creating a predictable and supportive environment are crucial for emotional healing. This helps children regain a sense of safety and control after the traumatic events they have endured.

Encourage open communication with the children. Let them know it's okay to talk about their feelings, even if it's difficult. Listen attentively to what they share, validating their emotions and never minimizing their experiences.

Avoid using judgmental language, instead focusing on providing empathy and understanding. Allow them to express their emotions freely, without fear of judgment or reprisal. Create a safe space where they feel comfortable sharing their thoughts and concerns.

In addition to professional therapy, maintaining routines and a sense of normalcy is crucial for children's recovery.

Establish a consistent schedule for meals, bedtime, and other daily activities. This structure provides a sense of order and predictability in their lives, reducing anxiety and fostering stability. Encourage participation in activities they enjoy, whether it's playing with friends, engaging in hobbies, or attending school. These activities contribute to their overall well-being, supporting their emotional healing. Positive

reinforcement can play a significant role in bolstering their resilience.

The long-term effects of trauma can be profound. Be vigilant in monitoring the children's emotional and behavioral changes. Seek immediate help if you notice any significant behavioral issues, such as withdrawal, aggression, or significant changes in sleep or appetite. Early intervention is key to mitigating potential long-term challenges associated with trauma exposure. Continued therapy is often necessary to help children process their experiences and develop healthy coping mechanisms. The healing process is gradual and ongoing, requiring patience, understanding, and unwavering support.

Education plays a vital role in protecting children. Teach them about safe and unsafe touch, body boundaries, and appropriate behavior from adults. Empower them to recognize and report any instances of abuse or discomfort. Equip them with the vocabulary to express their experiences effectively. Ensure they understand that it's not their fault if they experience any form of abuse or mistreatment.

Emphasize their right to safety and their right to say "no" to anything that makes them uncomfortable.

Collaboration with educational institutions is crucial. Inform the school officials about the situation and the children's needs. Request support for their academic and emotional well-being. Ensure the school is aware of any specific requirements, such as individualized learning plans or additional support services. Collaboration creates a supportive environment for the children, ensuring consistency and continuity of care.

Building a strong support network is essential for both parents and children. Reach out to family, friends, support

groups, or community organizations to provide emotional and practical support. Lean on trusted individuals for assistance with childcare, household tasks, or emotional support. Sharing experiences and support with other survivors can offer a sense of community and validation. Remember, you are not alone in this journey, and there are numerous people and resources available to help.

The escape from an abusive sociopath is a challenging undertaking, particularly when children are involved. Meticulous planning, proactive legal actions, and sustained emotional support are vital for ensuring the safety and well- being of the children. Remember, placing the children's welfare at the forefront of your actions is essential for their recovery and long-term emotional health. Their resilience and future happiness depend on your steadfast commitment to their safety and well-being. This commitment demands constant vigilance, proactive planning, and unrelenting dedication to their healthy development. The process is long, but the rewards of safeguarding their innocence and fostering their healing are immeasurable.

Seeking Child Custody and Legal Protection

Navigating the legal system after escaping a sociopathic abuser can feel like entering a minefield, especially when children are involved. The immediate priority is to ensure their safety and well-being, and this often requires seeking legal protection and custody arrangements. Understanding the process and securing competent legal representation is crucial. Remember, the legal system is designed to protect victims and their children, but you must actively engage with it to reap its benefits.

The first step is to find a lawyer specializing in family law and domestic violence cases. This isn't a situation where you can afford to compromise on expertise. A lawyer experienced in dealing with sociopaths understands their manipulative tactics and can anticipate their strategies in court. They will be equipped to counter these strategies effectively, protecting your children's interests. Do your research; ask for referrals from domestic violence shelters, women's advocacy groups, or trusted friends. Read online reviews and compare different lawyers' experience and success rates in similar cases. The initial consultation is often free or low-cost, allowing you to assess their suitability before committing. Don't hesitate to interview several lawyers until you find one you trust and feel comfortable with. The rapport you build with your lawyer is crucial throughout the legal process, particularly when dealing with the high-stakes emotional turmoil involved.

Your lawyer will guide you through the process of filing for custody and obtaining protective orders. Custody orders dictate the legal rights and responsibilities of each parent regarding their children – physical custody (where the

children live) and legal custody (decision-making authority on matters such as education and healthcare). In situations of abuse, the courts heavily favor the safety and well-being of the children, and a judge is likely to grant you primary custody if sufficient evidence of the abuse is presented. This evidence might include police reports, medical records documenting injuries, photographs of bruises or other injuries, witness testimonies, and any documentation of the abuser's manipulative behaviors. Your lawyer will help you gather and organize this evidence in a way that is legally sound and persuasive.

Protective orders, often called restraining orders, are crucial for preventing further contact between the abuser and you and your children. These orders legally prohibit the abuser from coming within a certain distance of your home, workplace, or your children's school. They can also restrict the abuser's ability to contact you or your children by phone, email, or through any other means. Violating a protective order is a serious crime with potentially severe consequences. Obtaining a protective order is generally a relatively straightforward legal process if sufficient evidence of abuse exists. However, the process can still be emotionally draining, and having a strong legal team is critical to ensure the order is granted and effectively enforced.

Preparing for court proceedings is crucial. Your lawyer will prepare you for what to expect and will help you practice your testimony. They will guide you on how to answer questions clearly and concisely, focusing on the facts and avoiding emotionally charged language. Remember, the goal is to present a clear and compelling case emphasizing the danger the abuser poses to you and your children. The judge will base their decision on the evidence presented, so being prepared and providing clear, concise information is key to a

favorable outcome. This includes anticipating the abuser's potential arguments and preparing counterarguments.

Sociopaths are masters of manipulation, and they will likely try to distort the facts to portray themselves in a positive light or to undermine your credibility. Your lawyer will help you anticipate these attempts and craft appropriate responses.

The court process can be lengthy and emotionally taxing. Be prepared for delays, setbacks, and the inevitable emotional roller coaster. Maintaining a strong support system is critical during this period. Lean on your friends, family, support groups, and therapist for emotional support and practical assistance. Remember, you are not alone in this journey, and there are people who want to help. Your therapist can provide guidance on coping strategies to manage the stress and anxiety associated with court proceedings. Consider joining a support group for victims of domestic violence; sharing experiences with others who understand can provide validation and strength.

Financial considerations are another significant aspect of seeking legal protection. Legal representation can be expensive, and court costs can accumulate quickly. Explore financial assistance options such as legal aid societies or pro bono services offered by lawyers in your area. Many organizations dedicated to assisting victims of domestic violence offer financial assistance for legal fees. Do not let financial constraints prevent you from seeking legal help.

Your children's safety and well-being are paramount, and securing competent legal representation is a non-negotiable step in protecting them.

Beyond custody and protective orders, your lawyer may also advise you on other legal avenues to secure your children's safety and well-being. This could include exploring options

for changing your address, obtaining security systems for your home, or even seeking assistance from law enforcement in conducting regular welfare checks. Your lawyer will work with you to develop a comprehensive plan to ensure your children are safe and protected from future harm. The objective is not merely to escape the abuse, but to create a safe and stable environment where your children can heal and thrive.

The long-term implications of the legal process should also be considered. Even after achieving a favorable outcome in court, the process might require ongoing vigilance.

Regularly check in with your lawyer to address any new developments or concerns. Keep detailed records of all communications, court orders, and any instances of contact or attempted contact from the abuser. This documentation is crucial in case of future violations or disputes. Remembering that the fight for your children's safety is an ongoing process, not a single victory, ensures you continue to build a protective structure around them. Even years later, you might need to revisit the legal framework to adjust custody arrangements based on the children's evolving needs or the abuser's actions. Continued vigilance and legal counsel is not just a safeguard, but a critical component of rebuilding their lives and providing them the stability and safety they need to heal.

Ultimately, seeking child custody and legal protection is a multifaceted process requiring careful planning, legal expertise, and unwavering determination. It's a fight for your children's future, a battle against manipulation and abuse.

Remember that this is not about blame; it's about protecting your children from harm. By equipping yourself with the knowledge, support, and legal resources necessary, you're actively creating a safe and nurturing environment for your children to heal and grow. The journey is arduous, but the

ultimate goal - their safety and well-being - makes every step worthwhile. Your resilience and unwavering commitment to protecting them will significantly impact their healing and their future.

Helping Children Heal from Trauma

The legal battles to secure your children's safety are only one part of the healing journey. The emotional scars of witnessing or experiencing abuse run deep, and addressing these wounds requires a multifaceted approach focusing on their emotional well-being. Creating a stable and nurturing environment is paramount; a sanctuary where they feel safe, understood, and loved. This involves far more than simply removing them from the abusive situation; it's about actively fostering their healing and building their resilience.

First, understand that children process trauma differently than adults. Their expressions of distress might not align with our expectations. They may exhibit behavioral changes, such as increased aggression, withdrawal, anxiety, or nightmares. Academic performance might suffer; they may struggle to concentrate or experience unexplained absences from school. Physical symptoms, like headaches, stomachaches, or sleep disturbances, are also common manifestations of underlying trauma. It's crucial to recognize that these are not signs of misbehavior, but rather the outward expression of their inner turmoil. Avoid labeling their behavior as "bad" or "difficult"; instead, view it as a symptom requiring understanding and professional help.

Seeking professional help is not a sign of failure; it's a crucial step in the healing process. A therapist specializing in trauma-informed care is uniquely equipped to assess your child's specific needs and develop an individualized treatment plan. This therapist will use techniques that acknowledge the child's experience and provide a safe space for emotional expression. Therapy might involve play therapy for younger children, who often communicate their

feelings through play rather than words. For older children and adolescents, trauma-focused cognitive behavioral therapy (TF-CBT) is a highly effective approach that teaches coping mechanisms and helps process traumatic memories.

Remember, choosing the right therapist is crucial; ensure the therapist is experienced in working with children who have experienced parental abuse or witnessed domestic violence. A good therapist will create a rapport with your child, building trust and a sense of safety.

Creating a safe and predictable routine is another cornerstone of healing. Children thrive on consistency and structure, which provides a sense of security and control in a world that may have felt chaotic and unpredictable.

Establishing a clear daily schedule, including consistent bedtimes, mealtimes, and homework routines, can significantly reduce anxiety and improve overall well-being. This structured environment offers a sense of stability, a stark contrast to the unpredictable nature of life with an abusive parent. Incorporate activities that your child enjoys, creating opportunities for fun and relaxation. This balance between structure and enjoyment fosters a sense of normalcy and promotes emotional well-being.

Open communication is vital, but it should be age- appropriate and sensitive. Avoid pressuring your child to talk about the trauma before they're ready. Instead, create an environment where they feel comfortable expressing their feelings without judgment or pressure. Let them know that it's safe to talk about anything that's bothering them, and that you're there to listen without interruption or judgment. Even simple acts of listening and validating their feelings - acknowledging the validity of their emotions - can have a profound impact. You can use open-ended questions to encourage them to share their thoughts and feelings, such as

"How are you feeling today?" or "What was the best part of your day?"

Encourage healthy self-expression through various creative outlets. Art therapy, music, dance, or writing can provide a non-threatening way for children to process their emotions. These activities allow them to express themselves without the pressure of verbal communication, providing a safe space for emotional release. Moreover, it provides them with a sense of accomplishment and boosts their self-esteem.

Participation in extracurricular activities, such as sports or clubs, can also be incredibly beneficial. These activities provide opportunities for socialization, positive peer interactions, and a sense of belonging, counteracting the isolation that often accompanies trauma.

Building a strong support system is crucial, extending beyond immediate family. Connect with support groups specifically designed for children who have experienced parental abuse or domestic violence. These groups provide a safe and supportive environment where children can share their experiences with others who understand and validate their feelings. The shared experience fosters a sense of community and reduces feelings of isolation and shame.

Participation in these groups can also help build their self- esteem and resilience. Furthermore, connecting with other parents navigating similar situations can provide invaluable support and practical advice, combating the sense of isolation often experienced by those who have escaped abuse.

Remember that healing from trauma is not a linear process. There will be ups and downs, good days and bad days. Be patient, understanding, and supportive throughout the journey. Celebrate their progress and offer comfort during setbacks. Positive reinforcement and praise for their efforts

are essential to encourage self-confidence and build their resilience. Avoid using harsh disciplinary measures or punishment, particularly if their behavior reflects their trauma. Instead, focus on guiding them toward healthier coping mechanisms, working with their therapist to develop effective strategies.

Educate yourself about childhood trauma and its impact. The more you understand about the effects of abuse on children, the better equipped you'll be to support their healing. Read books, articles, and attend workshops focused on trauma- informed care for children. Understanding the complexities of trauma will help you respond appropriately to your child's needs and behaviors. This knowledge base will also strengthen your communication with their therapist, allowing you to work collaboratively to support your child's healing process.

Finally, take care of yourself. Supporting a child through trauma is emotionally draining. Prioritize self-care, ensuring you have the support you need to manage your own stress and emotions. Regularly engage in activities that promote your well-being, whether it's exercise, meditation, spending time in nature, or connecting with supportive friends and family. Remembering to care for yourself ensures you have the emotional resources necessary to support your child's healing journey. This self-care is not selfish; it's essential for your own well-being and ultimately strengthens your ability to support your child. The journey to healing from trauma is a marathon, not a sprint, and nurturing yourself allows you to endure and continue supporting your child's journey. This long-term commitment to healing, both yours and your child's, will cultivate a strong foundation for a healthier and happier future.

Accessing Resources for Children and Families

Accessing the right resources is crucial in navigating the aftermath of abuse. The journey to healing is often long and complex, and having a strong support system is paramount. For children, who are particularly vulnerable, access to specialized care and support is not merely beneficial—it's essential. This section focuses on identifying and accessing these vital resources for both children and their families.

The first, and often most immediate, need is safe shelter. Domestic violence shelters offer temporary refuge for families fleeing abusive situations. These shelters provide more than just a roof over their heads; they offer a safe space, counseling services, and assistance with essential needs like food and clothing. The National Domestic Violence Hotline website (thehotline.org) is an excellent starting point to locate shelters in your area. Many shelters offer specialized programs for children, including play therapy, art therapy, and educational resources to help them process their experiences. Remember that the location of the shelter should be kept confidential to ensure the safety and security of the family. It is imperative to inform the shelter of any potential threats or the abuser's knowledge of your location.

Beyond emergency shelter, counseling services are a cornerstone of recovery. Finding a therapist specializing in trauma-informed care is critical. Trauma-informed therapy recognizes the profound impact of trauma on a person's mind and body and utilizes approaches that minimize re- traumatization. For children, play therapy is often a highly effective method. It uses play as a medium for expression and exploration, allowing children to communicate their

emotions in a safe and non-threatening way. Older children and adolescents may benefit from trauma-focused cognitive behavioral therapy (TF-CBT), which is designed to help them understand and manage their trauma responses. The Childhelp USA National Child Abuse Hotline (1-800-422- 4453) can provide referrals to qualified therapists in your area. Your primary care physician can also make referrals, and many insurance providers offer directories of mental health professionals within your network.

Support groups offer a powerful sense of community and shared understanding. Connecting with other families who have navigated similar experiences can be incredibly validating and empowering. The shared experience reduces the feelings of isolation and shame that often accompany abuse. These groups allow for the exchange of practical advice, coping strategies, and emotional support.

Organizations such as the National Coalition Against Domestic Violence (ncadv.org) and Childhelp USA can offer information about local support groups and other community resources. Remember to research groups thoroughly to ensure they are trauma-informed and utilize appropriate practices for working with children and families who have experienced abuse.

Legal resources are vital for securing protection and ensuring safety. Legal aid organizations and attorneys specializing in family law and domestic violence can provide invaluable assistance in obtaining restraining orders, custody arrangements, and other legal protections. The National Network to End Domestic Violence (nnedv.org) provides information and referrals to legal professionals specializing in these areas. Many jurisdictions have specialized domestic violence courts designed to process cases efficiently and offer a safety-centered approach. Knowing your rights and

options can be empowering, and legal guidance ensures your family is safeguarded against future harm.

Financial assistance is often a critical need for families leaving abusive situations. Many organizations provide financial aid for housing, food, clothing, and other necessities. The Salvation Army, local churches, and charitable organizations frequently provide such assistance. Government assistance programs, such as Temporary Assistance for Needy Families (TANF) and the Supplemental Nutrition Assistance Program (SNAP), can also provide critical financial support. Eligibility requirements vary depending on your location and situation; contacting your local social services agency will help you navigate the application process.

Educational resources are paramount for both parents and children. Understanding the effects of trauma on children is crucial for supporting their healing. Numerous books, articles, and online resources are available, offering valuable insights into childhood trauma and its impact. Participating in workshops and educational programs offered by organizations specializing in trauma-informed care can enhance your understanding and equip you with the knowledge to effectively support your child's recovery. The knowledge you gain about childhood trauma will facilitate your communication with your child's therapist, allowing you to develop a collaborative approach to their healing.

Beyond professional resources, building a personal support network is crucial. Leaning on trusted friends, family members, and community members can provide vital emotional and practical support. Sharing your story with trusted individuals allows you to process your experiences and receive emotional validation. This personal network also offers valuable assistance with childcare, errands, and other

tasks, reducing stress and enabling you to focus on your healing and your child's. Remember that you are not alone in this journey; reaching out to your support network is a strength, not a sign of weakness.

Self-care is not a luxury but a necessity. Supporting a child through trauma can be emotionally draining, requiring parents to prioritize their own well-being. Engaging in activities that promote self-care, such as exercise, meditation, spending time in nature, or pursuing hobbies, can help manage stress and prevent burnout. Remember that you cannot pour from an empty cup; taking care of yourself ensures you have the emotional resources to support your child's healing process. This self-care is an investment in your family's well-being, ultimately strengthening your ability to support your child's journey toward healing.

Navigating the aftermath of abuse requires resilience, strength, and access to the right resources. The path to healing is a marathon, not a sprint. By understanding the available resources and proactively seeking assistance, you are taking a critical step toward rebuilding your lives and creating a safer, healthier future for you and your children. Remember that seeking help is a sign of strength, not weakness, and that healing is possible. With determination, support, and access to appropriate resources, you can escape the shadows of abuse and build a brighter future.

Rebuilding Family Relationships

Rebuilding trust after escaping abuse is a monumental task, especially within the family unit. The insidious nature of sociopathic manipulation often leaves deep wounds, impacting not only the primary victim but also children and other family members. The process requires patience, understanding, and a commitment from everyone involved to actively participate in healing. It's not a quick fix; it's a journey that demands consistent effort and a willingness to confront the lingering effects of the abuse.

One of the first hurdles is acknowledging the extent of the damage. The abuser often works tirelessly to isolate the family, creating a system of mistrust and control. Children, especially, may have witnessed abusive behaviors, internalized the abuser's manipulations, or even been directly victimized themselves. They may struggle to differentiate between reality and the distorted narrative presented by the abuser. Parents need to validate their children's experiences, acknowledging the trauma they've endured without judgment. Openly discussing the abuse, in age-appropriate terms, helps to break the cycle of silence and empowers children to reclaim their voices. This doesn't mean overloading them with graphic details, but rather ensuring they understand that what happened was wrong and that they are safe now.

Establishing clear and open communication is paramount. The family needs to create a safe space where everyone feels comfortable expressing their feelings, concerns, and anxieties without fear of judgment or reprisal. This requires active listening, empathy, and a willingness to understand each individual's perspective. It's crucial to create a culture

of respect where everyone's voice is valued, regardless of age or prior experiences. Family meetings, facilitated by a therapist or counselor specializing in trauma recovery, can provide a structured framework for these conversations.

These meetings offer a neutral space where family members can safely express their emotions, work through conflicts, and establish new patterns of communication.

Forgiveness, while a complex and personal process, plays a crucial role in healing. It's essential to understand that forgiveness doesn't mean condoning the abuser's actions or minimizing the harm inflicted. Rather, it's about releasing the anger, resentment, and bitterness that can consume individuals and prevent them from moving forward.

Forgiveness is primarily for the benefit of the person forgiving, allowing them to reclaim their emotional well- being and release the burden of carrying the weight of the past. This process might involve seeking individual therapy to address personal pain and anger before engaging in family-based forgiveness.

The process of rebuilding trust is gradual and iterative. It involves consistent actions that demonstrate commitment to creating a safe and healthy family dynamic. This may include establishing new routines, creating clear boundaries, and engaging in activities that promote connection and healing. Family therapy can be instrumental in this process, helping family members to learn effective communication skills, build healthy relationships, and develop coping mechanisms for dealing with the lingering effects of abuse. The therapist can provide guidance and support, helping the family to navigate difficult conversations and establish new patterns of interaction.

Children require specialized attention and support during this period. Their experiences may vary significantly depending

on their age and the nature of their exposure to the abuse. Some may exhibit behavioral problems, while others may withdraw or become excessively anxious. It's essential to ensure that children have access to age-appropriate therapeutic interventions that address their specific needs. Play therapy, art therapy, and trauma-focused cognitive behavioral therapy (TF-CBT) are all effective approaches for helping children process their trauma and develop healthy coping mechanisms.

Parental involvement is critical in supporting a child's healing. Parents need to understand the signs and symptoms of trauma in children and be able to provide consistent support and encouragement. This may involve adjusting parenting styles, establishing clear expectations, and providing consistent routines and structure. Maintaining a consistent disciplinary approach, free from anger and inconsistent punishment, can significantly enhance a child's sense of security and safety. It's important to work closely with the child's therapist to ensure a coordinated approach to their care and to understand the child's individual needs and emotional responses.

Re-establishing healthy boundaries is crucial. The abuser likely blurred or completely eliminated boundaries, creating an environment of control and manipulation. The family needs to establish clear and consistent boundaries to protect themselves from future harm. These boundaries might involve physical boundaries, such as limiting contact with the abuser, or emotional boundaries, such as refusing to engage in arguments or tolerate manipulative behavior.

Openly discussing these boundaries and ensuring everyone understands and agrees to them is paramount. The family should create a consistent set of rules and expectations that apply to everyone, emphasizing mutual respect and consideration.

Building new rituals and traditions can help to create a sense of normalcy and stability within the family. Creating positive family experiences can help to counteract the negative memories and experiences associated with the abuse. This might involve family dinners, game nights, or outings to the park. These activities provide opportunities for positive interaction, creating memories that are associated with safety, love, and support. Engaging in shared activities that foster laughter, connection, and cooperation are instrumental in rebuilding a positive family dynamic.

Incorporating self-care practices for all family members is critical. The experience of abuse can be emotionally draining and exhausting, leading to burnout and decreased resilience. Establishing self-care routines, such as regular exercise, meditation, or pursuing hobbies, can help to reduce stress and increase emotional well-being. Parents need to model healthy self-care behaviors for their children, demonstrating that taking care of oneself is not selfish, but essential for effective parenting and family well-being. Encouraging and supporting each other's self-care practices fosters a strong and supportive family unit.

The path to rebuilding healthy family relationships after escaping abuse is a challenging but rewarding journey. It demands patience, understanding, and a unwavering commitment from every family member. Seeking professional help from a therapist specializing in trauma recovery is crucial for navigating this complex process and ensuring that all members of the family receive the support they need. By actively working together, communicating openly, and establishing healthy boundaries, families can heal from the past and build a brighter, safer future.

Remember that healing is possible, and the journey toward rebuilding strong, healthy relationships is a testament to the resilience and strength of the family unit. The investment in therapy and family sessions will pay dividends in the long run, ensuring a foundation built on trust, respect, and genuine connection. The process requires time, understanding, and a consistent commitment to healing, but the result is a family strengthened by overcoming adversity. This is a testament to the family's resilience and a powerful example of human capacity for recovery and growth.

Understanding Legal Definitions of Abuse

Understanding the legal definitions of abuse is crucial for victims seeking protection and justice. The insidious nature of sociopathic abuse often makes it difficult to articulate the harm inflicted, especially when the abuser skillfully manipulates and gaslights their victim. Legal definitions provide a framework for understanding the severity of the abuse and the available legal recourse. It's important to remember that legal definitions vary across jurisdictions, so it's crucial to consult with a legal professional familiar with the specific laws in your area.

Physical abuse, the most readily identifiable form of abuse, involves any intentional act causing physical harm or injury. This ranges from slapping and hitting to more severe forms of violence resulting in serious bodily injury or even death. Bruises, cuts, broken bones, and other physical manifestations of violence are clear indicators. However, the subtle nature of some forms of physical abuse makes it harder to detect. For example, withholding necessary medication from a dependent person could also be considered physical abuse, as could controlling access to food or medical care. The intent to cause harm is a key element of the legal definition, and proving intent can sometimes be challenging. Documentation, such as photographs of injuries, medical records, and witness testimonies, becomes crucial evidence.

Emotional abuse, though less visible than physical abuse, is equally devastating. It involves a pattern of behavior designed to control, manipulate, and degrade a person's emotional well-being. Gaslighting, a common tactic employed by sociopaths, is a form of emotional abuse where

the abuser systematically distorts reality, making the victim question their own sanity and perception of events. Isolation from friends and family, constant criticism and belittling, threats and intimidation, and the manipulation of guilt and shame are all hallmarks of emotional abuse. Legally proving emotional abuse can be complex. It often requires building a case based on a pattern of behavior, corroborated by documentation like emails, text messages, and diary entries illustrating the abuser's manipulative tactics and the victim's emotional distress. Witness testimonies from family and friends who observed the abuser's behavior can also be vital.

Financial abuse involves the exploitation of a person's financial resources. This can manifest in various ways, from subtly controlling access to bank accounts and credit cards to outright theft and fraud. Forcing a victim to sign over assets, preventing them from working, controlling their spending, or using their money without their consent are all examples of financial abuse. The legal ramifications of financial abuse can be serious, involving charges such as theft, fraud, and embezzlement. Detailed financial records, bank statements, and legal documentation of any transactions are crucial for building a strong legal case. Understanding the financial aspects of the abuse and how the abuser manipulated the victim's resources is essential for restitution and preventing future financial exploitation.

Sexual abuse, a profound violation of personal boundaries, encompasses any form of non-consensual sexual contact.

This includes rape, sexual assault, sexual harassment, and any other act of a sexual nature imposed without consent. The legal definition of consent is crucial here, emphasizing that consent must be freely given, informed, and ongoing. Any form of coercion, intimidation, or manipulation to obtain sexual compliance is considered non-consensual and falls under the definition of sexual abuse. Gathering

evidence in cases of sexual abuse often requires a sensitive and thorough approach. Medical examinations, forensic evidence, and witness testimonies can all be vital in building a case. The psychological impact of sexual abuse is significant, and legal support can provide a path toward justice and healing.

Stalking, a form of abuse that frequently overlaps with other types, involves repeated harassment and unwanted pursuit that creates a reasonable fear of harm or death. This can manifest in various ways, from sending unwanted messages and emails to following the victim's movements, making threatening phone calls, or showing up unexpectedly at their home or workplace. The key element of stalking is the creation of fear and intimidation, regardless of the specific actions taken. The use of technology for stalking, such as tracking a victim's location through GPS or monitoring their online activity, adds another layer of complexity.

Documentation of the stalking behaviors, including dates, times, and specifics of each incident, is crucial for legal action. This could involve saving messages, emails, texts, and maintaining a detailed log of incidents.

Neglect, often overlooked as a form of abuse, involves the failure to provide necessary care or support to someone dependent on you. This can range from neglecting a child's basic needs like food, clothing, and shelter, to neglecting the care of an elderly parent or other vulnerable individual. The legal definitions of neglect often specify a duty of care and a failure to fulfill that duty, resulting in harm or potential harm to the victim. Evidence of neglect might include a lack of proper medical care, insufficient food, unsanitary living conditions, or a general failure to meet the needs of the dependent individual. Documentation of this failure to provide care, along with evidence of the resulting harm, is crucial for legal recourse.

Cyber abuse, a relatively new form of abuse enabled by technology, utilizes digital platforms to inflict harm. This can include cyberstalking, online harassment, the dissemination of intimate images without consent (revenge porn), or online threats and intimidation. The legal framework for cyber abuse is still evolving, but many jurisdictions recognize the severity of the harm inflicted and are enacting laws to protect victims. Preserving evidence of cyber abuse, such as screenshots of harassing messages, emails, and social media posts, is critical. Knowing the platforms where the abuse occurred and understanding the relevant terms of service is important for legal action.

Understanding the specific legal definitions of these various forms of abuse is only the first step. Seeking legal counsel is essential to navigate the complexities of the legal system and to ensure that victims' rights are protected. Legal professionals can help victims gather evidence, file for restraining orders, pursue criminal charges against abusers, and seek compensation for damages incurred. The process can be long and challenging, but having legal support is invaluable in achieving justice and securing a safe future.

Remember, you are not alone, and seeking help is a sign of strength, not weakness. The legal system offers avenues for protection and recourse, but navigating this system often requires professional assistance. The trauma of abuse can significantly impair one's ability to advocate effectively for themselves, underscoring the importance of seeking professional legal support.

Gathering Evidence and Documentation

Gathering and preserving evidence is paramount in cases of abuse, especially when dealing with a sociopath whose manipulative tactics often aim to discredit or undermine the victim's account. The goal is not just to remember what happened, but to create a comprehensive, verifiable record that stands up in a court of law or other legal setting. This process requires meticulous attention to detail and a systematic approach. The more organized and thorough your documentation, the stronger your case will be.

Start by creating a dedicated journal or digital document. This will be your central repository for recording every instance of abuse, no matter how seemingly insignificant it may appear at the time. Include dates, times, locations, and detailed descriptions of each incident. If possible, note the presence of any witnesses. The level of detail is crucial. For example, instead of simply writing "He yelled at me," write, "On July 15th, at 8:00 PM in the kitchen, he yelled at me for burning dinner. He used foul language, calling me incompetent and useless. His voice was loud enough that our neighbor, Mrs. Smith (apartment 3B), could likely hear it."

Beyond your journal, meticulously preserve any evidence that supports your claims. This includes:

Photographs and Videos: If you have sustained any physical injuries, photograph them immediately. Take multiple pictures from different angles, documenting the extent of the bruising, cuts, or other marks. If possible, take pictures before the injuries heal to capture their full extent. Similarly, if there is evidence of property damage caused by the abuser, document it with photographs. Video recordings,

if safely obtained, can be powerful evidence of abusive behavior. Remember to be mindful of your safety when capturing such evidence.

Text Messages, Emails, and Social Media Posts: Save every text message, email, and social media post that contains evidence of abusive behavior. Screenshot conversations and download messages to preserve them even if deleted by the abuser. Many messaging platforms offer ways to download conversation histories. Be aware that the content of such messages can be a double-edged sword, so it's best to carefully review everything and ensure that you are only submitting relevant and pertinent information to your legal team.

Voicemails: If you have received abusive voicemails, save them. Most phones allow you to save voicemails directly, often storing them digitally in an accessible format.

Financial Records: Keep meticulous records of all financial transactions, especially those showing unusual activity or instances of financial control or manipulation. Gather bank statements, credit card statements, loan documents, and any other financial records that demonstrate the abuser's control over your finances. Note any instances where funds were withheld, misused, or improperly accessed.

Medical Records: If you've sought medical attention due to physical or emotional distress caused by the abuse, obtain copies of your medical records. These records will provide documentation of your injuries and the treatment you received, corroborating your claims of physical or emotional harm.

Witness Testimony: Identify anyone who witnessed incidents of abuse. Collect contact information and written

statements from those individuals willing to testify on your behalf. The more witnesses who can corroborate your account, the stronger your case will become. Consider speaking to these witnesses with your lawyer present.

Police Reports: If you have filed any police reports, keep copies of those reports as part of your evidence. Maintain a detailed record of every interaction with law enforcement, including dates, times, and the names of the officers involved.

Security Camera Footage: If there is security camera footage showing incidents of abuse or the abuser's behavior, request copies of this footage, if possible. This footage can act as an unbiased third-party account. Ensure you have permission to access and use the footage.

Legal Documents: Keep all legal documents relating to your case in a secure and organized manner. This includes restraining orders, protection orders, court documents, and correspondence with your attorney.

Diary Entries or Personal Writings: If you have kept a diary or journal where you documented your experiences, this can serve as a valuable source of evidence. Note that even if you did not write about events in a diary, recalling events from memory and recording them into your evidence journal can still act as helpful supplementary evidence.

Remember that consistency is key.

Remember, consistency is crucial throughout the evidence- gathering process. Try to maintain a chronological order, and ensure that all your documentation is accurate and factual.

Avoid speculation or emotional outbursts in your written records. Focus on presenting a clear, objective account of what occurred. Keep all your collected evidence in a secure

location, ideally inaccessible to the abuser. Consider using a cloud-based storage system with strong password protection, or a safety deposit box.

Consider consulting with a forensic psychologist or trauma specialist. These professionals can help you articulate the impact of the abuse on your mental and emotional well- being, which can be crucial for legal proceedings. They can provide professional corroboration for the impact of the abuse.

The legal process can be daunting, but having a strong evidentiary foundation increases your chances of a positive outcome. Remember to be patient, persistent, and prioritize your safety throughout this process. It is essential to understand that gathering evidence might take time and effort, but it is an invaluable investment in your safety and well-being. The goal is to build a comprehensive and compelling narrative that leaves no room for doubt regarding the reality of the abuse and its impact. This robust record will serve as a powerful testament to your experience and a crucial tool in seeking justice and reclaiming your life. Do not hesitate to seek help from professionals – lawyers, therapists, and support groups – who can guide you through this challenging process. Your safety and well-being are paramount.

Seeking Legal Representation and Advice

Navigating the legal system after experiencing abuse by a sociopath can feel overwhelming, but securing legal representation is a crucial step towards protecting yourself and securing your future. Finding the right lawyer is paramount, as their expertise and understanding of sociopathic manipulation will significantly impact the outcome of any legal proceedings. Don't underestimate the importance of this choice; the wrong lawyer could inadvertently undermine your case and potentially expose you to further harm.

First, prioritize finding a lawyer specializing in domestic violence or family law cases involving abuse. These lawyers possess a deep understanding of the dynamics of abusive relationships, including the manipulative tactics often employed by sociopaths. Their experience equips them to effectively navigate the complexities of your situation, anticipating the abuser's strategies and countering them effectively. General practice lawyers, while well-intentioned, may lack the specialized knowledge needed to handle the nuances of abuse cases. This specialized knowledge is critical; it's not simply a matter of presenting evidence; it's about presenting that evidence in a way that resonates with the court and counters the manipulative narratives often employed by abusers.

Your network can be a valuable resource in your search. Start by reaching out to trusted friends, family members, therapists, support groups, or domestic violence shelters. These individuals may have personal recommendations or know of lawyers with a proven track record of success in similar cases. Don't hesitate to ask for referrals; their insights

can save you valuable time and prevent you from inadvertently choosing an unqualified or unsuitable representative. Remember, word-of-mouth recommendations often offer a more realistic and reliable assessment of a lawyer's capabilities than online reviews alone.

Online directories and legal aid organizations can also assist in your search. Many bar associations maintain online directories of lawyers, often categorized by area of specialization. This allows you to filter your search to find lawyers specializing in domestic violence or family law in your geographic area. Similarly, legal aid organizations often provide referrals to attorneys who offer pro bono or reduced- fee services to individuals who cannot afford legal representation. Remember to thoroughly vet any lawyer you find through online resources, checking their credentials and reviews before contacting them. Always verify their license and any disciplinary actions taken against them.

Once you have a list of potential lawyers, schedule initial consultations. Most lawyers offer free or low-cost initial consultations, providing you with an opportunity to assess their suitability. During these consultations, pay close attention to the lawyer's demeanor, listening skills, and understanding of your situation. Do they actively listen to your experiences, validate your feelings, and demonstrate empathy? Or do they minimize your concerns or seem dismissive of the abuse you have endured? The attorney- client relationship is built on trust and mutual respect; if you don't feel comfortable with the lawyer, it's crucial to continue your search.

Ask prospective lawyers about their experience handling cases similar to yours. Inquire about their success rate in such cases and their strategies for addressing the specific challenges posed by sociopathic manipulators.

Understanding their approach to evidence presentation, witness examination, and cross-examination is crucial. Don't hesitate to ask detailed questions about their fee structure, payment plans, and the expected timeline of your case.

Transparency and clear communication are essential in building a productive attorney-client relationship.

Consider consulting with multiple lawyers before making a decision. This comparative approach allows you to evaluate different legal strategies, fee structures, and personality styles to find the best fit for your needs and preferences.

Your comfort level with the lawyer is critical; the legal process can be long and stressful, and having a lawyer you trust and feel comfortable with is vital for your emotional well-being.

Remember that obtaining legal representation is not just about winning a court case; it's about protecting your safety and well-being during and after the legal proceedings. A skilled lawyer can help you secure restraining orders, protection orders, or other legal protections against your abuser. They can also assist with custody disputes, property division, or other legal matters arising from the abusive relationship. Moreover, having a lawyer on your side provides a crucial layer of support and guidance during what can be an emotionally draining and complex process. They will act as your advocate, navigating the legal system on your behalf and ensuring that your rights are protected.

Beyond legal representation, consider exploring resources offered by local domestic violence shelters or advocacy groups. These organizations often provide legal advocacy services, assisting survivors in navigating the legal system and connecting them with pro bono attorneys or reduced-fee legal services. Their support extends beyond legal aid, often encompassing counseling, support groups, and safe housing options. Their staff typically has extensive experience working with survivors of abuse, providing emotional support and practical assistance throughout the challenging recovery process.

If you're struggling to afford legal representation, explore options such as legal aid societies, pro bono programs offered by bar associations, or government-funded assistance programs. These resources can provide access to legal services at reduced cost or completely free of charge. Don't let financial constraints prevent you from seeking the legal protection and support you deserve. Your safety and well- being should always be the priority.

The legal process is often complex and protracted. Be prepared for delays, setbacks, and potential emotional challenges. Your lawyer should be a reliable source of information and support throughout this process. Maintain open communication with your lawyer, promptly responding to requests for information and keeping them updated on any relevant developments. Remember that patience and persistence are crucial; the legal system may move slowly, but your perseverance will ultimately contribute to a more positive outcome.

Seeking legal representation is a significant step in reclaiming your life after experiencing abuse. It provides crucial protection, empowers you to assert your rights, and establishes a foundation for rebuilding your life free from fear and intimidation. Remember that you deserve support and justice, and finding the right legal counsel is a critical step towards achieving both. The road ahead may be challenging, but with the right support, you can navigate this process and emerge stronger and safer. Remember, your safety and well-being are paramount, and seeking legal counsel is a vital step in securing them.

Navigating Legal Procedures and Processes

The emotional toll of escaping an abusive relationship often overshadows the practical steps needed to secure your safety and future. While finding a skilled lawyer is crucial, the legal process itself presents a new set of challenges.

Understanding these procedures, from obtaining protective orders to navigating divorce and custody battles, is vital for reclaiming your life. This understanding empowers you to navigate the complexities of the legal system with greater confidence and clarity.

One of the most immediate concerns for many survivors is securing a restraining order or protection order. These legal instruments aim to create a physical barrier between you and your abuser, preventing further contact and ensuring your safety. The process for obtaining a restraining order varies by jurisdiction, but typically involves submitting a petition to a court detailing the abuse you've experienced. This petition will include specific instances of abuse, dates, locations, and any evidence you have supporting your claims. This evidence could include photos, texts, emails, medical records documenting injuries, police reports, and witness statements. The court will then review your petition and, if they find sufficient evidence, issue a temporary restraining order. This order will be served on the abuser, and a hearing will be scheduled to determine whether a permanent order should be granted. At this hearing, you'll have the opportunity to present your case before a judge. The abuser may also present their case and attempt to challenge the claims.

Preparing for this hearing requires careful organization and meticulous record-keeping. Document everything – dates, times, locations, descriptions of events, any witnesses, and

the impact of the abuse on you. Even seemingly insignificant details can become critical pieces of evidence when presented in a coherent and compelling narrative. A skilled lawyer can help you gather and organize this evidence, ensuring it's presented in the most effective manner. They will also advise you on what to expect during the hearing and coach you on how to testify clearly and convincingly, even under pressure. Remember, the judge's decision is based on the evidence presented; being thoroughly prepared is crucial for a successful outcome.

Beyond restraining orders, many survivors face the complex legal issues surrounding divorce and custody arrangements. If you're married to your abuser, the divorce process can be particularly challenging, fraught with emotional distress and legal complexities. Navigating property division, spousal support, and child custody agreements requires a deep understanding of family law and the ability to effectively present your case to the court. The emotional manipulation you've experienced from a sociopath will likely be mirrored in the courtroom as your abuser employs similar tactics to influence the outcome. Therefore, having legal counsel deeply familiar with these manipulative strategies is paramount.

Child custody arrangements, in particular, are high-stakes matters, often deeply entwined with the safety and well- being of the children involved. Judges prioritize the child's best interests, considering factors such as each parent's ability to provide a safe, stable, and nurturing environment. Evidence of abuse, whether physical, emotional, or financial, heavily influences the court's decision-making process. Your lawyer will meticulously document the instances of abuse, their effect on your children, and the potential risks associated with the abuser having access to them. They will utilize psychological evaluations, school records, and

witness statements to demonstrate the dangers of leaving the children in the abuser's custody. They will also help you develop a comprehensive parenting plan that prioritizes the children's safety, well-being, and stability.

Financial issues frequently arise during the legal proceedings. Sociopaths often exert significant control over finances within the relationship, leaving victims financially vulnerable upon separation. This can include hiding assets, controlling bank accounts, and manipulating financial records. Your lawyer will work to uncover any hidden assets, ensuring a fair and equitable division of marital property.

They will also guide you through the process of obtaining spousal support, addressing any financial inequalities created by the abuse. These financial aspects can be a protracted part of the legal process and require patience and meticulous documentation.

Navigating these legal procedures requires resilience and strength. The process can be lengthy, stressful, and emotionally demanding. However, remember that you are not alone. Support groups, therapists, and advocates can provide invaluable emotional support and guidance throughout this difficult time. They can help you process the trauma you've experienced, manage stress, and maintain hope during the legal proceedings. Moreover, they can offer practical assistance, such as connecting you with additional resources or helping you navigate bureaucratic hurdles.

Furthermore, understanding your rights is crucial. Familiarize yourself with your state's laws regarding domestic violence, restraining orders, divorce, and child custody. While a lawyer will handle the legal aspects, having a basic understanding of the legal framework enhances your ability to participate effectively in the process and advocate for your own needs and those of your children. The

information available online and through legal aid organizations can offer a starting point for this education.

The legal process after escaping abuse from a sociopath can be a long and arduous journey. However, by securing the right legal representation and understanding the procedures involved, you can significantly increase your chances of securing your safety and building a future free from fear and intimidation. Remember, seeking legal assistance is a critical step towards reclaiming your life and empowering yourself to move forward. Your safety, well-being, and the well-being of your children are paramount, and taking proactive legal steps is a powerful act of self-preservation. Don't underestimate the importance of this process; it is a crucial foundation for rebuilding your life and ensuring your future is safe and secure. The legal system, although imperfect, offers a means to protect yourself and to hold your abuser accountable. Taking these steps demonstrates your strength and your commitment to a life free from abuse.

Understanding Your Rights and Legal Protections

Understanding your rights is the first step towards reclaiming your power and securing your future after escaping an abusive relationship with a sociopath. The legal system, while often complex and frustrating, offers crucial protections and avenues for redress. This section outlines some of the key legal remedies and support systems available to survivors of abuse. Remember, the specifics of these laws and procedures vary by jurisdiction (state and even county), so it's vital to seek legal counsel in your specific area. This information is for educational purposes and not a substitute for professional legal advice.

One crucial area is the protection afforded by restraining orders, also known as protection orders or civil protection orders. These are court orders that legally prohibit an abuser from contacting you, coming near your home or workplace, or engaging in other specified behaviors. To obtain a restraining order, you'll generally need to file a petition with the court detailing the abuse you've suffered. This documentation is critical; meticulous record-keeping is your most powerful weapon. Keep a detailed journal, save all communications (texts, emails, voicemails), and collect any physical evidence of abuse, such as photographs of injuries or damaged property. If possible, obtain witness statements from friends, family, neighbors, or coworkers who have witnessed the abuse. Police reports, medical records, and therapy notes can also be invaluable evidence.

The petition process often involves detailing specific instances of abuse, providing dates, times, locations, and a description of the events. The clearer and more comprehensive your documentation, the stronger your case

will be. This is where the manipulative tactics of a sociopath become particularly challenging. They are masters of gaslighting and distortion, and they may attempt to discredit your claims, even presenting themselves as the victim.

Therefore, it is vital to present your evidence in a clear, organized, and unemotional manner, focusing solely on the facts. Your lawyer will be instrumental in guiding you through this process, helping you present a strong case to the court.

Once a petition is filed, the court usually issues a temporary restraining order, immediately barring the abuser from contact. A hearing is then scheduled to determine whether to grant a permanent restraining order. This hearing requires preparation. You might be required to testify, and the abuser may also present their version of events. Therefore, practice your testimony beforehand with your lawyer. Anticipate potential lines of questioning and rehearse your responses, focusing on factual accuracy and emotional composure.

Remember, the judge's decision is based on the evidence presented, not on emotional displays. Your calm, collected presentation strengthens your credibility. Moreover, during this time, consider seeking therapy to manage the stress and emotional turmoil of the legal proceedings, which can be emotionally taxing.

Beyond restraining orders, the legal process can extend to divorce proceedings if you were married to the abuser.

Divorce involving a sociopath presents unique complexities, often fueled by their manipulative tactics. They might attempt to control the process, hide assets, or use the children as pawns. Therefore, a strong legal team that understands the manipulative characteristics of sociopaths is crucial. Your lawyer will help navigate the intricacies of property division, spousal support, and child custody,

ensuring your rights are protected and your financial security is addressed.

The division of marital assets is a critical component of divorce proceedings. Sociopaths often exhibit financial manipulation, hiding assets, making fraudulent transactions, or using joint accounts to their advantage. Your lawyer will work to uncover any hidden assets, ensuring a fair and equitable division of marital property. This may involve financial investigations and forensic accounting. You will need to present comprehensive financial documents to the court, detailing your assets, debts, and income.

Child custody arrangements present another layer of complexity. The court's primary concern is always the child's best interests, and evidence of abuse—physical, emotional, or financial—heavily influences the judge's decision. Your lawyer will meticulously document the abuse, its impact on your children, and the potential risks of the abuser having access to them. This can include psychological evaluations of both parents and the children, school records demonstrating the children's emotional well-being, and witness statements from family, friends, or teachers. A comprehensive parenting plan that prioritizes the children's safety and stability is essential. The aim is not only to keep your children safe from harm but to minimize the disruption of their lives during this difficult period. You may consider having a neutral third-party professional such as a child psychologist prepare a report that is then presented to the court.

The financial aspects of separation are often intertwined with the emotional manipulation. Sociopaths might control the family finances, leaving the victim financially vulnerable after separation. Your lawyer will assist you in obtaining spousal support (alimony) to address any financial disparities

created by the abuse. They will help you navigate the complexities of obtaining any financial assistance you are legally entitled to and to safeguard your financial well-being. This may involve seeking additional legal expertise in areas of financial fraud, depending on the level of financial manipulation the sociopath exerted during the relationship.

Throughout these legal proceedings, remember that you are not alone. Support systems are critical. Support groups specifically for survivors of abuse can provide a sense of community and shared experience. They offer a safe space to share your feelings and experiences, and you can gain support and encouragement from others who understand what you're going through. Moreover, therapy can provide invaluable emotional support, helping you process the trauma and cope with the stress of the legal process. Therapy can also aid in rebuilding your self-esteem and reclaiming your sense of self after the manipulative tactics of your abuser have eroded your sense of worth.

Legal aid organizations can provide legal assistance and information to those who cannot afford a private attorney. These organizations offer free or low-cost legal services and can advocate for your rights in court. They may assist in preparing your legal documents, represent you in court, and provide crucial information about your rights. It's worth researching legal aid services in your local area to see what kind of support they can offer.

Remember, the legal process can be lengthy, complex, and emotionally challenging. It requires patience, resilience, and a strong support system. However, understanding your rights and accessing available legal resources is essential in protecting yourself and securing a safe future for yourself and your children. The legal system provides a framework for justice and a path towards healing and rebuilding your

life, free from fear and control. Don't hesitate to seek the support you need and remember that your safety and well- being are paramount. You deserve to live a life free from abuse.

Protecting Your Online Privacy and Security

Reclaiming your digital life after escaping abuse requires a proactive approach to online privacy and security. Your abuser, especially if they are a sociopath, may have had extensive access to your online accounts, devices, and personal information. This access could range from knowing your passwords and login details to having installed spyware or monitoring software on your devices. Securing your digital presence is a critical step in establishing a safe and independent life. It's not just about preventing further harassment; it's about regaining control over your personal information and rebuilding your sense of privacy.

The first step is a thorough audit of your online accounts. Start by listing every online account you can think of: email accounts (personal and work), social media platforms (Facebook, Instagram, Twitter, TikTok, LinkedIn, etc.), online banking portals, shopping accounts (Amazon, eBay, etc.), subscription services (Netflix, Spotify, etc.), cloud storage accounts (Google Drive, Dropbox, iCloud, etc.), and any other online services you use regularly. This process can be overwhelming, but it's crucial to identify every potential point of vulnerability. Don't be afraid to reach out to a trusted friend or family member for help with this process.

They can assist in identifying accounts you might have overlooked or forgotten.

Once you have a comprehensive list, it's time to begin securing each account individually. The most crucial element is changing your passwords. Don't simply change them to a slightly modified version of your old passwords. This is easily guessed by someone familiar with your past practices. Instead, create strong, unique passwords for each account.

This means using a combination of uppercase and lowercase letters, numbers, and symbols. Aim for passwords that are at least 12 characters long, or even longer if possible. Avoid using personal information like your birthday, pet's name, or address in your passwords. If this feels overwhelming, consider using a reputable password manager. Password managers generate strong, unique passwords and securely store them for you, eliminating the need to remember them all.

Beyond password complexity, consider the strength of your security questions. Many online services use security questions as a backup method for password recovery. These questions often seem straightforward, such as "What is your mother's maiden name?" However, a sociopath might know the answer. Instead, choose security questions with less common answers. For example, "What was the name of your first teacher?", "What was the title of your favorite childhood book?", or "What is your favorite type of tree?". The more obscure the answer, the harder it will be for someone to guess. If possible, use different answers for each account.

Next, enable two-factor authentication (2FA) wherever possible. 2FA adds an extra layer of security by requiring a second form of verification beyond your password, such as a code sent to your phone via text message or a notification from an authenticator app. Even if someone gains access to your password, they will still need your phone to log in. This significantly reduces the risk of unauthorized access.

Activating 2FA should be a top priority for all accounts that contain sensitive information, such as your banking details or email accounts. Check each account individually to ensure 2FA is activated; don't assume it's enabled by default.

Review your privacy settings on all social media and online platforms. Social media can be a breeding ground for

harassment and stalking, and careful management of your privacy settings can significantly reduce your vulnerability. Limit the visibility of your posts and information to only your close friends and family. Be mindful of the information you share online, particularly details that could be used to identify your location or personal habits. Avoid posting real- time location updates or details about your daily routines.

Remember that anything you post online can be used against you, so exercise caution and discretion.

Consider reviewing your social media connections. Are there any accounts connected to your abuser, or individuals who might share information with them? Removing or blocking such accounts could prevent your abuser from monitoring your online activity. Remember that an abusive relationship often involves a manipulation of your support networks. The abuser may have fostered relationships with people in your circle, either for social support or to gain information.

Assessing who you have online connections with is an important step in rebuilding your support networks and establishing firm boundaries.

Update the software on all your devices regularly. Software updates often include security patches that address vulnerabilities exploited by hackers and malware. Neglecting to update your software can make your devices vulnerable to attacks. This includes your computer, phone, tablet, and any other smart devices you use. Enable automatic updates wherever possible to ensure your devices are always running the latest and most secure software versions.

Regularly review your device's security settings. Make sure you have strong security measures in place, such as password protection and screen locks. Consider using biometric authentication, such as fingerprint or facial recognition, for additional security. For your computer,

enable a firewall to help protect against unauthorized access. Install reputable antivirus and anti-malware software and keep it updated.

Be cautious about clicking links or downloading attachments from unknown or untrusted sources. These can often contain malware or phishing scams designed to steal your personal information. Never open emails or messages from senders you don't recognize. If you're unsure about the legitimacy of a link or email, contact the sender directly through a known channel to verify its authenticity. Be particularly wary of emails or messages that ask for personal information, such as your passwords or bank details; legitimate organizations will rarely request this information via email.

Consider using a virtual private network (VPN) for enhanced online privacy. A VPN encrypts your internet traffic and masks your IP address, making it harder for others to track your online activity. This is especially important if you are using public Wi-Fi networks, which are often less secure. A VPN adds a layer of protection against surveillance and helps to safeguard your online privacy.

If you suspect your devices have been compromised, take immediate action. Change all your passwords, run a full scan with your antivirus software, and consider seeking professional assistance from a cybersecurity expert to help you identify and remove any malware or spyware.

Remember that removing malicious software from your system often requires specialized expertise and tools.

Finally, it's important to remember that online security is an ongoing process. Regularly review your security practices and stay updated on the latest threats and best practices. The digital landscape is constantly evolving, and staying informed is critical to maintaining your online safety and

privacy. Consider seeking help from a technology professional or computer support service. They may assist in updating and securing your devices, providing more peace of mind and increasing your comfort level with technology.

These resources can also provide training and guidance on establishing secure online habits.

The journey to recovery after escaping an abusive relationship is multifaceted. Securing your online privacy and security is not just a technical task; it's a crucial step towards reclaiming your autonomy, rebuilding your confidence, and creating a safer future for yourself. This process, while demanding, is an investment in your independence and well-being, and a powerful affirmation of your right to privacy and security. It demonstrates a clear boundary: you are no longer under the control of your abuser.

Detecting and Preventing Technological Stalking

The digital realm, while offering connection and convenience, can also become a tool for insidious control and surveillance in abusive relationships. Sociopaths and stalkers are adept at exploiting technology to maintain their hold over victims, even after the physical relationship has ended. Detecting and preventing this technological stalking requires vigilance, proactive measures, and a deep understanding of how abusers leverage technology for their manipulative purposes.

One of the most common methods of technological stalking involves monitoring online activity. This might range from directly accessing a victim's accounts – through password theft, phishing scams, or spyware – to subtly tracking their online behavior. Abusers might use tracking apps disguised as seemingly harmless productivity tools, monitor browsing history through routers or shared devices, or even utilize keyloggers to record every keystroke. The aim is not just to observe, but to control and intimidate. They might use this information to exert pressure, threaten exposure of private details, or even manipulate social interactions. For example, an abuser might discover a victim's plans to meet with friends through social media posts or calendar entries, creating a situation where they feel compelled to stay home to avoid conflict.

Therefore, understanding how an abuser could be tracking your online activity is crucial for prevention. Are they unusually interested in your computer, phone, or other devices? Do they constantly ask about your online interactions? Do they seem to know details about your activities that you haven't explicitly shared? These subtle

indications can be a red flag, demanding immediate attention. If you have any suspicions, it's vital to document these instances. Keeping a detailed journal of these behaviors, noting the dates, times, and specific actions, can be valuable evidence if legal action becomes necessary.

Beyond direct access, abusers might exploit features within social media platforms and other online services to track their victim's movements and connections. This is where understanding and maximizing privacy settings becomes paramount. Many platforms offer a range of options for controlling who can see your posts, location data, and friend list. It's essential to review these settings on each platform, tightening restrictions to limit visibility to trusted individuals only. For example, on Facebook, you can adjust the audience for your posts, ensuring that only friends or a selected group of people can view your content. Similarly, you can disable location tagging on Instagram and Twitter to prevent your abuser from tracking your movements. Remember, even seemingly insignificant details, like checking in at a gym or restaurant, can be used by an abuser to triangulate your location and activities.

In addition to privacy settings, be hyper-aware of what information you are sharing online. Avoid posting real-time location updates, details about your daily routine, or anything that could potentially reveal personal information that might be useful to someone intent on tracking or harassing you. Over-sharing personal information is a common vulnerability exploited by stalkers. Think carefully before uploading photos that show your home or workplace, and be cautious about disclosing sensitive personal details, even to those you trust, as information can spread far beyond your intended audience.

Security measures are equally critical in preventing technological stalking. This begins with strong, unique passwords for every online account. Avoid easily guessed passwords or those based on personal information. Password managers are invaluable tools for generating and managing strong, unique passwords for each account. These services not only create complex passwords, but also store them securely, relieving you of the burden of remembering them.

Two-factor authentication (2FA) should be activated wherever possible. This adds an extra layer of security, requiring a secondary verification step beyond your password, usually a code sent to your phone or a notification from an authenticator app. Even if someone gains access to your password, 2FA greatly reduces the chance of them successfully logging into your account. Ensure this is enabled on all sensitive accounts, such as your banking, email, and social media profiles.

Regularly reviewing and updating the software on all your devices is crucial for minimizing vulnerabilities. Outdated software often contains security flaws that hackers can exploit to gain access to your devices and information.

Enable automatic updates where possible for computers, phones, and tablets to ensure the latest security patches are installed promptly.

Similarly, maintaining up-to-date antivirus and anti-malware software is non-negotiable. Regular scans can detect and remove malicious programs that may have been installed without your knowledge. Consider professional cybersecurity services to conduct thorough scans and check for spyware.

Be cautious about clicking on unknown links or downloading attachments from untrusted sources. These can

contain malware designed to steal your data or compromise your devices. If you are unsure about the authenticity of a link or email, do not click on it. Instead, contact the sender through a known, legitimate channel to verify the message.

Consider using a virtual private network (VPN). A VPN encrypts your internet traffic, masking your IP address and making it significantly harder for others to track your online activity. This is particularly important when using public Wi- Fi, which is generally less secure than your home network. A VPN adds an essential layer of privacy and security, especially if you suspect you might be monitored.

If you suspect your devices have been compromised, take immediate action. Change all your passwords, run a full virus scan, and consider seeking professional help from a cybersecurity expert to thoroughly investigate and remove any malicious software. This is a critical step in regaining control over your digital life and preventing further harassment.

Beyond technological solutions, fostering a strong support network is essential. Trusted friends, family members, or support groups can offer emotional support and practical advice during this difficult time. Sharing your experiences with these individuals can help you feel less isolated and more empowered. These people can also serve as an important check on your safety and well-being. If you notice significant changes in behavior or access to your online accounts, consulting your support network can offer reassurance and assistance.

Finally, remember that the fight for safety and security extends beyond the technological realm. The emotional and psychological impact of stalking is substantial, and seeking professional support is highly recommended. A therapist

specializing in trauma and abuse recovery can provide a safe space to process your experiences and develop coping mechanisms. They can assist you in navigating the complex emotional landscape associated with stalking and rebuilding your sense of safety and self-worth.

Escaping the shadow of technological stalking is a journey that requires ongoing vigilance and proactive measures. It involves not just mastering the technical aspects of online security, but also developing a profound understanding of the manipulative tactics employed by abusers and cultivating a strong support network for emotional resilience. This journey toward reclaiming your digital life is a testament to your strength and a powerful assertion of your right to live free from fear and manipulation. The process of securing your online safety is as much about regaining control of your life as it is about preventing further abuse. It's a critical step towards building a future free from the shadow of fear.

Using Technology to Enhance Safety and Security

The previous sections have highlighted the insidious ways technology can be weaponized by abusers to maintain control and inflict harm. However, technology also offers powerful tools for enhancing our safety and security.

Learning to harness these tools is crucial for reclaiming our digital lives and building a future free from fear. This section focuses on leveraging technology proactively to bolster our safety and security.

One of the most readily available and impactful tools is the use of emergency alert apps. These apps provide quick and easy access to emergency services, often with location sharing capabilities. Many offer features beyond simple dialing, such as sending pre-programmed messages to trusted contacts, detailing your location and the nature of the emergency. Some apps even integrate with wearable technology, allowing for silent alerts in situations where making a call might be dangerous. Familiarize yourself with the emergency services numbers in your region, and explore the variety of apps available, choosing one that best suits your needs and smartphone operating system. Consider having multiple backup options, given the possibility of technical failure or the abuser disabling access to specific apps.

Location-sharing apps can also be invaluable tools, especially if you are feeling unsafe or anticipating a potentially dangerous interaction. Many platforms allow you to share your real-time location with trusted contacts, providing them with ongoing awareness of your whereabouts. This can be particularly helpful if you are meeting someone new, traveling alone, or engaging in

activities that might put you at risk. Remember, it's vital to select your trusted contacts carefully. Only share your location with individuals you implicitly trust and who understand the context of your sharing. Regularly review your contact list and remove anyone who no longer needs or should not have access to this sensitive information.

Beyond real-time location sharing, consider using apps that offer personal safety monitoring features. These apps can range from simple panic buttons to more sophisticated systems that track your activity patterns and automatically alert emergency contacts if deviations occur. Some of these advanced systems can detect falls, sudden stops, or other signs of distress, providing an extra layer of protection for individuals living alone or who are at increased risk of assault. Research thoroughly before choosing a personal safety app; read reviews, compare features, and choose one that offers a combination of reliable functionality and user- friendly interface. Ensure that the app's privacy policy aligns with your comfort level regarding data collection and usage.

Beyond dedicated safety apps, we can leverage the built-in features of our smartphones and other devices. For example, using the "find my phone" functionality can be crucial in locating a stolen or lost device, which may contain sensitive information that an abuser could exploit. Understanding how to remotely wipe your device's data is also essential, preventing the abuser from accessing your personal information even after they gain possession of the device.

Familiarize yourself with these features well in advance of any potential crisis; panic often hinders effective problem- solving.

The use of strong, unique passwords is non-negotiable, as outlined previously, but extends to all aspects of your digital life. This includes not only your online accounts but also

your smart home devices, which often provide access to sensitive information, such as security camera footage or smart lock access codes. Avoid using the same password across multiple platforms; consider utilizing a password manager to generate and securely store complex, unique passwords for each account. Regularly audit your password usage, updating passwords at least every three months or after any suspected security breach.

Two-factor authentication (2FA) adds an essential layer of protection against unauthorized access. Enable it on all your sensitive accounts, including your email, bank accounts, social media, and any cloud storage services. 2FA significantly increases the difficulty for an abuser to gain access to your accounts, even if they have obtained your password. It can also help mitigate the risks associated with phishing scams, whereby abusers attempt to trick you into revealing your login credentials.

Cybersecurity hygiene goes beyond passwords and 2FA. Regularly update your operating systems, apps, and antivirus software. These updates often include crucial security patches that address vulnerabilities that hackers could exploit. Turn on automatic updates whenever possible, ensuring your devices and software are consistently up-to-date. Regularly back up your data to cloud storage or an external hard drive. This ensures you won't lose valuable information even if your device is lost, stolen, or compromised.

Consider using a virtual private network (VPN) to encrypt your internet traffic and mask your IP address. This is particularly important when using public Wi-Fi networks, which are often less secure than your home network. A VPN provides an additional layer of privacy, making it more difficult for someone to track your online activity. Be aware

that even VPNs are not foolproof, and they should be considered part of a comprehensive security strategy, rather than a standalone solution. Research reputable VPN providers before making a selection.

Be vigilant about phishing scams, malicious links, and unsolicited emails. Never click on links from unknown senders or open attachments from untrusted sources. If you suspect something is suspicious, contact the sender through a known, legitimate channel to verify the message's authenticity.

Finally, educating yourself about technology's role in abuse is a crucial part of staying safe. Regularly review security updates and articles, stay informed about new threats, and adapt your security strategies accordingly. Recognize that technological abuse is constantly evolving, and our efforts to stay safe must also evolve.

Beyond specific apps and technologies, the most powerful tool is a supportive network. Confide in trusted friends, family members, and support groups. Their awareness of your situation can provide emotional support and practical help. They can also serve as a second pair of eyes, helping to identify potential red flags or signs of technological abuse.

Open communication is crucial to maintaining safety and ensuring that your network can assist when needed.

Remember, seeking professional help from a therapist or counselor specializing in trauma and abuse recovery is essential for both emotional healing and for building long- term safety strategies. These professionals can provide valuable insights, guidance, and support in navigating the complexities of recovery and building a life free from fear.

Managing Social Media and Online Presence

The previous sections focused on practical technological tools to enhance safety. However, our online presence – our digital footprint – is another significant area requiring careful management. Social media and online platforms, while offering connection and community, can also become avenues for harassment, stalking, and continued abuse.

Learning to navigate these spaces safely and strategically is crucial for reclaiming your digital life and building a future free from fear.

One of the first steps is a thorough review of your current social media accounts. This isn't about deleting everything; it's about assessing what information is publicly available and identifying potential vulnerabilities. Consider the images you've shared, the locations you've tagged, the personal details you've disclosed in posts or comments. Does this information inadvertently reveal your daily routine, address, workplace, or other sensitive information that could be exploited by an abuser? A sociopath or stalker can use this information to plan interactions, monitor your movements, or even gain access to your physical location.

Go through your friend lists, follower lists, and connections meticulously. Are there any accounts that seem suspicious or that you no longer interact with? Remove any connections that you feel uneasy about, even if it seems insignificant.

Remember, the goal is to minimize the amount of information available to anyone who might want to harm you. This includes removing connections with individuals who the abuser might use to relay information or manipulate you indirectly.

Next, examine your privacy settings on every platform you use. Most platforms offer granular control over who can see your posts, your profile information, your location data, and your contact information. Take the time to explore these settings thoroughly and adjust them to the most restrictive level that you are comfortable with. Remember, it's far better to err on the side of caution.

Consider limiting the information you share about your personal life. Avoid posting real-time updates about your location, especially if you're alone or engaging in activities that might make you vulnerable. Think carefully about the photos and videos you share; avoid images that reveal specific details about your home, workplace, or routines.

Regularly review your posts and activity. Are there any posts that reveal more information than you intended? If so, consider deleting them. Many platforms allow for the deletion of past posts. Remember, the goal is not perfection, but consistent efforts to reduce potential vulnerabilities.

Beyond your personal accounts, consider your online presence across various platforms. Do you have any public profiles on professional networking sites like LinkedIn?

Review these profiles carefully. While professional profiles require some personal information, be mindful about what you disclose and the level of detail you provide. Avoid sharing information that could be used to track your whereabouts or identify your physical location.

Managing your online presence extends beyond social media. Think about online reviews you've written, comments you've left on articles or forums, and even your online shopping history. All these contribute to your digital footprint. While complete anonymity is nearly impossible in the digital age, striving for a degree of privacy and limiting

unnecessary disclosures is a proactive step in protecting yourself.

If you have used dating apps or other online platforms for meeting people, take extra precautions. Never share your full name, address, or workplace before you have met someone in person in a public place and feel completely safe and secure. Be cautious about sharing personal information online, especially if you don't know the person well. Always meet in a well-lit and populated public space, and always let a trusted friend or family member know where you're going and who you're meeting.

Remember, these platforms often contain algorithms that can be exploited. Abusers might leverage these algorithms to find you, track your activity, or target you with specific content. Be aware of the potential for manipulative or deceptive tactics.

Consider creating separate email addresses and accounts for different purposes. For example, use one email address for sensitive communication like financial transactions or legal matters, and another for less sensitive communications like online shopping or social media. This approach helps to compartmentalize information and limit the impact of a potential security breach.

Another important step is to be vigilant about online harassment and surveillance. Understand that even with careful management of your online presence, you may still experience online harassment or stalking. Know your rights, and report any instances of harassment or abuse to the relevant platform and authorities. Many platforms have reporting mechanisms and procedures in place to address harassment and abuse. Document all instances of online harassment, including screenshots of messages, comments,

and other evidence. This documentation can be crucial if you decide to pursue legal action.

If you are experiencing cyberstalking or online harassment, consider seeking professional support. A therapist or counselor who specializes in trauma and abuse recovery can provide valuable support and guidance in navigating this challenging situation. They can help you develop coping mechanisms, and strategies for managing your online presence safely and securely. Remember, you are not alone, and help is available.

Finally, regularly educate yourself about online safety and privacy best practices. Technology is constantly evolving, so staying informed about the latest threats and security measures is essential. There are many reputable online resources that provide guidance on online safety and privacy, and staying informed can significantly improve your ability to protect yourself online. Regularly review your security settings, and be aware of potential vulnerabilities. By taking proactive steps to manage your digital footprint and protect your online presence, you're taking a vital step toward building a safer and healthier future for yourself. Remember, regaining control over your online presence is a significant part of your journey towards recovery and healing. It's a crucial component of establishing your autonomy and personal safety in a world increasingly intertwined with technology.

Reporting Online Harassment and Abuse

The previous sections emphasized proactive measures to minimize your online vulnerability. However, even with the most diligent precautions, you may still experience online harassment or abuse. This section focuses on the crucial steps you should take if you find yourself targeted.

Remember, reporting is not about weakness; it's about actively protecting yourself and holding perpetrators accountable. Your safety and well-being are paramount.

Reporting online harassment and abuse varies depending on the platform. Each site has its own reporting mechanisms and procedures. Familiarize yourself with these processes for each platform you use. These mechanisms typically involve locating a "Report" or "Flag" button, often found near offensive content or within the profile of the abuser. Clicking this button usually opens a reporting form where you'll provide details about the incident.

Be thorough and detailed in your reports. The more information you can provide, the better equipped the platform is to investigate and take appropriate action. Include the following information whenever possible:

Specific details of the incident: Clearly describe the nature of the harassment or abuse. Were you subjected to threats, insults, stalking, doxxing (revealing personal information), or other forms of abuse? Be precise in your descriptions, detailing the exact words or actions used. Dates and times are vital for context.

Links or screenshots: Whenever feasible, provide links directly to the offensive content, or screenshots capturing the

abusive messages, images, or videos. This irrefutable evidence significantly strengthens your report and increases the likelihood of a successful investigation.

Usernames or URLs: Include the usernames or URLs of the perpetrator's accounts. This allows the platform to quickly identify and locate the individual responsible. If you're unsure of the exact username, provide any details that might help in identification, such as profile pictures, and any other identifiers.

Impact on you: Detail the emotional and psychological impact the harassment has had on you. This isn't simply about stating the facts; it's about expressing the very real harm the abuser has inflicted. Describing the anxiety, fear, distress, or other emotional consequences demonstrates the seriousness of the situation and helps the platform understand the gravity of the offense.

Previous attempts at resolution: If you've already tried to resolve the issue directly with the perpetrator (perhaps by requesting they cease their behavior), document those attempts, including dates, times, and the outcomes. This provides further context and shows that you've already made efforts to address the problem independently.

After submitting your report, you might receive an automated acknowledgment, indicating the platform has received your complaint. This doesn't guarantee immediate action, but it confirms your report has been logged.

Platforms often have different response times, and the process can take days, weeks, or even longer. Maintain patience and understand that investigations require time.

If the initial response is insufficient or you aren't satisfied with the platform's resolution, escalate your report. Most platforms have escalation channels, whether through appeals processes or direct contact with their support teams.

Persistence is key. Don't hesitate to push for a more thorough investigation or stronger action if you believe it's warranted.

Remember, reporting online abuse is not a one-time action. If the harassment continues, you must continue to report each incident. Each report provides further evidence and strengthens your case for platform intervention and potential legal action. Document each incident meticulously, saving all evidence and keeping a detailed record of your interactions with the platform's support team.

Beyond reporting to the platform itself, consider reporting the abuse to law enforcement. While platforms primarily handle violations of their terms of service, law enforcement addresses potential criminal offenses, such as threats, stalking, or harassment that may cross legal boundaries.

Different jurisdictions have different reporting procedures, but most require a police report or a formal complaint.

Gathering all available evidence—screenshots, messages, and any other supporting documentation—is crucial when reporting to law enforcement.

Working with law enforcement can be a complex process. Be prepared to provide detailed information and cooperate fully with the investigation. If you feel overwhelmed or unsure of how to proceed, seek legal counsel from a lawyer specializing in cybercrime or harassment cases. They can guide you through the legal process, ensuring your rights are protected and that you are represented effectively.

The process of reporting online harassment and abuse can be emotionally draining. Remember to prioritize your own

well-being. Talk to a trusted friend, family member, or therapist. Sharing your experience and seeking support can

significantly improve your mental and emotional health during this difficult period.

Additionally, if you are feeling particularly vulnerable or experiencing intense emotional distress, consider seeking support from a mental health professional who specializes in trauma and abuse recovery. They can provide coping mechanisms and strategies for managing the psychological impacts of online harassment. Remember, seeking professional help is a sign of strength, not weakness.

The digital age presents unique challenges, but also offers tools for accountability. By understanding the reporting processes of different platforms, persisting in your efforts, and seeking support when needed, you can effectively combat online harassment and work towards reclaiming your online safety and well-being. Remember, your experience is valid, and you have the right to feel safe online. Do not hesitate to use the resources available to you to protect yourself.

Beyond immediate reporting, consider long-term strategies. This includes building a support network of friends, family, or online communities where you can find empathy and understanding. Maintaining open communication with these individuals can be invaluable during times of stress.

Consider seeking legal advice to establish preventative measures that might discourage future online harassment, such as restraining orders or cease-and-desist letters.

Understanding that online harassment is often a manifestation of underlying issues in the abuser's life does not excuse their actions. It is important to focus on protecting yourself and seeking help, not trying to understand or "fix" the perpetrator. Their actions are solely their responsibility.

Finally, remember that your experience is not unique. Many individuals experience online harassment and abuse. Seeking out support groups, either online or in person, can provide a sense of community and shared experience, reminding you that you are not alone in this struggle. These groups offer a platform for sharing experiences, advice, and mutual support. They can be invaluable resources in your journey towards recovery and reclaiming your digital life. Your recovery is a journey, and you have the power to navigate it with resilience and strength.

Identifying Local Resources and Services

Leaving an abusive relationship, especially one involving a sociopath, is only the first step on a long road to recovery. The emotional, psychological, and often physical toll can be immense. While the previous chapters focused on securing your safety and protecting yourself from further harm, this section focuses on actively building a support network and accessing resources that can assist in your healing process. Finding help within your local community is crucial for long-term recovery.

Your immediate priorities after escaping an abusive situation are likely to include securing safe housing, ensuring your financial stability, and addressing your immediate physical and emotional needs. Fortunately, various local services and organizations exist to provide support during this critical time. However, navigating the system can feel overwhelming, especially when you're grappling with the emotional trauma of abuse.

One of the first resources you should locate is a domestic violence shelter or safe house. These facilities offer temporary housing, providing a safe and secure environment away from your abuser. Shelters generally provide more than just a place to sleep; they typically offer a range of services designed to help you rebuild your life. These services can include:

Emergency shelter: A safe and secure place to stay, often with 24/7 security and support staff.

Counseling and therapy: Access to professional mental health services to address the trauma and emotional distress you've experienced. This is vital in processing the events and working through the emotional aftermath. Many shelters have counselors on-staff, or can provide referrals to outside therapists specializing in trauma and abuse recovery.

Legal assistance: Advice and support from legal professionals to help you navigate the legal system, including obtaining restraining orders, filing for divorce, or pursuing other legal options.

Financial assistance: Help with obtaining financial aid, food stamps, or other forms of government assistance to meet your immediate needs. Sociopaths often exert financial control over their victims, so regaining financial independence is a crucial aspect of recovery.

Job training and placement: Support in finding employment to achieve financial stability. This can include job skills training, resume writing assistance, and job placement services.

Childcare: If you have children, shelters usually provide childcare services, allowing you to focus on your recovery without worrying about childcare logistics.

Support groups: Opportunities to connect with other survivors of abuse, creating a supportive community and fostering a sense of shared experience.

Finding the nearest shelter requires research and might feel daunting in your current state. However, there are several ways to locate this crucial resource.

Online searches: Search online using terms such as "domestic violence shelter [your city/county]", "safe house [your city/county]", or "women's shelter [your city/county]". **National Domestic Violence Hotline:** The National Domestic Violence Hotline (1-800-799-SAFE) provides a 24/7 helpline that can connect you to local shelters and resources in your area. They can offer immediate support and guidance in locating nearby safe havens. Don't hesitate

to call; they are a valuable lifeline during this challenging time.

Local law enforcement: Police departments and sheriff's offices are often aware of the location and services of local shelters. They can provide direct referrals and assistance.

Hospitals and emergency rooms: If you present at a hospital or emergency room due to injuries sustained from abuse, the staff can connect you to local shelter services.

Social services agencies: Local social service agencies, such as your county's Department of Social Services or Human Services department, maintain databases of local resources and can assist in connecting you with appropriate shelters.

Beyond shelters, there are several other essential local resources available to support you. Support groups offer a crucial environment of shared experience and mutual understanding. Connecting with other survivors provides validation of your experiences, reduces feelings of isolation, and creates a community of support during your healing journey. Many local organizations and community centers offer support groups specifically designed for survivors of domestic violence or abuse from sociopaths. These groups provide a safe space to share your experiences, learn coping mechanisms, and find strength in the shared experiences of others.

Counseling and therapy are vital for processing the trauma of abuse. A qualified therapist specializing in trauma and abuse recovery can provide the tools and techniques to help you understand your experiences, heal from the emotional wounds inflicted by the abuse, and develop strategies for building a healthier future. Finding a therapist can be done through several means:

Your primary care physician: Your doctor can often provide referrals to therapists in your area.

Insurance provider: If you have health insurance, contact your provider to get a list of therapists in your network.

Online directories: Websites such as Psychology Today or Zocdoc allow you to search for therapists based on specialization, location, and insurance. It's important to look for therapists with specific experience in trauma and abuse recovery, as they have the expertise to address the unique challenges you face.

Local mental health centers: Your county or state may have a mental health center offering services at a reduced or sliding scale cost. This is particularly important if financial constraints are a factor in seeking professional help.

Remember, seeking professional help is a sign of strength, not weakness. Your mental and emotional health is paramount, and investing in your well-being is crucial for long-term recovery. The abuse you endured was not your fault, and seeking support is a vital step in reclaiming your life.

Legal resources are another important aspect of your recovery. If you need to obtain a restraining order, pursue legal action against your abuser, or address issues related to custody or divorce, legal aid services can provide invaluable assistance. Legal aid societies often offer free or low-cost legal representation to those who cannot afford an attorney. Bar associations also frequently maintain referral services to connect individuals with lawyers specializing in family law or domestic violence cases. If you have suffered financial abuse, exploring avenues for financial recovery, including reporting to relevant agencies, might be necessary.

Additionally, many local organizations provide a range of practical support services such as job training programs, financial assistance, and childcare. These services assist you in becoming financially independent and rebuilding your

life. The path to recovery is a journey, not a race. Take the time you need to heal and utilize the resources available to you. Don't hesitate to reach out for help; your well-being and safety are priorities.

Remember, the resources listed above are not exhaustive; the specific organizations and services available will vary based on your location and circumstances. However, the strategies for finding them remain consistent. By conducting online searches, contacting the National Domestic Violence Hotline, reaching out to your local law enforcement or social service agencies, or seeking help from medical professionals, you can access the support you need to begin the vital journey of healing and recovery. Your strength and resilience are evident in your willingness to seek help. This is a crucial step towards building a safer, healthier future for yourself and your family. Never forget that you deserve to live free from fear and manipulation.

Utilizing Hotlines and Emergency Services

Utilizing hotlines and emergency services is often the first crucial step in escaping and recovering from abuse by a sociopath. The initial shock and disorientation can make it difficult to know where to turn, but remember that help is readily available, and reaching out is a sign of strength, not weakness. These services offer immediate support, guidance, and crucial resources during this critical period.

The National Domestic Violence Hotline (NDVH) is a beacon of hope for countless victims. The number, 1-800- 799-SAFE (7233), is easily remembered and accessible 24 hours a day, 7 days a week. It's a lifeline connecting individuals to immediate support and local resources tailored to their specific needs and location. When you call the NDVH, trained advocates provide a non-judgmental listening ear, validate your experiences, and offer immediate crisis intervention. They can help you assess your situation, develop a safety plan, and locate nearby emergency shelters, legal aid services, and counseling resources. Beyond crisis support, the NDVH offers extensive online resources including safety planning tools, information about sociopathic behavior, and guidance on navigating the legal system. Don't hesitate to call; they can provide immediate support and direct you to resources that can begin the healing process immediately. The NDVH's website also offers a live chat option for those who prefer written communication.

Beyond the NDVH, the National Sexual Assault Hotline (RAINN) is another critical resource, especially if sexual assault is part of the abuse you've endured. Dialing 800-656- HOPE connects you with trained staff who can provide

immediate support, crisis intervention, and information about local resources. RAINN also operates a website with a wealth of information on sexual assault, recovery resources, and online support communities. The hotline and online resources can be invaluable tools during the initial stages of recovery, providing immediate emotional support and practical advice.

For situations requiring immediate medical attention, hospital emergency rooms are crucial. If you have experienced physical injury, or are experiencing a mental health crisis as a result of the abuse, seeking medical attention is paramount. Hospital staff are trained to identify signs of abuse, and many have protocols in place to ensure your safety and connect you with appropriate resources.

Emergency room personnel can provide immediate medical care, stabilize your condition, and connect you with local shelters, mental health professionals, and law enforcement as needed. Don't hesitate to seek medical attention for injuries or acute mental health crises, as your physical and emotional well-being is paramount.

Law enforcement agencies are another critical point of contact, particularly if you are in immediate danger. If you believe you are in imminent danger of physical harm, call 911 immediately. Police officers are trained to respond to domestic violence situations and can provide immediate protection, ensure your safety, and assist in apprehending your abuser. Even if you're not in immediate danger, reporting the abuse to law enforcement can be crucial in building a legal case against your abuser, obtaining a restraining order, and protecting yourself from future harm. Remember, your safety is the priority.

Local crisis centers are valuable resources that often provide immediate crisis intervention, counseling, and support

services. These centers frequently have 24/7 hotlines and provide a safe space to discuss your situation and develop a personalized safety plan. They offer immediate support and can connect you with longer-term resources as you begin your recovery journey. They can also provide vital information about shelters, counseling services, legal aid, and other critical support systems in your community. They often have multilingual staff and cater to a wide array of needs.

Your primary care physician (PCP) plays a crucial role in your overall well-being and can offer valuable support during this challenging time. Your PCP can provide referrals to therapists specializing in trauma and abuse, assist with accessing necessary medications, and advocate for your needs within the healthcare system. Your PCP can also help to document any physical injuries sustained as a result of the abuse, providing vital evidence for legal purposes. Their role extends beyond immediate medical needs; they can offer ongoing support and referrals to help you rebuild your life.

Remember, the process of escaping and recovering from abuse by a sociopath is not a solitary journey. There are countless individuals and organizations dedicated to providing support, guidance, and assistance. By utilizing the services mentioned above—the National Domestic Violence Hotline, the National Sexual Assault Hotline, hospital emergency rooms, law enforcement, local crisis centers, and your primary care physician—you are taking a proactive step towards reclaiming your safety, securing your future, and embarking on your healing journey. Your courage in seeking help is commendable, and the journey, while challenging, is filled with the potential for strength, resilience, and ultimately, freedom. Never underestimate the power of reaching out; it is a testament to your inherent strength and a vital step towards a brighter future. The resources are there,

waiting to provide the support you need and deserve. You are not alone.

Connecting with Support Networks and Groups

Beyond the immediate crisis response services, building a strong support network is crucial for long-term healing and recovery. Isolation is a common tactic employed by sociopaths, designed to weaken their victims and maintain control. Breaking free from this isolation and actively cultivating connections with supportive individuals is a powerful act of self-empowerment. This network can provide emotional sustenance, practical assistance, and a sense of belonging during the often-difficult journey of recovery.

The first step in building this network may involve confiding in trusted friends or family members. However, this can be challenging. Many victims hesitate to disclose their experiences due to fear of judgment, disbelief, or further manipulation by the abuser. Remember that your feelings are valid, and you deserve understanding and support. Choosing who to confide in is a personal decision; select individuals who have demonstrated empathy, trustworthiness, and a willingness to listen without judgment. If you're unsure who to approach, start with a close friend or family member you feel most comfortable with. Begin by sharing small details and gradually increase the level of disclosure as you feel more comfortable and secure.

If confiding in family or friends isn't an option, or feels too risky, consider seeking professional support from a therapist or counselor specializing in trauma and abuse recovery.

These professionals provide a safe and confidential space to process your experiences, explore your emotions, and develop coping mechanisms. They can offer invaluable guidance, support, and validation, helping you understand

the dynamics of the abuse and develop strategies for moving forward. Many therapists offer online sessions, which can provide a degree of anonymity and convenience for those who feel apprehensive about attending in-person appointments.

Support groups offer a unique form of healing, connecting you with others who share similar experiences. The shared experience fosters a sense of community, validation, and understanding often absent in other settings. Support groups provide a safe and non-judgmental environment to openly share your feelings, struggles, and triumphs without fear of ridicule or minimization. Listening to the stories of others who have overcome similar challenges can be incredibly empowering and instill hope for your own recovery. Many support groups are specifically designed for victims of sociopathic abuse, providing a space where your experiences are fully understood and validated. This understanding is crucial in dispelling feelings of isolation and shame that are often deeply ingrained by the abuser.

Finding a support group can be as simple as searching online for groups in your area or joining online forums and communities dedicated to supporting victims of abuse. Many organizations, including the National Domestic Violence Hotline and RAINN, maintain directories of support groups and resources. Attending a support group's meeting might feel daunting initially, but remember that everyone there understands the challenges you're facing. The supportive atmosphere and shared experiences often lead to meaningful connections and a sense of belonging. These connections can transform into invaluable friendships and long-term sources of support.

Beyond formal support groups, consider building informal connections with people who share your interests and values.

Reconnect with old friends, join community organizations, or take up new hobbies. These activities provide opportunities to meet new people, build positive relationships, and focus on aspects of your life unrelated to the abuse. These new connections can serve as a source of distraction, positive reinforcement, and a sense of belonging that counters the isolation imposed by the abuser. They offer a healthy counterbalance to the negative experiences and reinforce your sense of self-worth and self-confidence.

Rebuilding your life after escaping a sociopathic relationship requires a multifaceted approach, with community involvement playing a crucial role. Volunteering at a local charity or joining a community organization can offer a sense of purpose, contribute to your personal growth, and connect you with like-minded individuals. The act of giving back to the community can be incredibly therapeutic, fostering a sense of accomplishment and providing a healthy distraction from the trauma. Furthermore, it can offer new experiences and opportunities for personal growth, fostering independence and self-reliance.

Furthermore, engaging in creative activities can be tremendously beneficial for recovery. Writing, painting, music, and other artistic pursuits can offer an outlet for emotions, promoting self-expression and healing. Creating art allows you to process your experiences in a healthy way, translate feelings into tangible forms, and regain a sense of control over your life. Many community centers and organizations offer art therapy workshops and classes specifically designed for survivors of trauma. These provide guided support and a structured environment to explore these methods of healing.

It's important to remember that building a supportive network is an ongoing process. It's not a one-time event but

rather a continuous effort to cultivate healthy, positive relationships and connections. Some relationships may blossom quickly, while others may develop gradually over time. Be patient with yourself and the process, and prioritize relationships that provide genuine support, understanding, and encouragement. Avoid relationships that drain your energy, trigger negative emotions, or reinforce feelings of self-doubt.

Be selective in choosing your support network. Choose individuals who are supportive, understanding, and non- judgmental. Individuals who minimize your experience or blame you for the abuse should be avoided. Your support network should empower you, not hinder your progress. It's also important to remember that you don't have to share all the details of your experience with everyone in your support network. Gradually revealing information as you feel comfortable and trust the individuals is acceptable and often safer.

Your support network isn't limited to individuals; pets can also provide invaluable emotional support. The unconditional love and companionship of a pet can be incredibly healing, reducing feelings of loneliness and isolation. The routine of caring for a pet can provide a sense of structure and normalcy, which can be particularly beneficial after experiencing the chaos and instability of abuse.

Building a strong support network takes time and effort, but the rewards are immeasurable. The connection, empathy, and understanding you receive from others can be transformative, enabling you to heal, grow, and rebuild your life on your own terms. Remember, you are not alone, and there is a community of people who support you on your journey to recovery and empowerment. By actively

cultivating these connections, you are taking a crucial step towards reclaiming your life and building a future free from fear and manipulation. This is a vital step in your healing journey, one that underscores your inherent resilience and strength. Embrace the process, allow yourself to be vulnerable, and recognize the immense power of connection in your healing process. The support available to you is significant, and actively seeking it is a testament to your courage and commitment to a brighter future.

Accessing Government Assistance Programs

Navigating the aftermath of sociopathic abuse often involves significant financial and logistical challenges. The emotional toll is immense, but the practical realities of rebuilding your life can feel equally overwhelming. Fortunately, various government assistance programs are designed to help survivors like you regain stability and independence. These programs recognize the unique difficulties faced by those escaping abusive situations and offer a lifeline during this critical period. Accessing these resources is a vital step in your journey toward recovery, and understanding their availability can significantly alleviate the burden and empower you to move forward with greater confidence.

One of the most immediate needs for many survivors is safe and stable housing. Domestic violence shelters provide temporary refuge, but long-term housing solutions are crucial for sustained recovery.

The Department of Housing and Urban Development (HUD) offers various housing assistance programs, including Section 8 housing vouchers. These vouchers subsidize rent, making affordable housing accessible to low-income individuals and families. Eligibility criteria vary depending on location and specific program requirements, but generally include income restrictions and a demonstration of need. Many local HUD offices also have specialized programs designed to assist victims of domestic violence, offering expedited processing and greater flexibility in eligibility requirements. It's crucial to contact your local HUD office directly to inquire about available programs and the application process. They can guide you through the necessary paperwork and inform you of any specific requirements or deadlines.

Beyond Section 8, other HUD programs might provide support. For instance, the Public Housing program offers subsidized housing in government-owned or managed units. Eligibility is based on income limits, family size, and other factors. HUD also administers various programs for individuals experiencing homelessness or facing imminent eviction, often offering assistance tailored to domestic violence survivors. These programs can provide emergency shelter, rental assistance, and case management services to help you secure long-term housing stability.

In addition to HUD, many states and localities offer their own housing assistance programs specific to domestic violence survivors. These programs often provide additional support beyond basic rental assistance. Some might offer relocation assistance to help you move to a new location, increasing your safety and independence from your abuser. Others might include supportive services such as case management, counseling, and help with finding employment. Contacting your local social services agency or domestic violence shelter is an excellent way to learn about available state and local housing programs. Many shelters have dedicated case managers who can assist you in applying for and accessing these vital resources. Don't hesitate to reach out; their expertise in navigating the bureaucratic process can significantly ease the pressure during this challenging time.

Financial hardship is another common consequence of sociopathic abuse. Abusers often exert financial control, isolating their victims from personal funds and creating significant economic insecurity. Fortunately, several federal and state programs provide financial assistance to survivors. The Temporary Assistance for Needy Families (TANF) program provides cash assistance to low-income families, including those escaping domestic violence. TANF benefits

can help cover basic living expenses like rent, food, and utilities, providing a crucial safety net during this transition. Eligibility requirements vary by state, so contacting your state's TANF agency will provide the specifics for your area.

The Supplemental Nutrition Assistance Program (SNAP), formerly known as food stamps, provides food assistance to low-income individuals and families. SNAP benefits can significantly alleviate the financial burden of feeding yourself and your family, ensuring you have access to nutritious food during a period of significant upheaval and stress. The application process and eligibility criteria vary by state but are typically straightforward and accessible.

Beyond these broad-based programs, many states offer specialized financial assistance programs for domestic violence survivors. These may include emergency cash grants to cover immediate expenses, funding for job training programs to help survivors gain employment, and assistance with paying for childcare, allowing them to pursue employment or education opportunities. Many local domestic violence shelters and social service agencies can provide information about these programs and aid you in the application process. These programs are often designed to offer rapid assistance, addressing immediate needs and paving the path toward greater long-term financial independence.

Legal assistance is another critical component of recovery. Navigating the legal system after experiencing abuse can be daunting, and many survivors lack the financial resources to hire a lawyer. Legal Aid organizations offer free or low-cost legal services to those who qualify based on income and the nature of their legal issues. They can provide representation in cases involving restraining orders, custody disputes, divorce, or other legal matters related to escaping abuse.

Legal Aid's services also extend to helping survivors understand their rights and options, ensuring they navigate the legal system with confidence and support.

The Violence Against Women Act (VAWA) provides additional legal protections for survivors of domestic violence. VAWA offers crucial resources and support, including legal assistance, access to shelters, and other essential services. It also provides enhanced protections for immigrants who are survivors of domestic violence, enabling them to obtain legal status independent of their abuser.

Many states have additional legal aid programs specifically designed to assist domestic violence survivors. These programs can provide support in obtaining restraining orders, protective orders, and assistance with custody battles. Many domestic violence shelters and advocacy groups can connect survivors with these legal resources.

Beyond immediate financial and housing needs, survivors often require access to healthcare services, particularly mental health care. The Affordable Care Act (ACA) expands access to health insurance, making healthcare more affordable for millions of Americans, including survivors of abuse. Under the ACA, individuals can obtain health insurance through the marketplace or may qualify for Medicaid. Both plans cover essential health benefits, including mental health and substance abuse services, crucial for the healing process. Affordable healthcare access ensures survivors can address physical and mental health concerns without facing insurmountable financial barriers.

The process of accessing government assistance programs can often seem complex and daunting. However, many organizations are dedicated to helping survivors navigate these systems. Domestic violence shelters, legal aid organizations, and social service agencies all offer invaluable assistance. They can explain eligibility requirements, help with applications, and advocate on your behalf. Don't hesitate to contact these organizations. Their expertise and support can significantly ease the process and ensure you access the assistance you need.

Remember, seeking government assistance isn't a sign of weakness but rather a proactive step towards building a safer and more stable future. These programs are designed to help you reclaim your independence and rebuild your life after experiencing the trauma of sociopathic abuse. Navigating the application processes and understanding the nuances of each program can feel overwhelming, but know that you're not alone. There are individuals and organizations dedicated to supporting you every step of the way. Utilize the resources available to you; it is a testament to your strength and your commitment to creating a healthier future. By taking this proactive step, you are demonstrating resilience and a determination to emerge from the shadows and embrace a future of safety, security, and self-sufficiency.

Volunteering and Giving Back

The journey out of the shadow of sociopathic abuse is arduous, a climb out of a deep, dark pit. But as you begin to feel the sun on your face, a sense of empowerment takes hold. This empowerment isn't just about reclaiming your life; it's about sharing your strength with others who are still trapped in the darkness. Volunteering and giving back to your community is not only a powerful act of self-healing, but it's also a way to pay it forward, to help others avoid the pain you've endured.

Many survivors find solace and purpose in helping others. The act of extending a hand, of offering empathy and understanding to someone experiencing a similar struggle, can be deeply cathartic. It's a way of transforming your trauma into a force for good, turning a negative experience into a catalyst for positive change. This isn't about minimizing your experience or pretending it didn't happen; it's about channeling the strength you've gained through adversity.

Consider volunteering at a local domestic violence shelter. Your firsthand experience provides invaluable insight that professionals may not possess. You can offer peer support, share your story (at your own pace and comfort level, of course), and help other survivors navigate the complexities of escaping an abusive relationship. You can offer practical assistance – helping with administrative tasks, organizing events, or even just offering a listening ear. The act of supporting others creates a ripple effect of healing, benefiting both the recipient and the giver.

Your experience also offers a unique perspective in educating others about sociopathic abuse. Many people are unaware of the insidious tactics used by abusers, and your insights can help raise awareness. You can volunteer to speak at community events, schools, or support groups. You can share your story anonymously, if preferred, focusing on the signs of abuse and strategies for escape. Educating others is a crucial step in preventing future abuse and ensuring that survivors receive the support they need. The power of your testimony lies in its authenticity, its raw honesty, and its potential to save others from suffering similar experiences.

Perhaps your skills lie in other areas. If you have a background in writing or communications, you could volunteer to write articles or blog posts for organizations working with abuse survivors. If you're skilled in graphic design, you could help create awareness campaigns. If you're adept at fundraising, you could dedicate your time to raising crucial funds for shelters and support services. The opportunities are vast and varied, allowing you to leverage your talents while supporting a cause close to your heart.

Remember that even small contributions can make a significant impact.

Consider volunteering for crisis hotlines. These lines provide crucial support to individuals in immediate danger. The training provided will equip you with the skills to effectively listen and offer support to individuals in distress, helping them develop a safety plan and connect them with appropriate resources. While the work can be emotionally demanding, it provides a powerful sense of purpose, knowing you are directly helping those in immediate crisis.

It's a way to turn your pain into action, using your experiences to help save lives.

Beyond direct work with survivors, volunteering with organizations that advocate for policy changes surrounding domestic violence can be highly impactful. You can participate in lobbying efforts, campaign for better legislation, or raise public awareness about the need for increased funding for support services. By using your voice to advocate for policy reform, you are creating lasting change that can benefit countless survivors in the future.

This form of activism is a powerful way to turn personal experience into collective action, ensuring that others have access to the resources and support you may have lacked.

Many organizations actively seek volunteers with experiences relevant to domestic violence. These organizations are committed to providing comprehensive support for survivors and often provide training to their volunteers. This training not only helps volunteers develop essential skills but also offers a supportive community and a platform to connect with like-minded individuals.

Participating in such organizations offers a sense of belonging and camaraderie, easing feelings of isolation that often accompany trauma.

Your journey toward recovery is a testament to your strength and resilience. Sharing this strength with others by volunteering and giving back is a transformative act of healing. It's an opportunity to redirect your pain, empowering you to contribute positively to your community while simultaneously enriching your own life. It is a path towards reclaiming your narrative, not as a victim, but as a survivor, a beacon of hope, and a catalyst for change. This process is about more than just helping others; it is a crucial part of your ongoing healing journey.

Remember, there's no pressure to volunteer immediately or to engage in any activity that feels overwhelming. Recovery is a journey, and it progresses at your own pace. Take time to heal, to reflect, and to identify what feels right for you. Start small, maybe with just an hour a week or a few hours a month. Gradually increase your commitment as you feel more comfortable and confident.

Reaching out to local domestic violence organizations or searching online for relevant volunteer opportunities is an excellent starting point. Many organizations have specific volunteer roles that align with various skills and levels of experience. Some organizations offer flexible options, allowing you to volunteer remotely or on a schedule that fits your needs. The most important thing is finding a role that feels meaningful to you and allows you to contribute in a way that feels sustainable and fulfilling.

The impact of volunteering and giving back extends far beyond the immediate beneficiaries. It fosters a sense of purpose and meaning in your life, boosting self-esteem and promoting overall well-being. It creates a positive feedback loop, where your acts of kindness and compassion strengthen your own resilience and foster a sense of self-worth. It allows you to reconnect with your community and build positive relationships, counteracting the isolation often experienced by survivors of abuse.

In the process of helping others, you'll discover a renewed sense of agency and control over your life. This is not about replacing your past but integrating it into a larger narrative of empowerment and purpose. It is about finding your place in the world, using your experiences to build a better future for yourself and others. This journey of giving back is, in many ways, a continuation of your escape, a journey towards a life beyond the shadows, a life filled with purpose, meaning, and a profound sense of self-worth. Embrace this opportunity for growth and healing; your contribution will be invaluable.

Your strength is not only for your own survival; it is a gift to the world.

Embracing SelfForgiveness and Acceptance

The journey to healing after sociopathic abuse isn't solely about escaping the abuser; it's about reclaiming your sense of self. A crucial part of this reclamation is embracing self- forgiveness and self-acceptance. This isn't about condoning the abuse or minimizing its impact; it's about releasing the self-blame and shame that often accompany such experiences. Sociopaths are masters of manipulation, skillfully twisting narratives to make the victim feel responsible for the abuse. They plant seeds of doubt, whispering insidious suggestions that you deserved the treatment, provoked the anger, or somehow failed to prevent the harm. These insidious whispers linger long after the relationship ends, echoing in your mind and hindering your recovery.

Understanding this manipulative dynamic is the first step towards self-forgiveness. The abuse was never your fault. No one deserves to be manipulated, controlled, or abused. The responsibility for the abuse lies solely with the perpetrator.

Their actions, their choices, their calculated cruelty – these are what caused the harm, not any perceived failing on your part. Repeating this affirmation, both internally and aloud, can help break the cycle of self-blame.

Journaling can be an incredibly powerful tool in this process. Writing down your thoughts and feelings, acknowledging the pain and the self-criticism, allows you to externalize those negative emotions. It's a way to confront them directly, to examine their origins, and to challenge their validity. Don't censor yourself; let your raw emotions flow onto the page.

As you write, you might find patterns emerging, recurring thoughts and beliefs that stem from the manipulation of your

abuser. By recognizing these patterns, you can begin to dismantle them.

Consider writing a letter to your abuser, not to send, but to release your pent-up emotions. Pouring your anger, your hurt, your resentment onto paper can be incredibly cathartic. Don't hold back; let your feelings flow freely. Through this process, you'll likely discover the depth of the manipulation and the extent to which your abuser distorted your reality.

This letter is a tool for self-discovery, a way to uncover the truth and reclaim your narrative.

Self-acceptance is another crucial aspect of this healing process. This involves accepting all parts of yourself, including the scars left by the abuse. It's acknowledging that you've been through a traumatic experience that has impacted you deeply, without letting that experience define you. You are not your trauma; you are a survivor of trauma. This distinction is essential. Your experiences have shaped you, but they do not dictate your worth or your future.

Many survivors struggle with feelings of inadequacy and

self-doubt. These feelings are often amplified by the constant criticism and belittling that often accompany sociopathic abuse. Rebuilding self-esteem requires actively challenging these negative self-perceptions. This can involve setting small, achievable goals and celebrating your accomplishments, no matter how small they may seem. It's about focusing on your strengths and recognizing your resilience. Remind yourself daily of your positive qualities, your accomplishments, and your inherent worth.

Affirmations, both written and spoken, can be powerful tools in this process. Look in the mirror and speak kindly to yourself; treat yourself with the compassion and understanding you would offer a dear friend.

Forgiveness, both of yourself and your abuser, is a powerful, albeit challenging, step. Forgiving yourself isn't about forgetting the abuse or minimizing its impact; it's about releasing the burden of self-blame and allowing yourself to heal. It's about recognizing that you were a victim of manipulation and control, and that you are not responsible for the actions of your abuser. Forgiveness, in this context, is an act of self-compassion, a recognition of your own resilience and your capacity for healing.

Forgiving your abuser, however, is not a requirement for healing. It's a personal choice, and there's no timeline or pressure to do so. Some survivors find that forgiveness is an essential part of their recovery journey, while others find that it's simply not possible. Either path is valid and acceptable.

The focus should be on your own healing and well-being, not on the actions or feelings of your abuser. Their behavior was their responsibility; your healing is yours.

Therapy plays a vital role in this process. A therapist specializing in trauma and abuse recovery can provide a safe and supportive space to explore your feelings, challenge negative self-perceptions, and develop healthy coping mechanisms. They can guide you through the process of

self-forgiveness and self-acceptance, helping you to understand the impact of the abuse and to develop strategies for moving forward. Therapy provides a structure and a framework for navigating the complex emotions that often accompany sociopathic abuse. It offers validation, support, and a roadmap to healing.

Support groups can also be immensely helpful. Connecting with other survivors who understand your experiences can provide a sense of community and belonging. Sharing your story, listening to others' stories, and finding common ground can be incredibly validating and empowering. It's a reminder that you are not alone, that others have been through similar experiences and have found ways to heal. This shared experience can foster a sense of hope and resilience.

Self-care is crucial throughout this process. This isn't about indulging in luxuries; it's about prioritizing your physical and emotional well-being. This might involve regular exercise, healthy eating, sufficient sleep, spending time in nature, engaging in activities that bring you joy, and practicing mindfulness or meditation. These activities help regulate your nervous system, reduce stress, and promote a sense of calm and well-being. Prioritizing self-care isn't selfish; it's an act of self-respect, a commitment to your own healing and recovery.

Remember, the path to healing is not linear. There will be good days and bad days, moments of progress and moments of setbacks. Be patient with yourself; allow yourself to grieve the loss of the relationship, the betrayal, and the manipulation. Acknowledge the pain, but don't let it define you. Celebrate your small victories, and seek support when you need it. The journey to self-forgiveness and self- acceptance is a testament to your resilience and your strength. You are worthy of love, respect, and happiness.

Embrace your journey, and trust in your capacity for healing. The sun will rise again, and you will find your way back to the light. This is not just a hope; it is a promise you can keep to yourself. Believe in your capacity to heal, to thrive, and to build a life free from the shadows of the past. Your strength is remarkable, and your future is bright.

Developing a Positive SelfImage and SelfEsteem

Building a positive self-image and self-esteem after surviving sociopathic abuse is a crucial, yet often challenging, aspect of recovery. The manipulation and control exerted by a sociopath systematically erode a victim's sense of self-worth, leaving them feeling inadequate, unworthy, and deeply damaged. Rebuilding this sense of self requires a conscious and dedicated effort, a commitment to rediscovering your strengths, celebrating your accomplishments, and setting meaningful goals for the future. It's a journey of self-discovery and self-acceptance, one that unfolds gradually, with moments of progress interspersed with moments of doubt and setbacks. But the destination – a life filled with self-respect, confidence, and genuine joy – is worth the effort.

One of the most effective strategies in rebuilding self-esteem is to actively challenge the negative self-perceptions that have been ingrained by your abuser. Sociopaths are masters of manipulation, skillfully twisting reality to make you feel responsible for their actions. They might subtly (or not so subtly) criticize your appearance, your intelligence, your choices, constantly undermining your confidence and making you question your own judgment. These insidious criticisms linger long after the relationship ends, echoing in your mind and hindering your ability to see yourself accurately. To counteract this, you must actively challenge these negative voices.

Start by making a list of all the negative thoughts and beliefs about yourself that have surfaced since the abuse. Be honest and thorough; don't hold back. Once you have this list, examine each negative thought. Ask yourself: Is this thought

truly accurate? Is there evidence to support it? Or is this thought a product of the abuser's manipulation, a distortion of reality designed to control and diminish you? In most cases, you'll find that many of these negative thoughts are baseless, stemming from the abuser's calculated efforts to control you.

Next, create a counter-list. For each negative thought, write down a positive affirmation or a statement that challenges the negativity. For example, if a negative thought is "I'm unlovable," a counter-affirmation could be "I am worthy of love and respect, and I deserve to be treated kindly." If the negative thought is "I'm incompetent," a counter-affirmation could be "I have many skills and talents, and I am capable of achieving my goals." These affirmations should be specific, focusing on your strengths, your accomplishments, and your inherent worth.

Regularly review these lists. Read the negative thoughts to acknowledge their existence, but then immediately follow them with the counter-affirmations. Repeating these affirmations, both internally and aloud, can help reprogram your subconscious mind, gradually replacing the negative self-perceptions with more positive and realistic ones. This process takes time and consistency, but the results are well worth the effort.

In addition to challenging negative thoughts, focus on identifying and celebrating your personal strengths. Make a list of your positive qualities, skills, and talents. This might include traits like kindness, empathy, resilience, creativity, intelligence, or physical abilities. Think about past accomplishments, both big and small. Did you successfully navigate a difficult situation? Did you overcome a personal challenge? Did you achieve a goal you set for yourself? No matter how insignificant these accomplishments may seem,

acknowledge and celebrate them. They are proof of your strength, your resilience, and your capacity for growth.

Setting realistic goals is another crucial step in rebuilding self-esteem. Start with small, achievable goals. Don't try to tackle everything at once. Focus on one or two areas at a time, setting realistic goals that you can gradually achieve. As you accomplish these goals, celebrate your successes.

Acknowledge your efforts and reward yourself for your hard work. This positive reinforcement will build your confidence and encourage you to continue striving towards your goals.

Engage in activities that bring you joy and fulfillment. These activities should be things you enjoy doing, things that make you feel good about yourself. This could include anything from painting and writing to hiking and dancing. These activities can be a source of stress relief, self-expression, and a boost in self-esteem. Make time for these activities regularly, even if it's just for a few minutes each day.

Seek out support from trusted friends, family members, or support groups. Sharing your experiences and connecting with others who understand what you've been through can be incredibly validating and empowering. This shared experience can foster a sense of community and belonging, reminding you that you are not alone.

Remember, rebuilding your self-image and self-esteem is a journey, not a destination. There will be ups and downs, setbacks and breakthroughs. Be patient with yourself, celebrate your progress, and don't be afraid to seek professional help when needed. A therapist specializing in trauma and abuse recovery can provide valuable guidance and support during this process, helping you to challenge negative self-perceptions, develop healthy coping mechanisms, and build a stronger sense of self. The journey

may be long and challenging, but with perseverance and self-compassion, you can reclaim your sense of self and build a life filled with self-respect, confidence, and lasting joy. Believe in your strength, your resilience, and your capacity for healing. You are worthy of happiness and a life free from the shadows of the past. The journey to a positive self-image is an act of radical self-love; treat yourself with the kindness, patience, and understanding you deserve. This is not merely a hope; it is the foundation upon which you will build a healthier, happier future. You have survived unimaginable hardship; you are stronger than you think.

Embrace your strength, honor your journey, and celebrate your resilience. Your future is bright.

Celebrating Milestones and Achievements

Celebrating milestones and achievements is not merely a feel-good exercise; it's a crucial component of healing and reclaiming your life after surviving abuse. It's a powerful antidote to the insidious self-doubt and diminished sense of worth that sociopathic abuse inflicts. The constant negativity and manipulation designed to control and degrade you leaves a residue of self-criticism that can be exceptionally difficult to overcome. Actively celebrating your progress, no matter how small, serves as a vital counterbalance, reinforcing your inherent strength and resilience.

Think back to the moments when your abuser sought to diminish your accomplishments. Did they belittle your professional successes, dismissing them as luck or coincidence? Did they downplay personal victories, suggesting your achievements were insignificant or undeserved? This deliberate undermining was designed to control you, to keep you dependent and subservient. By actively celebrating your own achievements, you are directly challenging this manipulation and reclaiming your narrative. You are asserting your agency and affirming your self-worth.

Start by creating a "celebration journal." This isn't a diary in the traditional sense; it's a dedicated space to record your wins, both big and small. This might include completing a challenging task at work, sticking to your exercise routine for a week, finally tackling that daunting project you'd been putting off, or even something as seemingly insignificant as successfully navigating a grocery store without feeling overwhelmed. Every accomplishment, no matter how minuscule it may seem, deserves recognition.

The key is to shift your perspective. Instead of focusing on what you haven't achieved, focus on what you *have* accomplished. Celebrate the steps forward, the small victories that collectively contribute to your overall progress. Each entry in your celebration journal should be a testament to your resilience, your strength, and your capacity for growth. Don't minimize your achievements; detail the effort involved and the obstacles you overcame.

Consider setting aside specific time each week to review your journal. Re-read your entries, allowing yourself to fully appreciate your progress. This regular reflection helps reinforce your sense of accomplishment and provides tangible evidence of your growth. It's easy to forget the progress we've made, particularly when grappling with the lingering effects of trauma. The celebration journal acts as a constant reminder of your strength and capabilities.

Beyond the written word, consider incorporating other methods of celebration. Treat yourself to something you enjoy – a relaxing bath, a favorite meal, a new book, or a walk in nature. These small acts of self-care are essential for nurturing your well-being and reinforcing the message that you deserve to be happy and cared for.

The concept of celebrating milestones extends beyond personal achievements. It includes acknowledging the progress you make in your healing journey. This might involve completing a session with your therapist, attending a support group meeting, or successfully navigating a difficult interaction without succumbing to old patterns of behavior. These are significant steps that deserve recognition and celebration.

Remember, celebrating your achievements isn't about bragging or arrogance; it's about self-compassion and self-

validation. It's about acknowledging your hard work, your resilience, and your capacity for growth. It's about actively counteracting the negative self-talk ingrained by your abuser and replacing it with positive affirmation and self-belief.

Moreover, celebrate your resilience in unexpected ways. Perhaps you've learned a new skill, taken up a new hobby, or volunteered your time to a cause you care about. These actions, too, represent your strength and your commitment to rebuilding your life. They are tangible expressions of your recovery and deserve to be celebrated.

Let's examine some specific examples. Imagine you've successfully completed a challenging project at work, a project that previously would have filled you with anxiety and self-doubt. Instead of dismissing your success as "just luck," take time to acknowledge the effort, dedication, and skill you invested. Celebrate this achievement by rewarding yourself with something enjoyable, by sharing your success with a trusted friend or family member, or simply by taking a moment to savor your accomplishment.

Or perhaps you've finally left your abuser's home, a monumental step that required immense courage and determination. This achievement represents a significant turning point in your healing journey. Celebrate this milestone by acknowledging your bravery and strength. Treat yourself to something special, surround yourself with supportive people, and allow yourself to feel proud of your accomplishment.

Another example might be regaining your financial independence after being controlled by your abuser. This accomplishment represents a significant step toward self- sufficiency and freedom. Celebrate this by acknowledging your hard work and resilience. Mark this significant

milestone with a small celebratory gesture or reward to underscore your accomplishment.

It's crucial to understand that celebrating your achievements is not about minimizing the trauma you've endured. It's not about erasing the pain or pretending it didn't happen. Rather, it's about integrating your experience into your overall narrative in a way that empowers you, rather than defining you. It's about recognizing your strength, acknowledging your resilience, and affirming your capacity for growth and healing.

Think of it as creating a new story, a narrative that acknowledges the darkness but focuses on the light. It's a story of survival, resilience, and triumph. It's a story you write yourself, a story filled with accomplishments, both big and small, all celebrated and cherished. It is a story that reinforces your self-worth and reminds you of your innate strength.

Remember, the journey of healing is not linear. There will be setbacks, moments of doubt, and days when the weight of the past feels overwhelming. But through it all, continue to celebrate your progress. Celebrate the small victories, the milestones, and the moments of strength. These celebrations serve as reminders of your resilience and your capacity for healing. They are essential fuel for the journey ahead. They are proof that you are not just surviving; you are thriving.

Your future is a celebration of your strength, a testament to your unwavering spirit. Embrace it, own it, and let it guide you toward a future filled with hope, joy, and lasting peace.

Planning for the Future and Setting New Goals

Planning for the future after escaping an abusive relationship with a sociopath can feel daunting, even paralyzing. The very act of envisioning a future independent of your abuser might evoke fear, anxiety, and a sense of uncertainty. The years spent under their control might have left you feeling incapable of making your own decisions, fostering a deep- seated dependence and crippling self-doubt. However, reclaiming your agency and building a future on your own terms is entirely possible, and it's a crucial step toward lasting healing. It's about shifting from survival mode to thriving mode.

The first step is to acknowledge the enormity of what you've overcome. You've survived a profoundly damaging experience, and that alone is a testament to your strength and resilience. Don't underestimate the power of this accomplishment. You've escaped a web of manipulation and control, a feat that demands recognition and celebration.

Take time to reflect on your journey, acknowledging the bravery and determination it took to reach this point. This acknowledgment is vital in building the foundation for your future.

Now, it's time to start actively building that future. This process begins with setting goals, both large and small, short-term and long-term. These goals shouldn't be dictated by anyone else's expectations or ideals. Instead, they should reflect your own aspirations, desires, and ambitions. Think about what truly matters to you, what brings you joy, what ignites your passion. These are the things you should focus on.

Start with small, attainable goals. Perhaps it's something as simple as committing to a daily walk, learning a new skill, or joining a book club. These seemingly insignificant steps represent a shift in focus, a conscious decision to invest in your well-being and personal growth. The accomplishment of these smaller goals builds momentum, creating a sense of accomplishment and self-efficacy which can then be applied to larger, more challenging goals. Do not underestimate the power of small wins. They are the building blocks of a fulfilling future.

As you begin to set your goals, consider various aspects of your life:

Career: If your career was negatively impacted by the abuse, now is the time to explore new opportunities, pursue further education, or re-evaluate your professional path.

Perhaps you've always dreamed of a different career but lacked the courage or freedom to pursue it while under the control of your abuser. Now is your chance to explore those possibilities. Look for support groups or career counseling services specifically designed to help survivors of abuse.

They can provide guidance, resources, and encouragement as you navigate the next steps. Remember, you have skills and talents, even if your abuser tried to convince you otherwise.

Finances: Re-establishing financial independence is often a significant challenge after escaping an abusive relationship. If your abuser controlled the finances, you may need to rebuild your credit, establish new bank accounts, and learn about financial management. Seek guidance from financial professionals specializing in helping survivors of abuse.

They can provide strategies for debt management, budgeting, and financial planning. The path to financial stability might be long and require dedication but know that it is attainable.

Housing: Securing safe and stable housing is paramount. If you are currently in a shelter or temporary housing, start looking for long-term solutions. Connect with local organizations that provide assistance with housing for survivors of abuse. They can offer support and guidance in finding safe and affordable housing options. Ensure that your new living situation prioritizes your safety and sense of security.

Social Connections: Rebuild your support network. Reconnect with trusted friends and family members, or build new relationships with people who share your interests and values. Consider joining support groups for survivors of abuse or engaging in activities that help you connect with others in a positive and supportive environment. Allow yourself to be vulnerable, to share your experience with others who understand. Remember, you are not alone.

Physical and Mental Health: Prioritize your physical and mental well-being. Continue or start therapy, engage in regular exercise, eat healthy foods, and get enough sleep.

These are essential for your recovery and overall health. Explore different self-care techniques that bring you comfort and peace. Make time for activities that nourish your soul and help you relax.

Legal Matters: If necessary, seek legal counsel to protect yourself from further harm. This might involve obtaining restraining orders, pursuing legal action against your abuser, or addressing other legal issues related to the abuse. Do not hesitate to seek professional help to navigate the legal system. You have rights and deserve protection.

Personal Growth: Invest time in activities that promote personal growth and self-discovery. Explore your interests, hobbies, and passions. Learning new skills, taking up a new

hobby, or pursuing a creative outlet can be a powerful way to boost your self-esteem and foster a sense of accomplishment. This is an opportunity for self-discovery and growth – rediscovering your passions and exploring new avenues.

Setting goals for each of these areas of your life provides a roadmap for your future. These goals can be broken down into smaller, manageable steps, making the journey feel less overwhelming and more achievable. Regularly review and adjust these goals as your needs and priorities evolve.

Remember, this is your journey, and you have the right to adapt your path as you move forward.

One crucial aspect of planning for the future is envisioning your ideal life. This isn't just about setting goals; it's about creating a vision of the future you want to create. Imagine yourself living a life free from fear, manipulation, and control. What does that life look like? What does it feel like? Where do you live? What kind of work do you do? Who are the people in your life? This visualization can be a powerful tool in motivating you to achieve your goals. It is a powerful tool for building momentum and resilience.

Create a vision board. This can be a physical board filled with images, quotes, and affirmations that represent your ideal life. Or you can create a digital vision board using online tools. This visual representation serves as a constant reminder of what you are working towards.

Throughout this process, remember that setbacks are inevitable. There will be days when you feel overwhelmed, discouraged, or tempted to give up. But it's crucial to remember that these moments are temporary. Acknowledge your feelings, allow yourself to process them, and then refocus on your goals and your vision for the future. Be kind

to yourself. Celebrate your progress and learn from your setbacks. Your journey to healing is a marathon, not a sprint.

Seek professional support. Therapy is invaluable in this process. A therapist can help you process your trauma, build coping mechanisms, and develop strategies for managing your emotions. Support groups for survivors of abuse can also provide a sense of community and shared experience.

Finally, remember that you deserve a life filled with happiness, peace, and fulfillment. You deserve to live a life free from fear and manipulation. Your past does not define your future. You are resilient, capable, and deserving of a brighter tomorrow. Embrace the opportunity to rebuild your life, to create the future you deserve, and to find joy and peace along the way. This is your story, your future – write it with courage, determination, and unwavering self-belief.

Living a Life Free from Fear and Control

The journey from surviving abuse to thriving in freedom is a deeply personal one, filled with both challenges and incredible rewards. The road ahead might feel long and winding, perhaps even insurmountable at times. But remember, you've already conquered the most significant hurdle: escaping the clutches of your abuser. That act of courage is a testament to your inner strength, your resilience, and your unwavering will to live a life free from fear and control.

This freedom isn't merely the absence of abuse; it's the active creation of a life built upon your terms, guided by your aspirations, and filled with joy, peace, and self-worth. It's about reclaiming your agency, redefining your identity, and rewriting your narrative. It's about embracing the power you possess to shape your own destiny.

One of the most crucial steps in this process is fostering self- compassion. The abuse you endured wasn't your fault. The manipulation, the gaslighting, the constant control—none of it was deserved. It's imperative to release the burden of self- blame that your abuser meticulously cultivated. Forgive yourself for the choices you made while under their influence. Recognize that your survival instincts, even if they led to choices you now regret, were completely justifiable within the context of an abusive situation.

This self-forgiveness is not about condoning the abuser's actions; it's about releasing yourself from the shackles of guilt and self-criticism. It's about freeing yourself to move forward, to embrace the possibilities that lie ahead. Engage in practices that nurture self-compassion. These could

include mindfulness meditation, journaling, or simply taking time each day to engage in activities that bring you joy and peace.

Building healthy boundaries is equally crucial. This involves establishing clear limits on how others treat you and how you allow yourself to be treated. It requires recognizing your needs and communicating them assertively yet respectfully. It may involve saying "no" to requests that drain your energy, compromise your well-being, or violate your personal boundaries.

Setting boundaries might feel daunting, particularly after years of suppressing your needs and desires to appease your abuser. However, it's an essential component of creating a life free from fear and control. It allows you to protect your emotional, physical, and mental well-being. Begin by setting small, manageable boundaries, gradually expanding them as you gain confidence and assertiveness. For instance, you might start by setting clear limits on phone calls or social media interactions with people who drain your energy.

Developing a strong support system is also vital. Surround yourself with people who lift you up, encourage your growth, and offer unconditional love and support. These are individuals who respect your boundaries, value your voice, and champion your journey to healing. These could be family members, friends, fellow survivors, or members of a support group. Do not underestimate the power of connection and shared experience.

Actively seek out support groups specifically designed for survivors of sociopathic abuse. These groups provide a safe and confidential space to share your experiences, connect with others who understand your struggles, and receive validation and encouragement. They offer a sense of

community, a lifeline in the journey toward healing and empowerment. The shared experience within these groups can be profoundly healing, offering a sense of belonging and understanding that is often absent in other settings.

Remember, the healing process is not linear. There will be good days and bad days. There will be moments of profound progress and moments of setbacks. It's crucial to embrace this ebb and flow, recognizing that healing is a journey, not a destination. Be patient and kind to yourself throughout this process.

Another important aspect of living a life free from fear and control is cultivating resilience. Resilience is the ability to bounce back from adversity, to adapt to challenges, and to find strength in difficult times. It's the capacity to persevere despite setbacks and to emerge stronger from life's trials.

Resilience is not about ignoring pain or pretending everything is fine; it's about facing adversity head-on, learning from setbacks, and moving forward with renewed determination.

Cultivating resilience involves developing coping mechanisms, building self-esteem, and focusing on personal growth. It involves identifying and utilizing your inner strengths, developing healthy coping strategies, and learning to manage stress effectively. Engage in activities that promote your well-being, such as regular exercise, mindfulness practices, healthy eating, and sufficient sleep.

Furthermore, invest in your personal growth and self- discovery. Explore your interests, cultivate new skills, and pursue activities that bring you joy and fulfillment. These activities can help you reclaim your identity, build confidence, and reinforce your sense of self-worth. These activities are not mere distractions; they are fundamental to

your healing and growth, helping to reestablish your sense of self beyond the constraints imposed by your abuser.

As you move forward, remember that your journey towards a life free from fear and control is a testament to your courage, resilience, and unwavering spirit. It's a journey of self-discovery, healing, and empowerment. Embrace the challenges, celebrate your successes, and never underestimate the power of your own strength. You have the capacity to create a life filled with joy, peace, and lasting fulfillment. You deserve to live a life free from fear, a life where you are in control of your own destiny. This is your life, your story, and your future. Write it with boldness, authenticity, and unwavering self-belief. The future you envision is within your grasp. Embrace it, claim it, and live it fully.

Acknowledgments

This book would not exist without the unwavering support and contributions of many individuals. First and foremost, I extend my deepest gratitude to the brave survivors who shared their stories with me, granting me a glimpse into the profound strength and resilience of the human spirit in the face of unimaginable adversity. Their courage inspired every page.

My sincere appreciation goes to Dr. Daniel Fox, whose expertise and guidance proved invaluable in ensuring the accuracy and sensitivity of the information presented within these pages. HIs insights and unwavering commitment to supporting Cluster B personality disorders were instrumental in shaping this work.

A special thanks also to my children, whose tireless support during the writing process helped make this endeavor possible.

I offer my heartfelt gratitude to my family and friends, whose love and support provided a constant source of strength throughout this challenging journey. Their unwavering belief in me helped me navigate the complexities of this work.

Finally, to the one who sought to break me through **manipulation and malice: your actions revealed the depths of human resilience. Your pathology did not shatter me;it forged me. I stand stronger, wiser, and unyielding, a testament to the strength that emerges from surviving the storm. This book**

is not about you—it's about the triumph of the human spirit over darkness. JRoby

Appendix

This appendix provides a curated list of helpful resources for survivors of sociopathic abuse and stalking. These resources include national and international hotlines, support organizations, legal aid providers, and mental health professionals specializing in trauma and abuse recovery. It is important to remember that this list is not exhaustive, and the availability and suitability of these resources may vary depending on location and individual circumstances. It is crucial to research and select resources that best suit your specific needs and location. Please note that contact information is subject to change, so verifying details before use is recommended.

Percentage of proceeds from the sale of this book will go to organizations that help survivors!

List of Resources

Safe & Sound

Stalking Resource Center

National Domestic Violence Hotline RAINN (Rape, Abuse & Incest National Network)

Stalking Prevention, Awareness, and Resource Center (SPARC)

National Center for Victims of Crime Office on Violence Against Women (OVW)

Aftermath: Surviving Psychopathy Foundation Safe Horizon

MN Trauma Project Complextrauma.org

Open Path Psychotherapy Collective BuddyHelp Therapist Aid

National Alliance on Mental Illness (NAMI) Psychology Today's Therapy Directory

Glossary

This glossary defines key terms used throughout the book to ensure clarity and understanding.

Gaslighting: A form of psychological manipulation where a person seeks to sow seeds of doubt in a victim's mind, making them question their own memory, perception, and sanity.

Sociopath (or Psychopath): A person with a personality disorder characterized by a lack of empathy, remorse, and antisocial behavior. Note: This book uses these terms interchangeably for simplicity, acknowledging the nuanced differences in clinical diagnosis.

Stalking: Repeated, unwanted, and intrusive behavior directed at another person that causes the victim to feel fear, distress, or concern for their safety. This can include physical, online, or technological means.

Trauma Bonding: A paradoxical emotional attachment that can develop between victims and their abusers, despite the abusive nature of the relationship.

Cognitive Dissonance: The mental discomfort experienced by a person who holds two or more contradictory beliefs, ideas, or values. In the context of abuse, this can manifest as the victim struggling to reconcile the abusive behavior with their positive feelings for the abuser.

Hoovering: The attempt by an abuser to regain control over a victim after a period of separation. This may involve manipulation, promises, or displays of remorse.

Love Bombing: An intense and overwhelming display of affection and attention at the beginning of a relationship, used as a manipulative tactic to secure a victim's trust and commitment.

References

References

The Sociopath Next Door by Martha Stout: A deep dive into the traits and behaviors of sociopaths.

Understanding the Sociopath: Cause, Motivation, Relationship by Seth Meyers Psy.D., available on Psychology Today.

Differentiating Antisocial Personality Disorder, Psychopathy, and Sociopathy by Anthony Walsh and Huei-Hsia Wu, exploring the distinctions between these conditions.

Stalking: A Review of the Literature and Direction for the Future by Heather C. Melton, which examines the link between stalking and domestic violence.

Prosecutor's Guide to Stalking by the Stalking Awareness Organization, offering insights into legal and safety measures.

CDC'S OVERVIEW OF STALKING AS PART OF INTIMATE PARTNER VIOLENCE PREVENTION.

When a Sociopath Stalks You: Signs to Watch For and Steps to Protect Yourself by William Adams, available on Mind Psychiatrist. This article explores the behaviors of sociopaths and provides practical steps for protection.

Will a Sociopath Stalk You? Signs to Look Out For and How to Protect Yourself by William Adams, also on Mind Psychiatrist. It discusses red flags and protective measures against sociopathic stalking.

Coping with The Psychopath (Antisocial) Stalker by Sam Vaknin, available on HealthyPlace. This article delves into the psychological traits of stalkers and offers coping strategies.

When a Sociopath Stalks You : A detailed guide on recognizing sociopathic behavior and practical steps for protection.

Finding Support and Resources for Sociopaths: Insights into treatment options and support systems for individuals dealing with sociopathy.

Coping with The Psychopath (Antisocial) Stalker : Explores the psychological traits of stalkers and offers coping strategies.

IS LOVE BOMBING A RED FLAG?: **DISCUSSES THE DANGERS OF LOVE BOMBING, ITS IMPACT ON EMOTIONAL HEALTH, AND HOW TO DIFFERENTIATE IT FROM GENUINE AFFECTION.**

Love Bombing: 11 Warning Signs & Early Red Flags : This article explores the psychological manipulation behind love bombing, its connection to narcissistic abuse, and how to identify early warning signs.

Signs of Love Bombing: A guide to spotting behaviors like excessive compliments, over-the-top gestures, and boundary overstepping in relationships.

Author Biography

Jennifer is a survivor of sociopathic abuse, a licensed therapist in several states specializing in trauma and abuse recovery, and a writer of non-fiction works focused on mental health and recovery. Her personal experience combined with their professional expertise provides a unique perspective on the complexities of escaping and healing from this type of abuse. Jennifer is committed to providing support, education, and resources to individuals affected by sociopathic abuse and helping them navigate their journey towards healing and empowerment.

Jennifer is a therapist whose work is grounded in compassion, respect, and dedication to her clients' well- being. She specializes in trauma, addiction, personality disorders, and suicide prevention, while also addressing a broad range of concerns including depression, anxiety, relationship issues, parenting challenges, career stress, grief, and bullying. Jennifer's therapy style is warm and interactive, fostering collaboration with clients to help them reach their treatment goals in a safe and accepting environment.

With over 11 years of experience as a therapist, Jennifer skillfully adapts her approach to meet the unique needs of each individual. She integrates psychodynamic, humanistic, and existential principles, alongside Cognitive Behavioral Therapy, Client-Centered Therapy, Acceptance and Commitment Therapy (ACT), Mindfulness Therapy, and Inner Child Analytical Psychotherapy. Additionally, she is trained in advanced techniques such as Dialectical Behavior Therapy, Cognitive Processing Therapy, Prolonged Exposure Therapy, and Eye Movement Desensitization and

Reprocessing (EMDR). This diverse expertise enables her to guide her clients through life's challenges, helping them rediscover their emotional intelligence, inner wisdom, and capacity for self-compassion.

Jennifer's career includes extensive service to Veterans, Active-Duty Military members, and their families through her work in the Federal government. She has received numerous awards for her dedication, including the Presidential Volunteer Service Award from President Barack Obama, a VA Commendation from Secretary Robert McDonald, and the Making a Difference in the Community Spotlight from KGNS News, the Laredo Police Department, and the Laredo City Council. Jennifer has also been recognized with the Certificate of Special Recognition from Command Master Chief and the Certificate of Commitment from VCB VA Director Joe Perez, among many others.

These accolades reflect her tireless efforts to improve the lives of Veterans and their communities.

An accomplished author, Jennifer has written several treatment and self-help books, covering important topics such as suicide prevention, thriving after divorce, childhood trauma stemming from military service. Her works also include a guide for navigating passive-aggressive adult bullies, a self-help book for transcending others' perceptions to embrace your true self, and a beloved children's book series co-written with her own children, Johnny & his brothers: Adventures as a Military Child. Her writing offers hope, guidance, and practical tools for a diverse range of readers, addressing real-life challenges with compassion and insight.

Jennifer has delivered impactful clinical presentations at prominent conferences, such as "PTSD and Women Veterans" at the American Mental Health Counselors Association (AMHCA) in 2023 and "Veterans Suicide:

Prevention, Intervention, and Postvention" at the Texas Counseling Association State Conference in 2021. Her expertise has been sought by the Department of Defense and the Department of Veterans Affairs on topics ranging from PTSD and suicide to Veteran homelessness and dual diagnoses.

Beyond her professional life, Jennifer is a devoted and busy mother of five boys—Nicholas, William, Michael Anthony, Matthew, and Johnny. She finds immense joy and purpose in balancing her family life with her passion for helping others heal and thrive.

Jennifer is actively involved in numerous professional organizations, including the American Counseling Association, the Military and Government Counseling Association, the American Mental Health Counselors Association, and the Texas Counseling Association. She also serves on various committees, showcasing her commitment to fostering growth and advocacy in the field of mental health.

Jennifer believes that the process of psychotherapy is about exploring thoughts, feelings, beliefs, and behaviors to uncover strategies for change. She emphasizes the importance of understanding how actions, influenced by deeply held thoughts, impact oneself and others. She inspires courage by helping clients face their fears, work through them, and conquer them, all while creating a space for growth, healing, and transformation.

2

Dedication

Escaping Shadows: Surviving a Sociopath and Stalker

By: Jennifer E. Roby, LPC, NCC, BC-TMH, C-DBT, CMHC, CCTP, CCBT, CBGT, C-PD, CEAP

To all the survivors who have endured the pain and fear of living with a sociopath or being stalked—your courage and resilience inspire hope for healing and freedom. You are not alone, and your story matters. To myself—for finding my strength in the face of unimaginable challenges, for surviving the darkness brought by a sociopath and a stalker, and for reclaiming my life. I AM JROBY. I am unbroken, unstoppable, and free.

This book is dedicated to every survivor of sociopathic abuse. Your strength, resilience, and courage in the face of unimaginable cruelty inspire me deeply. This work is a testament to your inherent worth and the power you possess to heal, to thrive, and to build a life free from the shadows of manipulation and control. It is a tribute to your unwavering spirit, your capacity for forgiveness, and your journey towards a future filled with peace, joy, and self-love. May these pages offer solace, validation, and a path towards the brighter future you deserve. You are not alone. Your story matters. Your healing is possible.

JRoby

Preface

As a survivor of sociopathic abuse, and a therapist specializing in trauma and abuse recovery, I understand firsthand the insidious nature of this form of manipulation. The experiences detailed within these pages are not fiction; they are born from lived reality, meticulously researched, and woven together with clinical expertise. The manipulation, gaslighting, and systematic erosion of self-worth are not easily recognized. They are subtle, complex, and often leave victims feeling isolated, confused, and questioning their own sanity. My aim in writing Escaping Shadows is to provide a lifeline, a roadmap to freedom for those caught in the web of sociopathic control, and a resource for those who seek to understand this often-misunderstood form of abuse.

This book combines personal narrative with clinically- sound advice and practical tools. It is designed to empower you, the reader, to recognize the signs, create a safety plan, escape the abuse, and ultimately, rebuild your life. This is not a journey for the faint of heart, but remember, you are stronger than you think. Your recovery is possible, and your future is waiting.

Introduction

Sociopathic abuse is a uniquely insidious form of trauma. Unlike physical abuse, its wounds are often invisible, leaving victims grappling with self-doubt and a pervasive sense of confusion. The abuser, often charming and charismatic, expertly manipulates their partner, eroding their sense of self and control. This book is not merely a theoretical exploration of sociopathic behavior; it's a practical guide designed to help you navigate the complexities of escaping such a relationship and beginning the long process of healing. Within these pages, you will find a detailed exploration of the tactics used by sociopaths, from gaslighting and financial control to technological stalking.

We will delve into the devastating psychological impact of this abuse and provide evidence-based strategies for recognizing the red flags early on. More importantly, *Escaping Shadows* offers a concrete action plan for creating a safety net, securing resources, and legally protecting yourself. The journey to recovery is long and challenging, but know that you are not alone. This book offers validation, hope, and a detailed roadmap to navigate this difficult path. Take your time, work through each chapter, and remember that reclaiming your life is not only possible, it is your right. This is your journey to healing and empowerment. Begin here.

Defining Sociopathy and its Traits

Sociopathy, also known as antisocial personality disorder (ASPD), is a complex personality disorder characterized by a pervasive pattern of disregard for and violation of the rights of others. It's crucial to understand that sociopathy isn't simply a matter of being "bad" or "selfish." It represents a deeply ingrained personality structure that significantly impairs an individual's ability to form genuine emotional connections, experience empathy, and conform to societal norms.

This isn't to excuse the actions of a sociopath, but rather to contextualize the nature of the abuse they inflict.

Understanding the disorder helps survivors recognize the patterns of behavior and understand that the abuse they suffered wasn't their fault.

One of the most defining characteristics of sociopathy is the profound lack of empathy. Sociopaths struggle, often fail entirely, to understand or share the feelings of others. They don't experience the emotional pain or distress of their victims, making manipulation and abuse easier. This lack of empathy isn't simply a lack of compassion; it's a fundamental inability to comprehend the emotional experiences of other people. They may mimic empathy, expressing remorse or concern when it suits them, but this is usually a calculated performance, a tool for further manipulation rather than a genuine expression of feeling.

Closely linked to the lack of empathy is a profound ability to manipulate and deceive. Sociopaths are often masters of manipulation, using charm, charisma, and flattery to gain trust and control over their victims. They are adept at exploiting vulnerabilities and using emotional manipulation to achieve their self-serving ends. This manipulation can be

subtle and insidious, making it difficult for victims to recognize the abuse until considerable damage has been done. For instance, a sociopathic partner might consistently criticize a victim's appearance or accomplishments, gradually eroding their self-esteem until they become entirely dependent on the abuser for validation. This slow, methodical degradation of self-worth is a hallmark of sociopathic abuse.

Another key trait is a disregard for rules and consequences. Sociopaths often exhibit a pattern of impulsive and reckless behavior, disregarding the rights and well-being of others without remorse. They may lie, cheat, steal, or engage in other criminal activities without feeling any guilt or shame. This lack of moral compass is often paired with a sense of entitlement, believing they are above the law or societal expectations. Their actions are driven by a desire for immediate gratification, without considering the long-term consequences for themselves or others. For example, a sociopathic individual might repeatedly break promises, abandon responsibilities, or violate legal agreements without hesitation.

While charm is often associated with sociopaths, it's important to understand it is a manipulative tool, not a genuine reflection of personality. They can appear incredibly charming and likeable, making it difficult for victims to see the darkness beneath the surface. This façade of charm can mask their manipulative and exploitative behaviors, often lulling victims into a false sense of security. They may use charm to gain the trust of friends, family, and coworkers, reinforcing their image as a respectable and trustworthy individual, furthering their ability to conceal their abusive behavior. This charm is a carefully constructed persona, designed to serve their needs, and is easily discarded once their goals are achieved.

The diagnosis of sociopathy requires a specific pattern of behavior, not just a single instance of impulsive or unethical behavior. Professionals use established diagnostic criteria, typically from the Diagnostic and Statistical Manual of Mental Disorders (DSM-5) or the International Classification of Diseases (ICD-11), to assess for ASPD. Meeting the diagnostic criteria usually requires a history of exhibiting several key behaviors since the age of 15. These behaviors often include a pattern of deceitfulness, impulsivity, irritability, recklessness, consistent irresponsibility, and a lack of remorse. It's important to note that these diagnostic tools are just one piece of the puzzle in understanding sociopathic behavior and should be considered alongside an individual's entire history and context.

Differentiating sociopathy from other personality disorders is crucial. Narcissistic personality disorder, for instance, is characterized by an inflated sense of self-importance and a need for admiration, while sociopathy focuses on a pervasive pattern of disregard for the rights of others. While some overlap may exist, the core motivations and behaviors differ significantly. Similarly, borderline personality disorder involves intense fear of abandonment and unstable relationships, contrasting with the manipulative and exploitative nature of sociopathic interactions. A qualified mental health professional can make the necessary distinctions based on a comprehensive evaluation of the individual's history, behaviors, and interpersonal relationships.

Understanding the differences between these disorders isn't just an academic exercise; it's essential for victims of abuse to grasp the nature of the manipulation they've experienced. Recognizing the specific patterns of sociopathic behavior

allows survivors to validate their experiences, understand why they were targeted, and begin the crucial process of healing. The self-awareness gained from understanding sociopathy empowers survivors to establish healthier boundaries and build stronger defenses against future abuse.

It is crucial to remember that while the characteristics described provide a framework for understanding sociopathic behavior, it is not possible to definitively diagnose someone as a sociopath without a thorough professional evaluation. This chapter aims to provide information to help readers recognize potential red flags and seek appropriate support, not to label individuals.

The impact of sociopathic abuse extends far beyond the immediate physical or emotional harm. The subtle yet persistent manipulation can profoundly damage a victim's sense of self, leading to feelings of isolation, confusion, and self-doubt. Gaslighting, a tactic frequently used by sociopaths, systematically erodes a victim's trust in their own perception of reality. Victims may begin to question their sanity and memory, believing the abuser's version of events even when it contradicts their own experiences. This constant undermining of their self-perception can lead to significant psychological distress, including anxiety, depression, and post-traumatic stress disorder (PTSD). The isolating tactics employed by sociopaths further intensify this feeling of disconnect, leaving victims feeling alone and increasingly dependent on their abuser.

Furthermore, the financial control exerted by many sociopathic abusers can leave victims financially vulnerable and dependent, making it extremely difficult to escape the abusive relationship. This financial dependence is often coupled with threats and intimidation, further trapping victims in a cycle of abuse. The erosion of independence

extends beyond finances; it often includes control over social contacts, limiting the victim's ability to seek support or build alternative relationships. The pervasive nature of this control creates a suffocating environment that prevents victims from accessing the resources and support necessary to break free.

The long-term effects of sociopathic abuse can be devastating. Many survivors grapple with lasting psychological trauma, impacting their self-esteem, relationships, and overall well-being. They may struggle with trust issues, difficulty forming healthy relationships, and a persistent fear of future abuse. The process of healing is complex and often requires professional intervention, such as therapy or counseling specializing in trauma and abuse recovery. The crucial first step, however, is recognizing the abuse for what it is—not the victim's fault but a result of the abuser's actions and disordered personality. Understanding the nature of sociopathic abuse empowers survivors to begin their journey towards healing and reclaiming their lives. The path to recovery is challenging but achievable, and help is always available.

Tactics of Manipulation and Control

The insidious nature of sociopathic abuse lies not just in its overt acts of cruelty, but in the subtle, pervasive tactics of manipulation and control employed to systematically dismantle the victim's sense of self. These tactics are rarely singular events; they are woven together into a complex web designed to isolate, confuse, and ultimately subdue the victim. Gaslighting, a cornerstone of this manipulative strategy, involves twisting reality to make the victim doubt their own perceptions and sanity. It's a slow, insidious poison, chipping away at the victim's confidence until they question their own memories and experiences, accepting the abuser's distorted version of events as truth. For example, a sociopathic partner might deny making a cruel remark or promise, insisting the victim is imagining things, creating a constant state of cognitive dissonance and confusion. The victim, overwhelmed by this constant undermining, begins to question their own sanity and relies increasingly on the abuser for validation.

Beyond gaslighting, emotional abuse is a core element of the sociopath's arsenal. This involves a range of tactics, from constant criticism and belittling to subtle put-downs designed to erode the victim's self-esteem. These comments aren't random outbursts; they're carefully calibrated to target the victim's vulnerabilities, chipping away at their confidence until they become entirely dependent on the abuser for validation. A sociopathic partner might consistently criticize a victim's appearance, intelligence, or accomplishments, making them feel inadequate and unworthy. This subtle, persistent negativity slowly breaks down the victim's self-worth, leaving them vulnerable and susceptible to further manipulation.

Isolation is another powerful tool used by sociopaths to exert control. This isn't simply about physical separation; it's about gradually severing the victim's ties to their support network. Sociopaths often work to alienate the victim from friends and family, convincing them that these relationships are negative influences or sources of conflict. They might spread lies or create false narratives to damage the victim's reputation amongst their loved ones, creating further isolation and dependency on the abuser. They might control access to communication, monitoring calls and texts, or even forbidding contact with certain individuals. The victim, left increasingly alone and isolated, becomes more dependent on the abuser for companionship and emotional support, making it more difficult to escape the abusive relationship.

Financial control is a common and devastating tactic. Sociopaths often exert control over the victim's finances, restricting their access to money, forcing them to seek the abuser's permission for even small purchases. They might conceal joint accounts, open secret credit cards, or manipulate the victim's income to maintain financial dependence. This financial control is not just about economic dominance; it's about power and control over the victim's life. The financial dependence leaves the victim trapped, unable to leave the relationship without facing severe financial hardship. This dependence is often accompanied by subtle threats or intimidations, which further entrenches the victim's fear and prevents them from seeking help. The loss of financial independence is a significant barrier to escaping the abuse, leaving victims feeling powerless and trapped.

Control over communication is another tactic that reinforces the victim's isolation. This extends beyond monitoring calls and messages; it encompasses the manipulation of

information. The sociopath might control what the victim is allowed to read, watch, or listen to, limiting their access to information that could challenge the abuser's narrative or expose their manipulative behavior. They might filter information selectively, presenting only what suits their agenda and obscuring anything that could threaten their control. The victim's access to outside perspectives is curtailed, reinforcing their dependence on the abuser for information and interpretation of the world.

The impact of these tactics is cumulative and devastating. Each act of gaslighting, each instance of emotional abuse, each step towards isolation, each act of financial control further erodes the victim's sense of self and independence. The victim's reality is distorted, their confidence shattered, their support network dismantled, and their financial freedom curtailed. This systematic dismantling leaves the victim feeling helpless, confused, and deeply dependent on the abuser, making it extremely difficult to recognize the abuse, let alone escape it.

Consider the case of Sarah, a successful professional who fell prey to a charismatic sociopathic partner. Initially, he charmed her with his wit and apparent generosity. However, over time, he began subtly criticizing her work, her appearance, and her friendships. He manipulated her into isolating herself from her friends and family, convincing her they were jealous of their relationship. He exerted control over their finances, handling all the household bills and limiting her access to money. He would subtly gaslight her when she questioned his actions, implying she was too emotional or misunderstanding his intentions. Sarah found herself increasingly isolated, confused, and dependent on her partner, her sense of self completely eroded. She gradually lost confidence in her own judgment and accepted her

partner's distorted reality as truth, making it extremely difficult for her to recognize the abuse or seek help.

Another example is Mark, who experienced a different but equally insidious form of manipulation. His partner controlled the household narrative, consistently telling Mark he was ungrateful, lazy, or incompetent. This constant negativity, devoid of specific examples, was designed to break down Mark's self-esteem. His partner gradually isolated him from his friends by spreading malicious gossip and then took over managing his finances. This resulted in Mark becoming entirely financially dependent. He began to doubt his own perceptions, wondering if he was truly as flawed as his partner portrayed him to be. Mark's case illustrates how the insidious nature of sociopathic manipulation can manifest differently, subtly eroding a person's confidence and self-worth.

These examples underscore the subtle and insidious nature of sociopathic manipulation. The tactics are rarely blatant acts of aggression; instead, they're a series of carefully planned maneuvers designed to gain control and maintain dominance. The victim is gradually conditioned to accept the abuser's reality, making it difficult to recognize the abuse and escape its grip. The effects of this manipulative behavior are profound and long-lasting, impacting every aspect of the victim's life. Recognizing these tactics is the first critical step towards recovery and reclaiming one's life. Understanding the mechanisms of manipulation empowers survivors to break free from the cycle of abuse and begin the journey towards healing. The path to recovery is long and challenging, but with support and understanding, it is entirely possible. The knowledge gained from understanding these tactics is invaluable, providing the tools necessary to break the cycle and build a healthier, safer future.

The Impact of Sociopathic Abuse on Victims

The insidious nature of sociopathic abuse leaves a deep and lasting scar on the victim's psyche, extending far beyond the immediate physical and emotional trauma. The psychological and emotional consequences are profound and multifaceted, often manifesting as a complex array of symptoms that can significantly impair daily life. It's crucial to understand that these symptoms are not a sign of weakness or fault on the victim's part; they are entirely predictable and understandable responses to the systematic dismantling of one's sense of self, security, and reality. The experience is the result of the abuser's actions, not the victim's inherent flaws.

One of the most common consequences of sociopathic abuse is the development of Post-Traumatic Stress Disorder (PTSD). PTSD, traditionally associated with war or natural disasters, can also be triggered by the prolonged trauma of living with a sociopath. The constant fear, unpredictability, and emotional manipulation create a state of hypervigilance, leaving the victim constantly on edge, anticipating the next outburst or manipulation. Symptoms can include flashbacks, nightmares, intrusive thoughts related to the abusive relationship, and emotional numbness. Even seemingly mundane events or situations can trigger overwhelming feelings of anxiety or panic, transporting the victim back to the trauma. The inability to escape the emotional and mental grip of the abuser contributes significantly to the development of PTSD.

Anxiety disorders are another prevalent outcome. The constant uncertainty and fear created by the abuser's unpredictable behavior create a state of chronic anxiety.

Victims may experience generalized anxiety, characterized by persistent worry and nervousness, or panic attacks, characterized by intense fear and physical symptoms such as rapid heartbeat, shortness of breath, and trembling. The inability to trust one's own perceptions or judgment, a common consequence of gaslighting, further exacerbates anxiety, as the victim constantly questions their own reality and experiences. The resulting hyper-awareness of potential threats, even in safe environments, contributes to the persistent and debilitating effects of anxiety.

Depression is a common comorbid condition among survivors of sociopathic abuse. The systematic erosion of self-worth, the constant criticism and belittling, and the isolation imposed by the abuser contribute to feelings of hopelessness, worthlessness, and despair. Victims may experience persistent sadness, loss of interest in activities they once enjoyed, changes in appetite and sleep patterns, fatigue, and difficulty concentrating. The feeling of being trapped and powerless, coupled with the pervasive sense of shame and guilt often instilled by the abuser, deepens the depression, creating a vicious cycle of negativity and despair. The isolation often orchestrated by the abuser further prevents access to vital support networks, compounding the victim's distress.

Low self-esteem is a hallmark of the aftermath of sociopathic abuse. The abuser's constant criticism, subtle put-downs, and manipulation systematically erode the victim's confidence, making them question their judgment, abilities, and worth. The victim internalizes the abuser's negative messages, believing themselves to be flawed, inadequate, and unworthy of love and respect. This pervasive self-doubt extends to all aspects of their life, impacting their relationships, career, and overall well-being. The victim may struggle to make decisions, fearing they are incapable of making the right choices. The erosion of self- esteem is one of the most enduring and devastating legacies of sociopathic abuse.

Beyond these specific diagnoses, sociopathic abuse leaves a broader impact on the victim's sense of self and their ability to navigate the world. Trust issues are widespread. The consistent betrayal and manipulation experienced in the abusive relationship make it difficult for the victim to trust others, even those who genuinely care about them. This distrust can extend to close friends, family members, and even professionals, creating barriers to seeking help and support. The constant deception and manipulation make establishing genuine connections difficult, resulting in feelings of isolation and loneliness, even within supportive environments.

Difficulties with intimacy and forming healthy relationships are also common. The victim may struggle to form close attachments, fearing the repetition of the abusive dynamics. They may subconsciously seek out partners with similar traits to the abuser, recreating the familiar, albeit toxic, pattern. Alternatively, they may become overly cautious and avoid intimacy altogether, fearing vulnerability and betrayal. The experience of abuse distorts the perception of healthy relationships, making it challenging to differentiate between healthy boundaries and abusive behavior.

Cognitive impairment, often subtle and overlooked, can also result from chronic stress and emotional manipulation. The victim may struggle with concentration, memory, and decision-making due to the persistent cognitive dissonance created by gaslighting. The constant questioning of one's perceptions and reality can impair cognitive function, making it challenging to process information and make sound judgments. This mental fatigue can contribute to feelings of overwhelm and further impede recovery.

Somatic symptoms, physical manifestations of psychological distress, are frequently reported by survivors. These symptoms can include chronic pain, gastrointestinal issues, sleep disturbances, headaches, and fatigue. The prolonged stress and anxiety associated with the abuse manifest physically, taking a toll on the victim's overall health. The body's inability to effectively manage the constant state of stress can lead to a range of physical ailments.

The recovery process from sociopathic abuse is a journey, not a destination. It requires patience, self-compassion, and access to appropriate support systems. Therapy plays a crucial role, offering a safe space to process the trauma, rebuild self-esteem, and develop healthy coping mechanisms. It is essential to validate the victim's experience, acknowledging the reality of the abuse and helping them understand that the symptoms they are experiencing are not their fault. Therapy provides the necessary tools to challenge the internalized negative messages and reclaim their sense of self.

Support groups offer invaluable peer support, creating a community where survivors can share their experiences, find validation, and learn from others who understand the intricacies of recovering from sociopathic abuse. Connecting with others who have lived through similar experiences can significantly reduce feelings of isolation and provide a sense of hope and resilience.

Rebuilding a sense of self requires active engagement in self-care. This includes prioritizing physical health through exercise, healthy eating, and sufficient sleep; engaging in activities that bring joy and foster a sense of

accomplishment; setting healthy boundaries and learning to say no to demands that compromise personal well-being. It involves cultivating self-compassion and recognizing one's own strength and resilience. The path to recovery involves challenging the ingrained beliefs and behaviors shaped by the abuse and creating a new narrative centered on self- worth, safety, and agency. The process is challenging, but with perseverance and the right support, a fulfilling and healthy life free from the shadow of abuse is entirely possible. The journey of healing is unique to each individual, but recognizing the common impact of sociopathic abuse is the crucial first step. Understanding that these experiences are not a reflection of personal weakness, but rather the direct consequence of abuse, is fundamental in embarking on the path towards recovery and reclaiming a life free from fear and manipulation.

Recognizing the Red Flags and Warning Signs

Recognizing the insidious nature of sociopathic abuse often proves challenging due to the abuser's mastery of manipulation and deception. They rarely reveal their true selves outright; instead, they employ a complex web of tactics designed to slowly erode the victim's sense of self and control their behavior. Identifying these red flags requires careful observation and a willingness to question seemingly innocuous behaviors. It's crucial to remember that not all of these signs will be present in every abusive relationship, and the presence of one or two doesn't automatically mean you're in an abusive relationship. However, the consistent presence of multiple red flags should serve as a serious cause for concern.

One of the most prominent red flags is a pervasive pattern of **gaslighting** . This involves systematically manipulating the victim's perception of reality, making them question their own sanity and memory. The abuser might deny events that happened, twist their words, or subtly alter the narrative to suit their agenda. For example, an abuser might deny making a specific promise, claim the victim is misremembering a conversation, or insist the victim is overly sensitive or imagining things. The cumulative effect of these manipulations can leave the victim feeling confused, disoriented, and increasingly dependent on the abuser for validation. The gaslighting isn't a single incident; it's a repeated pattern of undermining the victim's sense of self and truth.

Closely related to gaslighting is the abuser's tendency to **control and manipulate** the victim's life. This control can manifest in numerous ways: restricting access to friends and

family, monitoring phone calls and emails, controlling finances, dictating clothing choices, or limiting access to transportation or personal possessions. This control is often subtle at first, presented as concern or protectiveness.

However, over time, it becomes increasingly restrictive, isolating the victim and diminishing their independence. For instance, an abuser might initially claim to be concerned about the victim's safety when limiting their contact with family or friends. Later, this could escalate into preventing them from seeing loved ones altogether, under the guise of 'protecting them'. Financial control is another common form of abuse, where the abuser might withhold money, control all joint accounts, or prevent the victim from working.

The **lack of empathy and remorse** is a defining characteristic of sociopathic abusers. They rarely show genuine concern for the victim's feelings or well-being. They might dismiss the victim's emotions as irrational, overblown, or manipulative, further eroding the victim's sense of self- worth. Even when directly confronted with their hurtful actions, they may show little to no remorse, offering superficial apologies or blaming the victim for their own behavior. For example, an abuser might react to a victim expressing hurt feelings with a dismissive comment like, "You're too sensitive," or "You're making a big deal out of nothing." They lack the ability to genuinely understand and share the victim's emotional experience.

Another significant red flag is the abuser's **charming and charismatic** facade. They often present themselves as charming, intelligent, and successful, masking their manipulative and abusive tendencies. This initial charm helps to draw victims into the relationship and make it more difficult to recognize the abuse. The abuser may be exceptionally skilled at making a good first impression, leaving others unaware of their true nature. This duality makes it difficult for victims and those around them to identify the abuser's abusive patterns.

Isolation is a tactic frequently employed by sociopathic abusers to increase their control and prevent the victim from seeking help or support. They might subtly undermine the victim's relationships with friends and family, creating distance and making them more reliant on the abuser. This isolation can be gradual, starting with criticisms of the victim's friends or family, leading to outright prohibitions on contact. The abuser might also make it difficult for the victim to leave the house, attend social events, or maintain their own independent social circle.

Pathological lying is a key component of the manipulative tactics used by sociopaths. They frequently lie, often without any apparent motive beyond the manipulation itself. These lies can be about big or small things, further eroding the victim's trust and confidence in their perception of reality.

The victim may find themselves constantly questioning the abuser's words and actions, further contributing to the confusion and disorientation caused by the abuse. Over time, this consistent deceit damages the victim's sense of security and self-trust.

Paranoia and projection are common mechanisms employed by sociopathic abusers. They often accuse the victim of behaviors that they themselves are guilty of, a tactic known as projection. This deflection shifts blame and distracts from their own actions. Similarly, they may display intense paranoia, distrusting the victim's intentions or accusing them of plotting against them. These behaviors are designed to confuse the victim and maintain control. For example, an abuser might accuse their partner of cheating when they are the one engaging in infidelity.

Threats, intimidation, and coercion can take many forms. These range from subtle threats to overt acts of violence or intimidation. The abuser might threaten to harm the victim, their family, or their pets; threaten to reveal embarrassing information; or use financial control to coerce compliance. These tactics are designed to create fear and maintain control over the victim. The constant fear generated through such threats impacts every aspect of the victim's daily life.

Controlling behavior extends beyond restricting social contacts and finances; it encompasses controlling every facet of the victim's life. This can include dictating what the victim wears, how they spend their time, who they can speak to, and even controlling their diet or sleep patterns. The abuser seeks to strip the victim of their autonomy, making them completely dependent.

Emotional volatility is another common red flag. The abuser's emotions can shift dramatically and unpredictably. They might switch from being overly charming and affectionate to angry and abusive within minutes or even seconds. This unpredictable behavior keeps the victim on edge, constantly anticipating the next outburst. This emotional rollercoaster creates a high level of stress and anxiety for the victim.

Lack of accountability and a refusal to take responsibility for their actions are crucial indicators. They will deflect blame, minimize the impact of their behavior, or rationalize their actions, shifting responsibility onto the victim or external factors. This prevents the relationship from ever being truly resolved and allows the abuse to continue.

Exploitation is a common element in sociopathic abuse. The abuser may exploit the victim financially, emotionally, or sexually. They might manipulate the victim into providing

money, favors, or emotional support without reciprocity. This exploitation is often intricately woven into the overall pattern of manipulation and control.

Love bombing , a period of intense affection and attention at the beginning of the relationship, is used to reel the victim in and create a false sense of security. This intense period of romantic gestures and compliments is then followed by periods of coldness, criticism, or abuse. This cyclical pattern of idealization and devaluation is a classic characteristic of sociopathic relationships.

Triangulation involves involving a third party in the relationship to create conflict and undermine the victim's sense of security. The abuser might talk to other people about the victim, pitting them against each other. They could also involve another person romantically to create jealousy or insecurity. This serves to weaken the relationship and increase the abuser's power.

Recognizing these red flags is a critical step towards escaping the cycle of abuse. While the presence of some of these warning signs doesn't automatically indicate sociopathic abuse, a consistent pattern of multiple red flags should be taken seriously. It's important to trust your instincts and seek help if you feel unsafe or manipulated.

Remember, escaping this kind of abuse is possible. The first step is identifying the problem and seeking professional support. The path to recovery is long and challenging, but it is a path worth pursuing. You deserve a life free from fear and manipulation.

Breaking the Cycle of Abuse The First Step

Breaking the cycle of abuse is a monumental task, often fraught with fear, uncertainty, and self-doubt. The insidious nature of sociopathic abuse leaves victims feeling trapped, their sense of self eroded, and their ability to make rational decisions compromised. However, understanding that you are not alone and that the abuse is not your fault is the crucial first step towards reclaiming your life. The manipulative tactics employed by sociopaths are designed to isolate and control, making it feel impossible to escape. But escape *is* possible. The path to freedom begins with recognizing the reality of your situation and accepting that you deserve better.

This isn't about blame; it's about empowerment. For years, I, like many others, struggled with the crippling guilt and self- reproach that accompany abuse. I replayed every conversation, every interaction, searching for my own flaws, the things I "could have done differently" to prevent the abuse. This is a classic manipulation tactic. Sociopaths expertly deflect blame, making you question your own sanity and perceptions. They'll paint you as the problem, the instigator, the emotionally unstable one, while they remain the seemingly rational, unaffected party. Let me assure you: this is a lie. The responsibility for the abuse rests entirely on the abuser's shoulders. Their actions are a reflection of their pathology, not a consequence of your shortcomings.

The decision to leave is rarely simple. It's often a process, a gradual awakening to the reality of the abuse and the recognition of its devastating impact. Fear is a powerful tool used by abusers, and it's understandable to feel terrified of the unknown. What will happen if you leave? Will you be

safe? Will you be able to support yourself? These are legitimate concerns, and addressing them is crucial to making a safe and successful exit.

Often, the first step isn't a dramatic escape but a series of small, incremental changes that gradually shift the balance of power. These subtle shifts can create space for self- reflection, allowing you to reassess the situation more clearly and begin to formulate a plan. Perhaps it's creating a secret email address, a discreet way to communicate with a trusted friend or family member outside the abuser's knowledge.

Maybe it's opening a separate bank account, securing a small amount of money to use for an eventual escape. Or it might be subtly researching local shelters or support organizations, learning about the resources available to you without alarming the abuser. These seemingly insignificant actions are actually steps towards reclaiming your agency, building a foundation for your escape.

Remember, creating a safety plan is paramount. This plan needs to be as detailed as possible, considering every aspect of your life. Where will you go? Who will you contact? Do you have access to transportation? What about your belongings? How will you secure your finances? Do you need to involve law enforcement? Creating a comprehensive safety plan minimizes risks and maximizes your chances of a successful escape. Don't underestimate the importance of having a detailed plan; it's the roadmap to your freedom.

It's imperative to start building a support network. Reach out to trusted friends, family members, or colleagues. Confiding in someone you trust, even if it's just one person, can make a world of difference. Sharing your experiences can provide validation, emotional support, and practical assistance. They might offer a safe place to stay, help with logistics, or simply provide a listening ear. This support network is crucial for

navigating the emotional and logistical challenges of leaving an abusive relationship. Don't be afraid to reach out; people who care about you want to help.

Connecting with support organizations specifically designed to help victims of domestic violence and abuse is also critical. These organizations offer a range of services, from emergency shelter and legal assistance to counseling and support groups. They provide a safe space to share your experiences without judgment and offer expert guidance on navigating the legal and emotional complexities of your situation. They can connect you with resources that you might not be aware of and help you develop strategies for moving forward. There is no shame in seeking help; it's a sign of strength and resilience.

Remember, the feeling of shame and guilt is a deliberate tactic used by abusers to keep you trapped. They want you to believe that you are somehow responsible for their behavior. You are not. The actions of the abuser are a reflection of their own character and personality disorders; your worth is not diminished by their actions. You deserve a life free from fear and manipulation. You deserve respect, kindness, and love.

The process of leaving an abusive relationship and rebuilding your life is a journey, not a destination. There will be setbacks, moments of doubt, and emotional challenges.

Healing takes time, patience, and self-compassion. Allow yourself to grieve the loss of the relationship you imagined, to feel the anger, the sadness, the confusion. These feelings are valid, and it's crucial to process them healthily, with the support of therapists or support groups.

Professional help is invaluable during this process. A therapist specializing in trauma and abuse recovery can

provide the necessary tools and techniques to cope with the emotional fallout of the abuse, to understand the impact on your mental and emotional well-being, and to develop healthy coping mechanisms. Therapy can help you unravel the complexities of the manipulation and rebuild your sense of self-worth. It offers a safe space to process your experiences without judgment and provides guidance on regaining your emotional equilibrium.

The path to recovery is paved with small victories, moments of self-discovery, and increasing self-confidence. It's about reclaiming your autonomy, your voice, your life. It's about redefining what a healthy relationship looks and feels like and setting boundaries to ensure you never fall prey to such manipulation again. It's about remembering your strength, your resilience, your inherent worth. This is your story, and you are writing the next chapter, a chapter filled with hope, healing, and a future free from the shadows of abuse.

Leaving an abusive relationship is never easy, but it is always possible. You are not alone. There are people who care, resources that can help, and a future waiting for you, a future where you can thrive and flourish. The first step, the most critical step, is recognizing the abuse, understanding that it's not your fault, and choosing to break free. That choice is the beginning of your journey to healing and recovery, a journey that is worth taking, a journey that leads to a life filled with love, respect, and peace. Remember your worth, believe in yourself, and know that you deserve a life free from the shadows.

Assessing Your Current Situation and Risks

Before embarking on the actual escape, a crucial step involves a thorough assessment of your present circumstances and the potential risks inherent in leaving. This isn't about dwelling on fear, but about strategically mitigating it. Understanding the potential dangers allows you to proactively build a safety plan that significantly increases your chances of a successful and safe transition.

Begin by honestly evaluating your living situation. Does your abuser have access to firearms or other weapons? Is there a history of violence or threats of violence? This information is critical for determining the level of immediate risk you face. If weapons are present, consider whether they are easily accessible, stored securely, or even hidden in places you wouldn't immediately suspect. The presence of weapons dramatically alters the safety equation, necessitating a more cautious and potentially more immediate escape strategy.

Next, analyze the level of control your abuser exerts over your daily life. This encompasses various aspects, from financial control to social isolation. Does your abuser control your finances, limiting your access to funds or preventing you from having a separate bank account? This financial dependence creates a significant barrier to escape, as it can leave you feeling trapped and unable to afford independent living. If this is the case, meticulously document any financial transactions, and begin subtly accumulating even small amounts of money. Consider creating a secret savings account, perhaps using a different financial institution, or utilizing prepaid cards.

Assess the extent of your social isolation. Have you been systematically cut off from friends and family? Does your abuser monitor your communications, restrict your access to technology, or control your movement? This isolation is a deliberate tactic to minimize your support network and increase your dependence on the abuser. If you're isolated, prioritize rebuilding contact with trusted individuals, even if it's initially through discreet methods, such as secret email addresses or coded messages. Re-establishing these connections is essential for providing emotional support and practical assistance during your escape.

Consider your abuser's personality and behavior patterns. Are they impulsive and prone to fits of rage? Do they exhibit a pattern of escalating aggression or violence?

Understanding these patterns allows you to anticipate potential reactions to your departure and factor those reactions into your safety plan. If they have a history of unpredictable behavior, you may need to take additional precautions, such as arranging for a temporary stay in a safe house or shelter, rather than going straight to a friend or family member's home.

Technological surveillance is a prevalent tool used by abusers. Assess your abuser's access to your digital devices, email accounts, and social media. Do they monitor your online activity? Do they have access to your passwords or location data through tracking apps? If so, take immediate steps to secure your digital privacy, changing all your passwords, deleting tracking apps, and limiting the personal information you share online. Consider using secure messaging apps that offer end-to-end encryption and using a different device if possible. It might be useful to research different applications and operating systems to better protect your privacy.

Your physical safety is paramount. Assess your home environment for potential escape routes and safe spaces. Identify potential escape routes from your home, noting the quickest ways to exit your apartment, house, or building safely. If you're staying in a shared residence, plan alternative routes. If you are being stalked, identify places where you are most vulnerable, and make plans to minimize your exposure to your stalker. Identify safe spaces within your home that offer a degree of privacy or refuge in case of an altercation. These safe spaces could be a locked room, a well-lit area, or a place where you can easily call for help.

Once you've conducted this self-assessment, it's crucial to identify specific risks associated with leaving. These risks can range from direct threats of violence to the more subtle forms of intimidation and harassment. It's imperative to recognize and address these risks systematically, incorporating preventive measures into your safety plan. The most crucial aspect of mitigating risk is careful planning and meticulous execution of that plan.

Consider the following potential risks and ways to mitigate them:

Physical violence: This is the most serious risk. If your abuser has a history of violence, leaving must be planned with utmost caution. Consider seeking assistance from law enforcement or a domestic violence shelter to ensure your safety during the escape.

Stalking and harassment: Your abuser may attempt to track your movements or harass you after you leave. Develop a plan to minimize your exposure and maintain your anonymity. This might involve changing your phone number, using a different email address, or temporarily relocating to a new address known only to a trusted few. Consider seeking a

restraining order to legally protect yourself from further harassment.

Financial hardship: If your abuser controls your finances, you'll need to secure your own financial resources before leaving. This might involve secretly opening a bank account, accumulating savings, or seeking assistance from family, friends, or social services.

Loss of housing and support systems: You may need to find a new place to live and rebuild your support network. Begin researching local shelters, affordable housing options, or the possibility of staying with friends or family.

Legal repercussions: If you're concerned about legal repercussions, consult with a lawyer specializing in domestic violence cases to understand your rights and options.

Emotional and psychological trauma: Leaving an abusive relationship is emotionally challenging. Begin building a support network of trusted friends, family, therapists, or support groups to provide emotional support and guidance throughout this process.

Your safety plan should be a detailed, personalized document addressing all these potential risks. It's not a single action but a multifaceted strategy covering every conceivable scenario. The more comprehensively you plan, the greater your chances of a successful and safe escape.

Begin creating your safety plan by listing all potential escape routes from your home, including alternative paths if your primary escape route is blocked. Consider the times of day when you are least likely to be observed or confronted and plan accordingly. If possible, consider having a backup plan in case your first attempt is unsuccessful. Don't

underestimate the importance of having a pre-determined location for your escape, whether it's a friend's house, a family member's home, or a domestic violence shelter.

This safety plan isn't static; it's a living document, subject to modification as circumstances evolve. Regularly review and update your plan based on any new information or changes in your situation. Remember, a dynamic, adaptable plan significantly improves your chances of a successful escape.

Remember that you are not alone in this, and seeking professional help is a sign of strength, not weakness. Therapists specializing in trauma and abuse recovery can provide invaluable support and guidance in developing a comprehensive safety plan and navigating the complexities of leaving an abusive relationship. They offer a safe space to process your fears, discuss your options, and develop coping strategies for the emotional challenges ahead.

The creation of a safety plan is a vital, life-affirming step toward reclaiming your life and breaking free from the abusive situation. It's a roadmap to your freedom, meticulously laid out to help you reach your destination safe and secure. Your journey towards freedom begins with one solid step: making a comprehensive safety plan.

Gathering Essential Resources and Support

Gathering the necessary resources and support is as crucial as crafting the safety plan itself. Your escape isn't just about leaving the abusive environment; it's about building a secure foundation for your future. This involves securing safe housing, assembling a dependable support network, and obtaining the legal and financial guidance you need to navigate this complex transition. Failing to adequately address these aspects can severely jeopardize your safety and well-being.

Let's begin with housing. Leaving an abusive situation often necessitates a change of address, even temporarily. The immediate priority is to find a safe place where your abuser cannot locate you. Domestic violence shelters offer a lifeline in these situations. These shelters provide temporary accommodation, meals, and often access to counseling and legal services. They are designed to offer a safe haven from immediate danger, giving you the space to assess your options and formulate a long-term plan. Finding a shelter requires research; many local organizations and hotlines can provide listings and referrals based on your geographical location and specific circumstances. Don't hesitate to utilize these resources; they are specifically designed to assist individuals in situations like yours. Remember, seeking help is a courageous act, not a sign of weakness.

If a shelter isn't immediately feasible, explore alternative temporary housing options. This could involve staying with trusted family or friends. Before approaching anyone, be sure you feel fully comfortable confiding in them. It's crucial to choose people who will prioritize your safety and offer unconditional support. Explain your situation honestly,

emphasizing the level of risk involved. This ensures they understand the gravity of the situation and can take appropriate precautions. It's vital to prepare your support network for potential contact attempts from your abuser. Provide them with strategies for deflecting any communication or visit attempts. If you have reason to believe your abuser may become violent or intrusive, your support network will need to be prepared to manage this possibility. A clear plan for handling any attempts from your abuser to contact them and you is crucial.

Finding long-term housing requires careful planning and consideration of your financial capabilities. Affordable housing options can be difficult to secure, especially if you lack financial independence. Explore housing assistance programs offered by your local government or non-profit organizations. These programs often provide subsidized housing or rental assistance to individuals in need. Research thoroughly and make sure you fully understand the eligibility criteria and application process. Be prepared to provide the necessary documentation, which might include proof of income, residency, and evidence of domestic violence.

Beyond housing, building a strong support network is vital. This network provides emotional and practical assistance during this difficult transition. Start by identifying trusted individuals who can offer unwavering support. This may include family members, close friends, colleagues, or members of your faith community. These individuals will offer a listening ear, practical help, and emotional strength during periods of vulnerability.

Reaching out to friends and family may feel daunting after a period of isolation imposed by your abuser. Remember, the isolation was a deliberate tactic designed to control you; it

does not reflect your true relationships. Your friends and family likely want to be helpful. Take the initiative to re- establish those connections. Start with short updates gradually explaining your situation. Don't feel pressured to reveal everything at once; take your time and share what you are ready to share. Prioritize those who you believe can be consistently supportive and understanding.

Consider joining a support group for survivors of domestic abuse. These groups offer a unique opportunity to connect with others who understand your experience. Sharing experiences and receiving empathetic support from others who've lived through similar situations can be incredibly powerful. Support groups provide a sense of community and validation. They can also offer practical advice and suggestions based on the lived experiences of others.

Finding professional support is essential. A therapist specializing in trauma and abuse recovery can offer invaluable guidance. Therapy provides a safe space to process the emotional trauma you've endured. A therapist can help you develop coping mechanisms to navigate the challenges of rebuilding your life. They can offer support and validation during this transition. Many therapists offer sliding-scale fees or pro bono services, ensuring access regardless of financial constraints.

Seeking legal counsel is also essential. A lawyer specializing in family law or domestic violence can advise you on your legal rights and options, particularly regarding restraining orders, child custody, and other relevant legal matters.

Having legal counsel can make a profound difference in securing your safety and protecting your rights during the separation and beyond. They can help you navigate the legal processes involved in severing ties with your abuser. A

lawyer can advise you on any potential legal repercussions related to the separation.

Financial independence is crucial for long-term safety and stability. If your abuser controlled your finances, you will need to begin rebuilding your financial security. Start by identifying your assets, including bank accounts, investments, and property. Secure these assets and take steps to prevent your abuser from gaining access to them.

Consider opening a new bank account and applying for credit cards in your name only. Explore financial assistance programs that offer grants or loans for survivors of domestic violence. These programs can assist in securing stable housing, paying off debts, or starting new careers.

Remember that rebuilding your life after escaping abuse is a marathon, not a sprint. Be patient with yourself and celebrate your progress along the way. It's important to acknowledge and validate the tremendous effort involved in creating a safe and stable future. Focus on taking small, manageable steps, one day at a time.

The process of gathering resources and support is integral to your safety and well-being. It's not a single step but a multifaceted strategy requiring ongoing effort. However, remember that each step you take is a demonstration of your resilience and strength. You are taking back control of your life, creating a foundation for your future free from fear and manipulation. This is a journey towards healing and empowerment, and you have the strength to succeed. Your commitment to rebuilding your life is a testament to your inner resilience and your determination to create a future free from abuse. Reach out to those who can support you, and remember that you are not alone.

Developing a Communication Strategy

Developing a communication strategy during the separation process from a sociopathic abuser requires careful planning and a deep understanding of their manipulative tactics. The goal is not to engage in protracted arguments or attempts at reconciliation, but rather to minimize contact while ensuring your safety and well-being. This means establishing clear boundaries and choosing communication channels strategically to protect yourself from further abuse or retaliation.

The first step involves recognizing that any communication with your abuser is inherently risky. Sociopaths are masters of manipulation, and even seemingly innocuous conversations can be used to exert control, gather information, or escalate conflict. Therefore, the ideal scenario is to eliminate direct contact entirely. This may involve utilizing a third party, such as a lawyer or a trusted friend, to handle all necessary communication. This approach removes the direct interaction that allows the abuser to exert their influence and minimizes the risk of emotional or psychological manipulation.

If direct communication is unavoidable—for example, regarding child custody arrangements or financial matters— it's crucial to maintain strict control over the interaction.

Choose a method that provides a written record, such as email or text messaging. Avoid phone calls, as they offer less control over the conversation and are more easily manipulated. Keep all communication concise, factual, and professional. Avoid emotional language or personal details that could be used against you. Respond only to essential

queries and refrain from engaging in lengthy discussions or arguments.

Before engaging in any form of communication, anticipate potential manipulative tactics. Sociopaths often employ gaslighting, blaming, and deflection to control the narrative and maintain their power. Prepare for these tactics by rehearsing your responses and having clear boundaries in mind. If the conversation veers into manipulation, immediately disengage. Politely but firmly state that you are not willing to engage in unproductive discussions and end the communication. Do not feel obligated to justify your actions or engage in debate.

Consider creating a template for your responses to frequently asked questions or common points of contention. This pre- prepared template ensures that your communications remain concise and avoids emotional responses. This is particularly helpful if you're dealing with multiple exchanges, ensuring consistency and preventing emotional outbursts that could fuel the abuser's manipulative behaviors. For instance, if the abuser repeatedly demands money, a prepared response outlining financial support arrangements and legal proceedings is more effective than a reactive, emotional response. Similarly, if questions arise about children, a consistent template that prioritizes the child's well-being and clearly outlines visitation plans minimizes the potential for manipulation.

Document every communication, including emails, texts, and any written notes. This record is crucial in case of future legal proceedings or if the abuser attempts to discredit your account of the abuse. It serves as irrefutable evidence of your interactions and demonstrates the pattern of their behavior.

Keep a detailed log of dates, times, the content of the communication, and any notable observations about the

abuser's tone or demeanor. This comprehensive documentation not only protects you legally but also reinforces your awareness of the dynamics at play.

If the communication involves a third party, ensure they fully understand the situation and the abuser's potential manipulative tactics. Provide them with background information to help them manage the interactions effectively. This includes details about the abuse, the abuser's manipulative tactics, and any specific concerns about their safety. This collaboration helps to protect you and provides additional layers of support during the separation process.

It's essential to maintain emotional distance during all communications. Avoid showing any vulnerability or emotional reactivity that the abuser can exploit. This means responding to their communication in a calm, detached, and businesslike manner. This emotional detachment limits their opportunity to exert their control and minimizes the risk of emotional escalation. Remember, your emotional state is your responsibility. Do not let their communications dictate your emotions.

Establish a clear communication protocol. Decide on the preferred method of communication, the frequency, and the topics to be discussed. This helps establish boundaries and prevents the abuser from dictating the terms of interaction. Stick to this protocol strictly and do not deviate from it, even if pressured to do so. This consistency reinforces your boundaries and protects you from unpredictable escalation.

For example, you might stipulate that communication only occurs through a designated attorney and is limited to twice a week to discuss specific legal matters.

Consider seeking guidance from a therapist or counselor specializing in trauma and abuse recovery. They can offer

support and strategies for managing communications with your abuser. They can help you identify potential triggers, develop coping mechanisms for dealing with the emotional fallout from the interaction, and provide valuable insights on recognizing and responding to manipulative behaviors. This professional support helps you maintain emotional equilibrium and prevents the abuser's manipulations from undermining your progress.

After any communication, allow yourself time to process the interaction. Engage in self-care activities that help you regain emotional balance and manage the stress. This could involve spending time in nature, practicing mindfulness, engaging in creative pursuits, or talking with a trusted friend or family member. This self-care routine helps regulate emotional responses, preventing the abuser from further controlling your emotional well-being.

Finally, remember that you have the right to protect your safety and well-being. Prioritize your emotional and physical health over the needs of the abuser. If the communication becomes emotionally or psychologically damaging, disengage immediately. Don't hesitate to seek support from legal counsel or law enforcement if necessary. Your safety and well-being are paramount, and your strength and resilience will guide you through this challenging process.

The process of disengaging from a sociopathic abuser requires patience, resilience, and a strong commitment to self-preservation. By implementing a well-defined communication strategy, you're taking control of the situation, protecting yourself from further harm, and paving the way for a healthier and safer future. Remember, you deserve to live a life free from fear and manipulation.

Protecting Yourself from Technological Stalking

Protecting yourself from technological stalking requires a proactive and multi-layered approach. Sociopaths and stalkers are adept at using technology to monitor and control their victims, often employing sophisticated methods that require careful attention to detail to counter. This isn't about paranoia; it's about safeguarding your privacy and well-being in the face of deliberate, malicious surveillance. The first step involves a complete overhaul of your digital security practices.

Begin by changing all your passwords. This isn't just about changing them; it's about creating strong, unique passwords for every online account. Avoid easily guessable passwords like birthdays, pet names, or sequential numbers. Instead, opt for a combination of uppercase and lowercase letters, numbers, and symbols. Consider using a password manager to generate and securely store these complex passwords.

Password managers generate robust passwords and can auto- fill login credentials securely, making this crucial task much more manageable. Remember to enable two-factor authentication (2FA) wherever possible, adding an extra layer of security to your accounts. This authentication method typically requires a second verification code, sent to your phone or email, in addition to your password. This significantly reduces the likelihood of unauthorized access even if your password is compromised.

Next, review and adjust your privacy settings on all social media platforms, email accounts, and online services. Most platforms offer detailed control over who can see your posts, messages, and location data. Limit the visibility of your personal information to trusted contacts only. Be particularly mindful of location services. While convenient, sharing your location in real-time makes you vulnerable to stalking.

Disable location sharing on apps and services unless absolutely necessary, and check the settings of any apps you've downloaded, as some will continue to share location data even when it's not explicitly enabled. Even seemingly innocuous apps might have these features, so thoroughly review their privacy policies.

Consider the apps on your phone and computer. Many apps have access to far more information than you might realize. Review your installed applications and remove any that you no longer use or that you suspect might be used for tracking or monitoring your activity. Pay close attention to apps with broad permissions, including access to your contacts, location, microphone, or camera. If you're unsure about an app's function, research it thoroughly online before continuing to use it. Uninstall any apps you deem suspicious and ensure that you are aware of every app installed on your devices.

Beyond reviewing your current apps, be vigilant about downloading new apps. Only download apps from reputable app stores, and carefully read reviews before installation.

Avoid apps from unknown or untrusted sources. Consider using a VPN (Virtual Private Network) to encrypt your internet traffic and mask your IP address. This makes it more difficult for someone to track your online activity and location. A VPN is a vital tool in preserving your digital anonymity and security, and it's a worthwhile investment.

Regularly scan your devices for malware and spyware. Use reputable antivirus and anti-malware software and keep it updated. These security programs can detect and remove harmful software that might be installed on your devices without your knowledge, potentially providing access to

your personal data and enabling surveillance. Ensure your operating systems are also updated regularly as these updates often include security patches to protect against known vulnerabilities.

Take extra precautions with your email. Be cautious about opening emails from unknown senders or clicking on links within emails, as these can lead to malware infections or phishing scams. Use strong and unique passwords for your email accounts and enable 2FA for added security. Consider setting up email filters to automatically move suspicious emails to your spam folder. Regularly review the "sent" folder and delete unwanted messages to prevent those messages from being easily accessible.

Be aware of smart home devices. Many modern homes are equipped with devices like smart speakers, security cameras, and smart televisions that can collect and transmit data about your activities. Be mindful of these devices and their privacy settings. Ensure you understand how they collect and use your data, and adjust their privacy settings to minimize the amount of data collected. In some cases, consider disabling these devices entirely if there is a significant risk of technological stalking. If you're unsure about the security implications of your smart home devices, consult a tech- savvy friend or professional.

Consider purchasing a new phone and/or computer. If you suspect your devices have been compromised by spyware or tracking software, it's wise to replace them. This is a significant step, but it's essential to ensure your complete digital security. While it requires an investment, the peace of mind gained by knowing you have devices that are truly yours and completely free of spyware is invaluable.

Finally, document everything. Keep a record of all suspicious activity, including emails, messages, and any unusual behavior of your devices. This documentation is crucial if you need to seek legal assistance or report the stalking to law enforcement. Note the dates, times, and details of any suspicious incidents. This detailed record will serve as crucial evidence of the abuser's actions and will greatly assist authorities in bringing them to justice.

This comprehensive approach to protecting yourself from technological stalking is crucial. It's a continuous process that demands vigilance and proactive measures. By adopting these strategies, you are significantly reducing your vulnerability and reclaiming control over your digital life and, by extension, your personal safety and well-being.

Remember, your safety is paramount. Don't hesitate to seek assistance from professionals – tech support, legal counsel, or a therapist specializing in trauma and abuse recovery – if you need help implementing these measures or feel overwhelmed. Your strength and resilience will guide you through this process. You deserve to live a life free from fear and manipulation.

Securing Legal Protection

Securing legal protection is a crucial step in escaping the clutches of a sociopathic abuser. It provides a tangible barrier against further harm and offers a pathway towards reclaiming your safety and autonomy. However, navigating the legal system can be daunting, especially when dealing with the manipulative tactics often employed by sociopaths. This section aims to equip you with the knowledge and strategies to effectively obtain legal protection and secure your future.

The first critical step involves understanding the types of legal protection available to you. In most jurisdictions, restraining orders and protective orders are the primary legal avenues for shielding yourself from abusive individuals.

While the specific terminology and requirements might vary slightly from state to state or country to country, the core purpose remains consistent: to prevent the abuser from contacting you, coming near your residence or workplace, and engaging in any other forms of harassment or intimidation.

Restraining orders, often referred to as temporary restraining orders or TROs, are typically granted quickly, often within a matter of days, following an initial court hearing. They provide immediate protection, but they are usually temporary in nature. A hearing is then scheduled to determine whether a permanent restraining order should be issued. To obtain a restraining order, you will need to demonstrate to the court that you are in immediate danger or have experienced credible threats of violence or harassment from the abuser. Detailed documentation of the abuse, including dates, times, specific incidents, and any

corroborating evidence (such as text messages, emails, photographs, witness statements, police reports, medical records), will be essential in supporting your application.

Protective orders, on the other hand, are often broader in scope and duration. They are frequently granted in cases involving domestic violence, stalking, or other forms of intimate partner abuse. They often include provisions beyond simple restrictions on contact, such as stipulations regarding child custody, visitation rights, firearm ownership, and access to shared property or finances. The application process for protective orders usually involves a more extensive investigation and hearing, but they offer stronger and more comprehensive protection.

Gathering evidence of abuse is paramount in your quest for legal protection. This evidence serves as the foundation upon which your case will be built. It is crucial to maintain detailed records of every interaction with your abuser, no matter how seemingly insignificant. This includes:

Detailed written accounts of every incident: Document the date, time, location, and a comprehensive description of what happened. Include specific details such as the abuser's words, actions, and any physical or emotional consequences you experienced. Be as specific as possible. Instead of saying "he yelled at me," write "on October 26th at 8:00 PM, in the kitchen, he yelled at me, calling me names including [specific names] and accusing me of [specific accusations]."
Copies of text messages, emails, and social media messages: Save all communication, regardless of whether it's abusive or seemingly

benign. These digital records often serve as irrefutable evidence of the abuser's behavior.

Screenshot everything. Don't delete anything; it can be used against you in court.

Photographs and videos: If you have any photographs or videos documenting injuries, property damage, or instances of harassment, these are powerful visual aids. If you take photos, ensure you take them immediately after the incident. **Medical records:** Document any injuries sustained due to the abuse. This includes physical injuries such as bruises, cuts, or broken bones, as well as psychological and emotional trauma. Make sure your doctor's records note the cause of your injuries.

Police reports: File a police report with every incident of violence or harassment. Keep a copy of the police report for your records. Even if the police don't make an arrest, the report serves as crucial documentation.

Witness statements: If anyone witnessed the abuse, obtain written or sworn statements from them. The testimony of independent witnesses can significantly strengthen your case.

Financial records: Document any financial control or manipulation by the abuser. This might include unauthorized withdrawals from joint accounts, control over finances, or preventing you from accessing money.

Organize all your documentation meticulously. Create a secure system for storing your evidence, and regularly back up your electronic files to the cloud. You might consider creating a dedicated file or folder, organized chronologically or by type of evidence. The goal is to have it readily available and easy to access when you're ready to approach the court system. Consider working with a therapist or advocate who can help you organize these materials into a cohesive and readily understandable file.

Beyond gathering evidence, seeking legal counsel is crucial. A lawyer specializing in domestic violence, stalking, or family law can provide expert advice, guide you through the legal process, represent you in court, and ensure that your

rights are protected. They can help you navigate the complexities of the legal system, explain your options, and help you develop a strategy for obtaining the most effective legal protection. Many legal aid organizations offer free or low-cost services to victims of domestic violence. Do not hesitate to seek professional legal assistance. This isn't a process to face alone.

It is imperative to understand your rights. You have the right to be safe, to be free from harassment and violence, and to seek legal recourse against those who abuse you. Familiarize yourself with your state's laws regarding restraining orders and protective orders. You are entitled to request an interpreter if you do not speak the language of the court and to be accompanied by a support person throughout the proceedings.

The process of obtaining legal protection might feel overwhelming and emotionally taxing. Remember that you are not alone, and seeking help is a sign of strength, not weakness. Lean on your support network—friends, family, therapists, support groups, or advocacy organizations—for emotional support and practical assistance. Take your time, focus on your well-being, and don't hesitate to seek help from professionals throughout this process. Securing legal protection is a crucial step in your journey towards safety and healing, and it's a testament to your resilience and your determination to build a life free from fear and control.

Remember that your safety and well-being are paramount. Never underestimate the power of seeking professional assistance; the support of qualified professionals can make all the difference in successfully navigating this challenging phase of your life.

The Escape Strategy A StepbyStep Guide

Leaving an abusive relationship with a sociopath is rarely a simple matter of packing a bag and walking out. It requires careful planning, meticulous execution, and a deep understanding of the potential risks involved. Your safety is paramount, and a well-defined escape strategy is crucial for minimizing danger and maximizing your chances of a successful and safe exit. This section will provide a detailed, step-by-step guide to help you navigate this challenging process.

First, understand that there's no one-size-fits-all approach. The best escape strategy will depend on your unique circumstances – the severity of the abuse, your abuser's personality and behavior patterns, your access to resources, and your personal support system. Some individuals might need to leave in a matter of hours, while others may require weeks or even months of careful planning. Don't feel pressured to follow a rigid timeline. Prioritize your safety and well-being above all else.

Assessing the Risks and Your Options:

Before you begin planning your escape, take some time to assess the level of risk you face. How unpredictable is your abuser? Are there instances of physical violence? Does your abuser have access to weapons? Have they threatened to harm you or others if you leave? Have they made threats via text or email? The answers to these questions will significantly influence your escape strategy. If you perceive an imminent threat of physical harm, prioritize contacting emergency services or a domestic violence hotline

immediately. They can provide immediate assistance and guidance on how to secure your safety.

Consider your available options for leaving. Do you have a safe place to go? This could be the home of a trusted friend or family member, a domestic violence shelter, or a safe house. If you don't have a pre-arranged safe haven, start identifying potential options now. Reach out to your support network and explain your situation. Don't be afraid to ask for help; it's a sign of strength, not weakness. Domestic violence shelters offer confidential accommodations and support services for victims of abuse. They can provide a safe space, counseling, and assistance with finding housing and other resources.

The Escape Plan: A Step-by-Step Guide:

1. **Gathering Essential Documents and Items:** Begin by compiling a list of essential documents and personal items you will need after you leave. This includes identification cards (driver's license, passport, social security card), birth certificates, bank information, medical records, legal documents (such as restraining orders or divorce papers), and any other crucial paperwork. Make copies of these documents and store them securely – ideally, outside your home and inaccessible to your abuser. Consider using a cloud storage service or a safety deposit box. Pack a small bag containing a few changes of clothing, toiletries, medication, and any other necessities. Leave this bag hidden, ready for a quick escape. Don't forget your phone and charger.
2. **Securing Financial Resources:** If your abuser controls your finances, discretely begin moving money to a separate account or securing access to emergency funds. This might involve opening a new bank account in your name only,

contacting your financial institution, or reaching out to trusted family or friends for financial assistance. This is crucial for your independence and safety post-escape. Keep records of all financial transactions, no matter how small. If your finances are intertwined and you require legal assistance to separate them, reach out to a lawyer immediately.

1. **Choosing the Right Time and Method of Escape:** The ideal time to leave will depend on your specific situation. If you live with your abuser, you might choose a time when they

are not home, such as during their work hours or social engagements. If they are consistently home, leaving may require greater subtlety and more extensive planning. Leaving during the day might feel safer than leaving at night, depending on your specific circumstances. If you have children, carefully coordinate their safety and care in your escape plan. Consider involving a trusted friend, relative, or social service agency to assist with this.

Consider your transportation options. Do you have access to a vehicle? If not, arrange for alternative transportation, such as a taxi, rideshare service, public transportation, or a trusted friend or family member. Plan your route carefully, and avoid routes that your abuser might anticipate.

1. **Creating a Communication Plan:** Develop a secure communication plan with trusted individuals who can provide assistance and support. This might include friends, family, neighbors, your therapist, or a domestic violence advocate. Establish a code word or phrase that indicates you need immediate help. Keep your phone charged and readily accessible. If using your phone seems too risky, create alternate contact points, such as using a friend's phone to reach out to support.
2. **Seeking Support After Escape:** Once you're safe, reach out to your support network immediately. Let them know you've left, and seek the assistance you need. Consider connecting with a domestic violence shelter or support organization to access resources, such as housing assistance, counseling, and legal aid. Remember that recovery is a journey, and it's crucial to have a support system in place.
3. **Dealing with Potential Reactions from the Abuser:** Be prepared for potential reactions from your abuser after you leave. They may attempt to contact you, harass you, or even try to

physically harm you. If you have a restraining order or protective order in place, make sure you understand its provisions, and report any violations to the authorities immediately. Maintain your safety plan and consistently follow its guidelines.

4. **Taking Care of Yourself:** The aftermath of escaping an abusive relationship is often overwhelming, both emotionally and physically. Prioritize self-care and seek professional help to process the trauma and rebuild your life. Trauma-informed therapy can provide you with the tools and support you need to heal and move forward. Don't underestimate the power of self-compassion; this is a monumental achievement and it's vital to celebrate that fact.

This step-by-step guide is intended to empower you, not overwhelm you. Remember that every situation is unique and there's no one-right answer. Adapt these steps to your specific circumstances. This escape plan is a testament to your strength and courage, and it's a critical step in reclaiming your life and your future. Don't hesitate to seek help from professionals, friends, and family—their support is invaluable. Your safety and well-being are your top priorities. Remember, you deserve to live a life free from fear and abuse.

Dealing with Immediate Threats and Emergencies

Dealing with immediate threats requires a different approach than the carefully planned escape outlined previously. While meticulous preparation is crucial for long-term safety, immediate danger necessitates swift action. Your priority in these situations is to get yourself and any dependents to safety. There is no room for hesitation; your well-being is paramount.

If you are facing an immediate threat of physical harm, your first course of action should always be to contact emergency services. This is not a time to hesitate. Dial 911 (or your country's equivalent) immediately. Clearly and concisely explain your situation, providing your location and describing the threat. Stay on the line with the dispatcher until help arrives. Even if you believe the situation might escalate if you call the police, prioritize your safety. Your life is far more important than potentially angering your abuser. The police can intervene and potentially provide immediate protection. If possible, safely leave the premises before the police arrive, but only do so if it is safe to do so.

If contacting emergency services feels impossible due to the immediate threat or your abuser's control, utilize any means available to get help. Texting a trusted contact with a pre- arranged code word ("Emergency - Code Red," for instance) can be effective, especially if you're unable to speak openly. This individual can then call emergency services on your behalf. Social media messaging, while potentially slower, can also work if your abuser doesn't monitor those accounts closely. However, be aware that evidence from social media messaging may not be admissible in court, but it can be helpful in building a history of abuse. Remember, even a

seemingly small action—a quick text, a silent alarm—can be a lifesaver.

The location you choose to flee to is vital in an immediate- threat situation. Your pre-planned safe house is your best bet; however, if that's not accessible, your options will depend on the specific circumstances. A neighbor's house, a nearby public space like a library or coffee shop, or even a crowded street can offer more immediate safety than staying in the current dangerous environment. Prioritize proximity and the visibility of other people.

Once you've reached safety, regardless of your location, inform the authorities and any relevant support networks. Detailed accounts of the incident are critical for legal action. If you have photographic or video evidence of abuse or threats—even if this information isn't currently accessible— note its existence and find a way to preserve it securely. This might involve uploading it to a cloud-based storage location accessed via a device other than your own, or confiding in a trusted individual to help you secure and preserve the evidence.

Creating a rapid response plan for urgent threats should be a crucial part of your overall safety strategy. This goes beyond the long-term escape plan discussed earlier. Think of it as your "Plan B" for when Plan A—a calm and meticulously executed exit—isn't feasible. This plan should include:

Pre-identified escape routes: Map out several different ways to leave your home or current location quickly and discreetly. Include alternative routes to avoid your abuser's anticipated path. This may involve exiting through different doors, windows, or even using back alleys if available.

Designated safe havens: Identify several locations besides your pre-planned safe house where you could go if an immediate escape is necessary. This could be a trusted friend's or family member's home, a public space with many people, or a 24-hour business that provides a safe environment.

Communication methods: Identify various communication strategies in case your primary method is compromised. This might include a pre-arranged signal with a neighbor, alternative phone numbers, or using public computers to contact support networks.

Emergency supplies kit: Keep a small bag containing essential items such as identification, medications, some money, and a phone charger in a readily accessible, hidden location. This kit is for quick grabs if you need to flee suddenly.

Pre-written emergency contact list: Keep a list of crucial contact numbers and information readily accessible, either physically or digitally. Include emergency services, domestic violence hotlines, trusted friends and family, and legal professionals.

Self-defense strategies: While not always ideal, learning some basic self-defense moves can provide a sense of empowerment and might give you a better chance to escape safely. There are many self-defense techniques available online or through community organizations that can provide this training. However, your primary goal is to escape, not engage in a physical confrontation.

Remember, your rapid response plan is a safeguard, a tool to help you get out of immediate danger, not a guaranteed solution. The plan should be flexible and adaptable to the

ever-changing circumstances of your situation. Regularly review and update it as your situation evolves.

Beyond these immediate actions, consider the long-term implications of the abuse. Seek professional help; a therapist specializing in trauma and abuse can help you process the experience, develop coping mechanisms, and create a more robust long-term safety plan. This help is not a sign of weakness but a testament to your strength and resilience.

The ability to acknowledge and address the damage done is essential to starting the long journey to healing and rebuilding your life.

The trauma you've experienced warrants significant support. Don't underestimate the depth of the impact. You may experience symptoms such as anxiety, panic attacks, depression, difficulty sleeping, flashbacks, and hypervigilance. These are all normal reactions to abnormal circumstances. It is imperative to seek professional help to navigate these challenges. A therapeutic alliance can offer a safe space to explore these feelings, unravel their root causes, and develop strategies to cope with them effectively.

Moreover, building a strong support network is crucial. Lean on your loved ones; let them be there for you. Explain to them what you've gone through in detail so they can understand the situation and provide the most appropriate level of support. They can become crucial allies in your recovery journey.

Healing from abuse by a sociopath is a marathon, not a sprint. There will be ups and downs, setbacks and progress. Be patient with yourself and celebrate your achievements along the way. Your ability to identify the abuse, to plan your escape, and to seek help are monumental steps toward reclaiming your life and your future. Remember, you deserve

to live a life free from fear and control, and the support is available to help you get there. It's a testament to your courage and strength that you've made it this far. Never forget that.

Managing the Aftermath of Escape

The adrenaline rush of escape often gives way to a profound sense of emptiness and disorientation. The immediate threat might be gone, but the emotional aftermath can be just as overwhelming, even more so. This isn't a time for self- criticism or second-guessing your decisions. You've survived. You've escaped. Now, it's about navigating the complex landscape of recovery. This phase involves a multitude of challenges, from dealing with the emotional trauma of the abuse to securing financial stability and rebuilding a life free from fear.

The first few weeks, even months, can feel like a blur. Sleep disturbances are common. You might find yourself constantly on edge, hyper-vigilant to any perceived threat, even in safe environments. Flashbacks – sudden, vivid memories of the abuse – can be terrifying and debilitating, pulling you back into the traumatic experiences you've worked so hard to leave behind. Anxiety and panic attacks may strike without warning, leaving you breathless and overwhelmed. These are not signs of weakness; they are normal responses to an abnormal situation. Your nervous system has been on high alert for a prolonged period, and it takes time for it to readjust.

It is crucial to understand that your emotional state is a direct consequence of the abuse you endured. Sociopathic abusers meticulously dismantle their victims' sense of self, creating a deep-seated feeling of inadequacy and self-blame.

Rebuilding self-esteem is a lengthy process, requiring patience, self-compassion, and professional support. Consider this phase as a marathon of healing, not a sprint. There will be moments of profound progress interspersed

with periods of regression. This is expected. The important thing is to keep moving forward.

One of the most immediate practical concerns is often financial instability. Sociopathic abusers frequently exert control over finances, leaving victims with little or no independent resources. This financial vulnerability can add another layer of anxiety and fear to an already precarious situation. Seek help immediately from local agencies dedicated to assisting victims of domestic violence. Many organizations provide emergency financial assistance, including temporary housing, food, and clothing. They can connect you with resources to help you open bank accounts, establish credit, and obtain essential necessities. Don't hesitate to reach out; these services are designed to help you regain your footing.

Finding secure housing is another critical step. If you left your home abruptly, you might find yourself without a place to live. Local shelters can provide temporary accommodation, offering a safe and supportive environment while you search for permanent housing. These shelters often offer additional services, such as counseling, legal assistance, and job training programs. Explore government assistance programs for subsidized housing; numerous options are often available depending on your location and circumstances. Reaching out to trusted friends or family members may also be a viable solution, but always prioritize your safety and comfort levels. Avoid situations that could put you at risk.

Navigating the legal system can seem daunting, but seeking legal assistance is vital to protecting yourself from future harassment and potential legal actions from your abuser.

Legal aid organizations offer pro bono or low-cost legal services, particularly in cases of domestic violence. These

services can help you obtain restraining orders, file for divorce (if applicable), and address any legal issues related to custody, child support, or property division. It is crucial to document every interaction with your abuser, keeping detailed records of any communication (emails, text messages, voicemails) and any instances of harassment or threats. This documentation will be essential in any legal proceedings.

Beyond the immediate practical issues, addressing the deeper emotional wounds left by the abuse is crucial for long-term healing. Therapy, preferably with a therapist specializing in trauma and abuse recovery, is paramount. This is not a sign of weakness; it's a testament to your strength and commitment to healing. A therapist can provide a safe and non-judgmental space to process the trauma, explore the impact on your self-esteem, and develop coping mechanisms to manage the emotional challenges you face.

They will help you understand the dynamics of the abuse and challenge the self-blame and negative self-talk that often accompany such experiences.

Cognitive Behavioral Therapy (CBT) is often highly effective in treating the psychological effects of trauma. CBT focuses on identifying and changing negative thought patterns and behaviors that contribute to anxiety, depression, and other symptoms related to trauma. Eye Movement Desensitization and Reprocessing (EMDR) is another effective therapy designed to treat trauma. EMDR uses bilateral stimulation (such as eye movements or tapping) to help process traumatic memories and reduce their emotional impact.

Building a support network is just as essential as professional therapy. Confiding in trusted friends, family members, or support groups can provide a sense of

community and belonging, helping to combat the isolation that often follows escaping an abusive relationship. Sharing your experiences with others who understand what you've been through can be incredibly validating and empowering. Support groups specifically for survivors of abuse can offer a safe space to connect with others who have had similar experiences and offer mutual support and encouragement.

Rebuilding your life after escaping abuse is a journey, not a destination. It requires courage, resilience, and a steadfast commitment to healing. There will be days when you feel overwhelmed and discouraged, but remember that you are not alone. Professional help, support networks, and self- compassion are your allies in this process. Celebrate your accomplishments, no matter how small they may seem. Each step you take toward healing is a victory. You have survived; now focus on thriving. Your strength and resilience are undeniable. Embrace your future, and know that a life free from fear and control is within reach.

Remember that reclaiming your life involves redefining your boundaries and establishing healthy relationships. This will require conscious effort and potentially professional guidance. Learning to recognize and assert healthy boundaries is vital in preventing future exploitation. The ability to say "no" without guilt or fear is a powerful tool in building a life free from manipulation. This may involve setting limits on contact with family members who enable or condone the behavior of your abuser. This will also involve creating a safe space for yourself physically and emotionally.

The process of rebuilding can involve many different aspects of your life. This might include returning to education, pursuing new career paths, or engaging in activities that bring you joy and fulfillment. Engage in activities that foster self-care and well-being. Exercise, meditation, yoga, and

spending time in nature can all contribute significantly to mental and emotional health. Make conscious choices that prioritize self-compassion and kindness. Treat yourself with the same empathy and understanding that you would offer a dear friend.

Finally, remember that your experience is not your fault. You did not deserve the abuse you endured. This understanding is fundamental to healing. The blame rests solely with your abuser. You are worthy of love, respect, and happiness.

Embrace this truth, and let it guide you as you navigate the path toward a brighter future. Your journey to recovery is a testament to your strength and resilience. Never underestimate the power of your inner strength and your capacity for healing. The life you are building is a life of freedom and self-determination. And you deserve that life.

Building a Support Network PostEscape

Building a support network is not merely beneficial after escaping abuse; it's essential for survival and healing. The isolation deliberately cultivated by sociopaths leaves victims feeling vulnerable and alone, even after the abusive relationship ends. Rebuilding your life requires actively creating a web of support that provides emotional sustenance, practical assistance, and a sense of belonging.

This support network acts as a crucial buffer against the lingering effects of manipulation and trauma.

The first step in building this network is often the most daunting: seeking professional help. Therapy, particularly with a therapist specializing in trauma and abuse recovery, provides a safe and confidential space to process your experiences. This isn't about weakness; it's a courageous act of self-care. A skilled therapist can help you understand the dynamics of the abuse, dismantle the self-blame that often accompanies such experiences, and develop coping mechanisms for managing the emotional fallout.

Finding the right therapist is vital. Don't hesitate to interview several therapists before making a decision. Look for someone who makes you feel comfortable, understood, and respected. A good therapist will validate your experience, offer non-judgmental support, and work collaboratively with you to develop a personalized treatment plan. Consider therapists with experience in treating complex post-traumatic stress disorder (C-PTSD), which is commonly associated with prolonged abuse by sociopaths. They will understand the intricacies of the manipulation and gaslighting you've endured.

Beyond individual therapy, consider the benefits of group therapy or support groups. Connecting with others who have experienced similar trauma offers immense validation.

Sharing your story in a safe and supportive environment can help you realize you're not alone in your struggles. Hearing other survivors' stories, their coping mechanisms, and their journeys to healing can be incredibly empowering and instill a sense of hope. These groups offer a unique opportunity to foster a sense of community and shared understanding, helping to combat the isolation and shame that are often lasting consequences of abuse.

Reaching out to trusted friends and family members can also be a vital part of building your support network. However, this step requires careful consideration. If your friends or family members were unaware of the abuse, or if they minimized or dismissed your concerns, their initial reactions might be unexpected or even unhelpful. It is important to prepare for this possibility and to prioritize your own emotional well-being. It might be necessary to communicate your boundaries clearly and directly.

Explain the impact of the abuse, the need for your privacy, and your need for their unconditional support. Choose individuals who demonstrate empathy, understanding, and a willingness to learn about the complexities of sociopathic abuse. They will need to appreciate the subtlety of manipulation and the effects of gaslighting without minimizing your experiences. If you find that certain relationships are not providing the support you need, it's okay to create some distance or temporarily limit contact until you're in a stronger position emotionally.

Rebuilding healthy relationships is a significant part of recovery. These relationships must be based on mutual respect, trust, and clear boundaries. You'll need to learn to

identify red flags and establish healthy patterns of communication. This may involve setting limits on contact with those who enabled or excused your abuser's behavior. It may involve saying “no” to requests that compromise your well-being or your boundaries. This process requires assertiveness, setting limitations, and maintaining a deep commitment to your own self-worth.

Rebuilding your life requires a proactive approach to self- care. Engage in activities that nourish your body and soul. Exercise regularly – it's a powerful antidote to stress and anxiety. Practice mindfulness techniques like meditation or yoga, which can help calm your nervous system and promote emotional regulation. Spend time in nature, engage in hobbies that bring you joy, and prioritize activities that restore your sense of peace and well-being. Self-compassion is crucial during this process; treat yourself with the same kindness and understanding that you would offer a cherished friend.

Consider seeking support from specialized organizations dedicated to assisting survivors of abuse. These organizations offer a wealth of resources, including hotlines, support groups, legal assistance, and financial aid. Many provide crisis intervention services, offering immediate support during moments of distress. They can also connect you with therapists, attorneys, and other professionals who specialize in working with survivors of abuse. These organizations often have extensive experience and understanding of the complexities of sociopathic abuse, offering a level of support tailored to your specific needs.

Remember, building a strong support network is an ongoing process. It will evolve and adapt as you heal and grow. There will be times when you need more support than others, and that is perfectly acceptable. Don't hesitate to reach out for

help when you need it. Embrace the strength that comes from connecting with others who understand and care. Your support network is an investment in your healing journey, and a testament to your resilience and your commitment to a future free from abuse.

Learning to recognize and establish healthy boundaries is a vital skill in rebuilding your life. Boundaries protect your physical, emotional, and mental well-being. They create a sense of safety and control in your life, which can be especially important after experiencing the manipulation and control characteristic of a sociopathic relationship.

Boundaries are not about being selfish; they are about self- respect.

These boundaries can extend to many aspects of your life. They might involve setting limits on how much time you spend with certain people, limiting communication with those who are toxic, or refusing requests that compromise your values or well-being. Boundaries might also involve protecting your personal space, possessions, and time.

Learning to say "no" assertively and respectfully is crucial. Practicing self-advocacy, stating your needs clearly and directly, is important for establishing and maintaining boundaries.

Rebuilding trust takes time, and it's a process that involves both the people in your support network and yourself. You might find yourself hesitant to trust others, and that's understandable given your experiences. Be patient with yourself and allow yourself to rebuild trust gradually. As you engage in therapy and connect with supportive individuals, you'll gain the confidence to discern healthy relationships from unhealthy ones. Look for individuals who respect your boundaries, listen without judgment, and are supportive of

your healing journey. Focus on nurturing these relationships, knowing that they are integral to your long-term well-being.

The journey of recovery from sociopathic abuse is not linear; it's a process marked by both progress and setbacks. There will be days when you feel strong and empowered, and days when you feel overwhelmed by memories or anxieties.

Acknowledge and validate these feelings; they are a part of the healing process. Remember that setbacks don't negate your progress. They are opportunities to learn, adapt, and grow stronger. Celebrate the small victories, and be compassionate towards yourself during moments of difficulty. You deserve kindness and understanding during this transformative journey. Your resilience is a testament to your strength, and a foundation for the bright future you deserve.

Finding Stability and Independence

Finding a safe and stable place to live is often the first and most crucial step towards independence after escaping an abusive relationship. The sense of security a stable home provides is paramount in the healing process. If you've been forced to leave your home abruptly, you might initially find yourself in a shelter or temporary housing situation. This is perfectly normal, and these resources are available to help you transition. Don't hesitate to utilize them; they are a vital part of your safety net.

Many shelters offer a range of services beyond just a place to stay. They often provide assistance with finding permanent housing, connecting you with support services, and helping you navigate the legal processes associated with escaping an abusive situation. It's important to remember that these are temporary solutions designed to give you the time and space you need to build a foundation for your independent life.

Once you've secured temporary housing, begin the process of finding more permanent accommodation. This might involve searching for apartments, houses, or shared living spaces. Consider factors such as safety, affordability, proximity to support systems, and your personal comfort level. If possible, visit potential housing options before signing any lease agreements. Trust your instincts; if something feels wrong or unsafe, look for another option.

Securing stable employment is another cornerstone of independent living. The income you generate will provide financial security and a sense of accomplishment. If you have job skills and experience relevant to your desired field, start your job search immediately. If you need to acquire new skills or update your resume, consider taking advantage of resources available through local employment agencies, community colleges, or online training programs. Many organizations dedicated to assisting survivors of abuse offer job training and placement services.

During your job search, be prepared to address any employment gaps that may have occurred during your abusive relationship. Frame these gaps honestly but positively, focusing on the personal growth and resilience you gained during that challenging period. Highlight your transferable skills and your willingness to learn and contribute. Remember, your past experiences do not define your future potential. Employers often value resilience and adaptability, qualities you've undoubtedly developed.

Establishing financial stability goes hand-in-hand with secure employment. If you've experienced financial control during the abusive relationship, begin by creating a budget and tracking your income and expenses. This allows you to gain clarity about your financial situation and make informed decisions about your spending. Consider opening a separate bank account and obtaining credit cards in your own name, establishing your independent financial identity.

If you're struggling with debt or other financial difficulties, seek assistance from credit counseling agencies or non-profit organizations that provide financial literacy programs and guidance. These services offer a safe space to explore your financial challenges and develop a plan for long-term financial stability. They can often help you negotiate with creditors and explore options for debt management.

Remember, seeking help is a sign of strength, not weakness.

Beyond practical aspects like housing and employment, fostering your overall well-being is crucial for long-term

stability and independence. This is not merely about surviving; it's about thriving. Engage in activities that promote self-care and personal growth. Regular exercise is an excellent stress reliever and can contribute significantly to both physical and mental well-being. Even a short walk daily can make a difference.

Mindfulness practices, such as meditation or yoga, can help calm your nervous system and reduce feelings of anxiety or overwhelm. Numerous apps and online resources provide guided meditations suitable for all experience levels. Explore different techniques until you find what works best for you.

Remember, the goal is not to eliminate stress entirely, but to learn healthy ways to manage it.

Nutrition plays a pivotal role in your overall health. Focus on consuming a balanced diet rich in fruits, vegetables, and whole grains. Avoid excessive caffeine or alcohol, which can exacerbate stress and anxiety. Make time for regular meals, and try to cultivate mindful eating habits; pay attention to the flavors and textures of your food, savoring each bite.

Prioritize sleep. Adequate rest is essential for physical and mental restoration. Aim for 7-8 hours of quality sleep each night. Establish a regular sleep schedule, creating a relaxing bedtime routine to signal your body it's time to rest. A quiet, dark, and cool bedroom can also significantly contribute to better sleep.

Engage in activities you enjoy. Hobbies and leisure pursuits provide an outlet for stress, promote relaxation, and foster a sense of personal fulfillment. Whether it's reading, painting, gardening, or playing a musical instrument, make time for activities that bring you joy and replenish your energy. These activities are not luxuries; they are essential components of self-care and healing.

Consider reconnecting with old hobbies or exploring new ones. Learning a new skill can be a powerful source of self- esteem and accomplishment. This could involve taking a class, joining a club, or pursuing an online course. These pursuits provide structure, engagement, and a sense of purpose.

It is also essential to cultivate self-compassion during this process of rebuilding your life. Be patient and understanding with yourself. Recovery is a journey, not a race. There will be days when you feel overwhelmed or discouraged.

Acknowledge these feelings, and allow yourself to feel them without judgment. Remember, progress isn't always linear.

There will be setbacks and challenges along the way, but these are opportunities for growth and learning.

Celebrating your small victories along the way is incredibly important. Acknowledge and appreciate your progress, no matter how small it may seem. This could involve securing a job interview, paying a bill on time, or simply having a good night's sleep. These accomplishments contribute to your sense of self-efficacy and reinforce your belief in your ability to rebuild your life.

It's important to remember that you deserve a life free from fear and control. The journey towards independence and healing requires courage, resilience, and self-compassion. By focusing on your well-being, building a solid support system, and taking proactive steps to secure housing, employment, and financial stability, you can create a brighter future for yourself. Your strength and your journey are testaments to your resilience, and the life you create will be a testament to your remarkable capacity for healing and growth. This is not simply about escaping the past; it's about building a future that you deserve – a future defined by your

own strength, your own choices, and your own unshakeable self-worth.

Processing Trauma and Healing from Abuse

Processing trauma after escaping an abusive relationship with a sociopath is a deeply personal and multifaceted journey. There's no one-size-fits-all approach, and the healing process unfolds at its own pace. What's crucial is recognizing that healing is possible, and that you are not alone. Many resources and therapeutic approaches can support you in reclaiming your life and rebuilding your sense of self.

One of the most effective therapeutic approaches for trauma recovery is Cognitive Behavioral Therapy (CBT). CBT focuses on identifying and challenging negative thought patterns and behaviors that contribute to emotional distress. In the context of abuse, this often involves confronting the insidious lies and manipulations perpetuated by the abuser. CBT helps you reframe your understanding of the abuse, separating the abuser's distorted perceptions from your own reality. It equips you with coping mechanisms for managing triggers and flashbacks, allowing you to regain control over your thoughts and emotions. A skilled CBT therapist can help you understand how your responses to past trauma are impacting your present life, and guide you in developing healthier coping strategies. This may involve techniques like cognitive restructuring, where you actively challenge and replace negative thoughts with more balanced and realistic ones, and behavioral experiments, where you gradually confront feared situations in a safe and controlled manner.

Trauma-focused therapies, such as Eye Movement Desensitization and Reprocessing (EMDR) and somatic experiencing, are particularly effective in addressing the lingering effects of trauma on the body and mind. EMDR

uses bilateral stimulation, such as eye movements or tapping, to help process traumatic memories and reduce their emotional intensity. This technique assists in breaking the cycle of re-experiencing traumatic events and helps you develop a healthier perspective on the past. Somatic experiencing focuses on addressing the physical sensations associated with trauma. It helps you safely release trapped emotions and bodily tension that can manifest as physical symptoms, such as chronic pain, digestive issues, or sleep disturbances. These therapies recognize the interconnectedness of mind and body and provide tools to regain a sense of bodily safety and regulation.

Beyond formal therapy, various self-help techniques can complement your healing journey. Mindfulness practices, such as meditation and deep breathing exercises, can be profoundly beneficial in managing PTSD symptoms like anxiety, hypervigilance, and intrusive thoughts. Mindfulness encourages you to focus on the present moment without judgment, helping you to ground yourself in the here and now and reducing the power of distressing memories. Even short periods of mindful meditation can significantly reduce feelings of anxiety and overwhelm. Many guided meditation apps are readily available to support you in practicing mindfulness.

Journaling can be a powerful tool for processing emotions and gaining self-awareness. Writing down your thoughts and feelings, without the need for judgment or editing, provides a safe and private space for emotional expression. It can help you identify patterns of thinking and behavior, track your progress, and gain a deeper understanding of yourself.

Journaling can be particularly helpful in documenting your healing journey, providing a tangible record of your progress and reminding you of your strength and resilience.

Physical activity plays a crucial role in both physical and mental health, particularly in the context of trauma recovery. Exercise releases endorphins, which have mood-boosting and stress-reducing effects. Regular exercise can help regulate sleep patterns, reduce anxiety and depression, and improve overall energy levels. Finding an activity you enjoy, whether it's walking, swimming, dancing, or yoga, can be a powerful form of self-care. Exercise provides a healthy outlet for emotions and promotes a sense of physical well- being, which can be particularly helpful after experiencing the emotional and physical toll of abuse.

Building a strong support system is paramount during this process. Connecting with trusted friends, family members, or support groups provides a sense of belonging and reduces feelings of isolation. Support groups specifically for survivors of abuse offer a safe space to share experiences, connect with others who understand, and learn from one another's journeys. These groups can provide validation, empathy, and practical advice, fostering a sense of community and shared resilience. Remember, seeking support isn't a sign of weakness; it's a testament to your strength and desire for healing.

Healthy boundaries are essential in protecting your well- being and preventing further harm. Learning to assertively communicate your needs and limits helps you safeguard your emotional and physical safety. This might involve setting limits on contact with the abuser, declining invitations that feel unsafe, or expressing your discomfort when others overstep your boundaries. Setting boundaries takes practice, and it's important to be patient with yourself as you learn to advocate for your needs.

It's vital to remember that healing is not a linear process; there will be setbacks and good days, and moments where

you feel strong and moments when you feel vulnerable. Allow yourself to feel the full spectrum of emotions without judgment. Acknowledge your progress, no matter how small, and celebrate your victories along the way. Be kind to yourself, and remember that self-compassion is a crucial component of the healing journey. Recovery from trauma is a marathon, not a sprint. Be patient with your progress and remember that you deserve a life free from fear and abuse.

The journey to healing is profoundly personal, and the timeline varies greatly for each individual. Some individuals may require intensive therapy to fully process their trauma, while others may find sufficient support through self-help techniques and support groups. The key is to find what works best for you and to be persistent in your commitment to healing.

Remember, you are not alone in this journey. Numerous resources are available to support you, including therapists specializing in trauma and abuse, support groups, hotlines, and online resources. Don't hesitate to seek professional help; it's a sign of strength, not weakness. With patience,

self-compassion, and the right support, you can heal from the trauma of abuse and build a fulfilling and joyful life.

The process of rebuilding your life after escaping abuse involves more than just securing housing and employment. It involves reclaiming your sense of self, rediscovering your passions, and redefining your future on your own terms. This process requires courage, resilience, and a steadfast belief in your capacity for healing and growth. You deserve to live a life filled with joy, peace, and empowerment. The journey may be challenging, but the reward—a life free from fear and control—is worth every step of the way. Remember to celebrate every milestone you achieve, no matter how small, and to honor your own remarkable strength and resilience.

Your future is yours to create, and it will be a future built on your terms, a testament to your enduring spirit.

Recovering Your SelfEsteem and Identity

Recovering your self-esteem after the insidious erosion caused by a sociopathic abuser is a monumental task, but it is absolutely achievable. The manipulation you endured wasn't your fault; it was a deliberate tactic used to control and dominate you. Understanding this crucial fact is the first step towards reclaiming your sense of self. The process involves a multifaceted approach that incorporates self-compassion, positive self-talk, and a conscious effort towards self-discovery and personal growth. This isn't a quick fix; it's a journey of rebuilding, one brick at a time.

Self-compassion is paramount. You've endured unimaginable hardship, and it's vital to treat yourself with the kindness and understanding you would offer a close friend facing similar challenges. Forgive yourself for any perceived failures or weaknesses that the abuser exploited. Remember, you survived. Your survival is a testament to your resilience and strength, not a measure of your worth. Cultivate self- compassion by actively challenging negative self-talk, replacing it with affirmations of your inherent worth and capabilities.

Positive self-talk is a powerful tool for reshaping your internal narrative. The abuser likely bombarded you with negativity, criticism, and lies, designed to erode your confidence and self-worth. Counter this by consciously engaging in positive affirmations. Start small. Instead of dwelling on perceived inadequacies, focus on your strengths and accomplishments, no matter how insignificant they might seem. Did you manage to get out of bed today? That's a victory. Did you make a healthy meal? That's an

accomplishment. Celebrate these small victories, as they build momentum and reinforce your sense of agency.

Journaling can be a transformative tool in this process. Write down your thoughts and feelings without judgment. Explore the emotions that arise – the anger, the sadness, the fear – and allow yourself to feel them without trying to suppress them. Journaling allows you to process your experiences, identify patterns of negative self-talk, and track your progress as you begin to build a healthier self-image. Use your journal to chronicle your successes, no matter how small. Over time, you'll begin to see a pattern of resilience and growth. This tangible record will serve as a reminder of how far you've come.

Engage in activities that bring you joy and a sense of accomplishment. This might involve rediscovering old hobbies or exploring new interests. Anything that sparks your curiosity and allows you to express yourself creatively can be profoundly healing. Whether it's painting, playing music, writing, gardening, or hiking, prioritize activities that nurture your spirit and reconnect you with your passions.

Remember the things that brought you happiness before the abuse, and actively seek opportunities to engage with them again.

Self-discovery is an essential part of reclaiming your identity. The abuser worked to strip you of your individuality, making you dependent on them for validation and direction. Now is the time to rediscover who you are, independent of their influence. This process might involve exploring your values, beliefs, and aspirations. What truly matters to you? What are your goals and dreams? Consider seeking professional guidance through therapy or counseling, as a therapist can provide a safe and supportive space to explore these questions and work through any lingering emotional wounds.

Personal growth is a continuous process, and this is an opportunity to focus on self-improvement in areas where you feel you might have been held back. This might involve developing new skills, pursuing educational opportunities, or setting personal goals for physical and mental health.

Consider taking a class, learning a new language, or volunteering your time to a cause you care about. These activities not only build confidence and skills but also contribute to a stronger sense of self and purpose.

Building healthy relationships is another crucial aspect of rebuilding your life. Focus on cultivating connections with individuals who support and uplift you. Surround yourself with people who treat you with respect, empathy, and genuine care. Set healthy boundaries in these relationships, protecting your emotional and physical well-being. Don't hesitate to distance yourself from relationships that feel draining or toxic. Building a supportive network of friends and family, or joining a support group for survivors of abuse, can provide the validation and encouragement you need as you navigate this journey.

Remember, physical health is intrinsically linked to mental well-being. Prioritize self-care through regular exercise, a healthy diet, and sufficient sleep. Physical activity releases endorphins, which have mood-boosting and stress-reducing effects. Engage in activities you enjoy, whether it's walking, swimming, yoga, or dancing. Focus on nourishing your body with healthy foods that fuel your energy levels. Aim for a regular sleep schedule, ensuring adequate rest for your mind and body. These seemingly small acts of self-care are crucial to your overall well-being and contribute significantly to your emotional recovery.

Consider professional help. Therapists specializing in trauma and abuse recovery can provide invaluable support and guidance. They can help you process the trauma, develop healthy coping mechanisms, and build resilience. Don't hesitate to reach out for professional support; it's a sign of strength, not weakness. A therapist can offer a safe and non- judgmental space to explore your experiences, address lingering emotional wounds, and develop strategies for building a healthier and happier future.

The journey of rebuilding your self-esteem and reclaiming your identity is a marathon, not a sprint. There will be setbacks and challenges along the way. Be patient with yourself, celebrate your progress, and remember that you are worthy of love, respect, and happiness. You are stronger than you think, and you deserve to live a life free from fear and control. Embrace this journey of self-discovery and growth with courage and self-compassion, knowing that you are not alone, and a brighter future awaits you. Your strength and resilience are remarkable; never underestimate your capacity to heal and thrive. Trust in your ability to rebuild your life, on your terms, and create a future that reflects your strength and worth. This journey is about reclaiming your narrative, rewriting your story, and celebrating the incredible person you are.

Setting Healthy Boundaries and Relationships

Building healthy relationships after escaping an abusive situation requires a fundamental shift in how you interact with others and how you perceive yourself within those interactions. The trauma you experienced likely distorted your sense of self-worth and your ability to recognize healthy dynamics. Rebuilding trust and establishing healthy boundaries are crucial steps in creating a safe and fulfilling future.

One of the first and most vital steps is learning to recognize red flags. These aren't always obvious acts of aggression; subtle behaviors can be equally dangerous. For instance, excessive jealousy or possessiveness, even in the early stages of a relationship, is a significant warning sign. A healthy partner celebrates your independence and supports your personal growth; they don't try to control your friendships, your work, or your personal choices. Similarly, belittling comments disguised as "jokes" or constant criticism, however seemingly minor, erode your self-esteem and create an environment of negativity. Pay attention to how the person makes you feel; if you constantly feel anxious, insecure, or even slightly uncomfortable, take note. Your gut feeling is a powerful indicator; don't dismiss it. Remember the patterns of manipulation you experienced previously— learn to recognize these tactics in others before they escalate into abuse.

Furthermore, look for controlling behaviors. Does the person attempt to isolate you from friends and family? Do they monitor your communications, demanding access to your phone or social media accounts? Do they constantly check your whereabouts or make unreasonable demands on your

time? These actions aren't about care; they are about control. A healthy relationship respects individual autonomy and privacy. Control is a hallmark of abusive relationships, no matter how subtly it is presented. Another subtle but crucial sign is the constant need for validation or excessive reassurance. Someone who continuously seeks validation may be insecure, but a deeper issue might be their need for control and manipulation. They might use your need for reassurance against you, subtly manipulating your emotions to gain power.

Learning to say "no" is a powerful tool in setting boundaries. Many survivors of abuse struggle with assertiveness due to the constant pressure to comply with the abuser's demands.

Practice saying "no" in small ways, even to insignificant requests, to build confidence and solidify your boundaries. It's okay to decline invitations you don't feel comfortable attending or to refuse requests that make you feel uncomfortable or pressured. Start with low-stakes situations and gradually increase your comfort level. If someone pressures you to do something you don't want to do, it's a red flag. Remember, you have the right to refuse any request that violates your personal comfort level or goes against your values.

Communication is key to establishing healthy relationships. Be clear and direct about your needs and boundaries. Don't shy away from voicing your discomfort or displeasure if something bothers you. If someone is repeatedly disregarding your boundaries, it might be time to reconsider the relationship. Healthy communication is not just about expressing your needs but also about actively listening to the other person's perspective. This doesn't mean you have to agree with everything they say, but actively listening is essential for understanding and building trust. However, remember that in unhealthy relationships, there's often an

imbalance of communication where one person dominates the conversation or shuts down important dialogues.

Consider assertiveness training. Many resources are available online, including workshops and support groups, which focus on developing assertive communication skills. These programs help you learn to express your needs and opinions in a calm and respectful way without being aggressive or passive. They teach techniques for dealing with difficult conversations and setting clear boundaries, empowering you to take control of your interactions. Role- playing exercises can help you practice these skills in a safe and supportive environment. This is essential as it helps you navigate challenging interpersonal dynamics confidently and effectively.

Beyond individual assertiveness, it's important to establish clear and consistent boundaries within the relationship.

These boundaries should cover various aspects, including physical touch, emotional intimacy, time commitment, financial decisions, and personal space. Clearly articulate your limits to the other person and enforce them consistently. For example, if you're uncomfortable with physical affection in public, say so. If you need personal space to recharge after work, let them know. Don't feel obligated to explain yourself extensively; a simple, clear statement of your needs is sufficient. If these boundaries are consistently crossed, it signals a disregard for your wellbeing and an unhealthy dynamic.

Building a strong support system is essential for navigating the complexities of new relationships. Reach out to trusted friends and family members who provide emotional support and a safe space for expressing your feelings. They can help you process experiences, offer perspectives, and hold you accountable for maintaining your boundaries. Sharing your

experiences with others who understand what you've been through can be incredibly validating and empowering.

Consider joining a support group for survivors of abuse. These groups provide a community of like-minded individuals who share similar experiences, offering a unique level of understanding and encouragement. In a safe group environment, you can share your anxieties, successes, and challenges without judgment, gaining strength and inspiration from others on similar paths.

Don't underestimate the power of professional support. A therapist specializing in trauma and abuse recovery can provide invaluable guidance in identifying red flags, developing healthy communication patterns, and setting boundaries. They can provide a safe space to work through the emotional baggage from previous experiences and develop coping mechanisms for navigating difficult situations. They can help you understand why you might be drawn to certain patterns in relationships and guide you toward healthier, more fulfilling connections. Therapy is an investment in your well-being and provides a non- judgmental space to process your experiences and develop strategies to avoid future harm.

Remember, rebuilding your life and establishing healthy relationships is a process, not a destination. There will be setbacks and challenges along the way. Be patient with yourself, celebrate your progress, and trust that you're moving in the right direction. Learning to recognize red flags, setting clear boundaries, and practicing assertive communication are essential skills for building a future free from fear and control. Your journey to healing and happiness is a testament to your resilience and strength; embrace it with courage, self-compassion, and the unwavering knowledge that you deserve a life filled with respect, love, and healthy relationships. Your ability to build healthy

connections is not just possible; it's your birthright. Embrace the process, learn from each step, and celebrate the remarkable person you are becoming. Your future is bright, and it's yours to create.

Forgiving Yourself and Moving Forward

The journey out of the shadows of abuse is rarely a straight line. It's a winding path, sometimes arduous, sometimes exhilarating, but always leading toward a brighter future.

While escaping the immediate danger is a monumental achievement, the internal work of healing is equally, if not more, important. A significant part of that healing involves forgiving yourself. This isn't about condoning the abuser's actions; it's about releasing the self-blame, the guilt, and the shame that often accompany surviving abuse.

Many survivors struggle with the pervasive feeling that they somehow deserved the abuse, or that they could have prevented it. This is a common and deeply ingrained consequence of manipulative tactics used by abusers. They systematically erode your self-worth, twisting your perception of reality until you believe you are at fault. The insidious nature of gaslighting and other forms of manipulation means that you internalize their lies, accepting their distorted version of events as your own truth. This self- blame can be incredibly debilitating, hindering your ability to move forward and build a healthy life.

Understanding this is the first crucial step. Recognize that the abuse was not your fault. No one deserves to be subjected to the cruelty and manipulation inflicted by a sociopath. Your abuser's actions were a reflection of their own pathologies, not a judgment of your worth. Repeating this affirmation to yourself, daily, is a powerful tool. Write it down, say it aloud, believe it in your heart. The repetition helps solidify this truth in your mind, slowly chipping away at the layers of self-blame that have accumulated over time. Consider writing a letter to your past self, acknowledging the

pain and reassuring that individual that they are worthy of love and respect. This act of self-compassion can be remarkably healing.

Seeking professional help is invaluable in this process. A therapist specializing in trauma and abuse recovery can provide a safe and non-judgmental space to explore these feelings of guilt and shame. Through therapy, you can begin to unravel the tangled web of lies that your abuser spun, replacing them with a more accurate and compassionate understanding of your experience. Techniques like cognitive behavioral therapy (CBT) can help reframe negative thoughts and beliefs, replacing self-criticism with self- acceptance. Eye Movement Desensitization and Reprocessing (EMDR) can be particularly effective in processing traumatic memories and reducing their emotional intensity. Remember that seeking help is a sign of strength, not weakness. It takes courage to confront the pain of the past and work towards a healthier future.

Forgiveness, however, is not solely an act of self- compassion; it also involves understanding the dynamics of the abusive relationship. This understanding does not require empathy for the abuser, but rather, a cognitive understanding of how manipulation works and how it affects its victims.

Learning about the psychological mechanisms employed by sociopaths helps neutralize the power of their tactics.

Understanding that they skillfully exploit vulnerabilities and emotional triggers allows you to see the situation more objectively, removing the personalized shame and replacing it with a clearer understanding of the power dynamics at play. This knowledge empowers you to recognize the situation was not a personal failure, but rather, a carefully orchestrated manipulation.

Beyond therapy, journaling can be a profoundly effective tool. Writing down your thoughts and feelings allows you to process them in a safe and private space. This can be particularly helpful in identifying recurring patterns of self- blame and challenging those thoughts. Try to describe your feelings in detail, without judgment. Allow yourself to feel the emotions without trying to suppress them. The act of writing itself can be therapeutic, allowing you to externalize the internal chaos and begin to make sense of it. Consider starting a gratitude journal as well. Focusing on the positive aspects of your life, however small they may seem, helps shift your focus away from the negativity of the past and fosters a sense of hope for the future.

Developing healthy coping mechanisms is crucial for moving forward. This might include engaging in activities you enjoy, spending time in nature, practicing mindfulness or meditation, engaging in creative pursuits, or connecting with supportive friends and family. Anything that brings you joy and peace is a valuable tool for healing. Remember that self-care is not selfish; it's essential for your recovery and well-being. Engage in activities that nurture your mind, body, and spirit. It's a powerful step to actively choose activities that replenish your energy and bring a sense of calm and peace to your life. This active commitment to self- care is a crucial act of self-love.

Moving forward doesn't erase the past; it acknowledges it, learns from it, and uses that knowledge to build a stronger, healthier future. Setting realistic goals is a key element.

Don't try to overhaul your entire life overnight. Start with small, achievable goals. This could involve setting a routine, creating a budget, pursuing an educational goal, or simply committing to a daily walk. Each small victory builds confidence and momentum, paving the way for bigger achievements. Celebrate these accomplishments, no matter

how small they may seem; acknowledge your resilience and strength.

Forgive yourself for the things you couldn't control, and learn from the things you could. This journey involves introspection, understanding your own vulnerabilities, and recognizing that you are not defined by the abuse you endured. Your worth is inherent; it cannot be diminished by the actions of another. Remember the strength you showed in escaping the abuse; that same strength will guide you in rebuilding your life.

Creating a vision for your future is a powerful way to foster hope. Imagine the life you want to create, the person you want to become. Visualize yourself living a life free from fear and control, filled with joy, love, and fulfilling relationships. This vision should be specific and personal, reflecting your dreams and aspirations. Write it down, create a vision board, or simply hold it in your mind. This act of envisioning a brighter future provides direction and motivation, fueling your journey toward healing.

Remember, you are not alone. There are many people who understand your experience and want to support you. Reach out to friends, family, or support groups. Connect with others who have survived similar situations; sharing your story can be incredibly cathartic and empowering. Knowing that others have walked a similar path and emerged stronger offers invaluable hope and inspiration.

Rebuilding your life after escaping abuse is a testament to your incredible resilience. The journey will have its ups and downs, but your strength and determination will carry you through. Embrace the process, celebrate your progress, and remember that you deserve a life free from fear and control. You are worthy of love, happiness, and a future filled with

possibilities. The journey is long, but you are on the right path, towards a future filled with the kind of happiness you deserve.

Creating a Future Free from Fear

Creating a life free from the pervasive fear instilled by your abuser requires a multifaceted approach. It's not merely about escaping a physical situation; it's about reclaiming your autonomy, rebuilding your sense of self, and cultivating a future defined by your choices, not your abuser's manipulations. This process demands patience, self-compassion, and a commitment to personal growth, but the rewards—a life filled with genuine peace, joy, and authentic connections—are immeasurable.

One of the most crucial aspects of this rebuilding process is prioritizing self-care. This isn't about indulging in frivolous luxuries; it's about actively engaging in practices that nourish your mind, body, and spirit. This might involve establishing a regular sleep schedule, ensuring you eat nutritious meals, and incorporating regular physical activity into your routine. Exercise, in particular, serves a dual purpose. It not only improves physical health but also releases endorphins, which have mood-boosting effects and can help alleviate symptoms of anxiety and depression— common consequences of prolonged abuse. Find an activity you genuinely enjoy, whether it's yoga, swimming, dancing, or a brisk walk in nature. The key is consistency, even if it's just for a short period each day.

Beyond physical self-care, nurturing your mental and emotional well-being is paramount. This could involve engaging in mindfulness practices, such as meditation or deep breathing exercises. These techniques help to center you in the present moment, reducing the power of intrusive thoughts and anxieties related to the past trauma. Consider journaling as a means of emotional processing. Writing

down your thoughts and feelings allows you to externalize them, making them less overwhelming and providing a safe space to explore your emotional landscape without judgment. Don't worry about grammar or eloquence; the act of writing itself is therapeutic.

Cultivating a strong support system is equally essential. Lean on trusted friends, family members, or support groups.

Sharing your experiences with others who understand can be incredibly validating and empowering. Find a therapist specializing in trauma and abuse recovery who can provide a safe and non-judgmental space for you to process your emotions and develop coping mechanisms. Therapy provides a structured framework for healing, offering tools and techniques to navigate the complexities of trauma recovery. Group therapy, in particular, can offer a sense of community and shared experience, helping you to feel less alone in your journey.

Remember that establishing healthy boundaries is a crucial aspect of creating a future free from fear. This means learning to say "no" to requests or demands that compromise your well-being. It means protecting your time and energy, prioritizing your needs, and setting limits on interactions with individuals who are toxic or draining. This process may feel uncomfortable at first, especially if you're accustomed to placating others or prioritizing their needs above your own.

However, establishing these boundaries is an act of self- respect and a vital component of creating a life free from manipulation and control.

Setting and achieving goals is a powerful way to build self- esteem and a sense of accomplishment. Begin with small, attainable goals, gradually working your way up to larger aspirations. This could involve anything from completing a small home improvement project to pursuing a new hobby or

enrolling in a course. Each accomplishment, no matter how small, reinforces your sense of agency and reinforces the belief in your ability to create positive change in your life. As you achieve these milestones, celebrate your progress and acknowledge your resilience. This positive reinforcement helps to build momentum and instills confidence in your ability to overcome challenges.

Consider pursuing personal growth opportunities that align with your interests and passions. This might involve taking a class, learning a new skill, volunteering for a cause you believe in, or engaging in creative pursuits. These activities not only provide a sense of fulfillment but also help you to rediscover your passions and connect with your authentic self. They can help to shift your focus away from the past and towards a brighter future, fostering a sense of hope and purpose. Investing time in your personal growth is an investment in your future happiness and well-being.

As you begin to rebuild your life, remember that forgiveness —both of yourself and your abuser—is a crucial step in the healing process. Forgiving yourself is not about condoning the abuse; it's about releasing the self-blame, guilt, and shame that often accompany such experiences. It's about recognizing that you were a victim of manipulation and that your worth is not diminished by the actions of another.

Forgiving your abuser, on the other hand, is not about condoning their behavior; it's about releasing the anger, resentment, and negativity that they may still hold over you. This doesn't mean you need to reconcile or have contact with them; it simply means freeing yourself from the emotional weight of their actions. It's about choosing to move on and not letting their toxicity continue to impact your life.

Building financial independence is often a critical element in escaping and staying free from an abusive relationship. If you experienced financial control during the abuse, focus on regaining your financial autonomy. This might involve creating a budget, seeking financial counseling, or exploring educational opportunities to enhance your earning potential. Becoming financially independent empowers you to make your own choices, free from the manipulation and control of another. It is a powerful symbol of your newfound freedom and self-sufficiency.

It's essential to remember that the journey to rebuilding your life after escaping abuse is rarely linear. There will be setbacks, moments of doubt, and periods of intense emotion. Be patient and kind to yourself throughout this process.

Acknowledge your progress, celebrate your successes, and don't be afraid to seek support when you need it. The strength you demonstrated in escaping the abusive situation is a testament to your resilience, and that same strength will guide you as you navigate this next phase of your life.

Creating a future free from fear requires courage, determination, and self-compassion. It requires actively working to build a life that reflects your values, priorities, and dreams. It's a journey of self-discovery, healing, and personal growth. Remember that you are not defined by your past experiences; you are capable of creating a bright, fulfilling future filled with joy, peace, and genuine connection. Embrace the process, celebrate your progress, and know that you are worthy of a life free from fear and control. The path ahead may seem daunting, but with each step you take, you move closer to the life you deserve.

Remember, your strength is inherent; your value is undeniable; and your future is bright. The journey is long, but the destination—a life free from the shadows of abuse— is worth every step. You have survived the unimaginable; now, it's time to thrive.

Finding the Right Therapist or Counselor

Finding the right therapist is crucial in your journey to healing after escaping abuse. It's not a simple task; choosing a therapist is like choosing a partner—you need to feel comfortable, safe, and confident in their abilities. This section will guide you through the process, equipping you with the knowledge to make an informed decision. The wrong therapist can inadvertently retraumatize you; the right one can be your anchor in the storm. Remember, you deserve to be heard, understood, and supported by a professional who truly gets it.

The first step is researching therapists in your area who specialize in trauma and abuse recovery. Start by utilizing online directories such as Psychology Today, GoodTherapy, and the websites of professional organizations like the American Psychological Association (APA) or your country's equivalent. These platforms often allow you to filter your search by specialization, insurance acceptance, and even treatment modalities. You can refine your search by keywords such as "trauma-informed therapy," "complex PTSD," "sociopathic abuse," or "relationship abuse." Look for therapists with specific experience working with victims of the type of abuse you've endured.

Don't be afraid to cast a wide net initially. Look at several therapists' profiles, paying close attention to their bios. A good therapist's profile will clearly articulate their experience and approach. It should be more than just a list of credentials; it should offer insight into their philosophy and the types of clients they feel best equipped to serve. Look for statements reflecting an understanding of the nuances of

abuse dynamics, especially if you've experienced gaslighting, coercive control, or other manipulative tactics.

Once you've compiled a list of potential therapists, it's time to schedule initial consultations. Many therapists offer a free 15- to 30-minute introductory call or consultation. This initial contact is crucial; it's your opportunity to gauge the therapeutic rapport and determine if there's a good fit. Before the consultation, jot down questions that are important to you. These questions may include:

What is your experience working with survivors of sociopathic abuse or similar situations? Be specific about the type of abuse you experienced.

What therapeutic modalities do you utilize? (e.g., Cognitive Behavioral Therapy (CBT), Dialectical Behavior Therapy (DBT), Eye Movement Desensitization and Reprocessing (EMDR), Trauma-Focused Cognitive Behavioral Therapy (TF-CBT)). Different modalities cater to different needs and preferences. Research which modalities might be most helpful for your specific situation.

What is your approach to setting boundaries within the therapeutic relationship? This is crucial, especially if you've experienced difficulties setting boundaries in the past.

How do you handle emergencies or crises that might arise between sessions? What is your protocol for after-hours support?

What is your cancellation policy? This is a practical consideration, but also provides insight into the therapist's approach to their practice and client management.

What is your fee schedule, and what insurance plans do you accept?

Can you provide references? While unlikely to be explicitly offered, you can ask if you have significant concerns.

How long do you typically work with clients before considering termination of therapy? Understanding their

approach to the length of therapy helps in managing expectations.

What is your approach to working with trauma? How do you assess the impact of trauma on different facets of the client's life and personal relationships?

During the consultation, pay attention to your gut feeling. Do you feel safe and comfortable talking to this person? Do you feel judged or understood? A good therapist will create a safe and non-judgmental space for you to share your experiences, even if those experiences are extremely difficult to recount. They should listen attentively, validate your feelings, and avoid minimizing your trauma. They should not interrupt your narrative excessively, but respectfully guide the conversation. They should demonstrate empathy and a genuine interest in helping you heal.

It's vital to clarify their approach to confidentiality and mandated reporting. Understand the limits of confidentiality and under what circumstances they would be legally obligated to report information to authorities. This is essential for establishing trust and ensuring your safety.

If, during the consultation, you feel uncomfortable, uneasy, or that the therapist isn't a good fit, don't hesitate to end the session and seek out another professional. Finding the right therapist may take time and involve speaking to several practitioners before you find the right match. Don't lose heart; finding the right support is a critical part of healing. The time and effort spent searching for the correct professional is an investment in your long-term well-being.

It's also important to consider the therapist's cultural competency. If you identify with a specific cultural background or have unique cultural needs, ensure the therapist understands and respects your culture and beliefs.

Lack of cultural understanding can create barriers to effective treatment. If you feel unsure, directly inquire about their experience working with people from diverse backgrounds.

Beyond the initial consultation, consider researching the therapist's credentials. Verify their licenses and certifications with the relevant licensing board in your state or country.

Check online reviews, but remember that online reviews should be considered as one piece of information among many and not the sole determiner.

Once you find a therapist with whom you feel comfortable and confident, establish clear communication. Express your needs and expectations openly and honestly. Don't hesitate to provide feedback about your experience. A strong therapeutic relationship is built on mutual trust, respect, and open communication. Remember that the therapeutic relationship is a partnership, and both you and your therapist should be actively engaged in the healing process.

Finding a therapist is a journey in itself, a necessary step in your broader journey of healing. Be patient, persistent, and proactive in your search. Your mental and emotional well- being is worth the investment. The right therapist will provide a safe space to unpack the complexities of your trauma and equip you with the tools you need to navigate your recovery journey. Remember, healing is possible, and you deserve to experience a life free from the shadows of the past. You are strong, resilient, and deserving of a future filled with peace and happiness.

Types of Therapy for Abuse Survivors

Having found a therapist you trust, the next step is understanding the various therapeutic approaches available to help you process the trauma you've endured. There isn't a one-size-fits-all solution; the most effective therapy will depend on your individual needs, preferences, and the specific nature of your trauma. However, several therapeutic modalities have proven highly effective for survivors of abuse, particularly those perpetrated by sociopaths.

One widely used approach is **Cognitive Behavioral Therapy (CBT)**. CBT focuses on the interconnectedness of thoughts, feelings, and behaviors. In the context of abuse recovery, CBT helps you identify and challenge negative or distorted thought patterns that might be contributing to your emotional distress. For example, if you're struggling with feelings of self-blame or worthlessness – common after enduring abuse – CBT provides strategies to reframe these thoughts and replace them with more realistic and empowering ones. This might involve journaling, cognitive restructuring exercises, or behavioral experiments designed to test the validity of your negative beliefs. A CBT therapist will guide you in developing coping mechanisms to manage anxiety, depression, and other symptoms often associated with trauma. They might also help you establish healthy boundaries and develop assertive communication skills – skills often eroded during an abusive relationship. The strength of CBT lies in its practical, action-oriented approach, making it a highly effective tool for building resilience and self-efficacy.

Another highly effective modality is **Eye Movement Desensitization and Reprocessing (EMDR)**. EMDR is a

specialized therapy designed specifically to address trauma. It involves bilateral stimulation, often through eye movements, while you recall traumatic memories. The theory behind EMDR suggests that the bilateral stimulation helps your brain process the traumatic memories, reducing their emotional intensity. EMDR isn't just about remembering the traumatic event; it's about changing how your brain processes and stores that memory. While the exact mechanism isn't fully understood, research strongly supports EMDR's effectiveness in treating PTSD and other trauma-related conditions. It's particularly useful for processing specific traumatic events and reducing the intrusive thoughts, flashbacks, and nightmares often experienced by abuse survivors. Unlike some other therapies, EMDR often works relatively quickly, providing noticeable relief in a shorter timeframe. It's important to note that EMDR is usually not a standalone treatment and is often used in conjunction with other therapies such as CBT.

Trauma-Focused Cognitive Behavioral Therapy (TF- CBT) integrates elements of both CBT and EMDR, tailoring the approach to the specific needs of trauma survivors. It specifically addresses the cognitive, emotional, and behavioral consequences of trauma. This modality is especially effective in cases where trauma has significantly impacted a person's ability to function daily, affecting areas such as sleep, concentration, or relationships. TF-CBT uses a combination of techniques from CBT, including psychoeducation, relaxation techniques, and cognitive processing, to help survivors understand their trauma and develop healthy coping mechanisms. It incorporates aspects of EMDR to process traumatic memories directly, working to reduce the emotional impact of these experiences. The collaborative nature of TF-CBT—working closely with the therapist to establish goals and track progress—makes it a

powerful tool for regaining control and rebuilding one's life after abuse.

Dialectical Behavior Therapy (DBT) is another effective modality, particularly helpful for those struggling with intense emotions, self-harm, or suicidal ideation. DBT emphasizes mindfulness, emotional regulation, distress tolerance, and interpersonal effectiveness. These skills are crucial for managing the overwhelming emotions that often accompany trauma recovery. DBT helps you develop a broader range of emotional coping strategies, enabling you to manage intense feelings without resorting to self- destructive behaviors. The core principles of DBT involve acceptance of your current state alongside a commitment to making positive changes. This balanced approach is especially beneficial for individuals who might be struggling with feelings of shame or self-criticism, common after surviving abuse. It focuses on building a stronger sense of self, reducing reactivity, and improving relationships with others.

Somatic Experiencing (SE) is a body-oriented approach that focuses on the physical sensations associated with trauma. Unlike other therapies that primarily focus on cognitive or emotional processing, SE acknowledges that trauma is stored in the body. Through gentle movements and mindfulness techniques, SE helps you release the physical tension held within your body as a result of trauma. This can manifest as muscle tension, chronic pain, or other physical symptoms. SE helps you become more aware of your body's sensations and develop coping strategies for managing these physical manifestations of trauma. Because sociopathic abuse frequently involves physical and emotional control, SE can be particularly valuable in addressing the lingering physical effects of the abuse. It's a more gentle, non-invasive approach which can be particularly beneficial for individuals

who find traditional talk therapies triggering or overwhelming.

Beyond these core modalities, several other therapeutic techniques can be integrated into your treatment plan. These might include:

Narrative Therapy: This approach focuses on helping you reframe your story and create a more empowering narrative about your experiences. Instead of viewing yourself as a victim, narrative therapy helps you reclaim your agency and see yourself as a survivor who has overcome adversity.

Attachment-Based Therapy: This approach focuses on understanding how early childhood experiences and attachment patterns may have influenced your vulnerability to abuse and your responses to it. It helps to address underlying issues that might be perpetuating unhealthy relationship dynamics.

Group Therapy: Connecting with other survivors can be incredibly powerful. Group therapy provides a safe space to share your experiences, learn from others, and realize you're not alone in your journey.

The decision of which therapy, or combination of therapies, is best suited to your needs will be a collaborative process between you and your therapist. They will consider the nature of your trauma, your personal preferences, and your goals for therapy. It's crucial to be open and honest with your therapist about your experiences, your challenges, and what you hope to achieve through therapy. Don't hesitate to ask questions, voice concerns, and advocate for your needs. Your therapist is a partner in your healing journey, and the right therapeutic relationship is built on mutual trust, respect, and open communication. The path to healing is not always

linear; there may be setbacks and challenges along the way. Remember that progress is progress, and celebrate every step you take towards a healthier and more fulfilling life. Your resilience is a testament to your strength, and with the right support, you can reclaim your life and build a future free from the shadows of the past. You deserve to live a life filled with peace, happiness, and genuine connection. Don't underestimate the power of seeking help, and trust in your ability to heal and thrive. The journey is long, but the destination—a life free from the grip of abuse—is worth the effort. Remember, healing is a journey, not a destination, and it's okay to take your time, adapt your approach, and adjust your goals as you progress.

Support Groups and Peer Support

The therapeutic journey, as powerful as it is, doesn't exist in a vacuum. While individual therapy provides a deeply personal and focused space for healing, the added support of a community can be transformative. This is where support groups and peer support networks come in, offering a unique and invaluable dimension to your recovery. These groups provide a safe and understanding environment where you can connect with others who have lived through similar experiences. This shared understanding transcends the limitations of even the most empathetic therapist, offering a sense of validation, belonging, and hope that is incredibly powerful.

The value of connecting with fellow survivors cannot be overstated. It's a fundamental truth of trauma recovery that you are not alone. Feeling isolated and misunderstood is a common experience for survivors of sociopathic abuse, a consequence of the abuser's deliberate attempts to isolate their victims and erode their sense of self. Support groups actively counter this isolation, creating a space where sharing your story, hearing others' stories, and finding solidarity can be profoundly healing.

In a support group, you'll encounter others who understand the nuances of sociopathic manipulation, the insidious gaslighting, the pervasive control, and the lasting effects of the emotional and psychological damage. You'll hear stories that mirror your own, validating your experiences and helping you normalize your reactions. This shared validation can be incredibly powerful, dismantling the self-doubt and shame that often accompany abuse. You'll discover that your experiences are not unique, that your feelings are valid, and

that your reactions are completely understandable given the circumstances. This simple realization can be a monumental step toward healing.

Beyond validation, support groups provide practical support and advice. Members often share coping strategies, resources, and information about legal and other assistance. This exchange of knowledge and experience can be a valuable lifeline, especially during the early stages of recovery when you're still navigating the complexities of leaving an abusive relationship and rebuilding your life. The collective wisdom within a support group can help you navigate practical hurdles, from finding safe housing and securing financial independence to dealing with legal issues and rebuilding your support network.

Furthermore, the peer-to-peer support offered in these groups is unique and invaluable. While your therapist provides professional guidance, your fellow survivors offer a different kind of support – a shared experience of understanding. This doesn't diminish the importance of therapy, but it complements it. The shared experiences and empathy within the group offer a sense of camaraderie and understanding that can be both comforting and empowering. You'll find yourself less alone in your journey, empowered by the collective strength and resilience of the group. This can build confidence and create a sense of hope that extends far beyond the confines of individual therapy sessions.

Many support groups are specifically designed for survivors of domestic violence and abuse. These groups often offer specialized support tailored to the unique challenges faced by those who have survived relationships with sociopaths or narcissists. They often delve into the intricacies of manipulative behaviors and offer strategies for recognizing and avoiding similar patterns in future relationships. This

specialized focus provides a level of understanding that is simply unavailable in more general support groups. Finding a group that caters to your specific experience is crucial in finding a supportive and understanding community.

However, finding the right support group is critical. It's essential to find a group that feels safe and comfortable for you. Look for groups that are facilitated by trained professionals who understand trauma and abuse. A well- facilitated group will provide a structured and supportive environment, ensuring that conversations are respectful and productive, and that boundaries are maintained. It's equally important that the group environment fosters a sense of trust and mutual respect. Some groups might adopt a strict confidentiality policy, ensuring that shared information remains within the group. Others might have more flexible guidelines. Understanding these nuances before joining is essential in ensuring a positive and beneficial experience.

Investigate any group thoroughly before participating.

Finding these groups may involve some research. A good starting point is to search online for "support groups for survivors of sociopathic abuse" or "support groups for domestic violence survivors" in your local area. Many organizations dedicated to domestic violence prevention and support offer online and in-person support groups. Your therapist can also provide valuable recommendations or referrals to local groups, leveraging their knowledge of your specific circumstances and needs. It's not uncommon for therapists to suggest or even refer patients to support groups as part of a holistic treatment plan. This collaborative approach significantly enhances the effectiveness of therapy and strengthens your overall recovery.

Moreover, online support groups and forums offer a broader reach, connecting you with individuals across geographical

boundaries. This is especially valuable if local resources are limited or if you prefer the anonymity and flexibility that online platforms can offer. Online communities can also provide ongoing support outside of scheduled group meetings, offering a sense of connection and community 24/7. However, it's crucial to approach online support groups with caution. Ensure the platform prioritizes safety and has measures in place to address potential harassment or inappropriate behavior. Some platforms provide moderation to ensure a safe and respectful environment. Always prioritize your safety and well-being when participating in online communities.

Remember that finding the right support group might take time. Don't be discouraged if the first group you try isn't a good fit. It's crucial to find a group where you feel comfortable, accepted, and understood. The feeling of acceptance and belonging is fundamental for healing. A supportive environment can help you to share your story, process your emotions, and connect with others on a meaningful level. This process might require trying out several groups before finding the one that resonates with you and feels like a true sanctuary.

The benefits of support groups extend far beyond the immediate feeling of connection and validation. The ongoing support you receive can empower you to navigate challenges more effectively, build resilience, and maintain momentum in your recovery. The lasting connections forged within these groups can provide a powerful source of strength and encouragement during difficult times. By creating a community around you that understands your experiences, you are creating a safe space where your healing can flourish and ultimately lead to a future free from the shadows of your past. The collective resilience found in such groups can be a

significant driving force in your continued healing and personal growth.

Beyond formal support groups, you can also find valuable support through informal networks. This might involve connecting with trusted friends, family members, or colleagues who understand your situation and offer consistent support. Even casual conversations with people who have shown empathy and understanding can be helpful. This approach is especially useful if formal groups aren't readily accessible, or if you find group settings overwhelming or triggering. Remember that any support is valuable, and building a supportive network, however informal, can substantially contribute to your healing journey.

Cultivating a personal support network is a cornerstone of successful recovery. It doesn't have to be a large group; rather, it's the quality of the relationships that matter most. These individuals, whether friends, family, or colleagues, provide a sense of normalcy and stability in your life, helping you feel connected and understood. The support you receive from your personal network can act as a buffer, mitigating the negative impacts of trauma and promoting your sense of self-worth. It's crucial to build a network of people who will listen without judgment and provide unwavering support during challenging times.

In summary, seeking support from both formal groups and informal networks is a critical element of healing from the trauma of sociopathic abuse. The validation, practical advice, and emotional support you gain from these groups can be instrumental in your recovery, and their contribution shouldn't be underestimated. By embracing these supportive communities, you're taking a proactive step toward reclaiming your life, strengthening your sense of self, and building a future free from the grip of abuse. Remember, seeking help is a sign of strength, and you are not alone in this journey.

Working with Legal Professionals

Navigating the legal system after experiencing abuse from a sociopath can feel like entering a minefield. The complexities of the law, coupled with the emotional toll of the abuse, can be overwhelming. However, understanding your legal options and seeking skilled legal representation is crucial for protecting yourself and securing your future. This section will guide you through the process of working with legal professionals, empowering you to take control and safeguard your well-being.

The first crucial step is finding a lawyer specializing in domestic violence or abuse cases. These lawyers possess a deep understanding of the dynamics of abusive relationships and the specific legal challenges faced by survivors. They are equipped to handle the nuances of cases involving sociopathic abusers, who often employ sophisticated manipulation tactics to undermine their victims' credibility. Don't hesitate to interview several lawyers before making a decision. Ask about their experience with similar cases, their approach to working with trauma survivors, and their fee structure. A good lawyer will prioritize your safety and well- being, demonstrating empathy and understanding throughout the process.

One of the most effective legal tools available to survivors is a restraining order, also known as a protection order. A restraining order is a court order that legally restricts the abuser's contact with you. This can include prohibiting them from contacting you directly or indirectly, coming within a certain distance of your home or workplace, or even possessing a firearm. The specific terms of the order vary depending on your jurisdiction and the details of your case.

However, the primary goal is to create a physical and emotional barrier between you and your abuser, minimizing the risk of further harm.

Obtaining a restraining order requires providing evidence of abuse. This evidence can include photos, videos, medical records documenting injuries, police reports, emails, text messages, or even witness testimonies. Your lawyer will help you gather and organize this evidence, ensuring it is presented effectively in court. Be prepared to detail the instances of abuse, providing specific dates, times, and descriptions of the events. It is crucial to be accurate and consistent in your testimony, maintaining a calm and clear demeanor. Your lawyer will guide you through this process, offering support and reassurance along the way.

Remember that even if you've never reported the abuse to the police previously, you can still seek a restraining order. The court will consider all available evidence, even if it is solely based on your testimony and supporting documentation. Your lawyer can help you navigate the process of presenting your evidence effectively and persuasively. It's worth noting that obtaining a restraining order is not always a guarantee of complete safety, but it serves as a significant deterrent and provides a critical legal layer of protection.

Beyond restraining orders, legal professionals can play a vital role in securing your financial safety and independence. If you shared finances with your abuser, you might need assistance in disentangling your joint accounts, dividing assets, and obtaining financial support. This can involve seeking alimony, child support, or other forms of financial assistance. The process can be complex and legally demanding, requiring expert legal guidance. Your lawyer

will help you navigate the legal requirements, protecting your financial rights and ensuring a fair settlement.

Furthermore, if you experienced financial abuse – such as controlling access to funds, manipulating credit cards, or coercing you into financial decisions that benefited your abuser – your lawyer can help you address this specific aspect of your situation. This might involve seeking reimbursement for financial losses incurred during the abusive relationship, or addressing fraudulent activity. The legal process can help you reclaim financial control of your life, laying a secure foundation for your independent future.

In situations involving custody of children, legal representation is even more critical. Navigating child custody arrangements during and after a relationship with a sociopathic abuser can be incredibly challenging. Child custody cases are often highly emotional and contentious, requiring a strong legal team that understands the dynamics of abuse and can effectively advocate for your child's well- being. A lawyer specializing in family law can help you navigate the complexities of the legal process, ensuring the safety and best interests of your child are prioritized.

Your lawyer can help determine the most appropriate custody arrangement, considering the abuser's manipulative tendencies and any history of violence or abuse. They can assist in constructing a comprehensive parenting plan that safeguards your child's physical and emotional well-being, limiting the abuser's access if necessary. They can also advocate for your rights as a parent, ensuring that your voice is heard and that your concerns are addressed fairly and effectively.

Beyond individual legal action, your lawyer can also guide you through the potential benefits of seeking legal assistance

through domestic violence shelters or advocacy organizations. These organizations often provide pro bono or reduced-fee legal services to survivors, making legal representation more accessible. They can also offer comprehensive support services, including counseling, housing assistance, and financial assistance. Leveraging these resources can significantly enhance your ability to rebuild your life and secure your future.

Remember that the legal process can be long and emotionally draining. It's crucial to maintain open communication with your lawyer, keeping them informed of any new developments or concerns. Don't hesitate to ask questions or express your anxieties. Your lawyer's role extends beyond the courtroom; they are there to provide guidance, support, and a sense of stability during a challenging time. They are your advocate, helping you navigate a complex legal landscape while you focus on your healing and recovery.

Furthermore, consider the possibility of criminal charges against your abuser. If you have evidence of criminal activity, such as assault, stalking, or theft, you can report it to the police. Your lawyer can work with law enforcement to build a strong case, guiding you through the process of providing evidence and testimony. While it's not guaranteed that criminal charges will be filed, pursuing this avenue can provide a sense of justice and accountability, contributing to your healing process.

Finally, remember that seeking legal help is a sign of strength, not weakness. It's a proactive step toward protecting yourself and creating a safer future. Don't let fear or intimidation prevent you from accessing the legal support you deserve. With the help of a skilled and compassionate legal professional, you can navigate the complexities of the legal system, securing your safety and laying the foundation for a life free from abuse. Your journey towards healing and empowerment begins with taking this critical step. The support you receive from your lawyer will prove invaluable as you continue to rebuild your life and reclaim your future. You deserve peace, safety, and a life free from the shadow of your past.

Accessing Community Resources and Services

The legal process, as crucial as it is, forms only one part of your journey to recovery. Equally vital is accessing the wealth of support available within your community. These resources, often overlooked in the immediate aftermath of abuse, can provide the lifeline you need to rebuild your life and reclaim your sense of self. Domestic violence shelters, hotlines, and advocacy groups offer a network of support, practical assistance, and a safe haven where you can begin to heal.

Domestic violence shelters provide temporary safe housing for survivors of abuse, offering a refuge from immediate danger. These shelters vary in size and the services they offer, but typically include a safe, secure environment, meals, clothing, and basic necessities. More importantly, they often provide access to crucial support services, including counseling, legal advocacy, and assistance with finding employment and housing. The shelter environment itself offers a powerful sense of community, allowing survivors to connect with others who have shared similar experiences. This shared experience can be incredibly validating and empowering, reminding survivors that they are not alone in their struggles and that healing is possible.

Finding a shelter can be as simple as a quick online search, but it's also vital to be mindful of safety and discretion. If you're concerned about your abuser's ability to track your location, utilize a trusted friend or family member's computer or phone for your search, or seek assistance from a trusted professional who can provide resources without compromising your safety. Many shelters maintain confidential databases of available beds and services,

ensuring that your location and contact information remain private. This privacy is paramount, understanding that maintaining confidentiality is crucial to your safety and well- being. Shelter staff are trained to understand and respond to the unique needs of survivors, maintaining a strict confidentiality protocol and ensuring that your privacy is safeguarded at all times.

Beyond physical shelter, many organizations offer crisis hotlines. These hotlines operate 24/7, providing immediate support and guidance to individuals experiencing abuse. A call to a hotline can offer immediate emotional support, helping you to feel less isolated and alone. Hotline counselors are trained to provide crisis intervention, helping you to develop a safety plan, access resources, and navigate immediate challenges. They can offer a calming voice amidst the storm, providing a safe space to vent your emotions and process your experiences without judgment.

They are invaluable resources, offering immediate assistance and helping to connect you to more sustained support.

Remember that reaching out is a sign of strength, not weakness, and that there are people who care and want to help.

Advocacy groups play a crucial role in supporting survivors of abuse. These groups work to raise awareness about domestic violence, advocate for policy changes, and provide direct support to survivors. They often offer a wide range of services, including counseling, legal advocacy, support groups, and educational workshops. Participating in a support group can be incredibly therapeutic, allowing you to share your experiences with others who understand, providing mutual support and validation. These groups offer a safe space to process emotions, build resilience, and foster a sense of community. The shared experience within the

group can be transformative, allowing you to move forward in healing with the support of your peers.

Many advocacy groups also provide legal advocacy services, working in conjunction with legal professionals to ensure survivors have access to justice and appropriate legal representation. They may provide assistance with obtaining restraining orders, navigating custody battles, or securing financial assistance. These groups can be a powerful ally, navigating the complexities of the legal system alongside you and providing unwavering support. They often have strong networks within the legal community, ensuring that survivors have access to the best legal professionals available and can assist in finding lawyers who specialize in domestic violence and abuse cases.

Accessing these services can sometimes feel overwhelming, especially in the midst of trauma. However, it's essential to remember that you are not alone. There are people who care about your well-being and want to help. Don't hesitate to reach out to multiple organizations, explore various resources, and find the support systems that best fit your individual needs. Your safety and recovery are paramount, and taking the step to seek assistance is an act of incredible strength and courage.

Beyond shelters, hotlines, and advocacy groups, many community organizations offer additional support services relevant to your situation. Food banks can address immediate food insecurity, while housing assistance programs can help you find safe and affordable housing. Job training and placement services can help you rebuild your financial independence, and mental health services can provide ongoing support for your emotional well-being. Reaching out to your local community center or social services agency can provide information on these and other vital resources.

It's important to acknowledge that the process of accessing and utilizing these services might feel overwhelming, particularly during the initial stages of your recovery. The emotional impact of abuse can make it difficult to navigate complex systems and make crucial decisions. Allow yourself time, be patient with yourself, and remember that every small step forward is a victory. Don't hesitate to reach out to a trusted friend, family member, or therapist for support and guidance in navigating these resources. Their assistance can be invaluable in helping you to organize your thoughts, prioritize your needs, and access the support that you deserve.

Remember, seeking help is not a sign of weakness, it's a sign of strength and resilience. Taking this step demonstrates your commitment to healing and rebuilding your life. The road to recovery is not always easy, but it is a journey filled with hope and the possibility of a brighter future. By accessing the resources available within your community, you are taking control of your life and empowering yourself to move forward with strength and confidence.

Furthermore, consider the potential benefits of online support groups. These online communities offer a sense of anonymity and accessibility that can be particularly beneficial for survivors who may feel hesitant to participate in in-person support groups. These online platforms can provide a sense of connection and shared experience, offering opportunities to build resilience and learn from others who have overcome similar challenges. These online resources can be a valuable supplement to other forms of support, providing readily accessible emotional support and practical advice.

It is crucial to remember that the healing process is personal and takes time. There is no prescribed timeline, and it's important to be patient and compassionate with yourself throughout this journey. Celebrate small victories, acknowledge your progress, and allow yourself to grieve the losses you've experienced. Embrace the support of the community and continue to seek out resources and services as needed, recognizing that your needs will likely evolve as you heal and move forward. The path toward healing is unique to each individual, and the journey itself will contribute to shaping your sense of self and building a stronger, more resilient future. Your resilience and strength are undeniable; embrace them and celebrate the progress you make each day. You are capable of healing, and you deserve a life filled with peace, safety, and joy. The resources mentioned are stepping stones on your path to reclaiming your life and building a stronger, healthier future for yourself. Remember to reach out for assistance – you don't have to walk this path alone.

Assessing Your Financial Situation

Rebuilding your life after escaping an abusive relationship requires a multifaceted approach, and financial independence is a cornerstone of that process. While the emotional and psychological wounds of abuse can take time to heal, regaining control of your finances can provide an immediate sense of empowerment and security. This section will guide you through a process of assessing your current financial situation, identifying your assets and liabilities, and exploring potential avenues for financial stability.

Remember, this is a process, and it's crucial to be patient and kind to yourself throughout. Each step you take, no matter how small, contributes to your journey toward financial independence.

The first step is to take a deep breath and gather your resources. Find a quiet, safe space where you can focus without distractions. It may be helpful to have a notebook and pen, or to use a computer spreadsheet program, to keep track of your information. Don't feel pressured to complete this process in one sitting. If you feel overwhelmed, break it down into smaller, manageable tasks, taking breaks as needed. Remember to prioritize self-care throughout this process. Engage in activities that help you relax and de- stress; this will help you to stay focused and avoid feeling discouraged.

Begin by creating a comprehensive inventory of your assets. This includes any bank accounts, savings accounts, retirement funds, investment accounts, and other financial holdings. List the account numbers, the current balances, and the institution where the account is held. Include any physical assets such as vehicles, property, jewelry, or other

valuable possessions. Estimate the value of these assets, taking into account depreciation where necessary. If you are unsure about the value of a particular asset, you can seek assistance from a financial advisor or a trusted professional. Detailed records will be helpful if you decide to seek legal advice or need to support financial claims later. Keeping this information organized will not only help you understand your current financial standing but also assist you in making informed decisions moving forward.

Next, create a list of your debts. This includes credit card debt, loans (personal, student, auto, mortgage), medical bills, and any other outstanding financial obligations. For each debt, record the creditor's name, the amount owed, the interest rate, and the minimum monthly payment. This clear picture of your outstanding debts will be essential in developing a strategy to manage and ultimately eliminate them. It's important to be thorough, even if some debts seem insignificant. A complete record will assist you in evaluating your overall financial situation effectively.

Once you have a comprehensive list of your assets and debts, you can calculate your net worth. This is simply the difference between your total assets and your total liabilities (debts). A positive net worth indicates that your assets exceed your debts, while a negative net worth indicates the opposite. Your net worth provides a snapshot of your current financial health and can be a useful tool for tracking your progress as you work towards financial independence. Don't be discouraged by a negative net worth; this is a starting point, and with a plan, you can gradually improve your financial situation.

Now, turn your attention to your income. Identify all sources of current income, whether it's employment, alimony, child support, social security, disability benefits, or any other

forms of financial support. Record the amount of income you receive from each source, as well as the frequency of payment (weekly, bi-weekly, monthly, etc.). This comprehensive income analysis will help you accurately assess your budget and plan for the future. It's also important to consider potential future income sources; do you have skills or qualifications that would enable you to find new employment opportunities? Exploring job training programs or enhancing your resume might open the doors to new income streams.

After compiling the information, it's time to create a budget. This should be a realistic budget reflecting your actual spending habits. You can use budgeting apps or spreadsheets to track your income and expenses. Categorize your expenses (housing, food, transportation, utilities, healthcare, debt payments, entertainment, etc.). It's important to be honest with yourself about your spending habits. Identify areas where you can cut expenses and adjust your budget accordingly. Remember, even small adjustments to your spending habits can make a significant difference in your overall financial picture. Creating a detailed budget not only provides financial clarity but also allows you to plan for the future and prioritize your needs effectively.

Consider exploring resources available to assist you during this financial assessment and budgeting process. Financial literacy programs and workshops can provide guidance on budgeting, debt management, and financial planning. Local community organizations and non-profit agencies often offer free or low-cost financial counseling services. These resources can be invaluable in navigating the complexities of personal finance, providing support and guidance as you work toward achieving financial independence. Utilize these resources to equip yourself with the knowledge and skills necessary to take control of your financial future.

If you are facing overwhelming debt, consider seeking professional help. Credit counseling agencies can help you develop a debt management plan, negotiate with creditors, and explore options such as debt consolidation or bankruptcy. These agencies can provide valuable guidance and support in navigating your debt and securing your financial stability. Seeking help doesn't signal failure, but rather displays your proactive approach towards gaining control over your financial situation. Remember, addressing debt head-on, with the appropriate professional assistance, will enable you to rebuild your financial health effectively.

Protecting your credit is also crucial during this period. Regularly review your credit report for errors or signs of fraudulent activity. If you discover any inaccuracies, take immediate action to correct them. Understanding your credit score and working toward improving it is essential for securing loans, securing housing and gaining access to financial services. Taking proactive steps to improve and maintain your credit score can contribute greatly to your financial stability.

This detailed assessment will empower you to navigate the financial aspects of your recovery. Remember, this process is a journey, and it's important to celebrate your achievements along the way. As you gain financial stability, you'll build confidence and resilience, contributing to your overall well- being and creating a future free from financial anxieties. The path to financial independence is attainable;

with careful planning, persistence, and the utilization of available resources, you will achieve your financial goals. Your strength and perseverance in overcoming abuse extend to this new chapter of your life. Embrace this journey, acknowledge your progress, and celebrate the future you are

building for yourself, financially secure and independently empowered.

Creating a Budget and Managing Finances

Building a budget is more than just tracking income and expenses; it's about creating a roadmap for your financial future. This is particularly crucial after escaping an abusive relationship, where financial control may have been a significant tool of manipulation. Regaining control of your finances is a powerful step towards reclaiming your autonomy.

Start by meticulously documenting your income. This includes all sources—employment wages (including overtime and bonuses), alimony, child support, social security benefits, disability payments, rental income, any interest earned, and any other regular financial inflows. Note the frequency of each payment—weekly, bi-weekly, monthly, or annually. Be thorough; even small amounts add up. Consider setting up separate bank accounts for different purposes – one for necessities, another for savings, and perhaps a third for discretionary spending. This can improve your ability to track income and expenses. This segregation can also help you avoid overspending in one area while neglecting others.

Next, create a detailed list of your monthly expenses. Be brutally honest with yourself. Categorize your expenses to gain a clearer picture of your spending habits. Major categories often include:

Housing: Rent or mortgage payments, property taxes, homeowners insurance, renter's insurance, maintenance and repairs. If you're facing housing instability, explore options like subsidized housing, shelters, or transitional housing programs. Document all housing costs, even small ones, to

have a clear financial picture. If you shared housing with your abuser, you may have to reassess your housing needs and budget accordingly.

Food: Groceries, eating out, and any subscriptions to meal delivery services. Consider creating a meal plan to minimize food waste and reduce expenses. Look for budget-friendly recipes and explore options like bulk buying or utilizing food banks if your budget is particularly tight.

Transportation: Car payments, insurance, gas, public transportation fares, maintenance and repairs. If possible, consider carpooling, biking, or walking to reduce transportation costs. Explore public transportation options to cut down your costs.

Utilities: Electricity, gas, water, internet, phone, cable. Consider energy-efficient practices and negotiate with providers for better rates. Explore alternatives such as cheaper internet plans or switching to a more cost-effective phone provider.

Healthcare: Medical insurance premiums, co-pays, medications, dental care, vision care. If you're uninsured or underinsured, research available government programs like Medicaid or affordable care options in your area. Consider a health savings account (HSA) to plan for future medical expenses, a great tool for long-term savings.

Debt Payments: Minimum payments on credit cards, loans, and any other outstanding debts. List each debt separately, including the creditor, the balance, the interest rate, and the minimum monthly payment. This detailed information will assist you in formulating a comprehensive debt management strategy.

Childcare: If applicable, include daycare expenses, babysitting fees, or any other childcare-related costs. Research and find affordable childcare options such as subsidized programs or in-home care.

Personal Care: Toiletries, clothing, haircuts. Look for discounts and sales to minimize these expenses.

Entertainment: Movies, concerts, subscriptions, hobbies. This is often the first area to cut back on when budgeting is tight. Explore cost-effective alternatives like borrowing books from the library, enjoying free outdoor activities, or finding free or inexpensive community events.

Other Expenses: This category will encompass everything else, such as pet care, gifts, subscriptions, personal care products, and any miscellaneous expenses. A dedicated category for unforeseen expenses is wise.

Once you've compiled a complete list of your income and expenses, subtract your total expenses from your total income. A positive number indicates that you have a surplus, meaning you're earning more than you're spending. A negative number indicates a deficit, meaning you're spending more than you're earning. Don't panic if you have a deficit.

This is a common starting point and can be addressed through careful budgeting and financial planning.

If you have a deficit, you need to identify areas where you can reduce expenses. This may involve making difficult choices, but remember that this is a step towards financial independence and self-sufficiency. Examine each category closely, looking for areas where you can cut back without significantly impacting your quality of life. Consider reducing your entertainment budget, negotiating lower bills with service providers, or switching to cheaper alternatives for everyday items.

Creating a realistic budget requires honesty and self- discipline. Don't set unrealistic expectations for yourself. Start small, track your expenses diligently for at least one month to get a clear picture of your spending patterns, and gradually work towards your financial goals. There are many budgeting apps and tools available to help you track your spending. Many offer insights into your spending habits and help you identify areas for improvement.

Consider building an emergency fund. Aim for 3-6 months' worth of living expenses. This fund will provide a safety net in case of unexpected job loss, medical emergencies, or other unforeseen circumstances. Start small and gradually build up your emergency fund over time. Even small regular contributions will make a difference in the long run.

Managing debt is another crucial aspect of financial independence. If you have high-interest debt, prioritize paying it down as quickly as possible. Consider strategies like the debt snowball or debt avalanche method. The debt snowball involves paying off your smallest debt first, regardless of interest rate, to build momentum and motivation. The debt avalanche method involves paying off your highest-interest debt first to save money on interest in the long run.

Seek professional guidance if needed. Financial advisors and credit counselors can offer personalized advice and support. Many non-profit organizations offer free or low-cost financial counseling services. Don't hesitate to seek help if you're struggling to manage your finances.

Remember, rebuilding your financial stability after escaping an abusive relationship is a marathon, not a sprint. Celebrate your progress, no matter how small. Each step you take toward financial independence is a victory in reclaiming your life and your future. The journey towards financial empowerment will build your confidence and resilience, further solidifying your independence and setting the stage for a more secure and fulfilling life. This financial independence is a tangible manifestation of your strength and capacity for recovery.

Seeking Financial Assistance and Resources

Rebuilding your financial life after escaping an abusive relationship requires more than just budgeting; it necessitates accessing available resources and support systems. Many organizations and government programs are specifically designed to help survivors navigate the complex financial challenges that often accompany such situations.

Understanding and accessing these resources is a crucial step towards achieving lasting financial independence.

One of the first places to explore is your local government's social services department. These departments often administer various programs, including emergency financial assistance, housing subsidies, and food stamps (SNAP).

Eligibility requirements vary depending on location and individual circumstances, such as income level and family size. It is crucial to gather all necessary documentation, such as proof of income, identification, and proof of residence to ensure a smoother application process. The application process itself can be daunting, filled with complex paperwork and potential delays. However, many social service departments offer assistance in navigating this process. Don't hesitate to ask for help; their staff are often trained to support individuals in need. Consider seeking assistance from a local advocate or volunteer organization to help you navigate the bureaucracy. They can act as an intermediary, providing support and reducing the emotional strain often associated with applying for benefits.

Beyond local government assistance, several federal programs offer financial support to abuse survivors. One of the most significant is the Temporary Assistance for Needy Families (TANF) program. TANF provides temporary

financial assistance for low-income families, including those escaping domestic violence. The program often includes job training and placement services to help recipients become self-sufficient. Eligibility requirements are similar to those of state-level programs, emphasizing income level and household size. Again, assembling all necessary documentation is vital for a successful application. It's highly recommended to familiarize yourself with the specific requirements of your state's TANF program before starting the application.

Many states offer online applications and resources to guide you through the process.

Another crucial federal program is Medicaid, which provides healthcare coverage to low-income individuals and families. Healthcare costs can be substantial, and the lack of insurance can be a significant barrier to recovery. Medicaid helps alleviate this burden by covering essential medical, dental, and mental healthcare services. For those fleeing abusive situations, access to mental health services is particularly important, as trauma counseling is a vital part of the healing process. Navigating the Medicaid application process can be intricate, with varying eligibility requirements depending on your state. However, numerous resources are available online and through local health departments to assist in the application and understanding of the program.

In addition to government programs, many non-profit organizations across the country provide financial support specifically to victims of domestic violence. These organizations often offer a range of services, including emergency shelter, financial counseling, and assistance with job searching. Many of these organizations are locally based, offering a personalized approach to support. A simple online search for "domestic violence services [your city/state]" will likely yield a list of organizations in your area. These groups often have websites providing details about their services

and contact information. Don't hesitate to reach out to multiple organizations to explore the full range of support available. They often have a deep understanding of the unique financial challenges faced by survivors and can offer tailored solutions.

Some charitable organizations provide broader financial assistance, without necessarily focusing solely on domestic violence victims. Organizations like the Salvation Army and the United Way often offer emergency financial aid for various needs, including housing assistance and utility bill payments. Eligibility criteria vary, but these organizations often have flexible guidelines and prioritize assisting those facing immediate financial hardship. Their websites usually provide detailed information about their aid programs, including application processes and eligibility requirements. These broader charities may be particularly helpful if you are facing immediate financial emergencies while navigating the more specialized programs designed for domestic abuse survivors.

Beyond financial aid, many organizations provide crucial non-financial support. Legal aid societies often offer free or low-cost legal services to survivors, including assistance with obtaining protective orders or pursuing legal action against their abusers. Access to legal assistance is crucial for securing your safety and protecting your rights. Many legal aid societies offer services in various areas, such as housing law, family law, and employment law, areas often impacted by domestic abuse. Their services can alleviate the significant financial burden often associated with legal representation.

Job training programs are another invaluable resource for abuse survivors. Many organizations provide job skills training, resume building workshops, and job placement

assistance. These programs can help you gain the skills and confidence needed to secure stable employment, a crucial step towards financial independence. Many government agencies, such as the Workforce Development Boards, and non-profit organizations offer such programs, often with additional support such as childcare assistance and transportation assistance to help remove the barriers to obtaining employment. Check with your local workforce development board for available programs in your area.

They often offer a comprehensive list of services geared towards helping individuals achieve economic self- sufficiency.

Financial literacy workshops and counseling are also critical resources. Many organizations offer free or low-cost financial literacy workshops to help survivors learn about budgeting, debt management, and financial planning. These workshops can equip you with the tools you need to manage your finances effectively and build a secure financial future. These workshops are often offered through local community centers, libraries, and non-profit organizations. Look for workshops focusing on budgeting, saving, credit repair, and investing to build a solid financial foundation.

Remember, accessing these resources requires initiative and persistence. The application processes can be complex and time-consuming, and there may be initial rejections. Do not be discouraged. Seek help from advocates or caseworkers who can guide you through the process and provide emotional support. Their expertise in navigating these systems can significantly increase your chances of success. Consider keeping a detailed record of all your applications, communication, and deadlines. This will help you track your progress and ensure you don't miss any important steps. It is also helpful to keep a binder with all necessary

documentation to make the application process more efficient.

Finally, prioritize your mental and emotional well-being throughout this process. Rebuilding your life after escaping an abusive relationship is a marathon, not a sprint. Allow yourself time to grieve, heal, and adjust to your new reality. Support groups, therapy, and self-care practices can be invaluable tools during this challenging time. Remember that seeking financial assistance is not a sign of weakness but a sign of strength and resilience. You deserve to be safe, secure, and financially independent. Utilizing these resources is a testament to your commitment to building a brighter future for yourself and your family. The journey to financial freedom will be challenging, but with determination and access to the appropriate resources, it is entirely achievable.

Rebuilding Credit and Managing Debt

Rebuilding your credit after escaping an abusive relationship can feel like climbing a steep mountain, especially if your abuser controlled your finances. However, it is entirely possible, and vital for your long-term financial well-being.

The first step is obtaining a copy of your credit report from each of the three major credit bureaus: Equifax, Experian, and TransUnion. You can obtain these reports for free annually at AnnualCreditReport.com. This is crucial because it reveals the current state of your credit, identifying any negative marks left by your abuser or the financial challenges you faced during the relationship.

Examine your credit report meticulously. Look for accounts opened without your knowledge or consent, instances of fraudulent activity, late payments that might not reflect your own actions, and any inaccuracies. Dispute any entries you believe are incorrect. Each credit bureau provides a process for disputing information. You'll need to document your claims thoroughly with evidence, and be prepared for a potentially protracted process. While it may seem daunting, persistence is key. Remember, your abuser's manipulative behavior doesn't define your financial future.

Once you've cleaned up inaccuracies on your credit report, focus on rebuilding your credit score. This is a gradual process, but every positive step counts. Start by paying all your bills on time. This is the single most significant factor influencing your credit score. Set up automatic payments if necessary to avoid accidental late payments, a common pitfall during stressful periods of life. Consider using a budgeting app to track your spending and ensure you have

sufficient funds to meet your financial obligations each month.

Next, aim to keep your credit utilization ratio low. This ratio represents the percentage of your available credit that you're currently using. Ideally, you should aim to keep this ratio below 30%, and preferably even lower. For example, if you have a credit card with a $1,000 limit, try to keep your balance under $300. Paying down existing debt will significantly improve this ratio. Explore strategies for managing and paying down your existing debt. If you find yourself overwhelmed by the amount of debt, don't hesitate to seek professional guidance. Credit counseling agencies can provide personalized debt management plans, often offering debt consolidation or negotiation with creditors.

Debt consolidation can streamline your payments by combining multiple debts into a single loan with a potentially lower interest rate. This can simplify your finances and make it easier to stay on track with repayments. However, carefully evaluate the terms of any consolidation loan before agreeing to it. Some consolidation loans may carry significant fees or unfavorable interest rates, potentially making the situation worse in the long run.

Thoroughly compare offers from multiple lenders to ensure you're getting the best deal. Understand the implications before making any commitment. Do not rush into a deal simply because of the pressure to resolve debt quickly.

Negotiating with your creditors directly is another option, particularly if you're facing financial hardship. Many creditors are willing to work with individuals who demonstrate a sincere commitment to paying off their debt. You might be able to negotiate a lower monthly payment, a reduced interest rate, or even a settlement for a smaller amount than your total debt. Be prepared to provide

documentation of your financial situation and your willingness to stick to a repayment plan. Remember to keep a record of all communication with creditors.

Opening a secured credit card can be a helpful strategy for rebuilding credit. With a secured credit card, you make a security deposit, and your credit limit matches this deposit. This minimizes the risk to the lender, allowing individuals with poor credit history to build their credit gradually.

Consistent and responsible use of a secured credit card will gradually improve your credit score. However, remember to always pay your balance in full and on time to maximize the positive impact on your credit.

Building a positive credit history requires consistent effort and attention to detail. Set realistic goals, track your progress, and celebrate your successes along the way.

Remember, rebuilding your credit is a marathon, not a sprint. It will take time and patience, but the rewards of financial independence are well worth the effort. Financial independence is a powerful tool for protecting yourself from future abuse. It reduces your reliance on others, enabling you to make independent choices and maintain a sense of autonomy.

Beyond rebuilding your credit, it's crucial to develop strategies for protecting yourself from future financial exploitation. This involves understanding your financial rights and responsibilities, practicing responsible financial habits, and learning to identify and avoid potential financial scams or manipulative tactics. Develop a solid understanding of your personal finances. Keep accurate records of your income, expenses, and debts. Regularly check your bank accounts and credit reports for any unauthorized activity.

Educate yourself about common financial scams and manipulative techniques. Many predators target vulnerable individuals, using deception and coercion to exploit their finances. Learning to recognize these tactics can help protect you from falling victim to similar schemes in the future. This includes understanding how to identify and report identity theft, phishing scams, or other fraudulent activities.

Consider seeking professional financial advice. A qualified financial advisor can help you develop a personalized financial plan, providing guidance on budgeting, saving, investing, and debt management. Financial planning is essential for building a secure and independent future. They can provide insight and strategies for managing your finances efficiently and effectively. It also allows for a neutral evaluation of your financial situation, providing objective support and encouragement as you rebuild your financial life.

Finally, remember that your financial well-being is intrinsically linked to your overall mental and emotional health. The journey to financial recovery can be emotionally challenging, but it's important to prioritize self-care throughout this process. Don't hesitate to seek support from friends, family, or mental health professionals. Trauma therapy can be especially beneficial in addressing the emotional wounds that often accompany financial abuse.

Support systems can assist with dealing with the emotional stress involved in managing finances after experiencing abuse.

Financial independence is not merely about numbers on a balance sheet; it represents a fundamental aspect of personal freedom and safety. By actively rebuilding your credit, managing your debt effectively, and taking steps to protect yourself from future exploitation, you are reclaiming control

over your life and building a secure foundation for your future. This process might seem daunting initially, but remember that with resilience, resourcefulness, and the support available to you, you can achieve financial independence and live a life free from the shadow of financial control. Celebrate each small victory along the way, recognizing the strength and perseverance you are demonstrating in overcoming adversity. Your journey towards financial freedom is a testament to your strength and a powerful step towards lasting independence.

Gaining Financial Literacy and Independence

Gaining financial literacy isn't just about balancing a checkbook; it's about understanding the intricate web of financial systems and how they impact your life. After escaping an abusive relationship where financial control was a weapon, rebuilding your financial independence requires a deeper understanding than simply paying bills on time. It requires actively learning about budgeting, saving, investing, and debt management. Think of it as learning a new language – the language of money – to navigate a world that previously felt hostile and confusing.

The first step is acknowledging that you deserve this knowledge. Your abuser intentionally kept you in the dark about finances, fostering dependence and disempowerment. Reclaiming control starts with actively seeking out resources to understand how money works. This is not a sign of weakness, but an act of profound self-respect and empowerment.

There are numerous free and low-cost resources available to help you build this financial literacy. Many community colleges and universities offer free or discounted personal finance courses, often online. These courses often cover budgeting, debt management, investing, and retirement planning, providing a comprehensive foundation. Libraries also offer valuable resources, including books, workshops, and online databases with financial information. Don't underestimate the power of these readily available tools.

Online resources are another incredible source of financial knowledge. Websites like Investopedia offer clear explanations of complex financial concepts, while many

reputable financial institutions provide free guides and webinars on various financial topics. YouTube channels dedicated to personal finance offer engaging tutorials and advice from certified financial planners. While not all online information is trustworthy, research carefully, prioritizing information from established organizations and government agencies.

Budgeting is the cornerstone of financial literacy. It's about understanding where your money goes and making conscious decisions about how to allocate it. Many budgeting apps can simplify this process, automatically categorizing transactions and providing visual representations of your spending habits. These apps can highlight areas where you might be overspending, allowing you to make informed adjustments. A simple spreadsheet or notebook can also suffice if you prefer a more hands-on approach.

The 50/30/20 budgeting rule is a helpful guideline. It suggests allocating 50% of your after-tax income to needs (housing, food, transportation), 30% to wants (entertainment, dining out), and 20% to savings and debt repayment. This is just a guideline; adjust it based on your individual circumstances and financial goals. The key is to be mindful of your spending and to track your progress consistently.

Regularly reviewing your budget helps you stay on track and make necessary adjustments along the way.

Saving is crucial for building a financial safety net and achieving long-term financial goals. Even small, consistent savings can accumulate significantly over time, thanks to the power of compound interest. Automate your savings by setting up regular transfers from your checking account to a savings account. Treat these automated transfers as non- negotiable expenses, reinforcing the habit of saving.

Consider opening a high-yield savings account to maximize your returns.

Understanding debt is essential, particularly if you are carrying debt from your abusive relationship. Differentiate between good debt (like a low-interest student loan for a degree that enhances your earning potential) and bad debt (high-interest credit card debt). Prioritize paying down high- interest debt first to minimize the long-term cost. Explore different debt repayment strategies, such as the snowball method (paying off the smallest debt first for motivation) or the avalanche method (paying off the highest-interest debt first to save money). Explore options such as debt consolidation or negotiating with creditors, but always thoroughly research the implications before making any decisions.

Investing allows your money to grow over time, potentially outpacing inflation. Start by researching different investment options, such as stocks, bonds, mutual funds, and exchange- traded funds (ETFs). Understand the level of risk associated with each option and align your investments with your risk tolerance and financial goals. Consider starting with low- cost index funds or ETFs, which offer diversification and generally lower fees than actively managed funds. Avoid

get-rich-quick schemes, a common tactic used to exploit financially vulnerable individuals.

Protecting yourself from future financial exploitation is paramount. Monitor your credit reports regularly, checking for any unauthorized activity or errors. Regularly review your bank statements for suspicious transactions. Be wary of unsolicited financial advice or investment opportunities that sound too good to be true. Educate yourself about common scams, such as phishing emails or fraudulent websites, to avoid becoming a victim.

Building financial independence is a journey, not a destination. It requires patience, perseverance, and a commitment to continuous learning. Celebrate your small victories along the way, acknowledging the significant progress you've made. Remember that financial literacy empowers you to make informed decisions about your finances, ensuring a secure and independent future free from the manipulative control of others. It is a symbol of your resilience and your strength in overcoming adversity. Each step you take toward financial literacy is a powerful step toward building a life where you are in control of your destiny, financially and emotionally. You deserve financial freedom, and the path to achieving it begins with education and a commitment to your own empowerment. This is not just about numbers; it's about reclaiming your life.

Finding Safe and Affordable Housing

Finding safe and affordable housing after escaping an abusive situation can feel like navigating a minefield. The urgency to secure a safe space, coupled with the potential financial constraints and emotional distress, can be overwhelming. However, with careful planning and the utilization of available resources, finding a stable and secure home is achievable. This process requires patience, persistence, and a belief in your ability to rebuild your life. Don't be afraid to ask for help; there are people and organizations dedicated to supporting you.

One of the first steps is identifying your immediate needs. How much space do you need? Will you be alone, or will you be bringing children or pets? Do you require accessibility features? Knowing your requirements allows you to target your search effectively. This self-assessment is crucial to narrowing down the search and avoiding options that might not meet your specific needs. Start by making a list. Be realistic about your needs and priorities, recognizing that compromises might be necessary.

Shelters provide immediate safety and temporary refuge. Domestic violence shelters offer confidential, short-term accommodation, often including support services such as counseling, legal aid, and assistance with securing long-term housing. These shelters are specifically designed to protect survivors from further harm and provide a supportive environment to begin healing. Finding a shelter is often the first step in establishing a secure foundation. Their locations are usually kept confidential for the safety of residents, but local helplines or social services can provide referrals.

Remember, contacting a shelter is a brave step, and it

signifies your commitment to prioritizing your safety and well-being.

Transitional housing programs offer a bridge between emergency shelter and permanent housing. These programs typically provide longer-term accommodation, often with supportive services designed to help residents gain financial stability and develop life skills. They might offer assistance with job searching, budgeting, and life skills training, helping residents establish the foundations for long-term independence. These programs recognize that stable housing is only one piece of the puzzle. Access to resources and support is equally crucial for achieving long-term stability.

Research programs in your area to find one that best aligns with your individual needs and circumstances.

Affordable rental options are a crucial aspect of securing long-term housing. This requires researching different options, such as government-subsidized housing, Section 8 vouchers, and non-profit housing organizations.

Government-subsidized housing programs offer rent assistance to low-income families and individuals. Section 8 vouchers, administered by local housing authorities, provide rental subsidies that help pay a portion of the rent in privately owned housing. Non-profit organizations often offer affordable housing options, sometimes with additional support services. Thorough research is essential to understand the eligibility requirements and application processes for each program.

When searching for affordable rental options, it's essential to be cautious and thorough. Verify the legitimacy of any listing, confirming the landlord's identity and the property's availability. Avoid paying large deposits or fees upfront without proper verification. Inspect the property thoroughly before signing any lease agreement, ensuring it meets your

needs and is safe and habitable. Read the lease carefully before signing, understanding all terms and conditions to avoid unforeseen complications. Document everything, keeping copies of all contracts and correspondence. This proactive approach protects you from potential exploitation and ensures a smoother transition into your new home.

Beyond formal programs, networking can prove invaluable. Reach out to friends, family, and community organizations. Many individuals and groups are willing to offer assistance, providing information about available resources or even temporary accommodation. Don't underestimate the power of personal connections. People who have gone through similar situations can offer invaluable support and guidance, fostering a sense of community and shared experience.

Online resources and databases can aid your search. Websites such as Zillow, Trulia, and Apartments.com provide extensive listings of rental properties. Filter your search by price, location, and amenities to find properties that match your needs. However, always verify the legitimacy of any listing before contacting the landlord. Compare different options, and don't rush into a decision. Take your time to assess each option thoroughly before committing to a lease.

Safety is paramount. When viewing properties, bring a trusted friend or family member for support and an extra pair of eyes. Trust your instincts; if a property or landlord feels unsafe or makes you uncomfortable, don't hesitate to walk away. Prioritize locations that feel safe and secure, considering factors such as proximity to public transportation, well-lit streets, and a sense of community.

Remember, finding a safe home is essential for your well- being and recovery.

After securing housing, focus on establishing routines and creating a nurturing environment. Personalize your space to make it feel like home. This contributes significantly to your sense of security and stability. Declutter and organize your belongings to create a sense of calm and order. Incorporate elements that promote relaxation and well-being. Consider adding plants, soft lighting, calming colors, and personal items that bring you comfort and joy. This act of creating a haven for yourself is a powerful step in rebuilding your life.

Remember that this process takes time and patience. There will be challenges along the way, and setbacks are possible. However, focusing on your progress and celebrating small victories is essential. Each step you take toward finding safe and affordable housing is a significant step toward reclaiming your independence and building a life free from abuse. Don't hesitate to seek professional support. Therapists and counselors specializing in trauma can provide emotional support and guidance throughout this challenging process, helping you navigate the emotional complexities of rebuilding your life and creating a safe, stable future. You are not alone; there is support available to help you every step of the way. Believe in your strength and resilience; you deserve a safe and peaceful place to heal and thrive. The journey might be challenging, but the destination – a safe and stable home – is worth the effort. Keep moving forward, one step at a time. Your future is brighter than the shadows of the past.

Relocation Strategies and Safety Considerations

Relocation is often a crucial step in escaping an abusive situation, offering a chance to break free from the abuser's control and establish a safe haven. However, the planning and execution of a move require careful consideration, balancing the urgency of escape with the need for a well- thought-out strategy. The decision of where to relocate should not be taken lightly; it's a pivotal choice impacting your safety, well-being, and future. Several factors must be carefully weighed to ensure the relocation effectively protects you from further harm and provides a foundation for recovery.

First and foremost, the distance from your abuser is paramount. Consider the feasibility and necessity of moving far away. While escaping to a completely new state or even country may seem ideal, it also presents logistical challenges and may be financially impractical. The goal is to establish enough physical distance to deter the abuser while remaining within a manageable relocation budget and support network. Consider using online mapping tools to visualize the distance between your current location and potential new residences. Consult with law enforcement or victim advocacy groups to assess your risk level and determine the optimal distance to ensure your safety. They can offer valuable insights based on your specific circumstances and the abuser's behavior patterns. In some cases, even a move across town or to a different county might be sufficient to create the necessary buffer, especially if your abuser has limited resources or mobility.

Community safety is another critical factor. Research potential neighborhoods thoroughly before making a decision. Look for areas with low crime rates, well-lit streets, and a strong sense of community. Online resources, local police departments, and neighborhood watch programs can provide valuable information about the safety of different areas. Consider factors such as the proximity of police stations, hospitals, and 24-hour businesses – all of which can offer added safety and peace of mind. If you have children, research school districts and the overall family- friendliness of the community. Remember, selecting a safe and secure environment is paramount for your healing and recovery.

Access to support services is crucial during and after a relocation. Identify the availability of resources such as domestic violence shelters, therapists, support groups, and legal aid services in potential relocation areas. These services offer crucial assistance during the transition and help you navigate the emotional and practical challenges of escaping an abusive relationship. Online directories, local social service agencies, and victim advocacy organizations can provide information on the availability of these vital resources. The proximity to these services directly influences your ability to rebuild your life and manage the aftermath of abuse. Don't underestimate the value of a strong support network; having access to help nearby is essential during times of stress or crisis.

Financial resources significantly impact relocation planning. Create a realistic budget that considers moving costs, security deposits, first month's rent, and ongoing living expenses. Explore available financial assistance programs, such as government subsidies, rental assistance, and charitable organizations that aid victims of domestic violence. These programs can significantly reduce the financial burden and make relocation more feasible. Develop a detailed financial plan, tracking your income and expenses

to ensure you can maintain stability. Don't be afraid to ask for financial assistance from friends, family, or community support networks. Many organizations specialize in helping victims of abuse secure safe housing and financial stability.

Legal considerations are essential for your long-term safety and well-being. If you have a restraining order or other legal protection in place, ensure your new address is compliant with these legal requirements. Consult with an attorney specializing in domestic violence cases to discuss your legal options and ensure your relocation doesn't compromise your safety. They can help you understand your rights and navigate any potential legal issues that might arise. Consider consulting with a lawyer about changing your phone number, email address, and social media accounts to prevent your abuser from contacting you. This is particularly crucial if technology was used for stalking or harassment.

Securing a new place to live involves more than simply finding a house; it's about creating a safe environment. Prioritize features that enhance your security, such as sturdy doors and locks, working smoke detectors and alarms, and a secure neighborhood. Inspect the property thoroughly before signing a lease agreement, ensuring it meets your safety needs. If possible, visit the property at different times of the day to assess the neighborhood's level of activity and safety. Don't hesitate to ask questions about building security, and request information about the management company's procedures for handling safety concerns.

Maintaining confidentiality is vital during and after your relocation. Avoid sharing your new address or contact information with anyone who might inadvertently reveal it to your abuser. Inform only trusted individuals about your new location and take measures to protect your privacy online.

Consider using a PO Box for mail instead of your residential

address. Update your address with essential institutions like your bank and employer only once you're fully settled and confident in your safety. A proactive approach to maintaining confidentiality safeguards your privacy and reduces the risk of being discovered by your abuser.

The process of relocation, while essential, can be emotionally challenging. Consider the emotional toll it takes on yourself and any children or dependents. Seek professional support from a therapist or counselor specializing in trauma and abuse recovery. They can help you navigate the emotional complexities of leaving an abusive situation and provide coping mechanisms to deal with the stress and anxiety involved in relocation. Support groups for survivors of domestic violence can offer a sense of community and shared experience, helping you feel less isolated during this challenging transition. Remember, this is a journey, and it's okay to seek help along the way.

Remember that rebuilding your life after escaping an abusive situation is a marathon, not a sprint. There will be setbacks and challenges. Be patient with yourself, celebrate small victories, and never hesitate to ask for help. Finding safe and affordable housing is a significant step towards reclaiming your independence and building a future free from fear. Your safety and well-being are the top priorities; prioritize them throughout this process, and trust your instincts. You are stronger than you think, and you deserve a safe and peaceful life. The path ahead may seem daunting, but with careful planning, support, and self-belief, you can create a future free from the shadows of the past. Your journey to safety and healing begins with the brave step you've already taken; continue moving forward, knowing that a brighter future awaits.

Navigating Housing Applications and Rental Processes

Navigating the housing application process after escaping an abusive situation can feel overwhelming. The emotional toll of leaving behind a controlling environment often adds layers of complexity to what would already be a stressful task. However, understanding the process and preparing thoroughly can significantly alleviate some of the pressure and increase your chances of securing safe and stable housing.

First, familiarize yourself with the various housing options available to you. These might include subsidized housing programs, domestic violence shelters, transitional housing, affordable apartments, or renting a room in a shared house. Each option comes with its own set of requirements and procedures. Researching your local resources and understanding your eligibility for specific programs is crucial. Online searches, local government websites, and social service agencies are invaluable sources of information. Don't hesitate to contact several organizations to inquire about available assistance and eligibility criteria. Some agencies may even offer support throughout the application process, guiding you through the paperwork and providing additional resources.

Begin by gathering all the necessary documents well in advance of starting your applications. This usually includes a valid photo ID, proof of income (pay stubs, bank statements, social security benefits), references (previous landlords or employers), and possibly a background check. If you're applying for subsidized housing or assistance programs, you'll likely need additional documentation proving your

income, family size, and need for housing assistance. Keep all your documents organized in a secure place; consider creating a digital copy as a backup. This will streamline the application process and make it easier to respond to requests quickly. Missing even one document can delay the process significantly.

When completing applications, read each section carefully and provide accurate information. Any inaccuracies or omissions can lead to rejection, so take your time and double-check everything before submission. If you encounter any questions or sections you don't understand, don't hesitate to contact the housing provider or agency for clarification. They're often willing to assist in clarifying the application process and ensuring your application is complete and accurate.

Remember, honesty is essential, and seeking clarification is perfectly acceptable.

Understanding rental agreements is critical to securing safe and stable housing. Before signing any lease, meticulously read every clause. Pay close attention to the terms regarding rent, security deposits, lease duration, responsibilities for repairs and maintenance, and eviction procedures. If anything is unclear or seems unfavorable, don't hesitate to negotiate or seek legal advice. Many tenant rights organizations can provide guidance and assistance in interpreting rental agreements and ensuring fair treatment.

You have the right to understand your lease fully before committing to it. Take your time, and don't feel pressured to sign anything before you're entirely comfortable.

When inspecting potential housing, safety should be your top priority. Assess the security features, such as door locks, window locks, security systems, and neighborhood lighting. Note the overall condition of the property – look for signs of disrepair that could pose safety risks. Is the property well-

maintained? Are there adequate smoke detectors and carbon monoxide detectors? If you have children, prioritize properties that offer a safe and child-friendly environment. Don't hesitate to ask questions about the building's safety record, security measures, and the management company's procedures for addressing safety concerns. A thorough inspection can help you avoid potential problems and enhance your safety and peace of mind.

Beyond the physical safety aspects, consider the neighborhood's overall safety and security. Research the crime rates, proximity to police stations and hospitals, and the general atmosphere of the area. This can influence your sense of security and safety. Online resources, local police departments, and neighborhood watch programs can be invaluable sources of information. Visiting the neighborhood at different times of day can give you a better sense of its activity and safety levels. If possible, talk to neighbors to gauge their experience living in the area. Trust your instincts; if a property or neighborhood doesn't feel safe, don't hesitate to look elsewhere.

Finding affordable housing can be a significant challenge. Explore various resources and financial assistance programs available to assist victims of domestic violence.

Government-subsidized housing, rental assistance programs, and charitable organizations dedicated to helping victims of abuse can offer invaluable support. Research local and national programs to find options that align with your situation and needs. Many organizations offer guidance and assistance in navigating the application process for these programs. Don't be afraid to ask for help. Many individuals and organizations are committed to providing assistance to those escaping abusive situations.

Throughout the process, prioritize maintaining your confidentiality. Avoid disclosing your new address or contact information to anyone who could unintentionally reveal it to your abuser. Consider using a PO Box for mail instead of your residential address, particularly in the initial stages of relocation. Update your address with essential institutions such as your bank and employer only after you're settled and feel secure in your new environment. Remember, safeguarding your privacy is critical to your safety and well- being.

The emotional toll of finding new housing after escaping abuse should not be underestimated. The process can be extremely stressful and triggering. Seek support from a therapist or counselor specializing in trauma and abuse recovery. They can help you process your emotions, develop coping mechanisms, and navigate the practical challenges involved in securing safe and stable housing. Joining a support group for survivors of domestic violence can offer a sense of community and shared experience, reminding you that you are not alone in your journey. Don't hesitate to seek professional support and lean on your support network throughout this challenging process. Remember, you deserve a safe and peaceful place to heal and rebuild your life.

Finally, remember that securing safe and affordable housing is a significant step towards reclaiming your independence and building a future free from fear. Celebrate the progress you've made, no matter how small. Each step you take towards safety and independence is a victory. Be patient with yourself and trust in your ability to create a better life for yourself and your loved ones. The journey to recovery is not easy, but with perseverance, support, and self-compassion, you can build a life free from the shadows of the past. Your strength and resilience are commendable; believe in your

capacity to create the future you deserve. Remember, you are deserving of peace, safety, and a life free from abuse.

The complexities of navigating the housing application process can be daunting, even without the added burden of escaping an abusive situation. However, by taking a proactive, well-informed approach, and by accessing the abundant resources available to survivors, you can significantly increase your chances of securing a safe and stable living environment. Remember, your well-being is paramount, and seeking assistance is a sign of strength, not weakness. This is a journey, not a race, and taking each step with care and consideration is crucial to achieving long-term safety and stability. Your efforts and your bravery deserve to be celebrated; embrace your journey toward a brighter future. You are resilient, you are strong, and you deserve a safe haven.

Securing Housing Assistance Programs

Securing safe and stable housing is a fundamental step in escaping an abusive relationship, and thankfully, numerous resources exist to help survivors navigate this crucial process. This section will explore various government and community-based programs designed to provide housing assistance to those fleeing abusive situations. It's important to understand that eligibility criteria vary depending on your location and specific circumstances, so thorough research and direct contact with relevant agencies are essential.

One of the most commonly utilized programs is the **Housing Choice Voucher Program (Section 8)** , administered by the

U.S. Department of Housing and Urban Development (HUD). This program provides rental subsidies to low- income families, the elderly, and people with disabilities. While not exclusively for victims of domestic violence, it's a valuable resource for those who meet the income requirements and need financial assistance to secure affordable housing. The application process can be lengthy, often involving a waiting list. However, by submitting a complete and accurate application and maintaining regular contact with the housing authority, you can increase your chances of securing a voucher. Remember to clearly indicate your status as a survivor of domestic violence in your application, as this may expedite the process in some areas. Each local housing authority has its own specific procedures, so it's critical to contact your local office directly for detailed information.

Beyond Section 8, many communities offer **public housing** , which are government-owned and operated housing units for low-income individuals and families. These apartments often

have waiting lists, and eligibility is based on income and family size. Similar to Section 8, clearly indicating your status as a survivor of abuse can be beneficial in some locations. The application process will typically involve income verification, background checks, and an assessment of your housing needs. Contact your local public housing authority for specific information on eligibility and application procedures within your area.

Many states and municipalities also operate **state and local housing assistance programs** , which can offer various forms of support, including rental subsidies, down payment assistance, and mortgage assistance. These programs often target specific populations, such as families with children, seniors, or individuals with disabilities. However, many of these programs also consider victims of domestic violence for priority placement or expedited processing due to the urgent need for safe housing. To find these programs, search online using keywords like "[Your State/City] housing assistance," "[Your State/City] rental assistance," or "[Your State/City] domestic violence housing." The websites of your state's housing agency and your local government will be invaluable resources.

In addition to government-funded programs, several **non- profit organizations and charities** dedicate their resources to assisting survivors of domestic violence with housing.

These organizations often provide a range of services, including emergency shelter, transitional housing, and long- term housing support. They may offer assistance with finding affordable housing options, navigating the application process, and providing financial assistance with rent or security deposits. These organizations frequently work in collaboration with government agencies, offering a more comprehensive support system. Searching online for "domestic violence shelters [your city/state]" or "housing

assistance for domestic violence survivors [your city/state]" will help you locate these vital resources in your community.

Domestic violence shelters offer immediate refuge and support for survivors. They provide a safe, temporary place to stay while you develop a longer-term housing plan.

Shelters often provide a range of services beyond safe housing, including counseling, legal assistance, and help with securing employment. Finding a local shelter is often best done through a national domestic violence hotline or through local social services.

Transitional housing programs provide temporary housing for a specified period, usually six months to two years, helping survivors rebuild their lives and gain financial stability before transitioning to permanent housing. These programs often offer support services such as job training, life skills workshops, and counseling, aiding in long-term stability. Transitional housing programs are frequently connected with local non-profits or government agencies that work with victims of domestic violence.

For those who qualify, the **Veterans Affairs Supportive Housing (VASH) program** offers rental assistance and case management services to homeless veterans and their families. If you are a veteran, this program offers priority and may greatly reduce the housing-related stress associated with escaping abuse. Contact your local VA office to explore eligibility criteria.

It's crucial to be aware of potential **scams** related to housing assistance. Be cautious of any organization that requests payment upfront for housing assistance or asks for sensitive personal information before you have thoroughly vetted them. Always verify the legitimacy of any organization with

your local government agencies or trusted non-profit organizations.

Remember that the process of securing housing assistance can be complex and time-consuming. Be persistent, and don't hesitate to seek help from advocates and professionals specializing in domestic violence. These professionals can provide guidance, support, and assistance in navigating the bureaucratic processes and securing the resources you need to create a safe and stable future.

Furthermore, consider the emotional impact of this process. The stress of finding housing, dealing with applications, and managing the aftermath of an abusive relationship can be emotionally draining. It's essential to prioritize your emotional well-being throughout this time. Lean on your support system, seek professional counseling, and remember to practice self-care. Take breaks when needed, celebrate your small victories, and be patient with yourself.

Finally, remember that you are not alone. Many resources are available to help you navigate the complexities of securing housing and rebuilding your life after abuse. Reach out for help, and know that your strength and resilience will guide you toward a brighter future. Your safety and well- being are paramount, and seeking assistance is a sign of strength, not weakness. You deserve a safe and stable home, and with perseverance and the support available to you, you will find it.

Creating a Safe and Comfortable Home Environment

Creating a safe and comfortable home environment after escaping an abusive situation is crucial for healing and rebuilding your life. It's more than just finding a roof over your head; it's about establishing a sanctuary where you can feel safe, secure, and empowered. This process requires careful consideration of both physical and emotional aspects, creating a space that fosters self-care and promotes a sense of belonging.

One of the first steps is to declutter and purify your new space. The physical act of cleaning and organizing can be incredibly therapeutic. It allows you to remove any remnants of the past, symbolically and literally clearing away the negativity and manipulation you may have endured. Discard items that hold painful memories or represent the abuser's influence. Don't feel pressured to do this all at once; take it one step at a time, focusing on small, manageable tasks. The act of decluttering can itself be a powerful form of self-care, offering a sense of control and agency that may have been lacking during the abusive relationship. Consider inviting a trusted friend or family member to help; the support and shared experience can be profoundly beneficial.

Consider the scents in your environment. Strong, artificial air fresheners might mask unwanted smells but can also trigger headaches or allergies. Instead, opt for natural, calming scents such as lavender, chamomile, or sandalwood. These scents have been shown to have relaxing and therapeutic properties, creating a more peaceful atmosphere. Essential oil diffusers, candles (used safely), or simply a bowl of potpourri can effectively enhance the sensory experience of your space. Creating a pleasant aroma can be incredibly soothing after experiencing the often overwhelming stress of escaping an abusive relationship.

Lighting plays a critical role in creating a safe and comfortable atmosphere. Harsh, fluorescent lighting can be jarring and unwelcoming, while soft, warm lighting can be profoundly calming and relaxing. Use a combination of ambient lighting, task lighting, and accent lighting to create a layered effect that suits your needs. Lamps with adjustable brightness settings allow you to customize the lighting to match your mood and activity. Consider investing in dimmer switches to control the intensity of your overhead lights.

Remember that feeling safe and comfortable is paramount; the right lighting can be a significant contributor to this feeling.

Security measures are essential to building a sense of safety. Depending on your situation and resources, this might involve installing a security system, reinforcing doors and windows, or adding extra locks. Even simple measures, such as a sturdy door chain, can offer a sense of increased security. Consider getting to know your neighbors and building a supportive network within your community. If you have concerns about your safety, don't hesitate to contact local law enforcement or a domestic violence shelter for advice and support. Creating a safe physical environment is a foundation for emotional healing.

Beyond the physical aspects, cultivating a sense of emotional safety is paramount. This involves creating a space where you feel comfortable expressing your feelings without fear of judgment or reprisal. This might involve setting boundaries with others, prioritizing self-care activities, and engaging in therapy or support groups. Surrounding yourself with positive affirmations and inspiring quotes can help shift

your mindset from one of fear and self-doubt to one of hope and resilience. Consider creating a vision board that represents your goals and aspirations; a visual reminder of your progress can be incredibly motivating during the healing process.

Self-care is not a luxury; it's a necessity during this period of rebuilding. Prioritize activities that bring you joy and relaxation, whether it's reading, taking a bath, listening to music, spending time in nature, or engaging in creative pursuits. Remember that healing is a journey, not a destination, and self-compassion is crucial throughout this process. Allow yourself time to grieve the loss of the relationship, process your emotions, and adjust to your new reality. Don't be afraid to seek professional help; a therapist specializing in trauma can provide guidance and support as you navigate this challenging transition.

Creating a comfortable and supportive social network is equally important. Spend time with loved ones who offer unconditional support and understanding. Join support groups for survivors of domestic abuse, where you can connect with others who have shared similar experiences. Remember that you are not alone in this journey; connecting with others who understand can provide validation, hope, and a sense of community. Sharing your experiences and hearing others' stories can be incredibly validating and empowering.

Personalize your space to reflect your personality and interests. Hang artwork that inspires you, display family photos, and surround yourself with objects that bring you joy and comfort. Creating a visually appealing and aesthetically pleasing environment can significantly impact your mood and sense of well-being. Don't be afraid to express your creativity and individuality; this is an opportunity to reclaim

your identity and create a space that truly reflects who you are.

Consider incorporating elements of nature into your home. Plants have been shown to reduce stress and improve air quality. Choose plants that are easy to care for and that complement your decor. If you have a balcony or patio, consider creating a small outdoor garden. The act of nurturing plants can be incredibly therapeutic and a wonderful form of self-care. The presence of nature in your home can provide a sense of calm and connection to something larger than yourself.

As you create your new home, remember that this is a process of rebuilding, both physically and emotionally. There will be setbacks and challenges, but with perseverance and self-compassion, you can create a safe, comfortable, and nurturing environment where you can heal, grow, and thrive. Celebrate your progress, and remember that you deserve a space that reflects your strength, resilience, and potential.

Your home should be a haven, a place where you can feel secure, empowered, and free to live the life you deserve. This is your sanctuary, a testament to your journey of healing and your commitment to a brighter future. Never underestimate the power of creating a space that nourishes your mind, body, and soul. This space is your foundation for the next chapter of your life.

Identifying Career Goals and Skills

Rebuilding your life after escaping an abusive relationship involves many facets, and securing financial independence through meaningful employment is a crucial step. This process isn't merely about finding a job; it's about reclaiming your agency and building a future free from the control and manipulation you've endured. The journey starts with self- assessment – understanding your skills, interests, and aspirations. This self-discovery is empowering, as it allows you to define your future on your own terms, rather than based on the expectations or limitations imposed upon you by the abuser.

Begin by reflecting on your past experiences, not just the negative aspects, but also the positive contributions you've made. What were you good at in previous roles? What aspects did you enjoy? What tasks or responsibilities brought you a sense of accomplishment? Consider keeping a journal to help you track your thoughts and feelings. Write down specific instances where you excelled or felt fulfilled. This isn't about glorifying the past but about identifying your strengths and talents that can be leveraged in your future career. For instance, if you managed household finances effectively even amidst the chaos of an abusive relationship, that demonstrates strong organizational and budgeting skills – highly valuable assets in many job roles. Perhaps you excelled at multitasking, juggling household responsibilities with concealed attempts to plan your escape. These skills, honed under duress, are transferable and significant.

Don't underestimate the value of seemingly minor skills. Proficiency in specific software, strong communication abilities, or even meticulous attention to detail – all these

attributes can make you a strong candidate for various jobs. Remember, your abuser likely tried to diminish your abilities and self-worth. Now is the time to actively counter that narrative and recognize your capabilities. Create a comprehensive list of your skills, both hard skills (technical or quantifiable abilities) and soft skills (interpersonal or character-related traits). Be specific. Instead of writing "good communication skills," note "effectively communicated complex information to diverse audiences, both verbally and in writing." This level of detail makes your skills more impactful when presenting them to potential employers.

Next, consider your interests. What genuinely excites you? What activities make you feel engaged and motivated? Don't limit yourself to what you've done before; explore new avenues. The abusive relationship may have stifled your passions and personal growth; this is your chance to rediscover them. If you've always dreamed of pursuing creative writing, now is the time to explore that potential. If you find peace in helping others, consider roles in social work or community services. If you're fascinated by technology, research career paths in software development or data analysis. Exploring online resources like career aptitude tests can offer additional insight and direction. These tests aren't definitive, but they can help you identify career areas that align with your interests and abilities.

Once you have a clear understanding of your skills and interests, begin brainstorming potential career paths.

Research different occupations that utilize your strengths and align with your passions. Explore job descriptions and requirements to understand the specific skills and qualifications needed for each role. Consider using online job search engines to browse available positions and gain further insight into the job market. Don't be afraid to explore fields that seem outside your comfort zone. The process of

rebuilding empowers you to take calculated risks and explore paths you may have previously deemed unattainable.

Setting realistic employment goals is crucial for success. Avoid setting overly ambitious targets that can lead to disappointment. Instead, focus on smaller, achievable milestones. For example, your initial goal might be to secure part-time employment to gain experience and build confidence. This can then transition to a full-time position or a career advancement once you feel more established. Your goals should be specific, measurable, achievable, relevant, and time-bound (SMART goals). For instance, instead of saying "get a better job," set a goal like, "Secure a full-time position as a marketing assistant within the next six months, earning at least $X per year."

Consider your financial needs and circumstances when setting your employment goals. Will you need to secure immediate income to cover basic expenses, or do you have a safety net that provides some financial flexibility? This will influence the urgency and type of work you seek. Remember that starting small is perfectly acceptable. Many survivors find part-time or freelance work helpful in regaining a sense of independence and financial security before transitioning to full-time employment.

Networking is incredibly valuable during this process. Reach out to friends, family members, former colleagues, and mentors for support and guidance. Let your network know about your job search and the types of roles you're targeting. They may be able to offer leads or provide valuable insights into various industries. Attend industry events, workshops, or conferences to connect with potential employers and learn more about available opportunities. Remember, building connections is about fostering mutual support and collaboration.

Don't hesitate to seek professional guidance from career counselors or employment agencies. These services can provide personalized support and assistance throughout your job search. They can help you refine your resume and cover letter, practice interview techniques, and navigate the complexities of the job market. Many organizations offer free or low-cost career services specifically designed to support survivors of domestic abuse. Research your local resources and take advantage of these invaluable supports.

As you navigate your job search, remember that setbacks are inevitable. There will be days when you feel discouraged or overwhelmed. Don't let these moments define your journey. Focus on your strengths, celebrate your successes, and learn from any challenges you face. Maintaining self-compassion and believing in your ability to overcome obstacles is crucial during this transition. Remember that you are resilient, capable, and worthy of a fulfilling career. This is not just about finding a job; it's about reclaiming your life and building a future where you are in control, financially independent, and thriving. Your past experiences have shaped you, but they do not define your future. You have the power to create a new narrative, a future filled with purpose, accomplishment, and lasting happiness. Believe in yourself, and embrace this opportunity to build a career that reflects your strengths, passions, and unwavering spirit. This is your chance to rewrite your story and build a future free from the shadows of the past.

Job Searching Strategies and Techniques

Now that we've explored self-assessment and goal setting, let's delve into the practical strategies for your job search. Finding employment after escaping abuse is a significant undertaking, but with a structured approach, you can significantly increase your chances of success. This isn't just about securing a paycheck; it's about regaining your autonomy and building a foundation for a secure and fulfilling future.

First, let's focus on your resume and cover letter. These are your first impressions on potential employers, so crafting them effectively is crucial. Your resume should be concise, highlighting your most relevant skills and experiences.

Avoid lengthy paragraphs; use bullet points to showcase your achievements in a clear and impactful manner. Quantify your accomplishments whenever possible. Instead of saying "Improved customer service," say "Increased customer satisfaction ratings by 15% through implementation of a new training program." Such quantifiable results demonstrate your abilities more effectively.

Tailor your resume to each job application. Don't send a generic resume; adapt it to match the specific requirements and keywords mentioned in the job description. Use Applicant Tracking Systems (ATS) keywords strategically – these systems scan resumes for specific words and phrases, so including them increases your chances of getting past the initial screening. Spend time researching the company and the role to understand their values and priorities, and reflect this understanding in your resume and cover letter.

Your cover letter is your opportunity to tell your story. It shouldn't simply reiterate your resume; rather, it should provide context and demonstrate your enthusiasm for the specific position and company. Explain how your skills and experience align with their needs, and showcase your personality and passion. However, remember to keep it professional and concise, focusing on the most relevant aspects of your background. Avoid dwelling on the negative aspects of your past; instead, highlight your resilience and adaptability in overcoming challenges. Think of your cover letter as a narrative demonstrating how your past experiences have prepared you for this opportunity.

Next, let's address interview skills. The interview is a crucial stage, where you can showcase your personality and demonstrate your capabilities. Prepare thoroughly by researching the company and the interviewers. Practice answering common interview questions, focusing on your strengths and accomplishments. Prepare examples from your past work experience or volunteer activities to illustrate your skills and problem-solving abilities. Remember to frame your answers positively, highlighting your resilience and resourcefulness even when discussing challenging experiences. Never disclose details of your abuse unless you feel safe and comfortable doing so and it is directly relevant to the role.

Practice your responses out loud. This helps build confidence and fluency. Consider practicing with a friend or family member to get feedback. During the interview, maintain eye contact, speak clearly and concisely, and listen attentively to the interviewer's questions. Don't be afraid to ask clarifying questions if you're unsure about something. It demonstrates your engagement and interest. Remember to dress professionally and arrive on time, or even slightly early. Punctuality demonstrates respect for the interviewer's

time and professionalism. After the interview, send a thank- you note reiterating your interest and highlighting your key qualifications.

Networking is often overlooked, but it's a powerful tool. Leverage your existing network – friends, family, former colleagues, mentors – and inform them of your job search. They might have valuable contacts or insights into different industries. Attend industry events, workshops, or conferences to connect with professionals. Online platforms like LinkedIn offer excellent networking opportunities.

Remember, building connections is about fostering mutual support and collaboration. Be genuine and authentic in your interactions; don't be afraid to share your story if you feel comfortable, but always prioritize your safety and well- being.

Consider utilizing professional career services. Many organizations offer free or low-cost career counseling and job placement assistance, particularly for survivors of abuse. These services can provide personalized support, resume and cover letter review, interview preparation, and guidance on navigating the job market. Don't hesitate to seek this assistance; it's a valuable resource that can significantly enhance your job search efforts.

Remember to celebrate your successes along the way. Acknowledge every milestone, no matter how small. Finding a job after experiencing abuse is a significant achievement.

Be kind to yourself; the process takes time and effort. If you face setbacks, don't be discouraged. Learn from the experience, adapt your strategy, and keep moving forward. Maintaining a positive mindset and self-compassion is crucial for overcoming challenges. Remember your strength and resilience; you've already overcome immense obstacles.

Throughout your job search, prioritize your safety and well- being. If you feel uncomfortable or unsafe during an interview or networking event, remove yourself from the situation. Trust your intuition; your safety is paramount.

Remember, you deserve a job that values and respects you.

Beyond traditional job searches, consider alternative avenues. Freelancing or contract work might be excellent starting points, providing flexibility and allowing you to build your portfolio and gain experience. Volunteer work can also be beneficial, providing valuable skills and networking opportunities while contributing to your community. Starting your own small business, if feasible, allows you to be your own boss and build something according to your own terms and timelines. Explore all available options that suit your skills, interests, and overall well-being.

Remember, your journey toward financial independence and career success is a marathon, not a sprint. Be patient with yourself, and celebrate every small victory along the way.

Each step forward is a testament to your strength and resilience. You deserve a fulfilling career, a career that reflects your abilities and aspirations. This is your opportunity to rebuild your life on your terms, to create a future where you are empowered, independent, and thriving. Believe in yourself, your abilities, and your potential. Your future is yours to create, and you have the strength to build it. The shadows of the past may linger, but they do not define your future. You are capable, resilient, and deserving of a life filled with purpose and joy. This is your new beginning.

Embrace it with courage and confidence.

Accessing Job Training and Education Programs

Building a new career often requires acquiring new skills or enhancing existing ones. The trauma of abuse can leave individuals feeling depleted and unsure of their capabilities, making the prospect of returning to education or training seem daunting. However, many resources exist specifically designed to support survivors in acquiring the skills and qualifications they need for fulfilling employment. These programs understand the unique challenges faced by individuals escaping abusive situations and offer tailored support to help them navigate the process.

One vital resource is vocational training programs. These programs offer practical, hands-on training in a variety of skilled trades, from carpentry and plumbing to healthcare and technology. Many vocational schools offer flexible scheduling options, recognizing that survivors may have other commitments or need to adapt their learning around therapy appointments or other support services. Furthermore, these programs often provide supportive learning environments, fostering a sense of community and encouraging peer support among students. The focus on practical skills and immediate applicability makes vocational training an especially effective route for those seeking quick entry into the job market, offering a sense of accomplishment and tangible progress that can be incredibly empowering after experiencing the disempowerment of abuse.

Consider researching local community colleges and vocational schools. They often have dedicated counselors or advisors who can help assess your skills and interests and guide you toward suitable programs. Many offer financial

aid and scholarships, recognizing that financial constraints can be a major barrier for survivors. Don't hesitate to inquire about these options; they can make the difference between achieving your career goals and falling short. Don't be afraid to express your concerns about adjusting to a learning environment; many vocational schools are experienced in supporting learners with various backgrounds and challenges.

Adult education courses offer another avenue for skill development and career advancement. These courses cover a wide range of subjects, from basic literacy and numeracy to advanced computer skills and professional development training. The flexibility of many adult education programs allows for personalized learning plans, accommodating the varying schedules and learning styles of students. This flexibility is crucial for survivors who may be juggling multiple responsibilities or dealing with the lingering effects of trauma. Some programs specifically cater to adult learners, creating a supportive and understanding environment that encourages participation and success.

Many adult education programs offer free or low-cost courses, making them accessible to individuals with limited financial resources. These programs often partner with local organizations and businesses to provide job placement assistance and networking opportunities. Exploring your local community center or library is an excellent starting point for identifying available courses. Online learning platforms offer additional options, providing flexibility and accessibility for those who may not have access to in-person classes. Remember that many online courses provide certificates of completion, which can be valuable additions to your resume and demonstrate your commitment to professional development.

Beyond formal educational programs, consider the value of informal learning opportunities. Workshops, seminars, and online tutorials can provide valuable skills training in specific areas. These often focus on practical skills needed in today's job market, such as digital marketing, social media management, or graphic design. Many such workshops are offered at low cost or even for free, and they can provide a less intimidating entry point into learning new skills.

Government agencies often play a significant role in supporting job training and education for survivors of abuse. Agencies like your state's department of labor or workforce development often offer job training programs, financial assistance, and job placement services. These resources are specifically designed to help individuals re-enter the workforce after experiencing challenging life circumstances. Contacting these agencies can help you understand the specific benefits and services available in your area. They may offer financial assistance for tuition, childcare, transportation, or other expenses that could otherwise prevent you from accessing training or education opportunities.

Non-profit organizations dedicated to supporting survivors of abuse often offer job training and education programs tailored to their specific needs. These organizations frequently provide a holistic approach, addressing not only the skill development but also the emotional and psychological support necessary for successful reintegration into the workforce. They often offer individualized career counseling, resume building workshops, and interview preparation sessions. The supportive environment these organizations provide can be invaluable in building confidence and self-esteem, which are crucial for success in the job market after experiencing trauma.

When searching for appropriate programs, it's essential to consider your own individual needs and circumstances.

Assess your strengths, interests, and career goals. Identify the skills you already possess and the areas where you need additional training. The right program will align with your unique aspirations and provide the support you need to succeed.

Networking with other survivors can also be invaluable. Support groups and online communities provide platforms to share experiences and learn from others who have successfully navigated the process of job training and career development. Hearing success stories and receiving advice from those who understand your unique challenges can be incredibly motivating and empowering.

Remember, seeking help is a sign of strength, not weakness. Don't hesitate to reach out to the many resources available. Your journey toward career success is a testament to your resilience and determination. Believe in your capabilities, and know that with support and perseverance, you can achieve your goals. The path may be challenging at times, but the rewards of building a fulfilling and independent future are well worth the effort. Every step you take is a step toward reclaiming your life and building a future free from the shadows of the past. Your strength, resilience, and courage are undeniable; embrace them, and build the future you deserve. You are capable, you are resilient, and you deserve a life filled with purpose, joy, and professional fulfillment. This is your opportunity to write your own success story – embrace it.

Overcoming Barriers to Employment

Overcoming the barriers to employment after surviving abuse by a sociopath presents unique challenges. The trauma itself can manifest in various ways that directly impact job seeking and performance. Understanding these barriers is the first step towards overcoming them. Many survivors grapple with debilitating anxiety, panic attacks, and PTSD, making the structured environment of a workplace feel overwhelming and triggering. Simple tasks, such as answering the phone or interacting with colleagues, can become insurmountable obstacles. The constant fear of judgment or re-traumatization adds another layer of complexity. The intense manipulation and control exerted by a sociopath often leaves survivors with deeply ingrained self-doubt and a diminished sense of self-worth. This can lead to imposter syndrome, where they undervalue their skills and abilities, making it difficult to present themselves confidently during job interviews or in the workplace.

Moreover, the abuse often involves financial control, leaving survivors with limited resources and a lack of professional experience, which makes it incredibly hard to break free and rebuild their lives.

The insidious nature of sociopathic abuse often leaves its victims with a damaged credit history, limiting their access to housing, transportation, and other essential resources necessary for securing employment. The abuser might have intentionally sabotaged the survivor's career, damaging their professional reputation or preventing them from gaining experience. The lack of stable housing can also pose a significant barrier, making it difficult to attend interviews or maintain a regular work schedule. This instability creates a vicious cycle of hardship, hindering the survivor's ability to find and keep a job. It's vital to remember that these difficulties are not a reflection of personal shortcomings; they are direct consequences of the abuse suffered.

Addressing these multifaceted challenges requires a multi-pronged approach. Therapy plays a crucial role in helping survivors process the trauma, develop coping mechanisms, and regain their self-esteem. Cognitive Behavioral Therapy (CBT) and trauma-focused therapies like Eye Movement Desensitization and Reprocessing (EMDR) have proven particularly effective in addressing the psychological impact of abuse. These therapies can help survivors identify and challenge negative thought patterns, manage anxiety and panic attacks, and develop healthier coping strategies for dealing with stress. A supportive therapist can provide a safe space to unpack the emotions and experiences, fostering healing and strengthening self-belief, paving the way for greater self-confidence in navigating the job market.

Beyond therapy, practical support is essential. Financial assistance programs can help address immediate needs such as housing, transportation, and childcare. Many government agencies and non-profit organizations offer these services specifically tailored to assist survivors of domestic abuse.

These services often include emergency housing, food assistance, and job search support. Survivors should explore local and national resources available within their community, often publicized online or through advocacy groups focusing on victims' rights and support.

Building a strong support network is also critical. Connecting with other survivors, whether through support groups, online communities, or individual mentorships, provides a sense of belonging and validation. Sharing experiences and learning from others who have successfully navigated similar challenges can be incredibly empowering

and reassuring. This network can offer emotional support, practical advice, and encouragement during the job search process. The sense of community fostered in these groups can also help combat the isolation that often accompanies abuse.

Developing effective job search strategies is crucial, and this often begins with honestly assessing one's skills and qualifications. It's essential to focus on accomplishments and transferable skills gained from previous experiences. Even if those experiences were disrupted by the abuse, focusing on skills like problem-solving, adaptability, and communication can highlight valuable strengths. Resume and cover letter writing workshops offered by community organizations or career services can greatly aid in crafting compelling applications that highlight these transferable skills.

Interview skills are equally crucial. Practicing answering common interview questions with a trusted friend or therapist can help build confidence and prepare for the experience. Focusing on demonstrating resilience and adaptability, qualities often strengthened by overcoming past adversity, can be powerful selling points to potential employers. Many organizations that support survivors offer mock interviews to provide practice and feedback in a safe and supportive environment.

In some cases, survivors may find it beneficial to seek career counseling. A career counselor can help identify suitable career paths aligned with individual skills and interests, considering limitations and potential triggers related to the trauma. They can provide guidance on job searching, resume building, and interview preparation, offering tailored support for specific circumstances. The counselor's unbiased perspective can also help survivors identify and challenge negative self-beliefs hindering their job search.

Creating a safe and supportive work environment is crucial for survivors once they've secured a position. Open communication with employers about any specific needs or accommodations, such as flexible work arrangements or quiet spaces for breaks, can significantly improve the work experience. The Americans with Disabilities Act (ADA) protects employees with disabilities, including those with mental health conditions related to trauma. Under the ADA, employers are often legally obligated to provide reasonable accommodations to enable survivors to perform their jobs effectively. Knowing and understanding these rights is vital in creating a workplace where healing and professional growth can thrive.

Returning to the workforce after escaping a sociopathic relationship represents a significant accomplishment. It signifies the survivor's strength, resilience, and determination to rebuild their lives. Recognizing the profound impact of abuse and implementing the strategies outlined above – therapeutic support, financial assistance, building a support network, developing effective job search skills, and fostering a supportive work environment – empowers survivors to reclaim their lives and achieve professional fulfillment. The path might be challenging, but the ultimate reward – a life of independence and purpose – is well worth the effort. The journey to healing is a testament to personal strength and a vital step towards reclaiming a future free from the shadows of the past. Believe in your ability to succeed; you are stronger than you think.

Building a Successful and Fulfilling Career

Building a successful and fulfilling career after surviving the trauma of a sociopathic relationship requires a shift in perspective. It's not just about securing a job; it's about aligning your work with your values, passions, and newly discovered sense of self. The process of rebuilding your life after escaping abuse is a testament to your resilience, and your career should reflect this strength and newfound self- awareness.

One of the first steps is to engage in honest self-reflection. The manipulation and control experienced in an abusive relationship can distort your sense of self-worth and your understanding of your capabilities. Take time to rediscover your passions and talents. What did you enjoy doing before the abuse? What skills do you possess that you might not have fully appreciated? Consider creating a list of your strengths, both personal and professional, focusing on accomplishments rather than dwelling on perceived failures. Remember, your abuser likely actively minimized or sabotaged your aspirations, intentionally aiming to undermine your confidence and independence. Overcoming this sabotage is a huge victory.

Explore career paths that align with your values. After surviving such trauma, it's essential to build a career that resonates with your newfound sense of purpose and empowers you. This might mean choosing a career that aligns with your desire for autonomy, creativity, or social impact. Perhaps you've always wanted to work in a helping profession, inspired by your journey through therapy and recovery. Or maybe the experience has ignited a passion for advocating for victims of abuse. The possibilities are vast,

and choosing a path that aligns with your values will contribute to a far more satisfying career journey.

Consider the work environment. The aftermath of abuse often leaves survivors with heightened sensitivity to certain work dynamics. It's crucial to assess your tolerance for different work environments and prioritize your mental and emotional wellbeing. A supportive and understanding workplace culture is paramount. Research potential employers, seeking out organizations that prioritize employee well-being and have policies supporting mental health. Look for companies with strong anti-harassment policies and a culture of respect. Consider the physical work environment as well; is it calm and organized or chaotic and overwhelming? Will the work involve close contact with others that might make you feel anxious? These are important questions to consider during your job search.

Networking can be a powerful tool in your job search, but it requires a nuanced approach. Don't feel pressured to engage with people who make you uncomfortable. Build your network slowly and strategically, focusing on connections with people who are supportive and understanding. Online networking platforms can provide a safer space to connect with individuals in your field than in-person networking events. Remember, you're not obligated to disclose your past trauma if you're not comfortable, but connecting with others who have faced similar challenges can provide invaluable support and encouragement.

Develop strategies for managing stress and anxiety in the workplace. This might involve setting boundaries, prioritizing self-care, and seeking support from supervisors or colleagues when needed. Be open about your need for accommodations if necessary, but also remember that you are not defined by your trauma. Focusing on your strengths and your value as an employee is key to building confidence and maintaining a healthy work-life balance.

Continuously develop your skills and knowledge. The workplace is constantly evolving, and it's important to stay current in your field. Consider pursuing further education, attending workshops or conferences, or seeking out mentorship opportunities. This not only enhances your career prospects but also contributes to personal growth and self-esteem. It's a demonstration of your continued investment in yourself and your future, a powerful message of self-respect and resilience.

Celebrate your accomplishments, both big and small. Acknowledge the significant strides you've made in rebuilding your life and career. Every step forward, no matter how small, represents a triumph over adversity. Keep a journal to document your progress and celebrate your achievements. Acknowledge how far you've come, and remember that your strength and resilience are what got you here.

Seek mentorship and support. Connecting with a mentor or career counselor can provide invaluable guidance and support during this transition. They can offer personalized advice and resources to help you navigate the challenges of building a fulfilling career. Their perspective can be incredibly helpful in identifying potential career paths and developing the skills needed for success.

Remember that building a fulfilling career is a journey, not a destination. There will be setbacks and challenges along the way, but the goal is to create a career that is not only financially rewarding but also personally enriching and meaningful. Your resilience and strength will serve as your

guiding principles in creating a path that empowers you and honors your incredible journey of healing and self-discovery.

Don't underestimate the power of self-compassion. The process of rebuilding your life after abuse takes time and effort. Be patient with yourself and celebrate your progress. It's important to acknowledge that you may experience moments of self-doubt or anxiety along the way, and that's perfectly okay. Self-compassion allows you to acknowledge these feelings without judgment, allowing you to move forward with grace and understanding.

Consider volunteering or taking on freelance projects. This can provide valuable experience, build your confidence, and expand your network. Freelance opportunities offer flexibility and control, which can be particularly beneficial for survivors who may need to manage their time and energy levels effectively. Volunteering in a field you're passionate about allows you to make a difference while gaining experience and potentially discovering new career interests. Both avenues are great ways to test the waters and assess your suitability for different work environments.

Remember, your career is a reflection of your journey and a testament to your resilience. Your experiences have shaped you, and your path forward should celebrate your strength and empower you to build a life of purpose and fulfillment. It's a chance to reclaim your narrative, defining your future on your terms. The path may not always be easy, but the destination – a career that brings you both financial security and emotional satisfaction – is worth the journey. The freedom and independence you gain will be a powerful affirmation of your strength and a testament to your incredible journey of healing and recovery. Embrace this new chapter with courage and self-belief, knowing that you possess the inherent strength and resilience to achieve your

goals. The future is yours to shape, and you have the power to create a life that reflects your dreams and values.

Understanding Healthy Relationship Dynamics

Understanding healthy relationship dynamics is crucial for anyone emerging from the manipulative and controlling environment of a sociopathic relationship. The insidious nature of this abuse often distorts one's perception of what constitutes a healthy connection, leaving survivors vulnerable to repeating unhealthy patterns. Rebuilding trust and establishing healthy boundaries requires conscious effort and a deep understanding of what constitutes a truly supportive and equitable partnership.

First and foremost, mutual respect is the bedrock of any healthy relationship. This means valuing each other's opinions, feelings, and needs, even when they differ from your own. In a healthy relationship, partners actively listen to each other, seeking to understand rather than simply to respond. There's an absence of belittling, criticism, or attempts to control the other person's thoughts, actions, or choices. Respect extends to respecting each other's time, space, and personal boundaries. It acknowledges the individual autonomy of each partner and avoids the power imbalances inherent in abusive relationships. This respect manifests in everyday interactions: Considerate behavior, thoughtful gestures, and a willingness to compromise are all signs of a respectful partnership. It's about creating a safe space where both individuals feel valued and heard, free from the fear of judgment or intimidation. The absence of such respect—the consistent undermining of one's self- worth, the constant criticism and control—is a hallmark of the abusive relationship you've left behind. Learning to identify and actively cultivate this aspect is paramount to your healing journey.

Trust is another cornerstone of a healthy relationship. It involves a belief in the other person's integrity, honesty, and reliability. This is built over time through consistent actions that demonstrate dependability and trustworthiness. It's not simply about believing what someone says; it's about observing their behavior and witnessing their actions align with their words. In an abusive relationship, trust is systematically eroded, leading to a deep sense of insecurity and anxiety. Rebuilding trust requires patience and consistent effort. It's about choosing to believe in the potential for genuine connection, while also recognizing the importance of establishing clear boundaries to protect yourself. Start small. Trust can be built gradually, but it requires consistent reinforcement. This involves being truthful and transparent in your own actions, and carefully assessing the behavior of anyone you choose to be close to. If you've been betrayed consistently, building trust can feel nearly impossible, but it's not. Small acts of kindness, consistent reliability, and open communication will gradually rebuild it.

Open and honest communication is paramount in any healthy relationship. This goes far beyond simply talking; it's about actively listening, expressing your feelings honestly and respectfully, and working collaboratively to resolve conflicts. It means being able to share both positive and negative emotions without fear of judgment or retaliation. In abusive relationships, open communication is often stifled.

Manipulative tactics—gaslighting, silent treatment, or deflection—are employed to prevent honest dialogue. In a healthy relationship, you'll find a collaborative approach to resolving conflicts. Disagreements are addressed constructively, focusing on finding solutions rather than assigning blame. This process necessitates active listening, empathy, and a mutual commitment to understanding each other's perspective. It involves respectfully expressing your

own needs and feelings while being receptive to those of your partner. This involves learning to express your emotions clearly, calmly, and directly, while also developing skills in active listening and empathy.

Establishing and maintaining healthy boundaries is essential for protecting your emotional and psychological well-being. This means setting limits on what you are and are not willing to tolerate in a relationship. Boundaries should be clear, consistent, and communicated effectively. This might involve setting limits on time spent together, defining acceptable communication styles, or determining how disagreements will be handled. In abusive relationships, boundaries are frequently violated, leading to a sense of powerlessness and depletion. Rebuilding your capacity to set and maintain boundaries is a vital step in recovering from trauma. Start by identifying your needs and preferences, and then clearly communicate these limits to others. This might feel challenging initially, especially if you have a history of being compliant or people-pleasing. You need to learn to prioritize your well-being and refuse requests or behaviors that undermine your limits. Don't be afraid to say "no" if you feel uncomfortable or pressured. Practice setting smaller boundaries and gradually work your way up to larger ones.

Another crucial element of healthy relationships is emotional intimacy. This involves sharing your thoughts, feelings, and vulnerabilities with your partner in a safe and supportive environment. It's about feeling comfortable being your authentic self, without fear of judgment or rejection. This capacity for emotional intimacy is often damaged in abusive relationships, where emotional vulnerability is exploited and used against the victim. In the recovery process, it's essential to rebuild this capacity. Start by practicing self-compassion and self-acceptance. This foundation allows you to approach intimate connections with greater security. Then, start with

small steps, sharing with a trusted friend or therapist before engaging in emotional intimacy with a romantic partner.

Shared values and goals are also important for a healthy relationship. While differences can add richness to a partnership, having some shared values and aspirations can strengthen the bond. This doesn't mean you need to have identical life goals, but having some common ground creates a stronger foundation. For example, shared values regarding family, career aspirations, or ethical considerations can greatly enhance a relationship's resilience. However, the emphasis here is on *shared*, not forced conformity. You shouldn't feel compelled to compromise your core values to maintain a relationship.

Equitable distribution of power and responsibility is another critical aspect of a healthy relationship. In an abusive relationship, power is heavily skewed towards the abuser. In a healthy partnership, decisions are made collaboratively, with both partners having equal input and influence.

Responsibilities are shared fairly, and neither partner feels burdened disproportionately. This includes not just household chores or financial contributions, but also decision-making regarding important life choices. A fair and equitable distribution of responsibilities helps build a sense of partnership and mutual respect.

Finally, a healthy relationship allows for personal growth and independence. While intimacy and shared experiences are important, a supportive relationship also allows both partners to pursue their individual goals and interests. This means respecting each other's need for personal time, hobbies, and friendships. It allows space for individual self- discovery and growth without pressure to constantly be together or sacrifice personal aspirations. The ability to

maintain a healthy sense of self while nurturing a loving connection is a hallmark of a supportive relationship.

Recognizing these hallmarks of healthy relationships is the first step to creating them for yourself. Understanding the subtle differences between a healthy dynamic and a manipulative one will empower you to make informed choices about your future relationships, avoiding the pitfalls of the past. Remember, building healthy relationships takes time, effort, and self-reflection. Be patient with yourself and celebrate your progress along the way. The journey towards healthy connections is a testament to your resilience and a vital part of your recovery.

Identifying and Avoiding Toxic Relationships

Identifying and avoiding toxic relationships is paramount to your healing journey after escaping the clutches of a sociopathic partner. The insidious nature of abuse often leaves survivors with a distorted sense of normalcy in relationships, making them susceptible to falling into similar patterns. Recognizing the subtle—and not-so-subtle—red flags is a critical skill to develop, one that requires both self-awareness and a willingness to trust your instincts.

One of the earliest warning signs is a relentless pressure to isolate you from your support system. This can manifest in several ways. Your partner might subtly criticize your friends and family, sowing seeds of doubt about their loyalty or intentions. They might actively try to prevent you from spending time with them, creating obstacles or making you feel guilty for prioritizing your relationships. This isolation isn't accidental; it's a deliberate strategy to control you and make you more dependent on them. It's a way to sever your connection to people who might offer a different perspective or provide support if you ever choose to leave. Remember the feeling of being trapped? The sociopath created that by systematically eliminating your support structure. Do not repeat this mistake. If someone actively tries to distance you from your loved ones, take that as a colossal red flag.

Another crucial aspect to observe is the nature of the communication. In healthy relationships, communication is open, honest, and respectful. Disagreements are handled constructively, with both partners striving to understand each other's perspectives. In contrast, toxic relationships are often characterized by manipulative communication tactics.

Gaslighting—making you question your own sanity and

memory—is a classic example. Your partner might deny saying or doing something they clearly did, leaving you feeling confused and doubting yourself. Other manipulative tactics include silent treatment, constant criticism, blame- shifting, and deflection. These are not accidental communication errors; they are intentional tools used to control and undermine you. If you constantly feel like you're walking on eggshells, unsure of how to respond without provoking a negative reaction, that's a clear indication of a toxic dynamic.

Pay close attention to how your partner treats you emotionally. Do you feel consistently undermined, belittled, or criticized? Are your accomplishments dismissed or your feelings invalidated? Do you constantly feel the need to defend yourself or apologize for things that aren't your fault? Do you find yourself shrinking in your interactions with them to not trigger their displeasure? These are all signs of emotional abuse. A healthy relationship is built on mutual respect and support. If you feel consistently devalued and disrespected, it's a critical sign that the relationship is toxic.

The constant erosion of self-worth that you experienced during the abuse can be mimicked in other relationships, so paying attention to your emotional well-being in new contexts is critical.

Financial control is another common tactic in toxic relationships. Your partner might try to control your finances, limiting your access to money or making you feel guilty for spending on yourself. This financial control can take many forms, from preventing you from having a separate bank account to constantly criticizing your spending habits. This is not about shared finances; this is about control. In abusive relationships, this control can also extend to dictating your work choices, schooling, or volunteer work. It's not just about money; it's about the overall control they

exert over your independence and autonomy. This form of control is one of the most damaging aspects of the abuse, because it isolates you and ties your independence to their approval. Learn to be financially independent and safeguard your own financial security.

The ways in which your partner attempts to control your time is another significant indicator. Are you constantly being told what to do, how to spend your free time, or who to socialize with? Does this partner monopolize your free time, leaving you feeling suffocated and with no personal space? This constant intrusion on your time—along with attempts to dictate how you dress, what you eat, where you go—can be seen as control over your very life. This level of control is not about a "caring" relationship; it's about stifling your independence and reinforcing their dominance. This behavior is a stark departure from a healthy relationship where independence and personal space are respected and nurtured.

Consider the level of jealousy and possessiveness your partner displays. In healthy relationships, partners trust and support each other's autonomy. In contrast, toxic relationships are often characterized by excessive jealousy, possessiveness, and controlling behavior. Your partner might constantly check up on you, monitor your whereabouts, or interrogate you about your interactions with other people.

They might become irrationally angry if you spend time with friends or family or express any interest in activities that don't include them. This isn't a reflection of their love; it's a reflection of their desire to control and possess you. A healthy relationship respects personal boundaries and supports personal growth, not control and possessiveness.

Observe the patterns of behavior. Do you notice recurring cycles of abuse and remorse? Does your partner apologize

profusely after abusive incidents only to repeat the same behavior again and again? This pattern of abuse followed by a period of remorse is known as the cycle of violence. The apology is not genuine remorse; it's part of their manipulation tactic to retain control. It's essential to recognize this pattern and understand that it's unlikely to change unless the abuser seeks significant professional help. This is not your fault. Their actions are a reflection of their character, not a sign that you could have somehow avoided the abuse.

Stalking and monitoring are insidious forms of control and abuse that extend beyond the relationship itself. This can involve constantly checking your phone, social media accounts, or tracking your location. It can also involve showing up unexpectedly or contacting you incessantly. This behavior is a clear violation of your privacy and personal space, and it's a crucial red flag. If a partner exhibits any of this kind of intrusive behavior, removing yourself from the situation is crucial to your safety. Remember, even after escaping an abusive relationship, stalking can continue.

Understand and implement the digital safety measures described previously in the book.

Beyond these individual behaviors, pay close attention to the overall dynamic of the relationship. Does it feel balanced and equitable, or is it characterized by an imbalance of power? In a healthy relationship, both partners feel respected, valued, and heard. In a toxic relationship, one partner often holds disproportionate power, leading to a constant feeling of being controlled and manipulated. This power imbalance isn't always overt; it can be subtle and insidious. Recognize the patterns of control—the constant manipulation, the disregard for your feelings, and the pervasive sense of unease. This power imbalance isn't

something that you "created"; it's a direct result of their abusive behavior.

Remember, you are not responsible for the abusive behavior of others. It's crucial to understand that you did not cause the abuse, and you cannot cure it. Toxic relationships are not your fault, and leaving them is a sign of strength, not weakness. Taking the time to carefully assess your relationships and learn to identify the red flags, can protect you from future trauma and allow you to build healthier, more fulfilling relationships. If you encounter any of these warning signs, do not hesitate to seek professional help and support from trusted friends and family. Your safety and well-being are paramount. The journey to rebuilding your life after escaping abuse is challenging, but it's a journey worth undertaking. Remember that healing is possible, and a future filled with healthy, respectful relationships is within your reach. Trust your instincts. You deserve safety and happiness.

Building Healthy Communication Skills

Building healthy communication skills is not just about learning new techniques; it's about unlearning the patterns of manipulative communication you likely experienced in your abusive relationship.

The sociopath likely distorted communication to control and manipulate you—gaslighting, silent treatment, constant criticism, blame-shifting—were all tools used to undermine your sense of self and maintain their power. Rebuilding your ability to communicate effectively, authentically, and assertively requires conscious effort, patience, and self-compassion. It's a process of reclaiming your voice and learning to express yourself in a way that honors your needs and boundaries.

The first step is to become a more attentive listener. Active listening involves paying attention not only to the words being spoken but also to the nonverbal cues—body language, tone of voice, facial expressions. When you were in the abusive relationship, it's likely your attention was completely focused on attempting to preempt the next attack, rather than listening to what was being said. This often involves anticipating the sociopath's reaction to whatever you said and self-editing to avoid triggering negative responses. Now, you need to learn to receive information without the filter of fear.

In active listening, you reflect back what you hear to ensure you understand correctly. For example, if someone says, "I'm feeling overwhelmed by work," you might respond with, "So, it sounds like you're feeling stressed and burdened by your workload." This shows you are actively listening and validates the other person's feelings. This kind of validation was likely absent in your previous relationship. The

sociopath likely dismissed or invalidated your feelings consistently. Learning to actively listen, to truly hear someone, and to respond with empathy is a fundamental step toward building healthy communication.

Active listening isn't just about repeating words; it's about understanding the underlying emotions and needs.

Sometimes, what someone says is different from what they actually mean. It's crucial to listen for the underlying message. For instance, if someone says, "I'm fine," but their tone is flat and their body language is tense, they might not actually be fine. Paying attention to these incongruencies, which may have been normalized in the past, is crucial to understanding the true message. This requires you to become aware of your own emotional response to the communication as well. If you feel defensive or anxious listening to someone, consider this as a clue about what needs more attention.

Once you become comfortable with active listening, the next step is learning how to express your own needs effectively.

This is particularly important after experiencing abuse, where expressing your needs may have been met with criticism, punishment, or disregard. Assertiveness, the ability to express your needs and opinions respectfully and confidently, is a key communication skill. It's not about being aggressive or passive; it's about finding a healthy balance. Start with small steps. For instance, if you're in a restaurant and you don't like your meal, learn to politely and directly tell the waiter, instead of suffering in silence as you may have done in the past.

When expressing your needs, use "I" statements. Instead of saying, "You always make me feel bad," which is accusatory and likely to provoke a defensive response, try saying, "I feel hurt and misunderstood when..." This focuses on your own

feelings and experiences without blaming the other person. This technique helps create a more constructive conversation. Remember that your feelings are valid, and you deserve to have them acknowledged. This concept can be radically different from your experience with a sociopath, where your feelings were consistently invalidated or used against you.

Learning to resolve conflicts constructively is another essential communication skill. Disagreements are inevitable in any relationship, but how you handle them determines the health of the relationship. In your past relationship, conflicts were likely characterized by manipulation, aggression, or avoidance. Now, you must learn to approach disagreements with a focus on understanding, empathy, and collaboration. Avoid personal attacks; instead, focus on the issue at hand.

Negotiation is a crucial element of constructive conflict resolution. It involves finding solutions that meet the needs of both parties. Compromise and collaboration should replace the manipulative power dynamics from your previous relationship. It requires a willingness to listen to the other person's perspective, even if you disagree with it. This can be incredibly difficult after experiencing manipulation and control. You may have learned to anticipate and predict reactions, making open, honest dialogue a frightening prospect. Therapy can provide a safe and supportive environment to explore these anxieties.

Setting and maintaining boundaries is crucial for healthy communication. Boundaries are the limits you set to protect your emotional, physical, and mental well-being. This might involve saying "no" to requests that make you uncomfortable, limiting contact with people who are draining, or setting clear expectations for how you want to be treated. After surviving abuse, it is likely your boundaries

were constantly violated and ignored. Re-establishing healthy boundaries requires courage, self-awareness and consistency. Enforcing your boundaries will feel empowering and validating. It's an important part of self- care and healing.

Learning to communicate your boundaries effectively involves being direct, clear, and firm. Don't apologize for setting boundaries; you have the right to protect yourself. For example, if someone is constantly calling you late at night and you need sleep, tell them, "I appreciate you reaching out, but I need to set a boundary around my sleep schedule. Please call me before 9 p.m. if you need to talk." This is direct, clear, and expresses your needs without being accusatory. Reinforce your boundaries consistently. If someone crosses a boundary, calmly but firmly remind them of your limits.

Nonverbal communication is as important as verbal communication. Your body language, tone of voice, and facial expressions all communicate messages, often more powerfully than words. In your abusive relationship, you may have developed coping mechanisms—becoming withdrawn, subdued, or over-accommodating—that now need to be addressed. Focus on developing a confident and congruent posture, maintain eye contact, and use a calm and steady tone of voice. This will not only assist in communication, but also reflect your inner sense of strength and self-worth.

Another crucial aspect of healthy communication is learning to recognize and manage your emotions. Emotional regulation involves identifying your feelings, understanding their triggers, and responding to them in healthy ways. This may have been intentionally disrupted during your abusive relationship, creating chaos and confusion. Learning to

manage your emotional responses, recognizing the origins of this reactivity, and employing healthy strategies to cope with difficult emotions is essential. This might involve deep breathing exercises, meditation, or journaling. Remember, emotional intelligence is an important element of self-care.

Healthy communication is a skill that takes time and practice to develop. It's a journey of self-discovery and personal growth, and it's crucial for building healthy relationships.

Remember to be patient and compassionate with yourself. There will be setbacks, but each time you practice these skills, you are reinforcing your ability to communicate effectively and build stronger, more fulfilling relationships. The process of rebuilding healthy communication after abuse is vital, not just for future relationships but for your overall well-being. This is an essential step toward reclaiming your life and achieving a sense of peace and security. You deserve healthy relationships and communication—and you are capable of achieving them.

Setting and Maintaining Healthy Boundaries

Setting boundaries is not merely about saying "no"; it's about actively protecting your physical, emotional, and mental well-being. After enduring the insidious manipulation of a sociopath, where your boundaries were consistently violated and disregarded, reclaiming this sense of self-protection is paramount. It's about recognizing your inherent worth and establishing limits to prevent further harm. This process is often challenging, requiring courage, self-awareness, and unwavering consistency. It's a conscious act of self-care, a declaration that you will no longer tolerate mistreatment.

The first step in setting healthy boundaries is self-reflection. Consider your past experiences. Where were your boundaries violated? What situations, people, or behaviors consistently caused you pain or distress? Identifying these patterns is crucial because they provide valuable insights into your vulnerabilities. You need to recognize the red flags, the subtle manipulations that might have slipped by unnoticed in the past. These aren't isolated incidents; they are symptomatic of a larger pattern of abuse.

Journaling can be an invaluable tool in this process. Write down instances where you felt your boundaries were crossed. Detail the circumstances, your emotional responses, and the consequences. This process of externalizing your experience can illuminate the recurring themes and help you recognize your own vulnerabilities. This is not about dwelling on the past; it's about understanding it to move forward with a clear understanding of your needs.

Once you have identified your vulnerabilities, you need to start setting new boundaries. This doesn't happen overnight;

it requires a gradual process of re-education and reinforcement. Begin with small, manageable steps. For example, if you have a tendency to overcommit yourself, learn to say "no" to extra responsibilities. If someone consistently demands your time and attention, limit your availability. These small acts of self-preservation will reinforce your newfound strength and increase your confidence.

Communicating your boundaries effectively is equally important. This requires clarity, directness, and firmness. Avoid ambiguity or apologies. You are not obligated to justify your decisions. For instance, if someone is constantly texting or calling you late at night and disrupting your sleep, clearly communicate your need for rest. You might say, "I appreciate you reaching out, but I need to establish a boundary around my sleep. Please only contact me before 10 p.m. unless it's an emergency." This approach is assertive, respectful, and unambiguous.

It's crucial to anticipate potential pushback. Sociopaths and manipulative individuals thrive on bending and breaking boundaries. They may test your limits, attempt to guilt-trip you, or downplay the importance of your needs. In these situations, reaffirm your boundaries calmly but firmly.

Repeat your limits as needed. Don't engage in arguments or justifications; simply reiterate your position. Consistency is key. The more consistently you enforce your boundaries, the more likely it is that others will respect them.

Maintaining healthy boundaries is an ongoing process, not a one-time event. It requires vigilance and self-awareness. You might find yourself occasionally wavering or compromising your limits. This is perfectly normal; it's part of the healing journey. When this happens, don't beat yourself up; simply acknowledge the lapse and re-establish your boundaries. The important thing is to recognize the deviation and recommit to protecting yourself.

Setting boundaries extends beyond interpersonal relationships. It also encompasses your personal time, space, and emotions. Learn to prioritize your own needs and well- being. This might involve saying "no" to activities that drain your energy, creating personal space for reflection and relaxation, or simply taking breaks when you feel overwhelmed. These practices are not selfish; they are essential for your self-care and recovery. They demonstrate self-respect and demonstrate the value you place upon your own well-being.

Protecting your emotional space is crucial after experiencing abuse. This means setting limits on emotional burden. You are not responsible for the feelings or actions of others. If someone tries to offload their negativity onto you, set a boundary. You might say, "I understand you're feeling [emotion], but I can't carry that burden right now. I'm here to listen, but I need to focus on my own well-being." This response is both empathetic and assertive, acknowledging the other person's feelings while safeguarding your own emotional health.

Learning to say "no" can be incredibly liberating, particularly after a period of abuse where your needs were consistently ignored or disregarded. It is a powerful act of self-assertion, a reclaiming of your autonomy. It's also an opportunity to practice self-compassion; remember, saying "no" doesn't make you selfish; it makes you self-aware. You are learning to prioritize your well-being, to respect your limits, and to understand that it's perfectly acceptable to put your own needs first.

It's important to remember that setting boundaries doesn't mean isolating yourself from others. In fact, the opposite is true. Healthy boundaries allow for the development of authentic and supportive relationships. When you set boundaries, you communicate your needs and expectations, creating a space for healthy interaction. This is also a form of self-respect; it creates space for genuine connections based on mutual respect.

Establishing boundaries also extends to digital communication. This could mean limiting your interactions with certain individuals online, avoiding social media platforms that trigger negative emotions, or carefully curating your online presence to protect your privacy and personal information. In the digital age, boundary setting should be a priority, as we're often more vulnerable online than we realize.

Remember that setting boundaries is a journey, not a destination. There will be setbacks and challenges. There may be times when you feel uncomfortable or uncertain about your limits. In these moments, it's important to be patient and compassionate with yourself. Seek support from trusted friends, family members, or a therapist. They can provide encouragement, guidance, and accountability.

The process of rebuilding healthy relationships after abuse is complex and multifaceted. Setting and maintaining boundaries is a cornerstone of this process. It's about reclaiming your power, protecting your well-being, and creating a future free from manipulation and control. It's about valuing yourself, respecting your limits, and creating a life where your needs are honored and respected. This journey takes time and effort, but the rewards—a life lived on your terms—are well worth it. The freedom you will experience by setting and maintaining healthy boundaries is

truly liberating. Embrace this power and begin to build a life free from the shadows of the past.

Fostering Healthy Relationships with Family and Friends

Rebuilding trust and connection after escaping an abusive relationship is a crucial step in your healing journey. The damage inflicted by a sociopath extends far beyond the immediate relationship; it often fractures bonds with family and friends. They may have been alienated, manipulated, or even subtly pressured to doubt your account of the abuse.

Reconnecting with these individuals requires patience, understanding, and a carefully considered approach. It's not about forcing reconciliation; it's about rebuilding bridges based on honesty, transparency, and mutual respect.

The first step is self-assessment. Before reaching out, take time to reflect on your relationships before the abuse. Which connections were truly supportive, and which were more superficial or even subtly enabling of the abusive dynamic? Identifying those who consistently stood by you, offering unwavering support and understanding, is key. These are the relationships worth prioritizing as you begin to rebuild.

It's important to recognize that your friends and family might have been manipulated or misled. The sociopath likely engaged in a campaign of disinformation, portraying you in a negative light to undermine your credibility and sow seeds of doubt. They may have used charm, gaslighting, or even outright lies to influence their perception of you. This is not a reflection on your worth; it's a testament to the manipulative tactics employed by the abuser.

When you reconnect, be prepared for potential misunderstandings. Your loved ones may have questions or concerns that stem from the misinformation they've received.

Approach these conversations with empathy and patience. Explain your experience in a calm, clear, and concise manner, avoiding overly emotional outbursts or accusations. Remember that they may need time to process the information, to reconcile their previous understanding with your current account.

Providing evidence might be helpful, but don't force it. If you have documented instances of abuse, such as emails, texts, or photos, carefully consider whether sharing them would be beneficial. However, remember that your experience is valid even without concrete evidence. The focus should be on your emotional state and the impact of the abuse, rather than solely on proving the abuser's wrongdoing.

Don't expect immediate forgiveness or understanding. Some family members or friends may struggle to accept what you've been through, particularly if they've been close to the abuser. This is a reflection of their own biases and limited understanding, not a judgment on your character. Give them the space and time they need to process their feelings, without pressing them for immediate acceptance.

Consider approaching the reconciliation gradually. A short phone call, a brief email, or even a simple text message can be a good starting point. Gauge their response before committing to a face-to-face meeting. This approach allows you to assess their willingness to listen and understand without overwhelming yourself or them.

If you feel comfortable, consider seeking support from a therapist or counselor during this process. They can provide guidance on navigating these complex interactions, helping you communicate your needs effectively and develop healthy coping mechanisms for potential emotional setbacks.

They can also help you process any residual feelings of guilt, shame, or self-blame that may arise during these interactions.

Rebuilding relationships is not about blame; it's about healing. Forgiving those who didn't fully support you during the abuse may not be possible immediately, or ever.

However, focusing on your own healing and well-being is paramount. Acceptance of their limitations and your own emotional state is a sign of your strength.

The process of repairing family relationships might require a different approach than rebuilding friendships. Family dynamics are often more complex and emotionally charged. You might need to set stricter boundaries with certain family members, especially if they have historically enabled or minimized the abusive behavior. It's okay to distance yourself from individuals who continue to undermine your well-being or refuse to acknowledge the reality of your experiences.

Consider involving a neutral third party, such as a family therapist, to facilitate difficult conversations. This can create a safe space for open communication and help mediate disagreements. A therapist can offer tools for healthy communication and conflict resolution, fostering a more constructive environment for reconciliation.

Remember that rebuilding these relationships is a marathon, not a sprint. There will be setbacks, moments of frustration, and times when you feel like giving up. Be patient with yourself and allow yourself to grieve the loss of what you thought these relationships were. Celebrate small victories and acknowledge your strength in facing these challenges head-on.

It's essential to establish clear boundaries in your rekindled relationships. Communicate your needs clearly and directly, avoiding ambiguity or allowing yourself to be manipulated. This is not about controlling others; it's about protecting your emotional and mental health. It is your right to establish healthy boundaries, and these boundaries should be respected.

Avoid falling back into old patterns of behavior where you put others' needs before your own. The process of recovery requires prioritizing your own well-being. This is not selfishness; it is self-preservation. Healthy relationships are built on mutual respect and understanding, where each individual's needs are valued and honored.

If a relationship proves consistently damaging or unsupportive, despite your best efforts, accept that it may be necessary to sever ties, or at least significantly limit contact. This is not a sign of failure; it's a sign of self-respect and a commitment to your own well-being. You are prioritizing your healing journey, and that is a courageous and necessary step.

Throughout this process, remember that you are not alone. Seek support from a therapist, support groups, or trusted friends who understand the impact of sociopathic abuse.

These individuals can offer invaluable encouragement, validation, and practical strategies for navigating the challenges of rebuilding healthy relationships. Their support can be crucial in helping you maintain perspective and remain focused on your journey towards healing and wholeness.

The goal of rebuilding relationships is not to erase the past but to create a healthier future. By setting boundaries, communicating openly, and prioritizing your well-being, you can foster supportive and fulfilling connections with those who truly care about you. This process takes time, patience, and courage, but the reward—genuine connection and supportive relationships—is invaluable in your healing journey. Remember your strength, your resilience, and your unwavering determination to build a life free from the manipulation and control that defined your past. This new chapter of your life is a testament to your courage and commitment to a healthier, happier future.

Prioritizing SelfCare Practices

Prioritizing self-care after escaping a relationship with a sociopath is not a luxury; it's a necessity. The insidious nature of this abuse often leaves victims feeling depleted, emotionally exhausted, and struggling with a range of mental health challenges, including anxiety, depression, and PTSD. Rebuilding your life requires prioritizing your well-being, nurturing your physical and mental health, and establishing routines that support your recovery. This isn't about achieving perfection; it's about making small, consistent changes that accumulate over time, leading to significant improvements in your overall health and emotional stability.

One of the most powerful self-care tools is physical activity. Exercise isn't just about burning calories; it's a potent stress reliever, mood booster, and sleep regulator. Even moderate exercise, such as a brisk walk for 30 minutes most days of the week, can make a dramatic difference in your overall well-being. The endorphins released during physical activity have a natural mood-boosting effect, helping combat the feelings of anxiety and depression that often accompany trauma recovery. Finding an activity you enjoy is crucial.

Whether it's yoga, swimming, dancing, hiking, or simply walking in nature, the key is to find something that motivates you to move your body and engage in some form of physical exertion. Joining a fitness class can provide added social support and accountability, counteracting the isolation often imposed by an abusive partner.

Incorporating mindful movement practices, such as yoga or Tai Chi, can be particularly beneficial. These practices combine physical activity with mindfulness, encouraging you to focus on the present moment and release physical

tension. The deep breathing techniques often integrated into these practices can help calm your nervous system and reduce feelings of anxiety. It's not just about the physical postures; it's about the mental and emotional release they offer, helping to ground you in the present moment and interrupt cycles of negative thought patterns. Many free online resources and apps offer guided yoga and mindfulness meditations, making these practices accessible even if you have limited time or financial resources.

Alongside physical activity, nourishing your body with healthy food is crucial for recovery. The stress of escaping an abusive relationship can often lead to unhealthy eating habits. You might find yourself overeating, undereating, or relying on comfort foods high in sugar and processed ingredients. However, nourishing your body with nutrient- rich foods is essential for providing your body and mind with the energy and resources they need to heal. This doesn't mean strict dieting or deprivation; it's about making conscious choices to include more fruits, vegetables, whole grains, and lean protein in your diet. Prepare meals at home more often, reducing reliance on processed foods and takeout, which are often high in unhealthy fats, sugar, and sodium. Focus on whole, unprocessed foods and make gradual shifts towards a healthier eating pattern.

Consider keeping a food diary to track your eating habits and identify any patterns that might be contributing to emotional distress. This self-awareness can be a powerful tool for making healthier choices. If you struggle with disordered eating or have difficulty making healthy food choices, seek professional support from a registered dietitian or therapist specializing in eating disorders. They can provide guidance and support in developing healthy eating patterns tailored to your individual needs and circumstances. Remember that nutritional support is a vital part of your overall healing process.

Sleep is often disrupted after experiencing trauma. The constant state of hypervigilance and anxiety associated with abuse can make it challenging to fall asleep and stay asleep. Prioritizing good sleep hygiene is essential for promoting physical and mental recovery. This involves creating a relaxing bedtime routine, avoiding screen time before bed, ensuring your bedroom is dark, quiet, and cool, and maintaining a consistent sleep schedule, even on weekends. If you continue to struggle with sleep difficulties, consider consulting a healthcare professional to rule out any underlying medical conditions and explore potential treatments such as cognitive behavioral therapy for insomnia (CBT-I).

Mindfulness and meditation practices are powerful tools for managing stress, anxiety, and trauma. These techniques involve focusing on the present moment without judgment, allowing you to observe your thoughts and feelings without getting carried away by them. Regular meditation practice can help reduce rumination, improve emotional regulation, and increase self-awareness. There are many guided meditation apps and online resources available, catering to different experience levels and preferences. Start with short sessions (even five minutes) and gradually increase the duration as you become more comfortable with the practice.

Journaling can serve as a valuable tool for processing emotions and gaining insights into your experiences. Writing about your feelings can help you articulate what you're going through, identify patterns in your thoughts and behaviors, and gain a sense of perspective. It doesn't need to be a perfect or eloquent piece of writing; it's a private space for you to explore your emotions without judgment.

Engaging in creative activities can be a powerful way to express yourself and process your emotions. This could include anything from painting and drawing to playing music, writing poetry, or knitting.

Creativity provides an outlet for expressing emotions that might be difficult to articulate verbally. It allows for self-expression, distraction from negative thoughts, and a sense of accomplishment.

Connecting with others is essential for healing. Social isolation often exacerbates feelings of loneliness and anxiety. Reach out to trusted friends, family members, or support groups. Sharing your experiences with others who understand can provide comfort, validation, and a sense of community. Joining a support group specifically for survivors of sociopathic abuse can be particularly beneficial, providing a safe space to share experiences and learn from others who have gone through similar challenges.

Setting boundaries is crucial for protecting your well-being. This involves identifying your limits and communicating them clearly to others. It's about protecting yourself from further harm and ensuring your needs are respected. This might involve limiting contact with certain individuals or saying no to requests that drain your energy or compromise your well-being. Setting boundaries is an act of self-respect and self-preservation. It is not selfish; it is necessary.

Learning to say no is a vital component of self-care. It's often difficult after years of being manipulated to assert your needs. However, protecting your energy and well-being requires learning to politely but firmly decline requests that do not serve you. Practice saying no in low-stakes situations initially, building your confidence and ability to protect your time and emotional resources.

Remember that self-care is not a one-size-fits-all approach. Experiment with different activities and practices to find what works best for you. Be patient with yourself; healing is a process, not a destination. There will be good days and bad days. Celebrate your progress and be kind to yourself during setbacks. Remember that you deserve to prioritize your well- being and create a life free from fear and control. Your journey to recovery is a testament to your strength and resilience, and these self-care practices are essential tools to help you navigate this journey with grace, strength, and a renewed sense of self-worth. Seek professional support when needed; a therapist specializing in trauma can provide invaluable guidance and support during this process. Your healing journey is unique to you, and there is no one right way to heal. Embrace the process, celebrate your successes, and be compassionate with yourself as you rebuild your life.

Developing Healthy Coping Mechanisms

Developing healthy coping mechanisms is paramount in the aftermath of abuse by a sociopath. The manipulation and control experienced often leave survivors with a complex array of emotional challenges, making it crucial to develop strategies for managing difficult emotions and stressful situations. This isn't about suppressing feelings; rather, it's about learning healthy ways to process and navigate them, preventing them from overwhelming you.

One highly effective coping mechanism is journaling. The act of writing down your thoughts and feelings can be incredibly cathartic. It provides a safe space to explore your experiences without judgment, allowing you to untangle the complexities of your emotions. Don't worry about grammar or style; the goal is simply to express yourself honestly. You might find patterns emerging as you write, gaining valuable insights into your emotional responses and triggers. Consider dating your entries to track changes in your mood and emotional state over time. This can be a powerful tool for monitoring your progress and identifying areas needing further attention.

Journaling can also help to process traumatic memories in a safe and controlled environment. The act of writing can be a form of emotional release, allowing you to externalize painful memories and experiences. It's crucial to approach this gently, avoiding triggering memories that are too overwhelming. If you find yourself becoming excessively distressed while journaling, take a break and engage in a relaxing activity before returning to it later. Remember, the process is about self-discovery and healing, not causing further distress.

Beyond journaling, mindfulness and meditation offer invaluable tools for managing intense emotions. These practices encourage focusing on the present moment, gently redirecting your attention from distressing thoughts and feelings. Even a few minutes of daily meditation can help to calm your nervous system and reduce feelings of anxiety and overwhelm. Numerous guided meditations are readily available online or through apps, catering to all experience levels. Explore different styles to find one that resonates with you. The focus isn't about emptying your mind; it's about acknowledging thoughts and feelings without judgment, observing them as they arise and pass.

Mindfulness extends beyond formal meditation practices. You can incorporate mindful moments throughout your day, such as paying attention to your breath during stressful situations, noticing the sensations of your feet on the floor, or savoring the taste of your food. These small acts of mindful awareness can help you to ground yourself in the present moment and interrupt cycles of negative thinking.

They offer a subtle yet powerful antidote to the overwhelming rumination that can often accompany trauma recovery.

Creative expression is another powerful coping mechanism, providing an alternative outlet for processing intense emotions. This could involve any creative activity that you find engaging, whether it's painting, drawing, sculpting, playing a musical instrument, singing, writing poetry, photography, or knitting. The act of creation offers a form of emotional release and self-expression, allowing you to communicate emotions that might be difficult to articulate verbally. The process itself can be therapeutic, providing a sense of accomplishment and fostering self-esteem. It can be helpful to keep your creative work in a safe place, revisiting

it later to notice how your perspectives may change over time.

Engaging in creative activities can also be a way to reclaim your sense of self, reconnecting with aspects of yourself that may have been suppressed or neglected during the abusive relationship. The process of creation can be a deeply personal and empowering one, helping you to reconnect with your inner strength and resilience. Don't worry about producing a masterpiece; the focus should be on the process of creating and self-expression.

Physical activity remains a cornerstone of healthy coping. The endorphins released during exercise have a natural mood-boosting effect, helping to combat feelings of depression and anxiety. Regular physical activity can also improve sleep quality, further enhancing your overall well- being. Find an activity that you genuinely enjoy, whether it's dancing, swimming, hiking, cycling, or simply taking a brisk walk. The key is consistency rather than intensity. Even short bursts of activity throughout the day can accumulate to have a positive impact.

Consider joining a fitness class or group activity to foster a sense of community and social support. This can help counter the isolation often imposed by an abusive partner, providing a valuable opportunity to connect with others and build new, healthy relationships. The social interaction can be as beneficial as the physical activity itself.

Social connection is crucial for recovery. Isolation can exacerbate feelings of loneliness and vulnerability. Actively cultivate supportive relationships with trusted friends, family members, or support groups. Sharing your experiences with others who understand can provide validation, comfort, and a sense of community. Joining a support group specifically

for survivors of sociopathic abuse can be particularly beneficial, offering a safe and supportive environment where you can connect with others who have had similar experiences. The shared understanding and mutual support can be incredibly empowering.

Remember, recovery is not a linear process. There will be days when you feel stronger and more resilient, and other days when you experience setbacks. Be patient and kind to yourself throughout this journey. Celebrate your progress, no matter how small, and acknowledge that setbacks are a normal part of the healing process.

Learning to assert boundaries is essential for protecting your well-being. This involves identifying your limits and communicating them clearly and assertively to others. It is not selfish to prioritize your own needs and well-being. This may involve setting limits on contact with certain individuals or saying no to requests that drain your energy or compromise your well-being. This is an act of self-respect and self-preservation. Practice saying no in low-stakes situations first, building your confidence and ability to protect your time and emotional resources. Remember, healthy boundaries are a vital component of self-care.

Developing healthy coping mechanisms requires experimentation and self-discovery. Not every strategy will work for everyone, so it's essential to find what resonates with you and incorporates it into your daily routine. Be flexible, adapting your approach as your needs and circumstances change. The process of healing is a deeply personal one, and there is no one-size-fits-all approach. Seek professional support from a therapist specializing in trauma or abuse recovery if needed. Their guidance and expertise can provide invaluable support as you navigate your healing journey.

Remember, healing takes time. Be patient with yourself, celebrate your progress, and prioritize your well-being. Your resilience and strength are testaments to your ability to overcome this challenging experience, and you deserve to create a life free from fear and control. The tools and techniques discussed here are designed to empower you on your path to recovery, providing strategies for navigating difficult emotions, building resilience, and reclaiming your life. This is not just about surviving; it's about thriving.

Maintaining Physical and Mental Health

Maintaining physical and mental health is not a luxury after escaping an abusive relationship; it's a necessity. The trauma inflicted by a sociopath often leaves deep wounds, both visible and invisible.

Neglecting your well-being, in either aspect, will only hinder your recovery and allow the insidious effects of the abuse to linger. Prioritizing self-care in this context isn't selfish; it's an act of radical self- preservation. It's about rebuilding your life, brick by painstaking brick, and ensuring you have a strong foundation to support your future.

This begins with regular medical check-ups. The stress and emotional turmoil of escaping a sociopath can manifest physically in various ways – from digestive issues and chronic headaches to sleep disturbances and weakened immunity. Regular visits to your primary care physician allow for early detection of potential health problems, enabling prompt intervention before they escalate. Don't dismiss any physical symptoms; even seemingly minor ailments can be indicators of underlying stress or trauma.

Your doctor can perform necessary tests, offer advice on managing stress, and provide referrals to specialists if needed. Open and honest communication with your doctor is crucial; they can provide valuable support and guidance during this challenging time. Don't hesitate to explain the context of your life, the trauma you've endured, and how it's affecting your physical health. This information is vital in helping them provide the most effective care.

Beyond regular check-ups, be proactive in seeking medical attention when needed. Don't delay seeking help if you experience any significant physical or psychological

symptoms. This is especially important if you've experienced physical abuse. Delayed treatment can lead to more severe complications, both physically and emotionally. This proactive approach demonstrates self-respect and highlights the importance you place on your well-being. Remember, your health is your responsibility, and seeking medical assistance is a sign of strength, not weakness. Finding a doctor you trust and feel comfortable with is also crucial.

Choose a medical professional who is empathetic, understanding, and willing to listen to your concerns without judgment. A supportive doctor can become a valuable ally in your recovery journey.

Beyond physical health, mental well-being is equally, if not more, critical. The psychological impact of sociopathic abuse is profound and long-lasting. The manipulation, gaslighting, and emotional manipulation can leave deep scars, affecting your self-esteem, sense of self, and trust in others. Engaging in regular therapy is crucial for processing these traumatic experiences and developing coping mechanisms. Seek a therapist specializing in trauma and abuse recovery. This is not just about talking; a skilled therapist can provide you with specific techniques and strategies for managing trauma responses, such as flashbacks, nightmares, and intrusive thoughts.

Cognitive Behavioral Therapy (CBT) is frequently recommended for trauma recovery. CBT helps you identify and challenge negative thought patterns and develop healthier coping strategies. Eye Movement Desensitization and Reprocessing (EMDR) is another effective therapy for processing traumatic memories and reducing their emotional impact. Both of these therapies can help to reframe negative thoughts, reduce anxiety, and build resilience. A therapist can guide you through these techniques and help you adapt them to your specific needs and experiences. Remember,

finding the right therapist is paramount. It may take some time and effort to find a therapist with whom you feel comfortable and connected. Don't hesitate to try different therapists until you find one who meets your needs.

In addition to professional therapy, fostering self-compassion is essential. The self-doubt and low self-esteem that often result from abuse require deliberate counteraction. Practice self-affirmations, speaking kindly to yourself, and focusing on your strengths and accomplishments. Remind yourself that you are not to blame for the abuse you experienced, and that your worth is not determined by the actions of your abuser. This isn't a quick fix; it's a gradual process that requires consistent effort and patience. But over time, practicing self-compassion will significantly improve your self-esteem and empower you to move forward.

Building a strong support network is also vital for maintaining mental well-being. Isolation is a common tactic used by sociopaths to control and manipulate their victims. After escaping the abuse, actively cultivate relationships with trusted friends, family members, and support groups.

Sharing your experiences with others who understand can provide validation, comfort, and a sense of community.

Joining a support group for survivors of sociopathic abuse can be particularly beneficial. The shared understanding and mutual support within these groups can be incredibly powerful and healing. The opportunity to connect with others who have had similar experiences provides a sense of belonging and shared resilience.

Remember, there is no shame in seeking help. In fact, it demonstrates courage and strength. Reaching out for support shows your commitment to healing and well-being. This support network can provide crucial emotional support, practical assistance, and guidance during challenging times.

It's crucial to surround yourself with people who understand, support, and encourage your healing journey.

Prioritizing sleep is often overlooked but is fundamental to both physical and mental health. Trauma can significantly disrupt sleep patterns, leading to insomnia, nightmares, and fatigue. Establish a regular sleep schedule, creating a calming bedtime routine to promote relaxation and restful sleep. Avoiding caffeine and alcohol before bed, creating a quiet and dark sleep environment, and practicing relaxation techniques such as deep breathing or meditation can significantly improve sleep quality. If sleep problems persist, consult your doctor or therapist to explore potential underlying issues or consider seeking professional guidance on sleep hygiene. Sufficient sleep is essential for your body and mind to repair and rejuvenate, which is crucial for recovery.

Nutrition plays a vital role in overall well-being. A healthy diet provides the essential nutrients your body needs to heal and function optimally. Focus on consuming a balanced diet rich in fruits, vegetables, whole grains, and lean protein.

Limit processed foods, sugary drinks, and excessive caffeine, which can exacerbate anxiety and other symptoms. Regular hydration is also critical for both physical and mental health. Adequate water intake supports bodily functions and helps regulate mood. A well-balanced diet contributes to better physical and mental stamina, energy levels, and overall health, essential for navigating the challenges of recovery.

Finally, incorporating regular physical activity is another crucial element of self-care. Exercise releases endorphins, which have mood-boosting effects, helping combat feelings of depression, anxiety, and fatigue. Regular physical activity can also improve sleep quality, reduce stress, and boost overall energy levels. Find an activity you enjoy, whether it's

yoga, swimming, dancing, walking, or something else entirely. The key is consistency rather than intensity; even short bursts of activity throughout the day can accumulate to have a positive impact on your physical and mental health.

Remember, prioritizing your physical and mental well-being is an act of self-love and self-respect, critical for a full and meaningful recovery. This is not just about surviving; it is about thriving, building a life that is strong, healthy, and free from the shadow of abuse.

Practicing SelfCompassion and Forgiveness

Practicing self-compassion after escaping the clutches of a sociopath is not merely an act of self-care; it's a revolutionary act of self-preservation. The insidious nature of the abuse often leaves victims feeling profoundly flawed, responsible for the abuse they endured, and unworthy of happiness. This deeply ingrained sense of self-blame must be actively challenged and dismantled. Forgiveness, both of yourself and your abuser, plays a crucial, albeit complex, role in this process.

Self-compassion begins with acknowledging the profound impact of the abuse. It's about understanding that the manipulation, gaslighting, and control weren't your fault. The sociopath's actions were a reflection of their pathology, not a judgment of your worth. This understanding is the cornerstone of healing. It's a process of gently untangling the web of lies and distortions woven by your abuser, replacing them with the truth: you are worthy of love, respect, and a life free from fear.

One powerful tool for cultivating self-compassion is self- affirmations. These aren't superficial pronouncements; they're intentional statements designed to counter the negative self-talk instilled by the abuser. Start by identifying the most pervasive negative thoughts and beliefs about yourself—the ones that whisper doubts and insecurities.

Then, craft affirmations that directly challenge these thoughts. For instance, if you constantly berate yourself for not seeing the red flags sooner, an affirmation might be: "I am not responsible for my abuser's actions; I am learning and growing from this experience." Or, if you struggle with

feelings of inadequacy, an affirmation could be: "I am strong, resilient, and capable of overcoming this challenge."

Repeat these affirmations regularly—in the morning, before bed, or even throughout the day as needed. Write them down, say them aloud, or even record yourself saying them and listen back. The key is consistency. The more you repeat these positive statements, the more likely they are to replace the negative self-talk that has become deeply ingrained. It's like retraining your brain to recognize and value your inherent worth.

Beyond affirmations, practicing mindfulness can be profoundly beneficial. Mindfulness encourages you to focus on the present moment, without judgment. This can help to interrupt the cycle of negative thinking and self-criticism.

Simple mindfulness exercises, such as focusing on your breath or noticing the sensations in your body, can help ground you in the present and reduce feelings of anxiety and overwhelm. Numerous guided meditation apps are available to help you learn and practice mindfulness techniques. Even five minutes a day can make a significant difference.

Another vital aspect of self-compassion is self-soothing. This involves engaging in activities that bring you comfort and a sense of calm. These activities will differ from person to person, but they might include taking a warm bath, listening to soothing music, spending time in nature, reading a favorite book, engaging in a hobby, or connecting with a supportive friend or family member. Identify your personal self-soothing activities and make time for them regularly.

This is not a luxury; it's a necessity for healing and building emotional resilience.

Journaling can also be a powerful tool for cultivating self- compassion. Writing down your thoughts and feelings can

help you process your emotions, identify negative patterns, and challenge self-critical thoughts. It can provide a safe space to express your pain, anger, and grief without judgment. You don't need to write beautifully or eloquently; the act of writing itself is therapeutic. Simply let your thoughts and feelings flow onto the page. Over time, you might notice shifts in your self-perception and a growing sense of self-acceptance.

Forgiveness, both of yourself and your abuser, is another critical aspect of the healing process. Forgiving yourself doesn't mean condoning what happened or minimizing the trauma you endured. It means releasing the self-blame and self-hatred that can consume you. It's about recognizing that you were a victim of a manipulative and abusive person, and that you did the best you could given the circumstances. This is a process, not a destination. It might involve acknowledging your past mistakes, learning from them, and practicing self-compassion.

Forgiving your abuser is even more challenging, and it's not something you need to rush. It doesn't mean you condone their behavior or reconcile with them. It means releasing the anger, resentment, and bitterness that consume you and hinder your healing. Holding onto these negative emotions keeps you tethered to the past and prevents you from moving forward. Forgiveness doesn't erase the abuse; it simply frees you from its grip. You might find it helpful to visualize letting go of these negative emotions, perhaps by writing a letter to your abuser expressing your feelings without sending it, or through guided meditation or visualization exercises.

Remember that healing is a journey, not a destination. There will be setbacks, moments of doubt, and relapses. Be kind to yourself during these times. Don't judge yourself harshly for

feeling sad, angry, or scared. Allow yourself to experience these emotions without judgment and know that they are a natural part of the healing process. Recognize progress, no matter how small, and celebrate your victories along the way.

Self-compassion and forgiveness are not acts of weakness; they are acts of immense strength. They are essential steps in breaking free from the lingering effects of sociopathic abuse and building a life filled with self-love, self-respect, and well-being. This process requires consistent effort, patience, and self-awareness, but the rewards are immeasurable: a life free from the shadows of the past, filled with hope, happiness, and a renewed sense of self.

Consider seeking professional guidance in practicing self- compassion and forgiveness. A therapist specializing in trauma recovery can provide tailored strategies and support to help you navigate these complex emotional challenges. They can help you identify and challenge negative thought patterns, develop healthy coping mechanisms, and process the trauma you have experienced. Remember, you are not alone, and seeking professional help is a sign of strength, not weakness.

In addition to professional support, explore various self-help resources, such as books, workshops, or online support groups. These resources can offer valuable tools and strategies for fostering self-compassion and forgiveness.

Connect with other survivors of abuse; their shared experiences and support can be incredibly powerful and healing. The shared understanding and mutual support within these communities can offer a sense of belonging and shared resilience, reminding you that you are not alone in your journey.

It's crucial to remember that healing takes time. There is no set timeline for recovery, and your journey will be unique to your experiences. Be patient with yourself, celebrate your progress, and remember that you are worthy of a happy, healthy, and fulfilling life, free from the constraints of the past. The path to recovery is paved with self-compassion and forgiveness, leading to a future where you can finally escape the shadows and embrace the light.

Building Resilience and Strength

Building resilience after surviving abuse by a sociopath is not a passive process; it's an active, ongoing commitment to strengthening your inner self. It's about cultivating a deep- seated belief in your ability to overcome adversity, to learn from setbacks, and to emerge stronger on the other side. This involves more than just coping mechanisms; it's about fundamentally altering your relationship with yourself and the world. It's about recognizing your inherent strength, even in the face of overwhelming challenges.

One of the first steps in building resilience is to acknowledge and validate the trauma you've experienced. Minimizing or dismissing the abuse only serves to prolong the healing process. Allow yourself to feel the full spectrum of emotions – the anger, the sadness, the fear, the confusion. Don't try to suppress these feelings; instead, allow them to flow through you, acknowledging their presence without judgment. This acceptance is the bedrock upon which resilience is built. It's a recognition that you are not broken, but that you have been profoundly wounded and are actively working towards healing.

This acknowledgment often leads to a deeper understanding of your own strength and resourcefulness. Think back to moments during the abuse when you found inner strength, even if it was seemingly small acts of defiance or moments of quiet resistance. These moments are invaluable; they are proof that you possess an inner wellspring of fortitude that can be tapped into again and again. Recall specific instances: perhaps you subtly resisted a controlling demand, or you found a small way to maintain a connection with the outside world, or you silently planned your escape. These are crucial

victories that should be celebrated, no matter how seemingly insignificant they may appear in retrospect.

Learning to identify and challenge negative thought patterns is another crucial aspect of building resilience. Sociopaths are masters of manipulation, and their abuse often leaves victims with distorted perceptions of themselves and the world. These distortions often manifest as negative self-talk, self-doubt, and a pervasive sense of worthlessness. Actively challenge these thoughts. Ask yourself: are these thoughts based on facts or on the manipulations of your abuser? Are these thoughts serving me, or are they holding me back? By questioning the validity of these thoughts, you begin to reclaim your own narrative and create a more balanced perspective. Cognitive Behavioral Therapy (CBT) techniques are incredibly helpful in this process, teaching you to identify and reframe negative thoughts into more realistic and positive ones.

Developing healthy coping mechanisms is also essential for building resilience. This involves finding healthy and constructive ways to manage stress, anxiety, and other difficult emotions. This might involve physical activity, meditation, spending time in nature, engaging in creative pursuits, or connecting with supportive friends and family. It's crucial to find activities that truly resonate with you and that bring you a sense of peace and calm. Experiment with various approaches; what works for one person might not work for another. The key is to find strategies that help you regulate your emotions and feel empowered to navigate challenging situations.

Building a strong support network is paramount. Isolation is a common tactic used by sociopaths, leaving victims feeling alone and vulnerable. Actively seek out connections with supportive individuals who can offer understanding,

compassion, and a safe space for you to express your feelings. This might involve connecting with friends, family members, support groups, or therapists. Remember that you do not have to go through this alone. The empathy and shared understanding offered by others who have experienced similar trauma can be incredibly powerful.

Shared experiences often foster a deeper level of mutual support and understanding. Support groups offer a sense of community and belonging, reminding you that you are not alone in your journey of healing and recovery.

Setting boundaries is another critical step in building resilience. This involves learning to say no to requests or demands that compromise your well-being or safety. It's about prioritizing your own needs and establishing clear limits in your relationships. This may seem challenging initially, especially if you're accustomed to prioritizing the needs of others above your own. However, setting healthy boundaries is essential for protecting your emotional and mental health and creating a safe and empowering space for yourself. It requires both internal and external actions; internal strength to know what your boundaries are and the courage to communicate them clearly.

Forgiveness, while not a requirement for healing, can be an incredibly powerful tool in the process of building resilience. Forgiving your abuser doesn't mean condoning their behavior or forgetting what happened; it means releasing the anger, resentment, and bitterness that are holding you back from moving forward. It allows you to break free from the past and focus on building a brighter future. This is often a gradual process, and you don't have to forgive all at once.

Some may find that they never forgive their abuser and that's entirely acceptable. The key is to prioritize your own healing and well-being.

Self-care, often neglected during periods of abuse, is now paramount. Prioritizing your physical, emotional, and mental health is not a luxury; it's an essential component of your recovery. This encompasses all aspects of your well-being, including adequate sleep, healthy eating, regular exercise, engaging in activities you enjoy, and nurturing your spiritual side. It's about creating a life that is nourishing and supportive, replenishing your energy and vitality.

Finally, remember that building resilience is a process, not a destination. There will be setbacks, moments of doubt, and times when you feel overwhelmed. Be patient with yourself; celebrate your small victories and acknowledge the progress you've made. Don't be discouraged by setbacks; instead, use them as opportunities to learn and grow. Building resilience is a testament to your strength and determination. It's a testament to your ability to overcome adversity and create a life filled with hope, happiness, and a sense of self-worth.

You have survived, and you are capable of thriving.

Learning to recognize your strengths and acknowledging the progress you've made, no matter how small, builds confidence. Keep a journal, documenting not only the challenges but also your victories. Look back at past entries and see how far you've come. This self-reflection helps reinforce your progress and builds a sense of accomplishment. Remember, there's no competition in healing; it's a personal journey, and the pace is yours to set.

Embrace opportunities for self-discovery and personal growth. The trauma you've experienced has inevitably shaped your perception of yourself and your relationships. This is an opportunity to examine these perceptions with honesty and kindness. You might consider seeking additional therapy to address remaining issues, explore creative expression as a means of processing your experiences, or

delve into personal development resources. The focus is on creating a stronger, healthier, more authentic you.

Consider seeking professional help for Post-Traumatic Stress Disorder (PTSD) or other trauma-related conditions. A therapist can provide valuable support, equip you with coping strategies, and guide you through processing your trauma. Professional support can significantly enhance your journey toward resilience. Many different therapeutic approaches can assist in building resilience, including EMDR (Eye Movement Desensitization and Reprocessing), somatic experiencing, and trauma-focused Cognitive Behavioral Therapy.

Actively cultivate positive relationships with individuals who value and respect you. These relationships provide a sense of belonging, support, and understanding. Nurture these bonds, and choose to surround yourself with supportive and uplifting people who acknowledge and validate your experience. Remember that healthy relationships are reciprocal, providing mutual support and understanding.

Remember that you are not alone on this journey. There are many others who have survived similar experiences and can provide support and understanding. Seek out support groups or online communities where you can connect with others who have been through similar challenges. Shared experiences offer a powerful source of strength and healing.

Building resilience is not about forgetting the past; it's about integrating it into your life narrative in a way that empowers you, rather than defining you. It's about learning from your experiences, accepting your vulnerability, and celebrating your strength. It's about creating a future that is shaped by your resilience, not your trauma. You are a survivor, and you are capable of building a life that is meaningful, fulfilling, and free from the shadows of the past.

Protecting Children from Abuse

Protecting children is paramount when escaping an abusive situation involving a sociopath. The safety and well-being of children must be the absolute priority throughout the escape process and in the aftermath. Their innocence and vulnerability demand a meticulous and proactive approach, one that goes beyond simply leaving the abusive environment. The manipulative tactics of sociopaths often extend to controlling and isolating children, making their escape particularly complex and demanding.

The first step involves meticulous planning. This isn't a spontaneous decision; it requires careful consideration and strategy. Begin by creating a detailed safety plan, a document that outlines every step of the escape, including the timing, transportation, and destination. Identify safe houses or shelters specifically equipped to handle children's needs. These shelters provide a secure environment, often with trained personnel who understand the complexities of child trauma. Familiarize yourself with the resources available in your area, including child protective services and domestic violence shelters. Research these options well in advance to ensure a smooth and secure transition. Timing is crucial. Consider the sociopath's routine, their vulnerabilities, and any predictable patterns in their behavior to choose the most opportune moment for the escape. Ensure the children are well-prepared, with a change of clothes and any necessary medications or comfort items packed discreetly.

Financial security is another vital aspect. Sociopaths often control the family finances, leaving the victim with limited resources. Secretly secure funds, even small amounts, can be

a lifeline. Open a separate bank account, if possible, and deposit any money that can be moved without detection. Reach out to family or friends for financial assistance; let them know your situation in confidence and request their support in getting the children to safety. If immediate financial assistance is inaccessible, look into local charities and organizations that provide emergency financial aid to victims of domestic violence. Explore all avenues for support; even small contributions can make a significant difference.

Transportation plays a critical role in a successful escape. If you have access to a vehicle, ensure it's reliable and has enough fuel. Plan the escape route carefully, avoiding locations where the abuser might intercept you. If you don't have a car, arrange transportation in advance - a trusted friend, a taxi, or public transport. Ensure the children are aware of the escape plan, but only to the extent they can handle without undue anxiety. Keep the details simple, emphasizing their safety and the new, safe place they're going.

Upon reaching safety, immediate actions are necessary to safeguard the children's well-being. Report the abuse to the appropriate authorities. This involves contacting child protective services and law enforcement to file a formal report. Provide them with all the necessary details, including the abuser's identity, history of abuse, and evidence of the abuse. Cooperate fully with the investigation and follow their instructions diligently. Seeking legal counsel is also important. A lawyer can help secure a restraining order to prevent further contact with the abuser and assist with custody arrangements. Remember, the legal system is there to protect you and your children; use its resources to ensure their continued safety.

The emotional impact on children must not be underestimated. They have likely witnessed and experienced the abuse firsthand, suffering from trauma that requires specialized care. Seek professional help immediately from therapists experienced in treating child trauma. These therapists employ techniques designed to help children process their experiences in a safe and supportive environment, utilizing age-appropriate approaches. Child- centered therapy helps the children articulate their feelings, understand their experiences, and develop coping mechanisms. Providing a consistent routine, maintaining stability, and creating a predictable and supportive environment are crucial for emotional healing. This helps children regain a sense of safety and control after the traumatic events they have endured.

Encourage open communication with the children. Let them know it's okay to talk about their feelings, even if it's difficult. Listen attentively to what they share, validating their emotions and never minimizing their experiences.

Avoid using judgmental language, instead focusing on providing empathy and understanding. Allow them to express their emotions freely, without fear of judgment or reprisal. Create a safe space where they feel comfortable sharing their thoughts and concerns.

In addition to professional therapy, maintaining routines and a sense of normalcy is crucial for children's recovery.

Establish a consistent schedule for meals, bedtime, and other daily activities. This structure provides a sense of order and predictability in their lives, reducing anxiety and fostering stability. Encourage participation in activities they enjoy, whether it's playing with friends, engaging in hobbies, or attending school. These activities contribute to their overall well-being, supporting their emotional healing. Positive

reinforcement can play a significant role in bolstering their resilience.

The long-term effects of trauma can be profound. Be vigilant in monitoring the children's emotional and behavioral changes. Seek immediate help if you notice any significant behavioral issues, such as withdrawal, aggression, or significant changes in sleep or appetite. Early intervention is key to mitigating potential long-term challenges associated with trauma exposure. Continued therapy is often necessary to help children process their experiences and develop healthy coping mechanisms. The healing process is gradual and ongoing, requiring patience, understanding, and unwavering support.

Education plays a vital role in protecting children. Teach them about safe and unsafe touch, body boundaries, and appropriate behavior from adults. Empower them to recognize and report any instances of abuse or discomfort. Equip them with the vocabulary to express their experiences effectively. Ensure they understand that it's not their fault if they experience any form of abuse or mistreatment.

Emphasize their right to safety and their right to say "no" to anything that makes them uncomfortable.

Collaboration with educational institutions is crucial. Inform the school officials about the situation and the children's needs. Request support for their academic and emotional well-being. Ensure the school is aware of any specific requirements, such as individualized learning plans or additional support services. Collaboration creates a supportive environment for the children, ensuring consistency and continuity of care.

Building a strong support network is essential for both parents and children. Reach out to family, friends, support

groups, or community organizations to provide emotional and practical support. Lean on trusted individuals for assistance with childcare, household tasks, or emotional support. Sharing experiences and support with other survivors can offer a sense of community and validation. Remember, you are not alone in this journey, and there are numerous people and resources available to help.

The escape from an abusive sociopath is a challenging undertaking, particularly when children are involved. Meticulous planning, proactive legal actions, and sustained emotional support are vital for ensuring the safety and well- being of the children. Remember, placing the children's welfare at the forefront of your actions is essential for their recovery and long-term emotional health. Their resilience and future happiness depend on your steadfast commitment to their safety and well-being. This commitment demands constant vigilance, proactive planning, and unrelenting dedication to their healthy development. The process is long, but the rewards of safeguarding their innocence and fostering their healing are immeasurable.

Seeking Child Custody and Legal Protection

Navigating the legal system after escaping a sociopathic abuser can feel like entering a minefield, especially when children are involved. The immediate priority is to ensure their safety and well-being, and this often requires seeking legal protection and custody arrangements. Understanding the process and securing competent legal representation is crucial. Remember, the legal system is designed to protect victims and their children, but you must actively engage with it to reap its benefits.

The first step is to find a lawyer specializing in family law and domestic violence cases. This isn't a situation where you can afford to compromise on expertise. A lawyer experienced in dealing with sociopaths understands their manipulative tactics and can anticipate their strategies in court. They will be equipped to counter these strategies effectively, protecting your children's interests. Do your research; ask for referrals from domestic violence shelters, women's advocacy groups, or trusted friends. Read online reviews and compare different lawyers' experience and success rates in similar cases. The initial consultation is often free or low-cost, allowing you to assess their suitability before committing. Don't hesitate to interview several lawyers until you find one you trust and feel comfortable with. The rapport you build with your lawyer is crucial throughout the legal process, particularly when dealing with the high-stakes emotional turmoil involved.

Your lawyer will guide you through the process of filing for custody and obtaining protective orders. Custody orders dictate the legal rights and responsibilities of each parent regarding their children – physical custody (where the children live) and legal custody (decision-making authority on matters such as education and healthcare). In situations of abuse, the courts heavily favor the safety and well-being of the children, and a judge is likely to grant you primary custody if sufficient evidence of the abuse is presented. This evidence might include police reports, medical records documenting injuries, photographs of bruises or other injuries, witness testimonies, and any documentation of the abuser's manipulative behaviors. Your lawyer will help you gather and organize this evidence in a way that is legally sound and persuasive.

Protective orders, often called restraining orders, are crucial for preventing further contact between the abuser and you and your children. These orders legally prohibit the abuser from coming within a certain distance of your home, workplace, or your children's school. They can also restrict the abuser's ability to contact you or your children by phone, email, or through any other means. Violating a protective order is a serious crime with potentially severe consequences. Obtaining a protective order is generally a relatively straightforward legal process if sufficient evidence of abuse exists. However, the process can still be emotionally draining, and having a strong legal team is critical to ensure the order is granted and effectively enforced.

Preparing for court proceedings is crucial. Your lawyer will prepare you for what to expect and will help you practice your testimony. They will guide you on how to answer questions clearly and concisely, focusing on the facts and avoiding emotionally charged language. Remember, the goal is to present a clear and compelling case emphasizing the danger the abuser poses to you and your children. The judge will base their decision on the evidence presented, so being prepared and providing clear, concise information is key to a

favorable outcome. This includes anticipating the abuser's potential arguments and preparing counterarguments.

Sociopaths are masters of manipulation, and they will likely try to distort the facts to portray themselves in a positive light or to undermine your credibility. Your lawyer will help you anticipate these attempts and craft appropriate responses.

The court process can be lengthy and emotionally taxing. Be prepared for delays, setbacks, and the inevitable emotional roller coaster. Maintaining a strong support system is critical during this period. Lean on your friends, family, support groups, and therapist for emotional support and practical assistance. Remember, you are not alone in this journey, and there are people who want to help. Your therapist can provide guidance on coping strategies to manage the stress and anxiety associated with court proceedings. Consider joining a support group for victims of domestic violence; sharing experiences with others who understand can provide validation and strength.

Financial considerations are another significant aspect of seeking legal protection. Legal representation can be expensive, and court costs can accumulate quickly. Explore financial assistance options such as legal aid societies or pro bono services offered by lawyers in your area. Many organizations dedicated to assisting victims of domestic violence offer financial assistance for legal fees. Do not let financial constraints prevent you from seeking legal help.

Your children's safety and well-being are paramount, and securing competent legal representation is a non-negotiable step in protecting them.

Beyond custody and protective orders, your lawyer may also advise you on other legal avenues to secure your children's safety and well-being. This could include exploring options

for changing your address, obtaining security systems for your home, or even seeking assistance from law enforcement in conducting regular welfare checks. Your lawyer will work with you to develop a comprehensive plan to ensure your children are safe and protected from future harm. The objective is not merely to escape the abuse, but to create a safe and stable environment where your children can heal and thrive.

The long-term implications of the legal process should also be considered. Even after achieving a favorable outcome in court, the process might require ongoing vigilance.

Regularly check in with your lawyer to address any new developments or concerns. Keep detailed records of all communications, court orders, and any instances of contact or attempted contact from the abuser. This documentation is crucial in case of future violations or disputes. Remembering that the fight for your children's safety is an ongoing process, not a single victory, ensures you continue to build a protective structure around them. Even years later, you might need to revisit the legal framework to adjust custody arrangements based on the children's evolving needs or the abuser's actions. Continued vigilance and legal counsel is not just a safeguard, but a critical component of rebuilding their lives and providing them the stability and safety they need to heal.

Ultimately, seeking child custody and legal protection is a multifaceted process requiring careful planning, legal expertise, and unwavering determination. It's a fight for your children's future, a battle against manipulation and abuse.

Remember that this is not about blame; it's about protecting your children from harm. By equipping yourself with the knowledge, support, and legal resources necessary, you're actively creating a safe and nurturing environment for your children to heal and grow. The journey is arduous, but the

ultimate goal – their safety and well-being – makes every step worthwhile. Your resilience and unwavering commitment to protecting them will significantly impact their healing and their future.

Helping Children Heal from Trauma

The legal battles to secure your children's safety are only one part of the healing journey. The emotional scars of witnessing or experiencing abuse run deep, and addressing these wounds requires a multifaceted approach focusing on their emotional well-being. Creating a stable and nurturing environment is paramount; a sanctuary where they feel safe, understood, and loved. This involves far more than simply removing them from the abusive situation; it's about actively fostering their healing and building their resilience.

First, understand that children process trauma differently than adults. Their expressions of distress might not align with our expectations. They may exhibit behavioral changes, such as increased aggression, withdrawal, anxiety, or nightmares. Academic performance might suffer; they may struggle to concentrate or experience unexplained absences from school. Physical symptoms, like headaches, stomachaches, or sleep disturbances, are also common manifestations of underlying trauma. It's crucial to recognize that these are not signs of misbehavior, but rather the outward expression of their inner turmoil. Avoid labeling their behavior as "bad" or "difficult"; instead, view it as a symptom requiring understanding and professional help.

Seeking professional help is not a sign of failure; it's a crucial step in the healing process. A therapist specializing in trauma-informed care is uniquely equipped to assess your child's specific needs and develop an individualized treatment plan. This therapist will use techniques that acknowledge the child's experience and provide a safe space for emotional expression. Therapy might involve play therapy for younger children, who often communicate their

feelings through play rather than words. For older children and adolescents, trauma-focused cognitive behavioral therapy (TF-CBT) is a highly effective approach that teaches coping mechanisms and helps process traumatic memories.

Remember, choosing the right therapist is crucial; ensure the therapist is experienced in working with children who have experienced parental abuse or witnessed domestic violence. A good therapist will create a rapport with your child, building trust and a sense of safety.

Creating a safe and predictable routine is another cornerstone of healing. Children thrive on consistency and structure, which provides a sense of security and control in a world that may have felt chaotic and unpredictable.

Establishing a clear daily schedule, including consistent bedtimes, mealtimes, and homework routines, can significantly reduce anxiety and improve overall well-being. This structured environment offers a sense of stability, a stark contrast to the unpredictable nature of life with an abusive parent. Incorporate activities that your child enjoys, creating opportunities for fun and relaxation. This balance between structure and enjoyment fosters a sense of normalcy and promotes emotional well-being.

Open communication is vital, but it should be age- appropriate and sensitive. Avoid pressuring your child to talk about the trauma before they're ready. Instead, create an environment where they feel comfortable expressing their feelings without judgment or pressure. Let them know that it's safe to talk about anything that's bothering them, and that you're there to listen without interruption or judgment. Even simple acts of listening and validating their feelings – acknowledging the validity of their emotions – can have a profound impact. You can use open-ended questions to encourage them to share their thoughts and feelings, such as

"How are you feeling today?" or "What was the best part of your day?"

Encourage healthy self-expression through various creative outlets. Art therapy, music, dance, or writing can provide a non-threatening way for children to process their emotions. These activities allow them to express themselves without the pressure of verbal communication, providing a safe space for emotional release. Moreover, it provides them with a sense of accomplishment and boosts their self-esteem.

Participation in extracurricular activities, such as sports or clubs, can also be incredibly beneficial. These activities provide opportunities for socialization, positive peer interactions, and a sense of belonging, counteracting the isolation that often accompanies trauma.

Building a strong support system is crucial, extending beyond immediate family. Connect with support groups specifically designed for children who have experienced parental abuse or domestic violence. These groups provide a safe and supportive environment where children can share their experiences with others who understand and validate their feelings. The shared experience fosters a sense of community and reduces feelings of isolation and shame.

Participation in these groups can also help build their self- esteem and resilience. Furthermore, connecting with other parents navigating similar situations can provide invaluable support and practical advice, combating the sense of isolation often experienced by those who have escaped abuse.

Remember that healing from trauma is not a linear process. There will be ups and downs, good days and bad days. Be patient, understanding, and supportive throughout the journey. Celebrate their progress and offer comfort during setbacks. Positive reinforcement and praise for their efforts

are essential to encourage self-confidence and build their resilience. Avoid using harsh disciplinary measures or punishment, particularly if their behavior reflects their trauma. Instead, focus on guiding them toward healthier coping mechanisms, working with their therapist to develop effective strategies.

Educate yourself about childhood trauma and its impact. The more you understand about the effects of abuse on children, the better equipped you'll be to support their healing. Read books, articles, and attend workshops focused on trauma- informed care for children. Understanding the complexities of trauma will help you respond appropriately to your child's needs and behaviors. This knowledge base will also strengthen your communication with their therapist, allowing you to work collaboratively to support your child's healing process.

Finally, take care of yourself. Supporting a child through trauma is emotionally draining. Prioritize self-care, ensuring you have the support you need to manage your own stress and emotions. Regularly engage in activities that promote your well-being, whether it's exercise, meditation, spending time in nature, or connecting with supportive friends and family. Remembering to care for yourself ensures you have the emotional resources necessary to support your child's healing journey. This self-care is not selfish; it's essential for your own well-being and ultimately strengthens your ability to support your child. The journey to healing from trauma is a marathon, not a sprint, and nurturing yourself allows you to endure and continue supporting your child's journey. This long-term commitment to healing, both yours and your child's, will cultivate a strong foundation for a healthier and happier future.

Accessing Resources for Children and Families

Accessing the right resources is crucial in navigating the aftermath of abuse. The journey to healing is often long and complex, and having a strong support system is paramount. For children, who are particularly vulnerable, access to specialized care and support is not merely beneficial—it's essential. This section focuses on identifying and accessing these vital resources for both children and their families.

The first, and often most immediate, need is safe shelter. Domestic violence shelters offer temporary refuge for families fleeing abusive situations. These shelters provide more than just a roof over their heads; they offer a safe space, counseling services, and assistance with essential needs like food and clothing. The National Domestic Violence Hotline website (thehotline.org) is an excellent starting point to locate shelters in your area. Many shelters offer specialized programs for children, including play therapy, art therapy, and educational resources to help them process their experiences. Remember that the location of the shelter should be kept confidential to ensure the safety and security of the family. It is imperative to inform the shelter of any potential threats or the abuser's knowledge of your location.

Beyond emergency shelter, counseling services are a cornerstone of recovery. Finding a therapist specializing in trauma-informed care is critical. Trauma-informed therapy recognizes the profound impact of trauma on a person's mind and body and utilizes approaches that minimize re- traumatization. For children, play therapy is often a highly effective method. It uses play as a medium for expression and exploration, allowing children to communicate their

emotions in a safe and non-threatening way. Older children and adolescents may benefit from trauma-focused cognitive behavioral therapy (TF-CBT), which is designed to help them understand and manage their trauma responses. The Childhelp USA National Child Abuse Hotline (1-800-422- 4453) can provide referrals to qualified therapists in your area. Your primary care physician can also make referrals, and many insurance providers offer directories of mental health professionals within your network.

Support groups offer a powerful sense of community and shared understanding. Connecting with other families who have navigated similar experiences can be incredibly validating and empowering. The shared experience reduces the feelings of isolation and shame that often accompany abuse. These groups allow for the exchange of practical advice, coping strategies, and emotional support.

Organizations such as the National Coalition Against Domestic Violence (ncadv.org) and Childhelp USA can offer information about local support groups and other community resources. Remember to research groups thoroughly to ensure they are trauma-informed and utilize appropriate practices for working with children and families who have experienced abuse.

Legal resources are vital for securing protection and ensuring safety. Legal aid organizations and attorneys specializing in family law and domestic violence can provide invaluable assistance in obtaining restraining orders, custody arrangements, and other legal protections. The National Network to End Domestic Violence (nnedv.org) provides information and referrals to legal professionals specializing in these areas. Many jurisdictions have specialized domestic violence courts designed to process cases efficiently and offer a safety-centered approach. Knowing your rights and

options can be empowering, and legal guidance ensures your family is safeguarded against future harm.

Financial assistance is often a critical need for families leaving abusive situations. Many organizations provide financial aid for housing, food, clothing, and other necessities. The Salvation Army, local churches, and charitable organizations frequently provide such assistance. Government assistance programs, such as Temporary Assistance for Needy Families (TANF) and the Supplemental Nutrition Assistance Program (SNAP), can also provide critical financial support. Eligibility requirements vary depending on your location and situation; contacting your local social services agency will help you navigate the application process.

Educational resources are paramount for both parents and children. Understanding the effects of trauma on children is crucial for supporting their healing. Numerous books, articles, and online resources are available, offering valuable insights into childhood trauma and its impact. Participating in workshops and educational programs offered by organizations specializing in trauma-informed care can enhance your understanding and equip you with the knowledge to effectively support your child's recovery. The knowledge you gain about childhood trauma will facilitate your communication with your child's therapist, allowing you to develop a collaborative approach to their healing.

Beyond professional resources, building a personal support network is crucial. Leaning on trusted friends, family members, and community members can provide vital emotional and practical support. Sharing your story with trusted individuals allows you to process your experiences and receive emotional validation. This personal network also offers valuable assistance with childcare, errands, and other

tasks, reducing stress and enabling you to focus on your healing and your child's. Remember that you are not alone in this journey; reaching out to your support network is a strength, not a sign of weakness.

Self-care is not a luxury but a necessity. Supporting a child through trauma can be emotionally draining, requiring parents to prioritize their own well-being. Engaging in activities that promote self-care, such as exercise, meditation, spending time in nature, or pursuing hobbies, can help manage stress and prevent burnout. Remember that you cannot pour from an empty cup; taking care of yourself ensures you have the emotional resources to support your child's healing process. This self-care is an investment in your family's well-being, ultimately strengthening your ability to support your child's journey toward healing.

Navigating the aftermath of abuse requires resilience, strength, and access to the right resources. The path to healing is a marathon, not a sprint. By understanding the available resources and proactively seeking assistance, you are taking a critical step toward rebuilding your lives and creating a safer, healthier future for you and your children. Remember that seeking help is a sign of strength, not weakness, and that healing is possible. With determination, support, and access to appropriate resources, you can escape the shadows of abuse and build a brighter future.

Rebuilding Family Relationships

Rebuilding trust after escaping abuse is a monumental task, especially within the family unit. The insidious nature of sociopathic manipulation often leaves deep wounds, impacting not only the primary victim but also children and other family members. The process requires patience, understanding, and a commitment from everyone involved to actively participate in healing. It's not a quick fix; it's a journey that demands consistent effort and a willingness to confront the lingering effects of the abuse.

One of the first hurdles is acknowledging the extent of the damage. The abuser often works tirelessly to isolate the family, creating a system of mistrust and control. Children, especially, may have witnessed abusive behaviors, internalized the abuser's manipulations, or even been directly victimized themselves. They may struggle to differentiate between reality and the distorted narrative presented by the abuser. Parents need to validate their children's experiences, acknowledging the trauma they've endured without judgment. Openly discussing the abuse, in age-appropriate terms, helps to break the cycle of silence and empowers children to reclaim their voices. This doesn't mean overloading them with graphic details, but rather ensuring they understand that what happened was wrong and that they are safe now.

Establishing clear and open communication is paramount. The family needs to create a safe space where everyone feels comfortable expressing their feelings, concerns, and anxieties without fear of judgment or reprisal. This requires active listening, empathy, and a willingness to understand each individual's perspective. It's crucial to create a culture

of respect where everyone's voice is valued, regardless of age or prior experiences. Family meetings, facilitated by a therapist or counselor specializing in trauma recovery, can provide a structured framework for these conversations.

These meetings offer a neutral space where family members can safely express their emotions, work through conflicts, and establish new patterns of communication.

Forgiveness, while a complex and personal process, plays a crucial role in healing. It's essential to understand that forgiveness doesn't mean condoning the abuser's actions or minimizing the harm inflicted. Rather, it's about releasing the anger, resentment, and bitterness that can consume individuals and prevent them from moving forward.

Forgiveness is primarily for the benefit of the person forgiving, allowing them to reclaim their emotional well- being and release the burden of carrying the weight of the past. This process might involve seeking individual therapy to address personal pain and anger before engaging in family-based forgiveness.

The process of rebuilding trust is gradual and iterative. It involves consistent actions that demonstrate commitment to creating a safe and healthy family dynamic. This may include establishing new routines, creating clear boundaries, and engaging in activities that promote connection and healing. Family therapy can be instrumental in this process, helping family members to learn effective communication skills, build healthy relationships, and develop coping mechanisms for dealing with the lingering effects of abuse. The therapist can provide guidance and support, helping the family to navigate difficult conversations and establish new patterns of interaction.

Children require specialized attention and support during this period. Their experiences may vary significantly depending

on their age and the nature of their exposure to the abuse. Some may exhibit behavioral problems, while others may withdraw or become excessively anxious. It's essential to ensure that children have access to age-appropriate therapeutic interventions that address their specific needs. Play therapy, art therapy, and trauma-focused cognitive behavioral therapy (TF-CBT) are all effective approaches for helping children process their trauma and develop healthy coping mechanisms.

Parental involvement is critical in supporting a child's healing. Parents need to understand the signs and symptoms of trauma in children and be able to provide consistent support and encouragement. This may involve adjusting parenting styles, establishing clear expectations, and providing consistent routines and structure. Maintaining a consistent disciplinary approach, free from anger and inconsistent punishment, can significantly enhance a child's sense of security and safety. It's important to work closely with the child's therapist to ensure a coordinated approach to their care and to understand the child's individual needs and emotional responses.

Re-establishing healthy boundaries is crucial. The abuser likely blurred or completely eliminated boundaries, creating an environment of control and manipulation. The family needs to establish clear and consistent boundaries to protect themselves from future harm. These boundaries might involve physical boundaries, such as limiting contact with the abuser, or emotional boundaries, such as refusing to engage in arguments or tolerate manipulative behavior.

Openly discussing these boundaries and ensuring everyone understands and agrees to them is paramount. The family should create a consistent set of rules and expectations that apply to everyone, emphasizing mutual respect and consideration.

Building new rituals and traditions can help to create a sense of normalcy and stability within the family. Creating positive family experiences can help to counteract the negative memories and experiences associated with the abuse. This might involve family dinners, game nights, or outings to the park. These activities provide opportunities for positive interaction, creating memories that are associated with safety, love, and support. Engaging in shared activities that foster laughter, connection, and cooperation are instrumental in rebuilding a positive family dynamic.

Incorporating self-care practices for all family members is critical. The experience of abuse can be emotionally draining and exhausting, leading to burnout and decreased resilience. Establishing self-care routines, such as regular exercise, meditation, or pursuing hobbies, can help to reduce stress and increase emotional well-being. Parents need to model healthy self-care behaviors for their children, demonstrating that taking care of oneself is not selfish, but essential for effective parenting and family well-being. Encouraging and supporting each other's self-care practices fosters a strong and supportive family unit.

The path to rebuilding healthy family relationships after escaping abuse is a challenging but rewarding journey. It demands patience, understanding, and a unwavering commitment from every family member. Seeking professional help from a therapist specializing in trauma recovery is crucial for navigating this complex process and ensuring that all members of the family receive the support they need. By actively working together, communicating openly, and establishing healthy boundaries, families can heal from the past and build a brighter, safer future.

Remember that healing is possible, and the journey toward rebuilding strong, healthy relationships is a testament to the

resilience and strength of the family unit. The investment in therapy and family sessions will pay dividends in the long run, ensuring a foundation built on trust, respect, and genuine connection. The process requires time, understanding, and a consistent commitment to healing, but the result is a family strengthened by overcoming adversity. This is a testament to the family's resilience and a powerful example of human capacity for recovery and growth.

Understanding Legal Definitions of Abuse

Understanding the legal definitions of abuse is crucial for victims seeking protection and justice. The insidious nature of sociopathic abuse often makes it difficult to articulate the harm inflicted, especially when the abuser skillfully manipulates and gaslights their victim. Legal definitions provide a framework for understanding the severity of the abuse and the available legal recourse. It's important to remember that legal definitions vary across jurisdictions, so it's crucial to consult with a legal professional familiar with the specific laws in your area.

Physical abuse, the most readily identifiable form of abuse, involves any intentional act causing physical harm or injury. This ranges from slapping and hitting to more severe forms of violence resulting in serious bodily injury or even death. Bruises, cuts, broken bones, and other physical manifestations of violence are clear indicators. However, the subtle nature of some forms of physical abuse makes it harder to detect. For example, withholding necessary medication from a dependent person could also be considered physical abuse, as could controlling access to food or medical care. The intent to cause harm is a key element of the legal definition, and proving intent can sometimes be challenging. Documentation, such as photographs of injuries, medical records, and witness testimonies, becomes crucial evidence.

Emotional abuse, though less visible than physical abuse, is equally devastating. It involves a pattern of behavior designed to control, manipulate, and degrade a person's emotional well-being. Gaslighting, a common tactic employed by sociopaths, is a form of emotional abuse where

the abuser systematically distorts reality, making the victim question their own sanity and perception of events. Isolation from friends and family, constant criticism and belittling, threats and intimidation, and the manipulation of guilt and shame are all hallmarks of emotional abuse. Legally proving emotional abuse can be complex. It often requires building a case based on a pattern of behavior, corroborated by documentation like emails, text messages, and diary entries illustrating the abuser's manipulative tactics and the victim's emotional distress. Witness testimonies from family and friends who observed the abuser's behavior can also be vital.

Financial abuse involves the exploitation of a person's financial resources. This can manifest in various ways, from subtly controlling access to bank accounts and credit cards to outright theft and fraud. Forcing a victim to sign over assets, preventing them from working, controlling their spending, or using their money without their consent are all examples of financial abuse. The legal ramifications of financial abuse can be serious, involving charges such as theft, fraud, and embezzlement. Detailed financial records, bank statements, and legal documentation of any transactions are crucial for building a strong legal case. Understanding the financial aspects of the abuse and how the abuser manipulated the victim's resources is essential for restitution and preventing future financial exploitation.

Sexual abuse, a profound violation of personal boundaries, encompasses any form of non-consensual sexual contact.

This includes rape, sexual assault, sexual harassment, and any other act of a sexual nature imposed without consent. The legal definition of consent is crucial here, emphasizing that consent must be freely given, informed, and ongoing. Any form of coercion, intimidation, or manipulation to obtain sexual compliance is considered non-consensual and falls under the definition of sexual abuse. Gathering

evidence in cases of sexual abuse often requires a sensitive and thorough approach. Medical examinations, forensic evidence, and witness testimonies can all be vital in building a case. The psychological impact of sexual abuse is significant, and legal support can provide a path toward justice and healing.

Stalking, a form of abuse that frequently overlaps with other types, involves repeated harassment and unwanted pursuit that creates a reasonable fear of harm or death. This can manifest in various ways, from sending unwanted messages and emails to following the victim's movements, making threatening phone calls, or showing up unexpectedly at their home or workplace. The key element of stalking is the creation of fear and intimidation, regardless of the specific actions taken. The use of technology for stalking, such as tracking a victim's location through GPS or monitoring their online activity, adds another layer of complexity.

Documentation of the stalking behaviors, including dates, times, and specifics of each incident, is crucial for legal action. This could involve saving messages, emails, texts, and maintaining a detailed log of incidents.

Neglect, often overlooked as a form of abuse, involves the failure to provide necessary care or support to someone dependent on you. This can range from neglecting a child's basic needs like food, clothing, and shelter, to neglecting the care of an elderly parent or other vulnerable individual. The legal definitions of neglect often specify a duty of care and a failure to fulfill that duty, resulting in harm or potential harm to the victim. Evidence of neglect might include a lack of proper medical care, insufficient food, unsanitary living conditions, or a general failure to meet the needs of the dependent individual. Documentation of this failure to provide care, along with evidence of the resulting harm, is crucial for legal recourse.

Cyber abuse, a relatively new form of abuse enabled by technology, utilizes digital platforms to inflict harm. This can include cyberstalking, online harassment, the dissemination of intimate images without consent (revenge porn), or online threats and intimidation. The legal framework for cyber abuse is still evolving, but many jurisdictions recognize the severity of the harm inflicted and are enacting laws to protect victims. Preserving evidence of cyber abuse, such as screenshots of harassing messages, emails, and social media posts, is critical. Knowing the platforms where the abuse occurred and understanding the relevant terms of service is important for legal action.

Understanding the specific legal definitions of these various forms of abuse is only the first step. Seeking legal counsel is essential to navigate the complexities of the legal system and to ensure that victims' rights are protected. Legal professionals can help victims gather evidence, file for restraining orders, pursue criminal charges against abusers, and seek compensation for damages incurred. The process can be long and challenging, but having legal support is invaluable in achieving justice and securing a safe future.

Remember, you are not alone, and seeking help is a sign of strength, not weakness. The legal system offers avenues for protection and recourse, but navigating this system often requires professional assistance. The trauma of abuse can significantly impair one's ability to advocate effectively for themselves, underscoring the importance of seeking professional legal support.

Gathering Evidence and Documentation

Gathering and preserving evidence is paramount in cases of abuse, especially when dealing with a sociopath whose manipulative tactics often aim to discredit or undermine the victim's account. The goal is not just to remember what happened, but to create a comprehensive, verifiable record that stands up in a court of law or other legal setting. This process requires meticulous attention to detail and a systematic approach. The more organized and thorough your documentation, the stronger your case will be.

Start by creating a dedicated journal or digital document. This will be your central repository for recording every instance of abuse, no matter how seemingly insignificant it may appear at the time. Include dates, times, locations, and detailed descriptions of each incident. If possible, note the presence of any witnesses. The level of detail is crucial. For example, instead of simply writing "He yelled at me," write, "On July 15th, at 8:00 PM in the kitchen, he yelled at me for burning dinner. He used foul language, calling me incompetent and useless. His voice was loud enough that our neighbor, Mrs. Smith (apartment 3B), could likely hear it."

Beyond your journal, meticulously preserve any evidence that supports your claims. This includes:

Photographs and Videos: If you have sustained any physical injuries, photograph them immediately. Take multiple pictures from different angles, documenting the extent of the bruising, cuts, or other marks. If possible, take pictures before the injuries heal to capture their full extent. Similarly, if there is evidence of property damage caused by the abuser, document it with photographs. Video recordings,

if safely obtained, can be powerful evidence of abusive behavior. Remember to be mindful of your safety when capturing such evidence.

Text Messages, Emails, and Social Media Posts: Save every text message, email, and social media post that contains evidence of abusive behavior. Screenshot conversations and download messages to preserve them even if deleted by the abuser. Many messaging platforms offer ways to download conversation histories. Be aware that the content of such messages can be a double-edged sword, so it's best to carefully review everything and ensure that you are only submitting relevant and pertinent information to your legal team.

Voicemails: If you have received abusive voicemails, save them. Most phones allow you to save voicemails directly, often storing them digitally in an accessible format.

Financial Records: Keep meticulous records of all financial transactions, especially those showing unusual activity or instances of financial control or manipulation. Gather bank statements, credit card statements, loan documents, and any other financial records that demonstrate the abuser's control over your finances. Note any instances where funds were withheld, misused, or improperly accessed.

Medical Records: If you've sought medical attention due to physical or emotional distress caused by the abuse, obtain copies of your medical records. These records will provide documentation of your injuries and the treatment you received, corroborating your claims of physical or emotional harm.

Witness Testimony: Identify anyone who witnessed incidents of abuse. Collect contact information and written

statements from those individuals willing to testify on your behalf. The more witnesses who can corroborate your account, the stronger your case will become. Consider speaking to these witnesses with your lawyer present.

Police Reports: If you have filed any police reports, keep copies of those reports as part of your evidence. Maintain a detailed record of every interaction with law enforcement, including dates, times, and the names of the officers involved.

Security Camera Footage: If there is security camera footage showing incidents of abuse or the abuser's behavior, request copies of this footage, if possible. This footage can act as an unbiased third-party account. Ensure you have permission to access and use the footage.

Legal Documents: Keep all legal documents relating to your case in a secure and organized manner. This includes restraining orders, protection orders, court documents, and correspondence with your attorney.

Diary Entries or Personal Writings: If you have kept a diary or journal where you documented your experiences, this can serve as a valuable source of evidence. Note that even if you did not write about events in a diary, recalling events from memory and recording them into your evidence journal can still act as helpful supplementary evidence.

Remember that consistency is key.

Remember, consistency is crucial throughout the evidence- gathering process. Try to maintain a chronological order, and ensure that all your documentation is accurate and factual.

Avoid speculation or emotional outbursts in your written records. Focus on presenting a clear, objective account of what occurred. Keep all your collected evidence in a secure

location, ideally inaccessible to the abuser. Consider using a cloud-based storage system with strong password protection, or a safety deposit box.

Consider consulting with a forensic psychologist or trauma specialist. These professionals can help you articulate the impact of the abuse on your mental and emotional well- being, which can be crucial for legal proceedings. They can provide professional corroboration for the impact of the abuse.

The legal process can be daunting, but having a strong evidentiary foundation increases your chances of a positive outcome. Remember to be patient, persistent, and prioritize your safety throughout this process. It is essential to understand that gathering evidence might take time and effort, but it is an invaluable investment in your safety and well-being. The goal is to build a comprehensive and compelling narrative that leaves no room for doubt regarding the reality of the abuse and its impact. This robust record will serve as a powerful testament to your experience and a crucial tool in seeking justice and reclaiming your life. Do not hesitate to seek help from professionals – lawyers, therapists, and support groups – who can guide you through this challenging process. Your safety and well-being are paramount.

Seeking Legal Representation and Advice

Navigating the legal system after experiencing abuse by a sociopath can feel overwhelming, but securing legal representation is a crucial step towards protecting yourself and securing your future. Finding the right lawyer is paramount, as their expertise and understanding of sociopathic manipulation will significantly impact the outcome of any legal proceedings. Don't underestimate the importance of this choice; the wrong lawyer could inadvertently undermine your case and potentially expose you to further harm.

First, prioritize finding a lawyer specializing in domestic violence or family law cases involving abuse. These lawyers possess a deep understanding of the dynamics of abusive relationships, including the manipulative tactics often employed by sociopaths. Their experience equips them to effectively navigate the complexities of your situation, anticipating the abuser's strategies and countering them effectively. General practice lawyers, while well-intentioned, may lack the specialized knowledge needed to handle the nuances of abuse cases. This specialized knowledge is critical; it's not simply a matter of presenting evidence; it's about presenting that evidence in a way that resonates with the court and counters the manipulative narratives often employed by abusers.

Your network can be a valuable resource in your search. Start by reaching out to trusted friends, family members, therapists, support groups, or domestic violence shelters. These individuals may have personal recommendations or know of lawyers with a proven track record of success in similar cases. Don't hesitate to ask for referrals; their insights

can save you valuable time and prevent you from inadvertently choosing an unqualified or unsuitable representative. Remember, word-of-mouth recommendations often offer a more realistic and reliable assessment of a lawyer's capabilities than online reviews alone.

Online directories and legal aid organizations can also assist in your search. Many bar associations maintain online directories of lawyers, often categorized by area of specialization. This allows you to filter your search to find lawyers specializing in domestic violence or family law in your geographic area. Similarly, legal aid organizations often provide referrals to attorneys who offer pro bono or reduced- fee services to individuals who cannot afford legal representation. Remember to thoroughly vet any lawyer you find through online resources, checking their credentials and reviews before contacting them. Always verify their license and any disciplinary actions taken against them.

Once you have a list of potential lawyers, schedule initial consultations. Most lawyers offer free or low-cost initial consultations, providing you with an opportunity to assess their suitability. During these consultations, pay close attention to the lawyer's demeanor, listening skills, and understanding of your situation. Do they actively listen to your experiences, validate your feelings, and demonstrate empathy? Or do they minimize your concerns or seem dismissive of the abuse you have endured? The attorney- client relationship is built on trust and mutual respect; if you don't feel comfortable with the lawyer, it's crucial to continue your search.

Ask prospective lawyers about their experience handling cases similar to yours. Inquire about their success rate in such cases and their strategies for addressing the specific challenges posed by sociopathic manipulators.

Understanding their approach to evidence presentation, witness examination, and cross-examination is crucial. Don't hesitate to ask detailed questions about their fee structure, payment plans, and the expected timeline of your case.

Transparency and clear communication are essential in building a productive attorney-client relationship.

Consider consulting with multiple lawyers before making a decision. This comparative approach allows you to evaluate different legal strategies, fee structures, and personality styles to find the best fit for your needs and preferences.

Your comfort level with the lawyer is critical; the legal process can be long and stressful, and having a lawyer you trust and feel comfortable with is vital for your emotional well-being.

Remember that obtaining legal representation is not just about winning a court case; it's about protecting your safety and well-being during and after the legal proceedings. A skilled lawyer can help you secure restraining orders, protection orders, or other legal protections against your abuser. They can also assist with custody disputes, property division, or other legal matters arising from the abusive relationship. Moreover, having a lawyer on your side provides a crucial layer of support and guidance during what can be an emotionally draining and complex process. They will act as your advocate, navigating the legal system on your behalf and ensuring that your rights are protected.

Beyond legal representation, consider exploring resources offered by local domestic violence shelters or advocacy groups. These organizations often provide legal advocacy services, assisting survivors in navigating the legal system and connecting them with pro bono attorneys or reduced-fee legal services. Their support extends beyond legal aid, often encompassing counseling, support groups, and safe housing options. Their staff typically has extensive experience working with survivors of abuse, providing emotional support and practical assistance throughout the challenging recovery process.

If you're struggling to afford legal representation, explore options such as legal aid societies, pro bono programs offered by bar associations, or government-funded assistance programs. These resources can provide access to legal services at reduced cost or completely free of charge. Don't let financial constraints prevent you from seeking the legal protection and support you deserve. Your safety and well- being should always be the priority.

The legal process is often complex and protracted. Be prepared for delays, setbacks, and potential emotional challenges. Your lawyer should be a reliable source of information and support throughout this process. Maintain open communication with your lawyer, promptly responding to requests for information and keeping them updated on any relevant developments. Remember that patience and persistence are crucial; the legal system may move slowly, but your perseverance will ultimately contribute to a more positive outcome.

Seeking legal representation is a significant step in reclaiming your life after experiençing abuse. It provides crucial protection, empowers you to assert your rights, and establishes a foundation for rebuilding your life free from fear and intimidation. Remember that you deserve support and justice, and finding the right legal counsel is a critical step towards achieving both. The road ahead may be challenging, but with the right support, you can navigate this process and emerge stronger and safer. Remember, your safety and well-being are paramount, and seeking legal counsel is a vital step in securing them.

Navigating Legal Procedures and Processes

The emotional toll of escaping an abusive relationship often overshadows the practical steps needed to secure your safety and future. While finding a skilled lawyer is crucial, the legal process itself presents a new set of challenges.

Understanding these procedures, from obtaining protective orders to navigating divorce and custody battles, is vital for reclaiming your life. This understanding empowers you to navigate the complexities of the legal system with greater confidence and clarity.

One of the most immediate concerns for many survivors is securing a restraining order or protection order. These legal instruments aim to create a physical barrier between you and your abuser, preventing further contact and ensuring your safety. The process for obtaining a restraining order varies by jurisdiction, but typically involves submitting a petition to a court detailing the abuse you've experienced. This petition will include specific instances of abuse, dates, locations, and any evidence you have supporting your claims. This evidence could include photos, texts, emails, medical records documenting injuries, police reports, and witness statements. The court will then review your petition and, if they find sufficient evidence, issue a temporary restraining order. This order will be served on the abuser, and a hearing will be scheduled to determine whether a permanent order should be granted. At this hearing, you'll have the opportunity to present your case before a judge. The abuser may also present their case and attempt to challenge the claims.

Preparing for this hearing requires careful organization and meticulous record-keeping. Document everything – dates, times, locations, descriptions of events, any witnesses, and

the impact of the abuse on you. Even seemingly insignificant details can become critical pieces of evidence when presented in a coherent and compelling narrative. A skilled lawyer can help you gather and organize this evidence, ensuring it's presented in the most effective manner. They will also advise you on what to expect during the hearing and coach you on how to testify clearly and convincingly, even under pressure. Remember, the judge's decision is based on the evidence presented; being thoroughly prepared is crucial for a successful outcome.

Beyond restraining orders, many survivors face the complex legal issues surrounding divorce and custody arrangements. If you're married to your abuser, the divorce process can be particularly challenging, fraught with emotional distress and legal complexities. Navigating property division, spousal support, and child custody agreements requires a deep understanding of family law and the ability to effectively present your case to the court. The emotional manipulation you've experienced from a sociopath will likely be mirrored in the courtroom as your abuser employs similar tactics to influence the outcome. Therefore, having legal counsel deeply familiar with these manipulative strategies is paramount.

Child custody arrangements, in particular, are high-stakes matters, often deeply entwined with the safety and well- being of the children involved. Judges prioritize the child's best interests, considering factors such as each parent's ability to provide a safe, stable, and nurturing environment. Evidence of abuse, whether physical, emotional, or financial, heavily influences the court's decision-making process. Your lawyer will meticulously document the instances of abuse, their effect on your children, and the potential risks associated with the abuser having access to them. They will utilize psychological evaluations, school records, and

witness statements to demonstrate the dangers of leaving the children in the abuser's custody. They will also help you develop a comprehensive parenting plan that prioritizes the children's safety, well-being, and stability.

Financial issues frequently arise during the legal proceedings. Sociopaths often exert significant control over finances within the relationship, leaving victims financially vulnerable upon separation. This can include hiding assets, controlling bank accounts, and manipulating financial records. Your lawyer will work to uncover any hidden assets, ensuring a fair and equitable division of marital property.

They will also guide you through the process of obtaining spousal support, addressing any financial inequalities created by the abuse. These financial aspects can be a protracted part of the legal process and require patience and meticulous documentation.

Navigating these legal procedures requires resilience and strength. The process can be lengthy, stressful, and emotionally demanding. However, remember that you are not alone. Support groups, therapists, and advocates can provide invaluable emotional support and guidance throughout this difficult time. They can help you process the trauma you've experienced, manage stress, and maintain hope during the legal proceedings. Moreover, they can offer practical assistance, such as connecting you with additional resources or helping you navigate bureaucratic hurdles.

Furthermore, understanding your rights is crucial. Familiarize yourself with your state's laws regarding domestic violence, restraining orders, divorce, and child custody. While a lawyer will handle the legal aspects, having a basic understanding of the legal framework enhances your ability to participate effectively in the process and advocate for your own needs and those of your children. The

information available online and through legal aid organizations can offer a starting point for this education.

The legal process after escaping abuse from a sociopath can be a long and arduous journey. However, by securing the right legal representation and understanding the procedures involved, you can significantly increase your chances of securing your safety and building a future free from fear and intimidation. Remember, seeking legal assistance is a critical step towards reclaiming your life and empowering yourself to move forward. Your safety, well-being, and the well-being of your children are paramount, and taking proactive legal steps is a powerful act of self-preservation. Don't underestimate the importance of this process; it is a crucial foundation for rebuilding your life and ensuring your future is safe and secure. The legal system, although imperfect, offers a means to protect yourself and to hold your abuser accountable. Taking these steps demonstrates your strength and your commitment to a life free from abuse.

Understanding Your Rights and Legal Protections

Understanding your rights is the first step towards reclaiming your power and securing your future after escaping an abusive relationship with a sociopath. The legal system, while often complex and frustrating, offers crucial protections and avenues for redress. This section outlines some of the key legal remedies and support systems available to survivors of abuse. Remember, the specifics of these laws and procedures vary by jurisdiction (state and even county), so it's vital to seek legal counsel in your specific area. This information is for educational purposes and not a substitute for professional legal advice.

One crucial area is the protection afforded by restraining orders, also known as protection orders or civil protection orders. These are court orders that legally prohibit an abuser from contacting you, coming near your home or workplace, or engaging in other specified behaviors. To obtain a restraining order, you'll generally need to file a petition with the court detailing the abuse you've suffered. This documentation is critical; meticulous record-keeping is your most powerful weapon. Keep a detailed journal, save all communications (texts, emails, voicemails), and collect any physical evidence of abuse, such as photographs of injuries or damaged property. If possible, obtain witness statements from friends, family, neighbors, or coworkers who have witnessed the abuse. Police reports, medical records, and therapy notes can also be invaluable evidence.

The petition process often involves detailing specific instances of abuse, providing dates, times, locations, and a description of the events. The clearer and more comprehensive your documentation, the stronger your case

will be. This is where the manipulative tactics of a sociopath become particularly challenging. They are masters of gaslighting and distortion, and they may attempt to discredit your claims, even presenting themselves as the victim.

Therefore, it is vital to present your evidence in a clear, organized, and unemotional manner, focusing solely on the facts. Your lawyer will be instrumental in guiding you through this process, helping you present a strong case to the court.

Once a petition is filed, the court usually issues a temporary restraining order, immediately barring the abuser from contact. A hearing is then scheduled to determine whether to grant a permanent restraining order. This hearing requires preparation. You might be required to testify, and the abuser may also present their version of events. Therefore, practice your testimony beforehand with your lawyer. Anticipate potential lines of questioning and rehearse your responses, focusing on factual accuracy and emotional composure.

Remember, the judge's decision is based on the evidence presented, not on emotional displays. Your calm, collected presentation strengthens your credibility. Moreover, during this time, consider seeking therapy to manage the stress and emotional turmoil of the legal proceedings, which can be emotionally taxing.

Beyond restraining orders, the legal process can extend to divorce proceedings if you were married to the abuser.

Divorce involving a sociopath presents unique complexities, often fueled by their manipulative tactics. They might attempt to control the process, hide assets, or use the children as pawns. Therefore, a strong legal team that understands the manipulative characteristics of sociopaths is crucial. Your lawyer will help navigate the intricacies of property division, spousal support, and child custody,

ensuring your rights are protected and your financial security is addressed.

The division of marital assets is a critical component of divorce proceedings. Sociopaths often exhibit financial manipulation, hiding assets, making fraudulent transactions, or using joint accounts to their advantage. Your lawyer will work to uncover any hidden assets, ensuring a fair and equitable division of marital property. This may involve financial investigations and forensic accounting. You will need to present comprehensive financial documents to the court, detailing your assets, debts, and income.

Child custody arrangements present another layer of complexity. The court's primary concern is always the child's best interests, and evidence of abuse—physical, emotional, or financial—heavily influences the judge's decision. Your lawyer will meticulously document the abuse, its impact on your children, and the potential risks of the abuser having access to them. This can include psychological evaluations of both parents and the children, school records demonstrating the children's emotional well-being, and witness statements from family, friends, or teachers. A comprehensive parenting plan that prioritizes the children's safety and stability is essential. The aim is not only to keep your children safe from harm but to minimize the disruption of their lives during this difficult period. You may consider having a neutral third-party professional such as a child psychologist prepare a report that is then presented to the court.

The financial aspects of separation are often intertwined with the emotional manipulation. Sociopaths might control the family finances, leaving the victim financially vulnerable after separation. Your lawyer will assist you in obtaining spousal support (alimony) to address any financial disparities

created by the abuse. They will help you navigate the complexities of obtaining any financial assistance you are legally entitled to and to safeguard your financial well-being. This may involve seeking additional legal expertise in areas of financial fraud, depending on the level of financial manipulation the sociopath exerted during the relationship.

Throughout these legal proceedings, remember that you are not alone. Support systems are critical. Support groups specifically for survivors of abuse can provide a sense of community and shared experience. They offer a safe space to share your feelings and experiences, and you can gain support and encouragement from others who understand what you're going through. Moreover, therapy can provide invaluable emotional support, helping you process the trauma and cope with the stress of the legal process. Therapy can also aid in rebuilding your self-esteem and reclaiming your sense of self after the manipulative tactics of your abuser have eroded your sense of worth.

Legal aid organizations can provide legal assistance and information to those who cannot afford a private attorney. These organizations offer free or low-cost legal services and can advocate for your rights in court. They may assist in preparing your legal documents, represent you in court, and provide crucial information about your rights. It's worth researching legal aid services in your local area to see what kind of support they can offer.

Remember, the legal process can be lengthy, complex, and emotionally challenging. It requires patience, resilience, and a strong support system. However, understanding your rights and accessing available legal resources is essential in protecting yourself and securing a safe future for yourself and your children. The legal system provides a framework for justice and a path towards healing and rebuilding your

life, free from fear and control. Don't hesitate to seek the support you need and remember that your safety and well- being are paramount. You deserve to live a life free from abuse.

Protecting Your Online Privacy and Security

Reclaiming your digital life after escaping abuse requires a proactive approach to online privacy and security. Your abuser, especially if they are a sociopath, may have had extensive access to your online accounts, devices, and personal information. This access could range from knowing your passwords and login details to having installed spyware or monitoring software on your devices. Securing your digital presence is a critical step in establishing a safe and independent life. It's not just about preventing further harassment; it's about regaining control over your personal information and rebuilding your sense of privacy.

The first step is a thorough audit of your online accounts. Start by listing every online account you can think of: email accounts (personal and work), social media platforms (Facebook, Instagram, Twitter, TikTok, LinkedIn, etc.), online banking portals, shopping accounts (Amazon, eBay, etc.), subscription services (Netflix, Spotify, etc.), cloud storage accounts (Google Drive, Dropbox, iCloud, etc.), and any other online services you use regularly. This process can be overwhelming, but it's crucial to identify every potential point of vulnerability. Don't be afraid to reach out to a trusted friend or family member for help with this process.

They can assist in identifying accounts you might have overlooked or forgotten.

Once you have a comprehensive list, it's time to begin securing each account individually. The most crucial element is changing your passwords. Don't simply change them to a slightly modified version of your old passwords. This is easily guessed by someone familiar with your past practices. Instead, create strong, unique passwords for each account.

This means using a combination of uppercase and lowercase letters, numbers, and symbols. Aim for passwords that are at least 12 characters long, or even longer if possible. Avoid using personal information like your birthday, pet's name, or address in your passwords. If this feels overwhelming, consider using a reputable password manager. Password managers generate strong, unique passwords and securely store them for you, eliminating the need to remember them all.

Beyond password complexity, consider the strength of your security questions. Many online services use security questions as a backup method for password recovery. These questions often seem straightforward, such as "What is your mother's maiden name?" However, a sociopath might know the answer. Instead, choose security questions with less common answers. For example, "What was the name of your first teacher?", "What was the title of your favorite childhood book?", or "What is your favorite type of tree?". The more obscure the answer, the harder it will be for someone to guess. If possible, use different answers for each account.

Next, enable two-factor authentication (2FA) wherever possible. 2FA adds an extra layer of security by requiring a second form of verification beyond your password, such as a code sent to your phone via text message or a notification from an authenticator app. Even if someone gains access to your password, they will still need your phone to log in. This significantly reduces the risk of unauthorized access.

Activating 2FA should be a top priority for all accounts that contain sensitive information, such as your banking details or email accounts. Check each account individually to ensure 2FA is activated; don't assume it's enabled by default.

Review your privacy settings on all social media and online platforms. Social media can be a breeding ground for

harassment and stalking, and careful management of your privacy settings can significantly reduce your vulnerability. Limit the visibility of your posts and information to only your close friends and family. Be mindful of the information you share online, particularly details that could be used to identify your location or personal habits. Avoid posting real- time location updates or details about your daily routines.

Remember that anything you post online can be used against you, so exercise caution and discretion.

Consider reviewing your social media connections. Are there any accounts connected to your abuser, or individuals who might share information with them? Removing or blocking such accounts could prevent your abuser from monitoring your online activity. Remember that an abusive relationship often involves a manipulation of your support networks. The abuser may have fostered relationships with people in your circle, either for social support or to gain information.

Assessing who you have online connections with is an important step in rebuilding your support networks and establishing firm boundaries.

Update the software on all your devices regularly. Software updates often include security patches that address vulnerabilities exploited by hackers and malware. Neglecting to update your software can make your devices vulnerable to attacks. This includes your computer, phone, tablet, and any other smart devices you use. Enable automatic updates wherever possible to ensure your devices are always running the latest and most secure software versions.

Regularly review your device's security settings. Make sure you have strong security measures in place, such as password protection and screen locks. Consider using biometric authentication, such as fingerprint or facial recognition, for additional security. For your computer,

enable a firewall to help protect against unauthorized access. Install reputable antivirus and anti-malware software and keep it updated.

Be cautious about clicking links or downloading attachments from unknown or untrusted sources. These can often contain malware or phishing scams designed to steal your personal information. Never open emails or messages from senders you don't recognize. If you're unsure about the legitimacy of a link or email, contact the sender directly through a known channel to verify its authenticity. Be particularly wary of emails or messages that ask for personal information, such as your passwords or bank details; legitimate organizations will rarely request this information via email.

Consider using a virtual private network (VPN) for enhanced online privacy. A VPN encrypts your internet traffic and masks your IP address, making it harder for others to track your online activity. This is especially important if you are using public Wi-Fi networks, which are often less secure. A VPN adds a layer of protection against surveillance and helps to safeguard your online privacy.

If you suspect your devices have been compromised, take immediate action. Change all your passwords, run a full scan with your antivirus software, and consider seeking professional assistance from a cybersecurity expert to help you identify and remove any malware or spyware.

Remember that removing malicious software from your system often requires specialized expertise and tools.

Finally, it's important to remember that online security is an ongoing process. Regularly review your security practices and stay updated on the latest threats and best practices. The digital landscape is constantly evolving, and staying informed is critical to maintaining your online safety and

privacy. Consider seeking help from a technology professional or computer support service. They may assist in updating and securing your devices, providing more peace of mind and increasing your comfort level with technology.

These resources can also provide training and guidance on establishing secure online habits.

The journey to recovery after escaping an abusive relationship is multifaceted. Securing your online privacy and security is not just a technical task; it's a crucial step towards reclaiming your autonomy, rebuilding your confidence, and creating a safer future for yourself. This process, while demanding, is an investment in your independence and well-being, and a powerful affirmation of your right to privacy and security. It demonstrates a clear boundary: you are no longer under the control of your abuser.

Detecting and Preventing Technological Stalking

The digital realm, while offering connection and convenience, can also become a tool for insidious control and surveillance in abusive relationships. Sociopaths and stalkers are adept at exploiting technology to maintain their hold over victims, even after the physical relationship has ended. Detecting and preventing this technological stalking requires vigilance, proactive measures, and a deep understanding of how abusers leverage technology for their manipulative purposes.

One of the most common methods of technological stalking involves monitoring online activity. This might range from directly accessing a victim's accounts – through password theft, phishing scams, or spyware – to subtly tracking their online behavior. Abusers might use tracking apps disguised as seemingly harmless productivity tools, monitor browsing history through routers or shared devices, or even utilize keyloggers to record every keystroke. The aim is not just to observe, but to control and intimidate. They might use this information to exert pressure, threaten exposure of private details, or even manipulate social interactions. For example, an abuser might discover a victim's plans to meet with friends through social media posts or calendar entries, creating a situation where they feel compelled to stay home to avoid conflict.

Therefore, understanding how an abuser could be tracking your online activity is crucial for prevention. Are they unusually interested in your computer, phone, or other devices? Do they constantly ask about your online interactions? Do they seem to know details about your activities that you haven't explicitly shared? These subtle

indications can be a red flag, demanding immediate attention. If you have any suspicions, it's vital to document these instances. Keeping a detailed journal of these behaviors, noting the dates, times, and specific actions, can be valuable evidence if legal action becomes necessary.

Beyond direct access, abusers might exploit features within social media platforms and other online services to track their victim's movements and connections. This is where understanding and maximizing privacy settings becomes paramount. Many platforms offer a range of options for controlling who can see your posts, location data, and friend list. It's essential to review these settings on each platform, tightening restrictions to limit visibility to trusted individuals only. For example, on Facebook, you can adjust the audience for your posts, ensuring that only friends or a selected group of people can view your content. Similarly, you can disable location tagging on Instagram and Twitter to prevent your abuser from tracking your movements. Remember, even seemingly insignificant details, like checking in at a gym or restaurant, can be used by an abuser to triangulate your location and activities.

In addition to privacy settings, be hyper-aware of what information you are sharing online. Avoid posting real-time location updates, details about your daily routine, or anything that could potentially reveal personal information that might be useful to someone intent on tracking or harassing you. Over-sharing personal information is a common vulnerability exploited by stalkers. Think carefully before uploading photos that show your home or workplace, and be cautious about disclosing sensitive personal details, even to those you trust, as information can spread far beyond your intended audience.

Security measures are equally critical in preventing technological stalking. This begins with strong, unique passwords for every online account. Avoid easily guessed passwords or those based on personal information. Password managers are invaluable tools for generating and managing strong, unique passwords for each account. These services not only create complex passwords, but also store them securely, relieving you of the burden of remembering them.

Two-factor authentication (2FA) should be activated wherever possible. This adds an extra layer of security, requiring a secondary verification step beyond your password, usually a code sent to your phone or a notification from an authenticator app. Even if someone gains access to your password, 2FA greatly reduces the chance of them successfully logging into your account. Ensure this is enabled on all sensitive accounts, such as your banking, email, and social media profiles.

Regularly reviewing and updating the software on all your devices is crucial for minimizing vulnerabilities. Outdated software often contains security flaws that hackers can exploit to gain access to your devices and information.

Enable automatic updates where possible for computers, phones, and tablets to ensure the latest security patches are installed promptly.

Similarly, maintaining up-to-date antivirus and anti-malware software is non-negotiable. Regular scans can detect and remove malicious programs that may have been installed without your knowledge. Consider professional cybersecurity services to conduct thorough scans and check for spyware.

Be cautious about clicking on unknown links or downloading attachments from untrusted sources. These can

contain malware designed to steal your data or compromise your devices. If you are unsure about the authenticity of a link or email, do not click on it. Instead, contact the sender through a known, legitimate channel to verify the message.

Consider using a virtual private network (VPN). A VPN encrypts your internet traffic, masking your IP address and making it significantly harder for others to track your online activity. This is particularly important when using public Wi- Fi, which is generally less secure than your home network. A VPN adds an essential layer of privacy and security, especially if you suspect you might be monitored.

If you suspect your devices have been compromised, take immediate action. Change all your passwords, run a full virus scan, and consider seeking professional help from a cybersecurity expert to thoroughly investigate and remove any malicious software. This is a critical step in regaining control over your digital life and preventing further harassment.

Beyond technological solutions, fostering a strong support network is essential. Trusted friends, family members, or support groups can offer emotional support and practical advice during this difficult time. Sharing your experiences with these individuals can help you feel less isolated and more empowered. These people can also serve as an important check on your safety and well-being. If you notice significant changes in behavior or access to your online accounts, consulting your support network can offer reassurance and assistance.

Finally, remember that the fight for safety and security extends beyond the technological realm. The emotional and psychological impact of stalking is substantial, and seeking professional support is highly recommended. A therapist

specializing in trauma and abuse recovery can provide a safe space to process your experiences and develop coping mechanisms. They can assist you in navigating the complex emotional landscape associated with stalking and rebuilding your sense of safety and self-worth.

Escaping the shadow of technological stalking is a journey that requires ongoing vigilance and proactive measures. It involves not just mastering the technical aspects of online security, but also developing a profound understanding of the manipulative tactics employed by abusers and cultivating a strong support network for emotional resilience. This journey toward reclaiming your digital life is a testament to your strength and a powerful assertion of your right to live free from fear and manipulation. The process of securing your online safety is as much about regaining control of your life as it is about preventing further abuse. It's a critical step towards building a future free from the shadow of fear.

Using Technology to Enhance Safety and Security

The previous sections have highlighted the insidious ways technology can be weaponized by abusers to maintain control and inflict harm. However, technology also offers powerful tools for enhancing our safety and security.

Learning to harness these tools is crucial for reclaiming our digital lives and building a future free from fear. This section focuses on leveraging technology proactively to bolster our safety and security.

One of the most readily available and impactful tools is the use of emergency alert apps. These apps provide quick and easy access to emergency services, often with location sharing capabilities. Many offer features beyond simple dialing, such as sending pre-programmed messages to trusted contacts, detailing your location and the nature of the emergency. Some apps even integrate with wearable technology, allowing for silent alerts in situations where making a call might be dangerous. Familiarize yourself with the emergency services numbers in your region, and explore the variety of apps available, choosing one that best suits your needs and smartphone operating system. Consider having multiple backup options, given the possibility of technical failure or the abuser disabling access to specific apps.

Location-sharing apps can also be invaluable tools, especially if you are feeling unsafe or anticipating a potentially dangerous interaction. Many platforms allow you to share your real-time location with trusted contacts, providing them with ongoing awareness of your whereabouts. This can be particularly helpful if you are meeting someone new, traveling alone, or engaging in

activities that might put you at risk. Remember, it's vital to select your trusted contacts carefully. Only share your location with individuals you implicitly trust and who understand the context of your sharing. Regularly review your contact list and remove anyone who no longer needs or should not have access to this sensitive information.

Beyond real-time location sharing, consider using apps that offer personal safety monitoring features. These apps can range from simple panic buttons to more sophisticated systems that track your activity patterns and automatically alert emergency contacts if deviations occur. Some of these advanced systems can detect falls, sudden stops, or other signs of distress, providing an extra layer of protection for individuals living alone or who are at increased risk of assault. Research thoroughly before choosing a personal safety app; read reviews, compare features, and choose one that offers a combination of reliable functionality and user- friendly interface. Ensure that the app's privacy policy aligns with your comfort level regarding data collection and usage.

Beyond dedicated safety apps, we can leverage the built-in features of our smartphones and other devices. For example, using the "find my phone" functionality can be crucial in locating a stolen or lost device, which may contain sensitive information that an abuser could exploit. Understanding how to remotely wipe your device's data is also essential, preventing the abuser from accessing your personal information even after they gain possession of the device.

Familiarize yourself with these features well in advance of any potential crisis; panic often hinders effective problem- solving.

The use of strong, unique passwords is non-negotiable, as outlined previously, but extends to all aspects of your digital life. This includes not only your online accounts but also

your smart home devices, which often provide access to sensitive information, such as security camera footage or smart lock access codes. Avoid using the same password across multiple platforms; consider utilizing a password manager to generate and securely store complex, unique passwords for each account. Regularly audit your password usage, updating passwords at least every three months or after any suspected security breach.

Two-factor authentication (2FA) adds an essential layer of protection against unauthorized access. Enable it on all your sensitive accounts, including your email, bank accounts, social media, and any cloud storage services. 2FA significantly increases the difficulty for an abuser to gain access to your accounts, even if they have obtained your password. It can also help mitigate the risks associated with phishing scams, whereby abusers attempt to trick you into revealing your login credentials.

Cybersecurity hygiene goes beyond passwords and 2FA. Regularly update your operating systems, apps, and antivirus software. These updates often include crucial security patches that address vulnerabilities that hackers could exploit. Turn on automatic updates whenever possible, ensuring your devices and software are consistently up-to-date. Regularly back up your data to cloud storage or an external hard drive. This ensures you won't lose valuable information even if your device is lost, stolen, or compromised.

Consider using a virtual private network (VPN) to encrypt your internet traffic and mask your IP address. This is particularly important when using public Wi-Fi networks, which are often less secure than your home network. A VPN provides an additional layer of privacy, making it more difficult for someone to track your online activity. Be aware

that even VPNs are not foolproof, and they should be considered part of a comprehensive security strategy, rather than a standalone solution. Research reputable VPN providers before making a selection.

Be vigilant about phishing scams, malicious links, and unsolicited emails. Never click on links from unknown senders or open attachments from untrusted sources. If you suspect something is suspicious, contact the sender through a known, legitimate channel to verify the message's authenticity.

Finally, educating yourself about technology's role in abuse is a crucial part of staying safe. Regularly review security updates and articles, stay informed about new threats, and adapt your security strategies accordingly. Recognize that technological abuse is constantly evolving, and our efforts to stay safe must also evolve.

Beyond specific apps and technologies, the most powerful tool is a supportive network. Confide in trusted friends, family members, and support groups. Their awareness of your situation can provide emotional support and practical help. They can also serve as a second pair of eyes, helping to identify potential red flags or signs of technological abuse.

Open communication is crucial to maintaining safety and ensuring that your network can assist when needed.

Remember, seeking professional help from a therapist or counselor specializing in trauma and abuse recovery is essential for both emotional healing and for building long- term safety strategies. These professionals can provide valuable insights, guidance, and support in navigating the complexities of recovery and building a life free from fear.

Managing Social Media and Online Presence

The previous sections focused on practical technological tools to enhance safety. However, our online presence – our digital footprint – is another significant area requiring careful management. Social media and online platforms, while offering connection and community, can also become avenues for harassment, stalking, and continued abuse.

Learning to navigate these spaces safely and strategically is crucial for reclaiming your digital life and building a future free from fear.

One of the first steps is a thorough review of your current social media accounts. This isn't about deleting everything; it's about assessing what information is publicly available and identifying potential vulnerabilities. Consider the images you've shared, the locations you've tagged, the personal details you've disclosed in posts or comments. Does this information inadvertently reveal your daily routine, address, workplace, or other sensitive information that could be exploited by an abuser? A sociopath or stalker can use this information to plan interactions, monitor your movements, or even gain access to your physical location.

Go through your friend lists, follower lists, and connections meticulously. Are there any accounts that seem suspicious or that you no longer interact with? Remove any connections that you feel uneasy about, even if it seems insignificant.

Remember, the goal is to minimize the amount of information available to anyone who might want to harm you. This includes removing connections with individuals who the abuser might use to relay information or manipulate you indirectly.

Next, examine your privacy settings on every platform you use. Most platforms offer granular control over who can see your posts, your profile information, your location data, and your contact information. Take the time to explore these settings thoroughly and adjust them to the most restrictive level that you are comfortable with. Remember, it's far better to err on the side of caution.

Consider limiting the information you share about your personal life. Avoid posting real-time updates about your location, especially if you're alone or engaging in activities that might make you vulnerable. Think carefully about the photos and videos you share; avoid images that reveal specific details about your home, workplace, or routines.

Regularly review your posts and activity. Are there any posts that reveal more information than you intended? If so, consider deleting them. Many platforms allow for the deletion of past posts. Remember, the goal is not perfection, but consistent efforts to reduce potential vulnerabilities.

Beyond your personal accounts, consider your online presence across various platforms. Do you have any public profiles on professional networking sites like LinkedIn?

Review these profiles carefully. While professional profiles require some personal information, be mindful about what you disclose and the level of detail you provide. Avoid sharing information that could be used to track your whereabouts or identify your physical location.

Managing your online presence extends beyond social media. Think about online reviews you've written, comments you've left on articles or forums, and even your online shopping history. All these contribute to your digital footprint. While complete anonymity is nearly impossible in the digital age, striving for a degree of privacy and limiting

unnecessary disclosures is a proactive step in protecting yourself.

If you have used dating apps or other online platforms for meeting people, take extra precautions. Never share your full name, address, or workplace before you have met someone in person in a public place and feel completely safe and secure. Be cautious about sharing personal information online, especially if you don't know the person well. Always meet in a well-lit and populated public space, and always let a trusted friend or family member know where you're going and who you're meeting.

Remember, these platforms often contain algorithms that can be exploited. Abusers might leverage these algorithms to find you, track your activity, or target you with specific content. Be aware of the potential for manipulative or deceptive tactics.

Consider creating separate email addresses and accounts for different purposes. For example, use one email address for sensitive communication like financial transactions or legal matters, and another for less sensitive communications like online shopping or social media. This approach helps to compartmentalize information and limit the impact of a potential security breach.

Another important step is to be vigilant about online harassment and surveillance. Understand that even with careful management of your online presence, you may still experience online harassment or stalking. Know your rights, and report any instances of harassment or abuse to the relevant platform and authorities. Many platforms have reporting mechanisms and procedures in place to address harassment and abuse. Document all instances of online harassment, including screenshots of messages, comments, and other evidence. This documentation can be crucial if you decide to pursue legal action.

If you are experiencing cyberstalking or online harassment, consider seeking professional support. A therapist or counselor who specializes in trauma and abuse recovery can provide valuable support and guidance in navigating this challenging situation. They can help you develop coping mechanisms, and strategies for managing your online presence safely and securely. Remember, you are not alone, and help is available.

Finally, regularly educate yourself about online safety and privacy best practices. Technology is constantly evolving, so staying informed about the latest threats and security measures is essential. There are many reputable online resources that provide guidance on online safety and privacy, and staying informed can significantly improve your ability to protect yourself online. Regularly review your security settings, and be aware of potential vulnerabilities. By taking proactive steps to manage your digital footprint and protect your online presence, you're taking a vital step toward building a safer and healthier future for yourself. Remember, regaining control over your online presence is a significant part of your journey towards recovery and healing. It's a crucial component of establishing your autonomy and personal safety in a world increasingly intertwined with technology.

Reporting Online Harassment and Abuse

The previous sections emphasized proactive measures to minimize your online vulnerability. However, even with the most diligent precautions, you may still experience online harassment or abuse. This section focuses on the crucial steps you should take if you find yourself targeted.

Remember, reporting is not about weakness; it's about actively protecting yourself and holding perpetrators accountable. Your safety and well-being are paramount.

Reporting online harassment and abuse varies depending on the platform. Each site has its own reporting mechanisms and procedures. Familiarize yourself with these processes for each platform you use. These mechanisms typically involve locating a "Report" or "Flag" button, often found near offensive content or within the profile of the abuser. Clicking this button usually opens a reporting form where you'll provide details about the incident.

Be thorough and detailed in your reports. The more information you can provide, the better equipped the platform is to investigate and take appropriate action. Include the following information whenever possible:

Specific details of the incident: Clearly describe the nature of the harassment or abuse. Were you subjected to threats, insults, stalking, doxxing (revealing personal information), or other forms of abuse? Be precise in your descriptions, detailing the exact words or actions used. Dates and times are vital for context.

Links or screenshots: Whenever feasible, provide links directly to the offensive content, or screenshots capturing the

abusive messages, images, or videos. This irrefutable evidence significantly strengthens your report and increases the likelihood of a successful investigation.

Usernames or URLs: Include the usernames or URLs of the perpetrator's accounts. This allows the platform to quickly identify and locate the individual responsible. If you're unsure of the exact username, provide any details that might help in identification, such as profile pictures, and any other identifiers.

Impact on you: Detail the emotional and psychological impact the harassment has had on you. This isn't simply about stating the facts; it's about expressing the very real harm the abuser has inflicted. Describing the anxiety, fear, distress, or other emotional consequences demonstrates the seriousness of the situation and helps the platform understand the gravity of the offense.

Previous attempts at resolution: If you've already tried to resolve the issue directly with the perpetrator (perhaps by requesting they cease their behavior), document those attempts, including dates, times, and the outcomes. This provides further context and shows that you've already made efforts to address the problem independently.

After submitting your report, you might receive an automated acknowledgment, indicating the platform has received your complaint. This doesn't guarantee immediate action, but it confirms your report has been logged.

Platforms often have different response times, and the process can take days, weeks, or even longer. Maintain patience and understand that investigations require time.

If the initial response is insufficient or you aren't satisfied with the platform's resolution, escalate your report. Most platforms have escalation channels, whether through appeals processes or direct contact with their support teams.

Persistence is key. Don't hesitate to push for a more thorough investigation or stronger action if you believe it's warranted.

Remember, reporting online abuse is not a one-time action. If the harassment continues, you must continue to report each incident. Each report provides further evidence and strengthens your case for platform intervention and potential legal action. Document each incident meticulously, saving all evidence and keeping a detailed record of your interactions with the platform's support team.

Beyond reporting to the platform itself, consider reporting the abuse to law enforcement. While platforms primarily handle violations of their terms of service, law enforcement addresses potential criminal offenses, such as threats, stalking, or harassment that may cross legal boundaries.

Different jurisdictions have different reporting procedures, but most require a police report or a formal complaint.

Gathering all available evidence—screenshots, messages, and any other supporting documentation—is crucial when reporting to law enforcement.

Working with law enforcement can be a complex process. Be prepared to provide detailed information and cooperate fully with the investigation. If you feel overwhelmed or unsure of how to proceed, seek legal counsel from a lawyer specializing in cybercrime or harassment cases. They can guide you through the legal process, ensuring your rights are protected and that you are represented effectively.

The process of reporting online harassment and abuse can be emotionally draining. Remember to prioritize your own

well-being. Talk to a trusted friend, family member, or therapist. Sharing your experience and seeking support can

significantly improve your mental and emotional health during this difficult period.

Additionally, if you are feeling particularly vulnerable or experiencing intense emotional distress, consider seeking support from a mental health professional who specializes in trauma and abuse recovery. They can provide coping mechanisms and strategies for managing the psychological impacts of online harassment. Remember, seeking professional help is a sign of strength, not weakness.

The digital age presents unique challenges, but also offers tools for accountability. By understanding the reporting processes of different platforms, persisting in your efforts, and seeking support when needed, you can effectively combat online harassment and work towards reclaiming your online safety and well-being. Remember, your experience is valid, and you have the right to feel safe online. Do not hesitate to use the resources available to you to protect yourself.

Beyond immediate reporting, consider long-term strategies. This includes building a support network of friends, family, or online communities where you can find empathy and understanding. Maintaining open communication with these individuals can be invaluable during times of stress.

Consider seeking legal advice to establish preventative measures that might discourage future online harassment, such as restraining orders or cease-and-desist letters.

Understanding that online harassment is often a manifestation of underlying issues in the abuser's life does not excuse their actions. It is important to focus on protecting yourself and seeking help, not trying to understand or "fix" the perpetrator. Their actions are solely their responsibility.

Finally, remember that your experience is not unique. Many individuals experience online harassment and abuse. Seeking out support groups, either online or in person, can provide a sense of community and shared experience, reminding you that you are not alone in this struggle. These groups offer a platform for sharing experiences, advice, and mutual support. They can be invaluable resources in your journey towards recovery and reclaiming your digital life. Your recovery is a journey, and you have the power to navigate it with resilience and strength.

Identifying Local Resources and Services

Leaving an abusive relationship, especially one involving a sociopath, is only the first step on a long road to recovery. The emotional, psychological, and often physical toll can be immense. While the previous chapters focused on securing your safety and protecting yourself from further harm, this section focuses on actively building a support network and accessing resources that can assist in your healing process. Finding help within your local community is crucial for long-term recovery.

Your immediate priorities after escaping an abusive situation are likely to include securing safe housing, ensuring your financial stability, and addressing your immediate physical and emotional needs. Fortunately, various local services and organizations exist to provide support during this critical time. However, navigating the system can feel overwhelming, especially when you're grappling with the emotional trauma of abuse.

One of the first resources you should locate is a domestic violence shelter or safe house. These facilities offer temporary housing, providing a safe and secure environment away from your abuser. Shelters generally provide more than just a place to sleep; they typically offer a range of services designed to help you rebuild your life. These services can include:

Emergency shelter: A safe and secure place to stay, often with 24/7 security and support staff.

Counseling and therapy: Access to professional mental health services to address the trauma and emotional distress you've experienced. This is vital in processing the events

and working through the emotional aftermath. Many shelters have counselors on-staff, or can provide referrals to outside therapists specializing in trauma and abuse recovery.

Legal assistance: Advice and support from legal professionals to help you navigate the legal system, including obtaining restraining orders, filing for divorce, or pursuing other legal options.

Financial assistance: Help with obtaining financial aid, food stamps, or other forms of government assistance to meet your immediate needs. Sociopaths often exert financial control over their victims, so regaining financial independence is a crucial aspect of recovery.

Job training and placement: Support in finding employment to achieve financial stability. This can include job skills training, resume writing assistance, and job placement services.

Childcare: If you have children, shelters usually provide childcare services, allowing you to focus on your recovery without worrying about childcare logistics.

Support groups: Opportunities to connect with other survivors of abuse, creating a supportive community and fostering a sense of shared experience.

Finding the nearest shelter requires research and might feel daunting in your current state. However, there are several ways to locate this crucial resource.

Online searches: Search online using terms such as "domestic violence shelter [your city/county]", "safe house [your city/county]", or "women's shelter [your city/county]". **National Domestic Violence Hotline:** The National Domestic Violence Hotline (1-800-799-SAFE) provides a 24/7 helpline that can connect you to local shelters and resources in your area. They can offer immediate support and guidance in locating nearby safe havens. Don't hesitate

to call; they are a valuable lifeline during this challenging time.

Local law enforcement: Police departments and sheriff's offices are often aware of the location and services of local shelters. They can provide direct referrals and assistance.

Hospitals and emergency rooms: If you present at a hospital or emergency room due to injuries sustained from abuse, the staff can connect you to local shelter services.

Social services agencies: Local social service agencies, such as your county's Department of Social Services or Human Services department, maintain databases of local resources and can assist in connecting you with appropriate shelters.

Beyond shelters, there are several other essential local resources available to support you. Support groups offer a crucial environment of shared experience and mutual understanding. Connecting with other survivors provides validation of your experiences, reduces feelings of isolation, and creates a community of support during your healing journey. Many local organizations and community centers offer support groups specifically designed for survivors of domestic violence or abuse from sociopaths. These groups provide a safe space to share your experiences, learn coping mechanisms, and find strength in the shared experiences of others.

Counseling and therapy are vital for processing the trauma of abuse. A qualified therapist specializing in trauma and abuse recovery can provide the tools and techniques to help you understand your experiences, heal from the emotional wounds inflicted by the abuse, and develop strategies for building a healthier future. Finding a therapist can be done through several means:

Your primary care physician: Your doctor can often provide referrals to therapists in your area.

Insurance provider: If you have health insurance, contact your provider to get a list of therapists in your network.

Online directories: Websites such as Psychology Today or Zocdoc allow you to search for therapists based on specialization, location, and insurance. It's important to look for therapists with specific experience in trauma and abuse recovery, as they have the expertise to address the unique challenges you face.

Local mental health centers: Your county or state may have a mental health center offering services at a reduced or sliding scale cost. This is particularly important if financial constraints are a factor in seeking professional help.

Remember, seeking professional help is a sign of strength, not weakness. Your mental and emotional health is paramount, and investing in your well-being is crucial for long-term recovery. The abuse you endured was not your fault, and seeking support is a vital step in reclaiming your life.

Legal resources are another important aspect of your recovery. If you need to obtain a restraining order, pursue legal action against your abuser, or address issues related to custody or divorce, legal aid services can provide invaluable assistance. Legal aid societies often offer free or low-cost legal representation to those who cannot afford an attorney. Bar associations also frequently maintain referral services to connect individuals with lawyers specializing in family law or domestic violence cases. If you have suffered financial abuse, exploring avenues for financial recovery, including reporting to relevant agencies, might be necessary.

Additionally, many local organizations provide a range of practical support services such as job training programs, financial assistance, and childcare. These services assist you in becoming financially independent and rebuilding your

life. The path to recovery is a journey, not a race. Take the time you need to heal and utilize the resources available to you. Don't hesitate to reach out for help; your well-being and safety are priorities.

Remember, the resources listed above are not exhaustive; the specific organizations and services available will vary based on your location and circumstances. However, the strategies for finding them remain consistent. By conducting online searches, contacting the National Domestic Violence Hotline, reaching out to your local law enforcement or social service agencies, or seeking help from medical professionals, you can access the support you need to begin the vital journey of healing and recovery. Your strength and resilience are evident in your willingness to seek help. This is a crucial step towards building a safer, healthier future for yourself and your family. Never forget that you deserve to live free from fear and manipulation.

Utilizing Hotlines and Emergency Services

Utilizing hotlines and emergency services is often the first crucial step in escaping and recovering from abuse by a sociopath. The initial shock and disorientation can make it difficult to know where to turn, but remember that help is readily available, and reaching out is a sign of strength, not weakness. These services offer immediate support, guidance, and crucial resources during this critical period.

The National Domestic Violence Hotline (NDVH) is a beacon of hope for countless victims. The number, 1-800- 799-SAFE (7233), is easily remembered and accessible 24 hours a day, 7 days a week. It's a lifeline connecting individuals to immediate support and local resources tailored to their specific needs and location. When you call the NDVH, trained advocates provide a non-judgmental listening ear, validate your experiences, and offer immediate crisis intervention. They can help you assess your situation, develop a safety plan, and locate nearby emergency shelters, legal aid services, and counseling resources. Beyond crisis support, the NDVH offers extensive online resources including safety planning tools, information about sociopathic behavior, and guidance on navigating the legal system. Don't hesitate to call; they can provide immediate support and direct you to resources that can begin the healing process immediately. The NDVH's website also offers a live chat option for those who prefer written communication.

Beyond the NDVH, the National Sexual Assault Hotline (RAINN) is another critical resource, especially if sexual assault is part of the abuse you've endured. Dialing 800-656- HOPE connects you with trained staff who can provide

immediate support, crisis intervention, and information about local resources. RAINN also operates a website with a wealth of information on sexual assault, recovery resources, and online support communities. The hotline and online resources can be invaluable tools during the initial stages of recovery, providing immediate emotional support and practical advice.

For situations requiring immediate medical attention, hospital emergency rooms are crucial. If you have experienced physical injury, or are experiencing a mental health crisis as a result of the abuse, seeking medical attention is paramount. Hospital staff are trained to identify signs of abuse, and many have protocols in place to ensure your safety and connect you with appropriate resources.

Emergency room personnel can provide immediate medical care, stabilize your condition, and connect you with local shelters, mental health professionals, and law enforcement as needed. Don't hesitate to seek medical attention for injuries or acute mental health crises, as your physical and emotional well-being is paramount.

Law enforcement agencies are another critical point of contact, particularly if you are in immediate danger. If you believe you are in imminent danger of physical harm, call 911 immediately. Police officers are trained to respond to domestic violence situations and can provide immediate protection, ensure your safety, and assist in apprehending your abuser. Even if you're not in immediate danger, reporting the abuse to law enforcement can be crucial in building a legal case against your abuser, obtaining a restraining order, and protecting yourself from future harm. Remember, your safety is the priority.

Local crisis centers are valuable resources that often provide immediate crisis intervention, counseling, and support

services. These centers frequently have 24/7 hotlines and provide a safe space to discuss your situation and develop a personalized safety plan. They offer immediate support and can connect you with longer-term resources as you begin your recovery journey. They can also provide vital information about shelters, counseling services, legal aid, and other critical support systems in your community. They often have multilingual staff and cater to a wide array of needs.

Your primary care physician (PCP) plays a crucial role in your overall well-being and can offer valuable support during this challenging time. Your PCP can provide referrals to therapists specializing in trauma and abuse, assist with accessing necessary medications, and advocate for your needs within the healthcare system. Your PCP can also help to document any physical injuries sustained as a result of the abuse, providing vital evidence for legal purposes. Their role extends beyond immediate medical needs; they can offer ongoing support and referrals to help you rebuild your life.

Remember, the process of escaping and recovering from abuse by a sociopath is not a solitary journey. There are countless individuals and organizations dedicated to providing support, guidance, and assistance. By utilizing the services mentioned above—the National Domestic Violence Hotline, the National Sexual Assault Hotline, hospital emergency rooms, law enforcement, local crisis centers, and your primary care physician—you are taking a proactive step towards reclaiming your safety, securing your future, and embarking on your healing journey. Your courage in seeking help is commendable, and the journey, while challenging, is filled with the potential for strength, resilience, and ultimately, freedom. Never underestimate the power of reaching out; it is a testament to your inherent strength and a vital step towards a brighter future. The resources are there,

waiting to provide the support you need and deserve. You are not alone.

Connecting with Support Networks and Groups

Beyond the immediate crisis response services, building a strong support network is crucial for long-term healing and recovery. Isolation is a common tactic employed by sociopaths, designed to weaken their victims and maintain control. Breaking free from this isolation and actively cultivating connections with supportive individuals is a powerful act of self-empowerment. This network can provide emotional sustenance, practical assistance, and a sense of belonging during the often-difficult journey of recovery.

The first step in building this network may involve confiding in trusted friends or family members. However, this can be challenging. Many victims hesitate to disclose their experiences due to fear of judgment, disbelief, or further manipulation by the abuser. Remember that your feelings are valid, and you deserve understanding and support. Choosing who to confide in is a personal decision; select individuals who have demonstrated empathy, trustworthiness, and a willingness to listen without judgment. If you're unsure who to approach, start with a close friend or family member you feel most comfortable with. Begin by sharing small details and gradually increase the level of disclosure as you feel more comfortable and secure.

If confiding in family or friends isn't an option, or feels too risky, consider seeking professional support from a therapist or counselor specializing in trauma and abuse recovery.

These professionals provide a safe and confidential space to process your experiences, explore your emotions, and develop coping mechanisms. They can offer invaluable guidance, support, and validation, helping you understand

the dynamics of the abuse and develop strategies for moving forward. Many therapists offer online sessions, which can provide a degree of anonymity and convenience for those who feel apprehensive about attending in-person appointments.

Support groups offer a unique form of healing, connecting you with others who share similar experiences. The shared experience fosters a sense of community, validation, and understanding often absent in other settings. Support groups provide a safe and non-judgmental environment to openly share your feelings, struggles, and triumphs without fear of ridicule or minimization. Listening to the stories of others who have overcome similar challenges can be incredibly empowering and instill hope for your own recovery. Many support groups are specifically designed for victims of sociopathic abuse, providing a space where your experiences are fully understood and validated. This understanding is crucial in dispelling feelings of isolation and shame that are often deeply ingrained by the abuser.

Finding a support group can be as simple as searching online for groups in your area or joining online forums and communities dedicated to supporting victims of abuse. Many organizations, including the National Domestic Violence Hotline and RAINN, maintain directories of support groups and resources. Attending a support group's meeting might feel daunting initially, but remember that everyone there understands the challenges you're facing. The supportive atmosphere and shared experiences often lead to meaningful connections and a sense of belonging. These connections can transform into invaluable friendships and long-term sources of support.

Beyond formal support groups, consider building informal connections with people who share your interests and values.

Reconnect with old friends, join community organizations, or take up new hobbies. These activities provide opportunities to meet new people, build positive relationships, and focus on aspects of your life unrelated to the abuse. These new connections can serve as a source of distraction, positive reinforcement, and a sense of belonging that counters the isolation imposed by the abuser. They offer a healthy counterbalance to the negative experiences and reinforce your sense of self-worth and self-confidence.

Rebuilding your life after escaping a sociopathic relationship requires a multifaceted approach, with community involvement playing a crucial role. Volunteering at a local charity or joining a community organization can offer a sense of purpose, contribute to your personal growth, and connect you with like-minded individuals. The act of giving back to the community can be incredibly therapeutic, fostering a sense of accomplishment and providing a healthy distraction from the trauma. Furthermore, it can offer new experiences and opportunities for personal growth, fostering independence and self-reliance.

Furthermore, engaging in creative activities can be tremendously beneficial for recovery. Writing, painting, music, and other artistic pursuits can offer an outlet for emotions, promoting self-expression and healing. Creating art allows you to process your experiences in a healthy way, translate feelings into tangible forms, and regain a sense of control over your life. Many community centers and organizations offer art therapy workshops and classes specifically designed for survivors of trauma. These provide guided support and a structured environment to explore these methods of healing.

It's important to remember that building a supportive network is an ongoing process. It's not a one-time event but

rather a continuous effort to cultivate healthy, positive relationships and connections. Some relationships may blossom quickly, while others may develop gradually over time. Be patient with yourself and the process, and prioritize relationships that provide genuine support, understanding, and encouragement. Avoid relationships that drain your energy, trigger negative emotions, or reinforce feelings of self-doubt.

Be selective in choosing your support network. Choose individuals who are supportive, understanding, and non- judgmental. Individuals who minimize your experience or blame you for the abuse should be avoided. Your support network should empower you, not hinder your progress. It's also important to remember that you don't have to share all the details of your experience with everyone in your support network. Gradually revealing information as you feel comfortable and trust the individuals is acceptable and often safer.

Your support network isn't limited to individuals; pets can also provide invaluable emotional support. The unconditional love and companionship of a pet can be incredibly healing, reducing feelings of loneliness and isolation. The routine of caring for a pet can provide a sense of structure and normalcy, which can be particularly beneficial after experiencing the chaos and instability of abuse.

Building a strong support network takes time and effort, but the rewards are immeasurable. The connection, empathy, and understanding you receive from others can be transformative, enabling you to heal, grow, and rebuild your life on your own terms. Remember, you are not alone, and there is a community of people who support you on your journey to recovery and empowerment. By actively

cultivating these connections, you are taking a crucial step towards reclaiming your life and building a future free from fear and manipulation. This is a vital step in your healing journey, one that underscores your inherent resilience and strength. Embrace the process, allow yourself to be vulnerable, and recognize the immense power of connection in your healing process. The support available to you is significant, and actively seeking it is a testament to your courage and commitment to a brighter future.

Accessing Government Assistance Programs

Navigating the aftermath of sociopathic abuse often involves significant financial and logistical challenges. The emotional toll is immense, but the practical realities of rebuilding your life can feel equally overwhelming. Fortunately, various government assistance programs are designed to help survivors like you regain stability and independence. These programs recognize the unique difficulties faced by those escaping abusive situations and offer a lifeline during this critical period. Accessing these resources is a vital step in your journey toward recovery, and understanding their availability can significantly alleviate the burden and empower you to move forward with greater confidence.

One of the most immediate needs for many survivors is safe and stable housing. Domestic violence shelters provide temporary refuge, but long-term housing solutions are crucial for sustained recovery. The Department of Housing and Urban Development (HUD) offers various housing assistance programs, including Section 8 housing vouchers. These vouchers subsidize rent, making affordable housing accessible to low-income individuals and families. Eligibility criteria vary depending on location and specific program requirements, but generally include income restrictions and a demonstration of need. Many local HUD offices also have specialized programs designed to assist victims of domestic violence, offering expedited processing and greater flexibility in eligibility requirements. It's crucial to contact your local HUD office directly to inquire about available programs and the application process. They can guide you through the necessary paperwork and inform you of any specific requirements or deadlines.

Beyond Section 8, other HUD programs might provide support. For instance, the Public Housing program offers subsidized housing in government-owned or managed units. Eligibility is based on income limits, family size, and other factors. HUD also administers various programs for individuals experiencing homelessness or facing imminent eviction, often offering assistance tailored to domestic violence survivors. These programs can provide emergency shelter, rental assistance, and case management services to help you secure long-term housing stability.

In addition to HUD, many states and localities offer their own housing assistance programs specific to domestic violence survivors. These programs often provide additional support beyond basic rental assistance. Some might offer relocation assistance to help you move to a new location, increasing your safety and independence from your abuser. Others might include supportive services such as case management, counseling, and help with finding employment. Contacting your local social services agency or domestic violence shelter is an excellent way to learn about available state and local housing programs. Many shelters have dedicated case managers who can assist you in applying for and accessing these vital resources. Don't hesitate to reach out; their expertise in navigating the bureaucratic process can significantly ease the pressure during this challenging time.

Financial hardship is another common consequence of sociopathic abuse. Abusers often exert financial control, isolating their victims from personal funds and creating significant economic insecurity. Fortunately, several federal and state programs provide financial assistance to survivors. The Temporary Assistance for Needy Families (TANF) program provides cash assistance to low-income families, including those escaping domestic violence. TANF benefits

can help cover basic living expenses like rent, food, and utilities, providing a crucial safety net during this transition. Eligibility requirements vary by state, so contacting your state's TANF agency will provide the specifics for your area.

The Supplemental Nutrition Assistance Program (SNAP), formerly known as food stamps, provides food assistance to low-income individuals and families. SNAP benefits can significantly alleviate the financial burden of feeding yourself and your family, ensuring you have access to nutritious food during a period of significant upheaval and stress. The application process and eligibility criteria vary by state but are typically straightforward and accessible.

Beyond these broad-based programs, many states offer specialized financial assistance programs for domestic violence survivors. These may include emergency cash grants to cover immediate expenses, funding for job training programs to help survivors gain employment, and assistance with paying for childcare, allowing them to pursue employment or education opportunities. Many local domestic violence shelters and social service agencies can provide information about these programs and aid you in the application process. These programs are often designed to offer rapid assistance, addressing immediate needs and paving the path toward greater long-term financial independence.

Legal assistance is another critical component of recovery. Navigating the legal system after experiencing abuse can be daunting, and many survivors lack the financial resources to hire a lawyer. Legal Aid organizations offer free or low-cost legal services to those who qualify based on income and the nature of their legal issues. They can provide representation in cases involving restraining orders, custody disputes, divorce, or other legal matters related to escaping abuse.

Legal Aid's services also extend to helping survivors understand their rights and options, ensuring they navigate the legal system with confidence and support.

The Violence Against Women Act (VAWA) provides additional legal protections for survivors of domestic violence. VAWA offers crucial resources and support, including legal assistance, access to shelters, and other essential services. It also provides enhanced protections for immigrants who are survivors of domestic violence, enabling them to obtain legal status independent of their abuser.

Many states have additional legal aid programs specifically designed to assist domestic violence survivors. These programs can provide support in obtaining restraining orders, protective orders, and assistance with custody battles. Many domestic violence shelters and advocacy groups can connect survivors with these legal resources.

Beyond immediate financial and housing needs, survivors often require access to healthcare services, particularly mental health care. The Affordable Care Act (ACA) expands access to health insurance, making healthcare more affordable for millions of Americans, including survivors of abuse. Under the ACA, individuals can obtain health insurance through the marketplace or may qualify for Medicaid. Both plans cover essential health benefits, including mental health and substance abuse services, crucial for the healing process. Affordable healthcare access ensures survivors can address physical and mental health concerns without facing insurmountable financial barriers.

The process of accessing government assistance programs can often seem complex and daunting. However, many organizations are dedicated to helping survivors navigate these systems. Domestic violence shelters, legal aid

organizations, and social service agencies all offer invaluable assistance. They can explain eligibility requirements, help with applications, and advocate on your behalf. Don't hesitate to contact these organizations. Their expertise and support can significantly ease the process and ensure you access the assistance you need.

Remember, seeking government assistance isn't a sign of weakness but rather a proactive step towards building a safer and more stable future. These programs are designed to help you reclaim your independence and rebuild your life after experiencing the trauma of sociopathic abuse. Navigating the application processes and understanding the nuances of each program can feel overwhelming, but know that you're not alone. There are individuals and organizations dedicated to supporting you every step of the way. Utilize the resources available to you; it is a testament to your strength and your commitment to creating a healthier future. By taking this proactive step, you are demonstrating resilience and a determination to emerge from the shadows and embrace a future of safety, security, and self-sufficiency.

Volunteering and Giving Back

The journey out of the shadow of sociopathic abuse is arduous, a climb out of a deep, dark pit. But as you begin to feel the sun on your face, a sense of empowerment takes hold. This empowerment isn't just about reclaiming your life; it's about sharing your strength with others who are still trapped in the darkness. Volunteering and giving back to your community is not only a powerful act of self-healing, but it's also a way to pay it forward, to help others avoid the pain you've endured.

Many survivors find solace and purpose in helping others. The act of extending a hand, of offering empathy and understanding to someone experiencing a similar struggle, can be deeply cathartic. It's a way of transforming your trauma into a force for good, turning a negative experience into a catalyst for positive change. This isn't about minimizing your experience or pretending it didn't happen; it's about channeling the strength you've gained through adversity.

Consider volunteering at a local domestic violence shelter. Your firsthand experience provides invaluable insight that professionals may not possess. You can offer peer support, share your story (at your own pace and comfort level, of course), and help other survivors navigate the complexities of escaping an abusive relationship. You can offer practical assistance – helping with administrative tasks, organizing events, or even just offering a listening ear. The act of supporting others creates a ripple effect of healing, benefiting both the recipient and the giver.

Your experience also offers a unique perspective in educating others about sociopathic abuse. Many people are unaware of the insidious tactics used by abusers, and your insights can help raise awareness. You can volunteer to speak at community events, schools, or support groups. You can share your story anonymously, if preferred, focusing on the signs of abuse and strategies for escape. Educating others is a crucial step in preventing future abuse and ensuring that survivors receive the support they need. The power of your testimony lies in its authenticity, its raw honesty, and its potential to save others from suffering similar experiences.

Perhaps your skills lie in other areas. If you have a background in writing or communications, you could volunteer to write articles or blog posts for organizations working with abuse survivors. If you're skilled in graphic design, you could help create awareness campaigns. If you're adept at fundraising, you could dedicate your time to raising crucial funds for shelters and support services. The opportunities are vast and varied, allowing you to leverage your talents while supporting a cause close to your heart.

Remember that even small contributions can make a significant impact.

Consider volunteering for crisis hotlines. These lines provide crucial support to individuals in immediate danger. The training provided will equip you with the skills to effectively listen and offer support to individuals in distress, helping them develop a safety plan and connect them with appropriate resources. While the work can be emotionally demanding, it provides a powerful sense of purpose, knowing you are directly helping those in immediate crisis.

It's a way to turn your pain into action, using your experiences to help save lives.

Beyond direct work with survivors, volunteering with organizations that advocate for policy changes surrounding domestic violence can be highly impactful. You can participate in lobbying efforts, campaign for better legislation, or raise public awareness about the need for increased funding for support services. By using your voice to advocate for policy reform, you are creating lasting change that can benefit countless survivors in the future.

This form of activism is a powerful way to turn personal experience into collective action, ensuring that others have access to the resources and support you may have lacked.

Many organizations actively seek volunteers with experiences relevant to domestic violence. These organizations are committed to providing comprehensive support for survivors and often provide training to their volunteers. This training not only helps volunteers develop essential skills but also offers a supportive community and a platform to connect with like-minded individuals.

Participating in such organizations offers a sense of belonging and camaraderie, easing feelings of isolation that often accompany trauma.

Your journey toward recovery is a testament to your strength and resilience. Sharing this strength with others by volunteering and giving back is a transformative act of healing. It's an opportunity to redirect your pain, empowering you to contribute positively to your community while simultaneously enriching your own life. It is a path towards reclaiming your narrative, not as a victim, but as a survivor, a beacon of hope, and a catalyst for change. This process is about more than just helping others; it is a crucial part of your ongoing healing journey.

Remember, there's no pressure to volunteer immediately or to engage in any activity that feels overwhelming. Recovery

is a journey, and it progresses at your own pace. Take time to heal, to reflect, and to identify what feels right for you. Start small, maybe with just an hour a week or a few hours a month. Gradually increase your commitment as you feel more comfortable and confident.

Reaching out to local domestic violence organizations or searching online for relevant volunteer opportunities is an excellent starting point. Many organizations have specific volunteer roles that align with various skills and levels of experience. Some organizations offer flexible options, allowing you to volunteer remotely or on a schedule that fits your needs. The most important thing is finding a role that feels meaningful to you and allows you to contribute in a way that feels sustainable and fulfilling.

The impact of volunteering and giving back extends far beyond the immediate beneficiaries. It fosters a sense of purpose and meaning in your life, boosting self-esteem and promoting overall well-being. It creates a positive feedback loop, where your acts of kindness and compassion strengthen your own resilience and foster a sense of self-worth. It allows you to reconnect with your community and build positive relationships, counteracting the isolation often experienced by survivors of abuse.

In the process of helping others, you'll discover a renewed sense of agency and control over your life. This is not about replacing your past but integrating it into a larger narrative of empowerment and purpose. It is about finding your place in the world, using your experiences to build a better future for yourself and others. This journey of giving back is, in many ways, a continuation of your escape, a journey towards a life beyond the shadows, a life filled with purpose, meaning, and a profound sense of self-worth. Embrace this opportunity for growth and healing; your contribution will be invaluable.

Your strength is not only for your own survival; it is a gift to the world.

Embracing SelfForgiveness and Acceptance

The journey to healing after sociopathic abuse isn't solely about escaping the abuser; it's about reclaiming your sense of self. A crucial part of this reclamation is embracing self- forgiveness and self-acceptance. This isn't about condoning the abuse or minimizing its impact; it's about releasing the self-blame and shame that often accompany such experiences. Sociopaths are masters of manipulation, skillfully twisting narratives to make the victim feel responsible for the abuse. They plant seeds of doubt, whispering insidious suggestions that you deserved the treatment, provoked the anger, or somehow failed to prevent the harm. These insidious whispers linger long after the relationship ends, echoing in your mind and hindering your recovery.

Understanding this manipulative dynamic is the first step towards self-forgiveness. The abuse was never your fault. No one deserves to be manipulated, controlled, or abused. The responsibility for the abuse lies solely with the perpetrator.

Their actions, their choices, their calculated cruelty – these are what caused the harm, not any perceived failing on your part. Repeating this affirmation, both internally and aloud, can help break the cycle of self-blame.

Journaling can be an incredibly powerful tool in this process. Writing down your thoughts and feelings, acknowledging the pain and the self-criticism, allows you to externalize those negative emotions. It's a way to confront them directly, to examine their origins, and to challenge their validity. Don't censor yourself; let your raw emotions flow onto the page.

As you write, you might find patterns emerging, recurring thoughts and beliefs that stem from the manipulation of your

abuser. By recognizing these patterns, you can begin to dismantle them.

Consider writing a letter to your abuser, not to send, but to release your pent-up emotions. Pouring your anger, your hurt, your resentment onto paper can be incredibly cathartic. Don't hold back; let your feelings flow freely. Through this process, you'll likely discover the depth of the manipulation and the extent to which your abuser distorted your reality.

This letter is a tool for self-discovery, a way to uncover the truth and reclaim your narrative.

Self-acceptance is another crucial aspect of this healing process. This involves accepting all parts of yourself, including the scars left by the abuse. It's acknowledging that you've been through a traumatic experience that has impacted you deeply, without letting that experience define you. You are not your trauma; you are a survivor of trauma. This distinction is essential. Your experiences have shaped you, but they do not dictate your worth or your future.

Many survivors struggle with feelings of inadequacy and

self-doubt. These feelings are often amplified by the constant criticism and belittling that often accompany sociopathic abuse. Rebuilding self-esteem requires actively challenging these negative self-perceptions. This can involve setting small, achievable goals and celebrating your accomplishments, no matter how small they may seem. It's about focusing on your strengths and recognizing your resilience. Remind yourself daily of your positive qualities, your accomplishments, and your inherent worth.

Affirmations, both written and spoken, can be powerful tools in this process. Look in the mirror and speak kindly to yourself; treat yourself with the compassion and understanding you would offer a dear friend.

Forgiveness, both of yourself and your abuser, is a powerful, albeit challenging, step. Forgiving yourself isn't about forgetting the abuse or minimizing its impact; it's about releasing the burden of self-blame and allowing yourself to heal. It's about recognizing that you were a victim of manipulation and control, and that you are not responsible for the actions of your abuser. Forgiveness, in this context, is an act of self-compassion, a recognition of your own resilience and your capacity for healing.

Forgiving your abuser, however, is not a requirement for healing. It's a personal choice, and there's no timeline or pressure to do so. Some survivors find that forgiveness is an essential part of their recovery journey, while others find that it's simply not possible. Either path is valid and acceptable.

The focus should be on your own healing and well-being, not on the actions or feelings of your abuser. Their behavior was their responsibility; your healing is yours.

Therapy plays a vital role in this process. A therapist specializing in trauma and abuse recovery can provide a safe and supportive space to explore your feelings, challenge negative self-perceptions, and develop healthy coping mechanisms. They can guide you through the process of

self-forgiveness and self-acceptance, helping you to understand the impact of the abuse and to develop strategies for moving forward. Therapy provides a structure and a framework for navigating the complex emotions that often accompany sociopathic abuse. It offers validation, support, and a roadmap to healing.

Support groups can also be immensely helpful. Connecting with other survivors who understand your experiences can provide a sense of community and belonging. Sharing your story, listening to others' stories, and finding common ground can be incredibly validating and empowering. It's a

reminder that you are not alone, that others have been through similar experiences and have found ways to heal. This shared experience can foster a sense of hope and resilience.

Self-care is crucial throughout this process. This isn't about indulging in luxuries; it's about prioritizing your physical and emotional well-being. This might involve regular exercise, healthy eating, sufficient sleep, spending time in nature, engaging in activities that bring you joy, and practicing mindfulness or meditation. These activities help regulate your nervous system, reduce stress, and promote a sense of calm and well-being. Prioritizing self-care isn't selfish; it's an act of self-respect, a commitment to your own healing and recovery.

Remember, the path to healing is not linear. There will be good days and bad days, moments of progress and moments of setbacks. Be patient with yourself; allow yourself to grieve the loss of the relationship, the betrayal, and the manipulation. Acknowledge the pain, but don't let it define you. Celebrate your small victories, and seek support when you need it. The journey to self-forgiveness and self- acceptance is a testament to your resilience and your strength. You are worthy of love, respect, and happiness.

Embrace your journey, and trust in your capacity for healing. The sun will rise again, and you will find your way back to the light. This is not just a hope; it is a promise you can keep to yourself. Believe in your capacity to heal, to thrive, and to build a life free from the shadows of the past. Your strength is remarkable, and your future is bright.

Developing a Positive SelfImage and SelfEsteem

Building a positive self-image and self-esteem after surviving sociopathic abuse is a crucial, yet often challenging, aspect of recovery. The manipulation and control exerted by a sociopath systematically erode a victim's sense of self-worth, leaving them feeling inadequate, unworthy, and deeply damaged. Rebuilding this sense of self requires a conscious and dedicated effort, a commitment to rediscovering your strengths, celebrating your accomplishments, and setting meaningful goals for the future. It's a journey of self-discovery and self-acceptance, one that unfolds gradually, with moments of progress interspersed with moments of doubt and setbacks. But the destination – a life filled with self-respect, confidence, and genuine joy – is worth the effort.

One of the most effective strategies in rebuilding self-esteem is to actively challenge the negative self-perceptions that have been ingrained by your abuser. Sociopaths are masters of manipulation, skillfully twisting reality to make you feel responsible for their actions. They might subtly (or not so subtly) criticize your appearance, your intelligence, your choices, constantly undermining your confidence and making you question your own judgment. These insidious criticisms linger long after the relationship ends, echoing in your mind and hindering your ability to see yourself accurately. To counteract this, you must actively challenge these negative voices.

Start by making a list of all the negative thoughts and beliefs about yourself that have surfaced since the abuse. Be honest and thorough; don't hold back. Once you have this list, examine each negative thought. Ask yourself: Is this thought

truly accurate? Is there evidence to support it? Or is this thought a product of the abuser's manipulation, a distortion of reality designed to control and diminish you? In most cases, you'll find that many of these negative thoughts are baseless, stemming from the abuser's calculated efforts to control you.

Next, create a counter-list. For each negative thought, write down a positive affirmation or a statement that challenges the negativity. For example, if a negative thought is "I'm unlovable," a counter-affirmation could be "I am worthy of love and respect, and I deserve to be treated kindly." If the negative thought is "I'm incompetent," a counter-affirmation could be "I have many skills and talents, and I am capable of achieving my goals." These affirmations should be specific, focusing on your strengths, your accomplishments, and your inherent worth.

Regularly review these lists. Read the negative thoughts to acknowledge their existence, but then immediately follow them with the counter-affirmations. Repeating these affirmations, both internally and aloud, can help reprogram your subconscious mind, gradually replacing the negative self-perceptions with more positive and realistic ones. This process takes time and consistency, but the results are well worth the effort.

In addition to challenging negative thoughts, focus on identifying and celebrating your personal strengths. Make a list of your positive qualities, skills, and talents. This might include traits like kindness, empathy, resilience, creativity, intelligence, or physical abilities. Think about past accomplishments, both big and small. Did you successfully navigate a difficult situation? Did you overcome a personal challenge? Did you achieve a goal you set for yourself? No matter how insignificant these accomplishments may seem,

acknowledge and celebrate them. They are proof of your strength, your resilience, and your capacity for growth.

Setting realistic goals is another crucial step in rebuilding self-esteem. Start with small, achievable goals. Don't try to tackle everything at once. Focus on one or two areas at a time, setting realistic goals that you can gradually achieve. As you accomplish these goals, celebrate your successes.

Acknowledge your efforts and reward yourself for your hard work. This positive reinforcement will build your confidence and encourage you to continue striving towards your goals.

Engage in activities that bring you joy and fulfillment. These activities should be things you enjoy doing, things that make you feel good about yourself. This could include anything from painting and writing to hiking and dancing. These activities can be a source of stress relief, self-expression, and a boost in self-esteem. Make time for these activities regularly, even if it's just for a few minutes each day.

Seek out support from trusted friends, family members, or support groups. Sharing your experiences and connecting with others who understand what you've been through can be incredibly validating and empowering. This shared experience can foster a sense of community and belonging, reminding you that you are not alone.

Remember, rebuilding your self-image and self-esteem is a journey, not a destination. There will be ups and downs, setbacks and breakthroughs. Be patient with yourself, celebrate your progress, and don't be afraid to seek professional help when needed. A therapist specializing in trauma and abuse recovery can provide valuable guidance and support during this process, helping you to challenge negative self-perceptions, develop healthy coping mechanisms, and build a stronger sense of self. The journey

may be long and challenging, but with perseverance and self-compassion, you can reclaim your sense of self and build a life filled with self-respect, confidence, and lasting joy. Believe in your strength, your resilience, and your capacity for healing. You are worthy of happiness and a life free from the shadows of the past. The journey to a positive self-image is an act of radical self-love; treat yourself with the kindness, patience, and understanding you deserve. This is not merely a hope; it is the foundation upon which you will build a healthier, happier future. You have survived unimaginable hardship; you are stronger than you think.

Embrace your strength, honor your journey, and celebrate your resilience. Your future is bright.

Celebrating Milestones and Achievements

Celebrating milestones and achievements is not merely a feel-good exercise; it's a crucial component of healing and reclaiming your life after surviving abuse. It's a powerful antidote to the insidious self-doubt and diminished sense of worth that sociopathic abuse inflicts. The constant negativity

and manipulation designed to control and degrade you leaves a residue of self-criticism that can be exceptionally difficult to overcome. Actively celebrating your progress, no matter how small, serves as a vital counterbalance, reinforcing your inherent strength and resilience.

Think back to the moments when your abuser sought to diminish your accomplishments. Did they belittle your professional successes, dismissing them as luck or coincidence? Did they downplay personal victories, suggesting your achievements were insignificant or undeserved? This deliberate undermining was designed to control you, to keep you dependent and subservient. By actively celebrating your own achievements, you are directly challenging this manipulation and reclaiming your narrative. You are asserting your agency and affirming your self-worth.

Start by creating a "celebration journal." This isn't a diary in the traditional sense; it's a dedicated space to record your wins, both big and small. This might include completing a challenging task at work, sticking to your exercise routine for a week, finally tackling that daunting project you'd been putting off, or even something as seemingly insignificant as successfully navigating a grocery store without feeling overwhelmed. Every accomplishment, no matter how minuscule it may seem, deserves recognition.

The key is to shift your perspective. Instead of focusing on what you haven't achieved, focus on what you *have* accomplished. Celebrate the steps forward, the small victories that collectively contribute to your overall progress. Each entry in your celebration journal should be a testament to your resilience, your strength, and your capacity for growth. Don't minimize your achievements; detail the effort involved and the obstacles you overcame.

Consider setting aside specific time each week to review your journal. Re-read your entries, allowing yourself to fully appreciate your progress. This regular reflection helps reinforce your sense of accomplishment and provides tangible evidence of your growth. It's easy to forget the progress we've made, particularly when grappling with the lingering effects of trauma. The celebration journal acts as a constant reminder of your strength and capabilities.

Beyond the written word, consider incorporating other methods of celebration. Treat yourself to something you enjoy – a relaxing bath, a favorite meal, a new book, or a walk in nature. These small acts of self-care are essential for nurturing your well-being and reinforcing the message that you deserve to be happy and cared for.

The concept of celebrating milestones extends beyond personal achievements. It includes acknowledging the progress you make in your healing journey. This might involve completing a session with your therapist, attending a support group meeting, or successfully navigating a difficult interaction without succumbing to old patterns of behavior. These are significant steps that deserve recognition and celebration.

Remember, celebrating your achievements isn't about bragging or arrogance; it's about self-compassion and self-

validation. It's about acknowledging your hard work, your resilience, and your capacity for growth. It's about actively counteracting the negative self-talk ingrained by your abuser and replacing it with positive affirmation and self-belief.

Moreover, celebrate your resilience in unexpected ways. Perhaps you've learned a new skill, taken up a new hobby, or volunteered your time to a cause you care about. These actions, too, represent your strength and your commitment to rebuilding your life. They are tangible expressions of your recovery and deserve to be celebrated.

Let's examine some specific examples. Imagine you've successfully completed a challenging project at work, a project that previously would have filled you with anxiety and self-doubt. Instead of dismissing your success as "just luck," take time to acknowledge the effort, dedication, and skill you invested. Celebrate this achievement by rewarding yourself with something enjoyable, by sharing your success with a trusted friend or family member, or simply by taking a moment to savor your accomplishment.

Or perhaps you've finally left your abuser's home, a monumental step that required immense courage and determination. This achievement represents a significant turning point in your healing journey. Celebrate this milestone by acknowledging your bravery and strength. Treat yourself to something special, surround yourself with supportive people, and allow yourself to feel proud of your accomplishment.

Another example might be regaining your financial independence after being controlled by your abuser. This accomplishment represents a significant step toward self- sufficiency and freedom. Celebrate this by acknowledging your hard work and resilience. Mark this significant

milestone with a small celebratory gesture or reward to underscore your accomplishment.

It's crucial to understand that celebrating your achievements is not about minimizing the trauma you've endured. It's not about erasing the pain or pretending it didn't happen. Rather, it's about integrating your experience into your overall narrative in a way that empowers you, rather than defining you. It's about recognizing your strength, acknowledging your resilience, and affirming your capacity for growth and healing.

Think of it as creating a new story, a narrative that acknowledges the darkness but focuses on the light. It's a story of survival, resilience, and triumph. It's a story you write yourself, a story filled with accomplishments, both big and small, all celebrated and cherished. It is a story that reinforces your self-worth and reminds you of your innate strength.

Remember, the journey of healing is not linear. There will be setbacks, moments of doubt, and days when the weight of the past feels overwhelming. But through it all, continue to celebrate your progress. Celebrate the small victories, the milestones, and the moments of strength. These celebrations serve as reminders of your resilience and your capacity for healing. They are essential fuel for the journey ahead. They are proof that you are not just surviving; you are thriving.

Your future is a celebration of your strength, a testament to your unwavering spirit. Embrace it, own it, and let it guide you toward a future filled with hope, joy, and lasting peace.

Planning for the Future and Setting New Goals

Planning for the future after escaping an abusive relationship with a sociopath can feel daunting, even paralyzing. The very act of envisioning a future independent of your abuser might evoke fear, anxiety, and a sense of uncertainty. The years spent under their control might have left you feeling incapable of making your own decisions, fostering a deep- seated dependence and crippling self-doubt. However, reclaiming your agency and building a future on your own terms is entirely possible, and it's a crucial step toward lasting healing. It's about shifting from survival mode to thriving mode.

The first step is to acknowledge the enormity of what you've overcome. You've survived a profoundly damaging experience, and that alone is a testament to your strength and resilience. Don't underestimate the power of this accomplishment. You've escaped a web of manipulation and control, a feat that demands recognition and celebration.

Take time to reflect on your journey, acknowledging the bravery and determination it took to reach this point. This acknowledgment is vital in building the foundation for your future.

Now, it's time to start actively building that future. This process begins with setting goals, both large and small, short-term and long-term. These goals shouldn't be dictated by anyone else's expectations or ideals. Instead, they should reflect your own aspirations, desires, and ambitions. Think about what truly matters to you, what brings you joy, what ignites your passion. These are the things you should focus on.

Start with small, attainable goals. Perhaps it's something as simple as committing to a daily walk, learning a new skill, or joining a book club. These seemingly insignificant steps represent a shift in focus, a conscious decision to invest in your well-being and personal growth. The accomplishment of these smaller goals builds momentum, creating a sense of accomplishment and self-efficacy which can then be applied to larger, more challenging goals. Do not underestimate the power of small wins. They are the building blocks of a fulfilling future.

As you begin to set your goals, consider various aspects of your life:

Career: If your career was negatively impacted by the abuse, now is the time to explore new opportunities, pursue further education, or re-evaluate your professional path.

Perhaps you've always dreamed of a different career but lacked the courage or freedom to pursue it while under the control of your abuser. Now is your chance to explore those possibilities. Look for support groups or career counseling services specifically designed to help survivors of abuse.

They can provide guidance, resources, and encouragement as you navigate the next steps. Remember, you have skills and talents, even if your abuser tried to convince you otherwise.

Finances: Re-establishing financial independence is often a significant challenge after escaping an abusive relationship. If your abuser controlled the finances, you may need to rebuild your credit, establish new bank accounts, and learn about financial management. Seek guidance from financial professionals specializing in helping survivors of abuse.

They can provide strategies for debt management, budgeting, and financial planning. The path to financial stability might be long and require dedication but know that it is attainable.

Housing: Securing safe and stable housing is paramount. If you are currently in a shelter or temporary housing, start looking for long-term solutions. Connect with local organizations that provide assistance with housing for survivors of abuse. They can offer support and guidance in finding safe and affordable housing options. Ensure that your new living situation prioritizes your safety and sense of security.

Social Connections: Rebuild your support network. Reconnect with trusted friends and family members, or build new relationships with people who share your interests and values. Consider joining support groups for survivors of abuse or engaging in activities that help you connect with others in a positive and supportive environment. Allow yourself to be vulnerable, to share your experience with others who understand. Remember, you are not alone.

Physical and Mental Health: Prioritize your physical and mental well-being. Continue or start therapy, engage in regular exercise, eat healthy foods, and get enough sleep.

These are essential for your recovery and overall health. Explore different self-care techniques that bring you comfort and peace. Make time for activities that nourish your soul and help you relax.

Legal Matters: If necessary, seek legal counsel to protect yourself from further harm. This might involve obtaining restraining orders, pursuing legal action against your abuser, or addressing other legal issues related to the abuse. Do not hesitate to seek professional help to navigate the legal system. You have rights and deserve protection.

Personal Growth: Invest time in activities that promote personal growth and self-discovery. Explore your interests, hobbies, and passions. Learning new skills, taking up a new

hobby, or pursuing a creative outlet can be a powerful way to boost your self-esteem and foster a sense of accomplishment. This is an opportunity for self-discovery and growth – rediscovering your passions and exploring new avenues.

Setting goals for each of these areas of your life provides a roadmap for your future. These goals can be broken down into smaller, manageable steps, making the journey feel less overwhelming and more achievable. Regularly review and adjust these goals as your needs and priorities evolve.

Remember, this is your journey, and you have the right to adapt your path as you move forward.

One crucial aspect of planning for the future is envisioning your ideal life. This isn't just about setting goals; it's about creating a vision of the future you want to create. Imagine yourself living a life free from fear, manipulation, and control. What does that life look like? What does it feel like? Where do you live? What kind of work do you do? Who are the people in your life? This visualization can be a powerful tool in motivating you to achieve your goals. It is a powerful tool for building momentum and resilience.

Create a vision board. This can be a physical board filled with images, quotes, and affirmations that represent your ideal life. Or you can create a digital vision board using online tools. This visual representation serves as a constant reminder of what you are working towards.

Throughout this process, remember that setbacks are inevitable. There will be days when you feel overwhelmed, discouraged, or tempted to give up. But it's crucial to remember that these moments are temporary. Acknowledge your feelings, allow yourself to process them, and then refocus on your goals and your vision for the future. Be kind

to yourself. Celebrate your progress and learn from your setbacks. Your journey to healing is a marathon, not a sprint.

Seek professional support. Therapy is invaluable in this process. A therapist can help you process your trauma, build coping mechanisms, and develop strategies for managing your emotions. Support groups for survivors of abuse can also provide a sense of community and shared experience.

Finally, remember that you deserve a life filled with happiness, peace, and fulfillment. You deserve to live a life free from fear and manipulation. Your past does not define your future. You are resilient, capable, and deserving of a brighter tomorrow. Embrace the opportunity to rebuild your life, to create the future you deserve, and to find joy and peace along the way. This is your story, your future – write it with courage, determination, and unwavering self-belief.

Living a Life Free from Fear and Control

The journey from surviving abuse to thriving in freedom is a deeply personal one, filled with both challenges and incredible rewards. The road ahead might feel long and winding, perhaps even insurmountable at times. But remember, you've already conquered the most significant hurdle: escaping the clutches of your abuser. That act of courage is a testament to your inner strength, your resilience, and your unwavering will to live a life free from fear and control.

This freedom isn't merely the absence of abuse; it's the active creation of a life built upon your terms, guided by your aspirations, and filled with joy, peace, and self-worth. It's about reclaiming your agency, redefining your identity, and rewriting your narrative. It's about embracing the power you possess to shape your own destiny.

One of the most crucial steps in this process is fostering self- compassion. The abuse you endured wasn't your fault. The manipulation, the gaslighting, the constant control—none of it was deserved. It's imperative to release the burden of self- blame that your abuser meticulously cultivated. Forgive yourself for the choices you made while under their influence. Recognize that your survival instincts, even if they led to choices you now regret, were completely justifiable within the context of an abusive situation.

This self-forgiveness is not about condoning the abuser's actions; it's about releasing yourself from the shackles of guilt and self-criticism. It's about freeing yourself to move forward, to embrace the possibilities that lie ahead. Engage in practices that nurture self-compassion. These could

include mindfulness meditation, journaling, or simply taking time each day to engage in activities that bring you joy and peace.

Building healthy boundaries is equally crucial. This involves establishing clear limits on how others treat you and how you allow yourself to be treated. It requires recognizing your needs and communicating them assertively yet respectfully. It may involve saying "no" to requests that drain your energy, compromise your well-being, or violate your personal boundaries.

Setting boundaries might feel daunting, particularly after years of suppressing your needs and desires to appease your abuser. However, it's an essential component of creating a life free from fear and control. It allows you to protect your emotional, physical, and mental well-being. Begin by setting small, manageable boundaries, gradually expanding them as you gain confidence and assertiveness. For instance, you might start by setting clear limits on phone calls or social media interactions with people who drain your energy.

Developing a strong support system is also vital. Surround yourself with people who lift you up, encourage your growth, and offer unconditional love and support. These are individuals who respect your boundaries, value your voice, and champion your journey to healing. These could be family members, friends, fellow survivors, or members of a support group. Do not underestimate the power of connection and shared experience.

Actively seek out support groups specifically designed for survivors of sociopathic abuse. These groups provide a safe and confidential space to share your experiences, connect with others who understand your struggles, and receive validation and encouragement. They offer a sense of

community, a lifeline in the journey toward healing and empowerment. The shared experience within these groups can be profoundly healing, offering a sense of belonging and understanding that is often absent in other settings.

Remember, the healing process is not linear. There will be good days and bad days. There will be moments of profound progress and moments of setbacks. It's crucial to embrace this ebb and flow, recognizing that healing is a journey, not a destination. Be patient and kind to yourself throughout this process.

Another important aspect of living a life free from fear and control is cultivating resilience. Resilience is the ability to bounce back from adversity, to adapt to challenges, and to find strength in difficult times. It's the capacity to persevere despite setbacks and to emerge stronger from life's trials.

Resilience is not about ignoring pain or pretending everything is fine; it's about facing adversity head-on, learning from setbacks, and moving forward with renewed determination.

Cultivating resilience involves developing coping mechanisms, building self-esteem, and focusing on personal growth. It involves identifying and utilizing your inner strengths, developing healthy coping strategies, and learning to manage stress effectively. Engage in activities that promote your well-being, such as regular exercise, mindfulness practices, healthy eating, and sufficient sleep.

Furthermore, invest in your personal growth and self- discovery. Explore your interests, cultivate new skills, and pursue activities that bring you joy and fulfillment. These activities can help you reclaim your identity, build confidence, and reinforce your sense of self-worth. These activities are not mere distractions; they are fundamental to

your healing and growth, helping to reestablish your sense of self beyond the constraints imposed by your abuser.

As you move forward, remember that your journey towards a life free from fear and control is a testament to your courage, resilience, and unwavering spirit. It's a journey of self-discovery, healing, and empowerment. Embrace the challenges, celebrate your successes, and never underestimate the power of your own strength. You have the capacity to create a life filled with joy, peace, and lasting fulfillment. You deserve to live a life free from fear, a life where you are in control of your own destiny. This is your life, your story, and your future. Write it with boldness, authenticity, and unwavering self-belief. The future you envision is within your grasp. Embrace it, claim it, and live it fully.

Acknowledgments

This book would not exist without the unwavering support and contributions of many individuals. First and foremost, I extend my deepest gratitude to the brave survivors who shared their stories with me, granting me a glimpse into the profound strength and resilience of the human spirit in the face of unimaginable adversity. Their courage inspired every page.

My sincere appreciation goes to Dr. Daniel Fox, whose expertise and guidance proved invaluable in ensuring the accuracy and sensitivity of the information presented within these pages. HIs insights and unwavering com-

mitment to supporting Cluster B personality disorders were instrumental in shaping this work.

A special thanks also to my children, whose tireless support during the writing process helped make this endeavor possible.

I offer my heartfelt gratitude to my family and friends, whose love and support provided a constant source of strength throughout this challenging journey. Their unwavering belief in me helped me navigate the complexities of this work.

Finally, to the one who sought to break me through **manipulation and malice: your actions revealed the depths of human resilience. Your pathology did not shatter me;it forged me. I stand stronger, wiser, and unyielding, a testament to the strength that emerges from surviving the storm. This book is not about you—it's about the triumph of the human spirit over darkness. JRoby**

Appendix

This appendix provides a curated list of helpful resources for survivors of sociopathic abuse and stalking. These resources include national and international hotlines, support organizations, legal aid providers, and mental health professionals specializing in trauma and abuse recovery. It is important to remember that this list is not exhaustive, and the availability and suitability of these resources may vary depending on location and individual circumstances. It is crucial to research and select resources that best suit your specific needs and location. Please note that contact information is subject to change, so verifying details before use is recommended.

Percentage of proceeds from the sale of this book will go to organizations that help survivors!

List of Resources

Safe & Sound

Stalking Resource Center

National Domestic Violence Hotline RAINN (Rape, Abuse & Incest National Network)

Stalking Prevention, Awareness, and Resource Center (SPARC)

National Center for Victims of Crime Office on Violence Against Women (OVW)

Aftermath: Surviving Psychopathy Foundation Safe Horizon

MN Trauma Project Complextrauma.org

Open Path Psychotherapy Collective BuddyHelp Therapist Aid

National Alliance on Mental Illness (NAMI) Psychology Today's Therapy Directory

Glossary

This glossary defines key terms used throughout the book to ensure clarity and understanding.

Gaslighting: A form of psychological manipulation where a person seeks to sow seeds of doubt in a victim's mind, making them question their own memory, perception, and sanity.

Sociopath (or Psychopath): A person with a personality disorder characterized by a lack of empathy, remorse, and antisocial behavior. Note: This book uses these terms interchangeably for simplicity, acknowledging the nuanced differences in clinical diagnosis.

Stalking: Repeated, unwanted, and intrusive behavior directed at another person that causes the victim to feel fear, distress, or concern for their safety. This can include physical, online, or technological means.

Trauma Bonding: A paradoxical emotional attachment that can develop between victims and their abusers, despite the abusive nature of the relationship.

Cognitive Dissonance: The mental discomfort experienced by a person who holds two or more contradictory beliefs, ideas, or values. In the context of abuse, this can manifest as the victim struggling to reconcile the abusive behavior with their positive feelings for the abuser.

Hoovering: The attempt by an abuser to regain control over a victim after a period of separation. This may involve manipulation, promises, or displays of remorse.

Love Bombing: An intense and overwhelming display of affection and attention at the beginning of a relationship, used as a manipulative tactic to secure a victim's trust and commitment.

References

References

The Sociopath Next Door by Martha Stout: A deep dive into the traits and behaviors of sociopaths.

Understanding the Sociopath: Cause, Motivation, Relationship by Seth Meyers Psy.D., available on Psychology Today.

Differentiating Antisocial Personality Disorder, Psychopathy, and Sociopathy by Anthony Walsh and Huei-Hsia Wu, exploring the distinctions between these conditions.

Stalking: A Review of the Literature and Direction for the Future by Heather C. Melton, which examines the link between stalking and domestic violence.

Prosecutor's Guide to Stalking by the Stalking Awareness Organization, offering insights into legal and safety measures.

CDC'S OVERVIEW OF STALKING AS PART OF INTIMATE PARTNER VIOLENCE PREVENTION.

When a Sociopath Stalks You: Signs to Watch For and Steps to Protect Yourself by William Adams, available on Mind Psychiatrist. This article explores the behaviors of sociopaths and provides practical steps for protection.

Will a Sociopath Stalk You? Signs to Look Out For and How to Protect Yourself by William Adams, also on Mind Psychiatrist. It discusses red flags and protective measures against sociopathic stalking.

Coping with The Psychopath (Antisocial) Stalker by Sam Vaknin, available on HealthyPlace. This article delves into the psychological traits of stalkers and offers coping strategies.

When a Sociopath Stalks You : A detailed guide on recognizing sociopathic behavior and practical steps for protection.

Finding Support and Resources for Sociopaths: Insights into treatment options and support systems for individuals dealing with sociopathy.

Coping with The Psychopath (Antisocial) Stalker : Explores the psychological traits of stalkers and offers coping strategies.

IS LOVE BOMBING A RED FLAG?: DISCUSSES THE DANGERS OF LOVE BOMBING, ITS IMPACT ON EMOTIONAL HEALTH, AND HOW TO DIFFERENTIATE IT FROM GENUINE AFFECTION.

Love Bombing: 11 Warning Signs & Early Red Flags : This article explores the psychological manipulation behind love bombing, its connection to narcissistic abuse, and how to identify early warning signs.

Signs of Love Bombing: A guide to spotting behaviors like excessive compliments, over-the-top gestures, and boundary overstepping in relationships.

Author Biography

Jennifer is a survivor of sociopathic abuse, a licensed therapist in several states specializing in trauma and abuse recovery, and a writer of non-fiction works focused on mental health and recovery. Her personal experience combined with their professional expertise provides a unique perspective on the complexities of escaping and healing from this type of abuse. Jennifer is committed to providing support, education, and resources to individuals affected by sociopathic abuse and helping them navigate their journey towards healing and empowerment.

Jennifer is a therapist whose work is grounded in compassion, respect, and dedication to her clients' well- being. She specializes in trauma, addiction, personality disorders, and suicide prevention, while also addressing a broad range of concerns including depression, anxiety, relationship issues, parenting challenges, career stress, grief, and bullying. Jennifer's therapy style is warm and interactive, fostering collaboration with clients to help them reach their treatment goals in a safe and accepting environment.

With over 11 years of experience as a therapist, Jennifer skillfully adapts her approach to meet the unique needs of each individual. She integrates psychodynamic, humanistic, and existential principles, alongside Cognitive Behavioral Therapy, Client-Centered Therapy, Acceptance and Commitment Therapy (ACT), Mindfulness Therapy, and Inner Child Analytical Psychotherapy. Additionally, she is trained in advanced techniques such as Dialectical Behavior Therapy, Cognitive Processing Therapy, Prolonged Exposure Therapy, and Eye Movement Desensitization and

Reprocessing (EMDR). This diverse expertise enables her to guide her clients through life's challenges, helping them rediscover their emotional intelligence, inner wisdom, and capacity for self-compassion.

Jennifer's career includes extensive service to Veterans, Active-Duty Military members, and their families through her work in the Federal government. She has received numerous awards for her dedication, including the Presidential Volunteer Service Award from President Barack Obama, a VA Commendation from Secretary Robert McDonald, and the Making a Difference in the Community Spotlight from KGNS News, the Laredo Police Department, and the Laredo City Council. Jennifer has also been recognized with the Certificate of Special Recognition from Command Master Chief and the Certificate of Commitment from VCB VA Director Joe Perez, among many others.

These accolades reflect her tireless efforts to improve the lives of Veterans and their communities.

An accomplished author, Jennifer has written several treatment and self-help books, covering important topics such as suicide prevention, thriving after divorce, childhood trauma stemming from military service. Her works also include a guide for navigating passive-aggressive adult bullies, a self-help book for transcending others' perceptions to embrace your true self, and a beloved children's book series co-written with her own children, Johnny & his brothers: Adventures as a Military Child. Her writing offers hope, guidance, and practical tools for a diverse range of readers, addressing real-life challenges with compassion and insight.

Jennifer has delivered impactful clinical presentations at prominent conferences, such as "PTSD and Women Veterans" at the American Mental Health Counselors Association (AMHCA) in 2023 and "Veterans Suicide:

Prevention, Intervention, and Postvention" at the Texas Counseling Association State Conference in 2021. Her expertise has been sought by the Department of Defense and the Department of Veterans Affairs on topics ranging from PTSD and suicide to Veteran homelessness and dual diagnoses.

Beyond her professional life, Jennifer is a devoted and busy mother of five boys—Nicholas, William, Michael Anthony, Matthew, and Johnny. She finds immense joy and purpose in balancing her family life with her passion for helping others heal and thrive.

Jennifer is actively involved in numerous professional organizations, including the American Counseling Association, the Military and Government Counseling Association, the American Mental Health Counselors Association, and the Texas Counseling Association. She also serves on various committees, showcasing her commitment to fostering growth and advocacy in the field of mental health.

Jennifer believes that the process of psychotherapy is about exploring thoughts, feelings, beliefs, and behaviors to uncover strategies for change. She emphasizes the importance of understanding how actions, influenced by deeply held thoughts, impact oneself and others. She inspires courage by helping clients face their fears, work through them, and conquer them, all while creating a space for growth, healing, and transformation.

www.ingramcontent.com/pod-product-compliance
Lightning Source LLC
LaVergne TN
LVHW100246210926
848480LV00003B/840
* 9 7 9 8 3 4 9 2 3 6 8 8 4 *